MW01156810

DEVELOPMENT, MARKETING, AND OPERATION OF MANUFACTURED HOME COMMUNITIES

DEVELOPMENT, MARKETING, AND OPERATION OF MANUFACTURED HOME COMMUNITIES

GEORGE ALLEN
DAVID ALLEY
EDWARD HICKS
with JOSEPH OWENS

JOHN WILEY & SONS, INC.
New York / Chichester / Brisbane / Toronto / Singapore

This publication is designed to provide accurate and
authoritative information in regard to the subject
matter covered. It is sold with the understanding that
the publisher is not engaged in rendering legal, accounting,
or other professional services. If legal advice or other
expert assistance is required, the services of a competent
professional person should be sought.

Library of Congress Cataloging in Publication Data:

Allen, George (George F.)
    Development, marketing, and operation of manufactured home
  communities / George Allen, David Alley, Edward Hicks, with Joseph
  Owens.
        p.   cm.
    Includes bibliographical references and index.
    ISBN 0-471-59519-5 (alk. paper) : $65.00
    1. Mobile home parks—Management.   2. Prefabricated houses.
  3. Real estate development.   I. Alley, David.   II. Hicks, Edward,
  1939–   .   III. Title.
  TX1105.A38   1994
  643'.2—dc20   93-9091

Printed in the United States of America

10 9 8 7 6 5 4

This text is respectfully dedicated to

Herbert E. Tieder, publisher, and the late James M. Mack, editor,
of the *Manufactured Home Merchandiser*

who provided the first
forum for many of the concepts, ideas, and
methodology appearing in this book.

FOREWORD

On behalf of the Manufactured Housing Institute, I would like to congratulate George Allen, David Alley, and Edward Hicks on the publication of this important industry resource. The Manufactured Housing Institute, which is composed of manufacturers, retailers, suppliers, community owners/operators, and financial institutions, is dedicated to ensuring professionalism within the industry. This comprehensive work provides a practical tool for promoting professionalism in land development and management.

A book on the development, marketing, and operation of manufactured home communities is very timely. More and more developers are discovering manufactured homes as a viable alternative to site-built homes. Two factors have contributed greatly to this trend: the escalating cost of new site-built construction and the improved quality and appearance of manufactured homes.

Developers are finding that today's manufactured homes offer quality construction and are aesthetically compatible with and often indistinguishable from site-built homes. Moreover, because houses, like other items, can be built more efficiently in a factory, developers get more home for their investment dollar.

These factors have contributed to the present boom in manufactured housing. Manufacturers shipped 210,787 homes in 1992, an 23.5% increase over 1991. This represented 26% of all new single-family homes sold that year. Shipments are expected to reach 250,000 for 1993.

As more developers are recognizing the advantages of using manufactured homes, this book will serve as an excellent guide. George Allen and his co-authors have been involved in the manufactured housing industry for decades. Their understanding and depth of knowledge about the industry makes their book a valuable resource.

This text covers nearly every imaginable situation, from politics to marketing to technical operations. The authors are candid about the advantages and disadvantages of developing manufactured home communities, and warn the reader of common pitfalls. Covering every base, this book even provides components of a sample business plan, sample forms such as resident applications, and hard numbers and equations such as the table entitled "Ratios That Are Important to Lenders (Fig. 16.1)."

MHI is delighted that this book is now available. Developers and future home buyers alike will benefit from the dissemination of this timely and professional information on the development, marketing, and operation of manufactured home communities.

JERRY C. CONNORS

President
Manufactured Housing Institute

PREFACE

How to Build and Operate a Mobile Home Park was written by L.C. Michelon in 1955 and revised in 1964. Twenty-five years went by before the next book on the subject appeared. When *Mobilehome Park Management,* later retitled *Mobilehome Community Management,* made its debut, investment property owners and managers across the United States and Canada purchased the text in record numbers. It was obvious that this most unique of all income-property types was coming into its own as a profitable business worthy of study, documentation, and sharing beyond the traditional confines of the mom-and-pop operation and insider-favored investment arenas.

A frequently voiced question over the past 20 years has been, "Why doesn't someone write and explain how to plan, develop, and fill a manufactured home community?" Some individuals have tried, but with limited success. To do the subject justice would require a team effort. And it was not until I was acquainted with the feasibility and development projects and industry reputations of David Alley and Edward Hicks that I felt the three of us could produce the first comprehensive, practical answer to that 2-decades-old question.

Development, Marketing, and Operation of the Manufactured Home Community has a dual perspective. On a larger scale, the text describes the only income-property type that can be configured as a landlease community occupied by home owners, a bona fide housing subdivision, or even a condominium or cooperatively-owned multihousing community. The book is also a veritable project road map for the community planner, civil engineer, land developer, housing marketer, and would-be investor, owner, or property manager of any manufactured home community.

Drawing upon his speciality areas and technical expertise, engineer David Alley expounds upon site selection and acquisition, concept development, zoning matters, project engineering, and details of construction.

Edward Hicks, following an overview of the development process, describes the importance and role of feasibility studies, preparation of the Business Plan and related market development, and sources of acquisition and development financing, and concludes with guidance on the installation of manufactured homes.

A most enlightening chapter has to do with the specialized nature of manufactured housing finance—the first such overview ever published. Joe Owens of the Manufactured Housing Institute staff, who prepared this chapter, is recognized as a foremost authority on this technical subject.

The property management material presented during the final third of this text is drawn from firsthand experience as a manufactured home community owner and manager. Many industry peers will see the influence of their good ideas and "lessons learned" on the real estate management policies and procedures recommended.

There are three distinct ways to read this text, depending on one's motivation and perspective.

- A leisurely cover-to-cover reading will yield a comprehensive overview of the manufactured housing industry and the role of manufactured home communities. It also offers a good introduction to real estate development practice.
- The reader can refer to particular chapters, depending on planning and management needs at the time. Each chapter is written as a stand-alone segment, useful as how-to guidelines for developing, marketing, and operating multihousing projects in general, and manufactured home communities in particular.
- A methodical, sequential study of the 17 chapters, underlining and taking notes along the way, equips the reader with the most comprehensive step-by-step real estate development guide available on the market today for manufactured home communities.

This reference work is filled with every aid and help available. The chapters, appendices and bibliography are designed to complement one another, forming a comprehensive resource for developing, marketing, and operating every type of manufactured home community.

Real estate developers, investment property owners, urban planners, engineers, project managers, and academics across the United States and Canada have long awaited this text. PMN Publishing, the industry's sole distributor of manufactured home community-related texts, standard forms, and publications, is contacted regularly with requests for "anything pertaining to the development and operation of mobilehome parks."

How many times after reading a book, particularly a business text, have you wished to communicate with the author, or to ask questions? The authors of this text share that frustration. Collectively, they have more than 50 years of experience in the manufactured housing industry, and they are willing to share their expertise with readers and would-be developers, investors, and property managers. Here's how to contact them:

George Allen	Box 47024 Indianapolis, IN 46247 317-888-7156
David Alley	Box 897 Palm Harbor, FL 34682 727-447-1700
Edward Hicks	Box # 2795 Brandon, FL 33509 813-661-5901
Joe Owens	1745 Jefferson Davis Highway Arlington, VA 22202 703-413-6620

The authors would be especially gratified to learn of your ideas and constructive suggestions for improving future editions of this text.

Now you are ready to begin what will surely be one of the most instructive, helpful, and probably profitable, "reads" of your business career. The authors and publisher wish you best success with your manufactured home community development and management project. With the publication of this text, the manufactured housing industry has its first truly comprehensive, hardbound reference, describing the development, marketing, and operation of manufactured home communities.

GEORGE ALLEN

ACKNOWLEDGMENTS

Lawrence A. "Bud" Meyer, mentor and friend, motivated me to undertake this project, and Carolyn—my life partner and writing companion—encouraged me throughout. Nora Freese not only deciphered my handwriting, but also typed and retyped masterfully. I owe a debt of gratitude to *The Allen Letter* subscribers, International Networking Roundtable attendees, and management consulting clients across the United States and Canada, whose support and loyalty have enabled GFA Management, Inc., to prosper, and me to author this historic text.

GEORGE ALLEN

To the wind beneath my wings, Barbara Alley, my partner in life, my partner in business, and without whom my contribution to this book would not have happened, I offer my gratitude. Many thanks also to our sons, Steven and Mark, and to Gerald Walek, with whom I have been associated for more than 25 years in the planning and engineering of more than 200 manufactured home communities.

DAVID ALLEY

To my wife Lynne, a talented businessperson in her own right, who, when necessary, has taken the time from her busy schedule to support my writing efforts, I offer my thanks.

My appreciation also goes to Edward Loudenclos, who started in the manufactured housing business in 1946 and got me involved in 1963, and to Andy Seligman, who first taught me to be a businessman.

EDWARD HICKS

I would like to thank my Manufactured Housing Institute colleagues Erin Dillenbeck and Chris Busky for their help in assembling and editing this material. Thanks also to the people at HUD, VA, and the Farmers Home Administration for answering our many questions.

JOE OWENS

ABOUT THE AUTHORS

George F. Allen, Jr., CPM, is founder and president of GFA Management, Inc., Indianapolis, Indiana, the only real estate management consulting firm in the United States and Canada specializing in the marketing and operation of manufactured home communities. He has managed, fee-managed, and owned manufactured home communities since 1978.

George travels widely and frequently, researching and resolving marketing and management challenges for corporate and individual clients. He professionally evaluates all types of multifamily rental communities and facilitates training seminars for state and national trade associations, as well as tailored in-house programs for many income-property owners. He is past president and Manager of the Year of the Institute of Real Estate Management's Indianapolis chapter, and former board of governors member with the Indiana Manufactured Housing Association.

Ten years of Community Corner columns in the *Manufactured Home Merchandiser,* prize-winning features in the *Journal of Property Management,* and his syndicated "Ask George" real estate management advice column, popular *Allen Letter,* and widely read *Mobilehome Community Management* text have positioned George as the most widely read author in the manufactured housing industry and one of the most prolific writers in the real estate management profession.

George Allen earned his liberal arts degree at Eastern College in St. Davids, Pennsylvania. He served a combat tour in the Republic of Vietnam and retired from the U.S. Marine Corps Reserve as a lieutenant colonel. He and his wife Carolyn live in Greenwood, Indiana, and have two grown children and two grandchildren.

*   *   *

David I. Alley, PE, president of Alley & Associates and partner in Thompson/ Alley Associates, is a nationally recognized expert in planning, engineering, and constructing manufactured housing communities and large tract developments. During the past 25 years he has been responsible for the engineering design of more than 200 subdivisions, condominiums, and/or rental housing communities throughout the United States. Because of his national acceptance as an authority on economically oriented engineering and zoning, David has been a frequently published author.

A civil engineer with more than 25 years' experience throughout the United States and abroad, David is a Registered Professional Engineer in 17 states. He is a member of the National Society of Professional Engineers, the American Consulting Engineers Council, the Florida Institute of Consulting Engineers, and the Florida Engineering Society.

David attended the University of North Dakota, where he received a bachelor of science degree in civil engineering.

Edward Hicks is the president of Consultants Resource Group, Inc., a nationally known manufactured housing development consulting firm, founded in 1982, specializing in market analysis and economic planning.

During his 30 years in the industry, he has been a home builder and retailer, community developer as general partner, and sales manager for a major home manufacturer.

As a licensed mortgage broker, Edward is also active in assisting developers and mortgagees with the FHA 207(m) loan guarantee program under HUD.

In the past 11 years, he has assisted more than 150 developers, investors, and community owners in 35 states. He is a member of the Land Development Committee of the Manufactured Housing Institute and has previously served as vice president of the California Manufactured Housing Dealers Association and as chairman of the Mobile Home Committee of the California Association of Realtors.

Over the past 20 years, he has written more than 200 articles for various trade publications and has authored three books on manufactured housing land development subjects.

He is a licensed real estate broker in Florida and in Maine and has held a California license, actively functioning as "buyers' broker" for several major investment and development firms.

Edward was previously active in the aerospace industry as a senior computer systems analyst. He attended Santa Barbara City College and Brigham Young University.

William J. (Joe) Owens has been the Manufactured Housing Institute's in-house specialist on manufactured housing finance since 1981. It is safe to say that no one, in or out of the industry, knows more about this subject than Joe. He is a graduate, of George Mason University in Virginia with a Bachelor of Science degree.

CONTENTS

CHAPTER 1

INTRODUCTION TO MANUFACTURED HOUSING AND THE MANUFACTURED HOME COMMUNITY

Manufactured housing is the most versatile and affordable housing type available in the United States and Canada today. The versatility of manufactured housing stems from two main factors:

- It can be designed and constructed in a variety of sizes, configurations, and quality gradients, and with the widest selection of features.
- It can be temporarily or permanently sited in landlease or subdivision communities and on private scattered lot homesites.

Manufactured housing is truly America's most affordable housing option. It costs less per square foot than conventional site-built housing, yet is constructed in a controlled factory environment to exacting federally mandated standards.

Manufactured home communities account for the siting of half of each year's production. The slim majority of manufactured homes are sited in landlease communities, and a small but growing percentage in subdivisions. The remaining percentage of each year's manufactured housing production is sited on scattered, privately owned homesites.

WHAT IS MANUFACTURED HOUSING?

The Manufactured Housing Institute says it best in the introduction to its annual industry update entitled *Quick Facts.*

Manufactured housing is defined as any home that is constructed in a factory and whose construction standards are enforced by the U.S. Department of Housing and

Urban Development. Manufactured homes are different from other types of factory-built housing because of the building codes with which manufacturers must comply. In 1974, Congress passed the National Manufactured Home Construction and Safety Standards, a law which not only changed the name from mobile homes to manufactured homes, but requires any company producing manufactured homes to comply with these federally regulated codes. All manufactured homes built after 1976 when the law was enacted, comply with these standards. Manufacturers of other types of factory-built housing, which include modular, panelized and kit homes, are required to meet codes regulated by state and local agencies. The standards by which manufactured homes are built account for durability, wind and fire safety, as well as energy efficiency. Since the enactment of this law, standards have become even more stringent, resulting in homes that are safer, more attractive and more affordable.[1]

The American Planning Association too has influenced the differentiation between the aforementioned housing terms. Their umbrella moniker, *factory-built housing,* is used to describe collectively:

- Manufactured homes
- Mobilehomes or mobile homes
- Modular homes[2]

Some industry experts have pointed out that a synonym for *factory-built housing* is *site-delivered housing.* The APA thus defines the three variants:

- *Manufactured home.* A factory-built structure that is manufactured or constructed under the authority of United States Code 42 Sec. 5401 and is to be used as a place for human habitation, but which is not constructed or equipped with a permanent hitch or other device allowing it to be moved other than for the purpose of moving to a permanent site, and which does not have permanently attached to its body or frame any wheels or axles. A mobile home is not a manufactured home, except as hereinafter provided.[3]
- *Mobile home.* A transportable, factory-built home, designed to be used as a year-round residential dwelling and built prior to enactment of the National Manufactured Housing Construction and Safety Standards (NMHCSS) Act of 1974, which became effective June 15, 1976.[4]
- *Modular home.* Factory-built housing certified as meeting the (local or) state building code as applicable to modular housing. Once certified by the state, modular homes are subject to the same standards as site-built homes.[5]

---

[1] Bruce Savage, ed., 1991–1992 Quick Facts (Arlington, Va.: Manufactured Housing Institute, 1991). Used by permission.
[2] Welford Sanders, *Regulating Manufactured Housing,* Report 398 Chicago, Ill.: American Planning Association, 1986.
[3] Welford Sanders.
[4] Welford Sanders.
[5] Welford Sanders.

Two additional variants of factory-built housing, outside the scope of this text, include:

- *Panelized home.* Housing consisting of wall panels fabricated in a factory as "closed" (complete with windows, doors, and siding installed) or "open" (simply with studs and plates nailed together and sometimes with sheathing attached to one side, but window and door openings left open) and shipped to the building site for final assembly and erection. These homes too must meet state or local building code requirements where constructed.
- *Precut homes.* Simply packages of building materials, factory-cut to design specifications, transported to the building site and assembled. Precut homes include kit, log, and dome homes. These too must meet local or state building codes. According to *Automated Builder* magazine statistics, the "1991 U.S. Housing Pie" showed the following percentages:[6]

Production or site builders	42%
Panelized home manufacturers	37%
HUD-Code (mobile)*	15%
Modular home manufacturers	6%
	100%

*Note: By strict definition, "mobile" as labeled here, should be "manufactured home." "Mobilehome" generally refers to pre-1976 manufactured homes. This simply demonstrates the confusion with terms that persists in the manufactured housing industry.

WHY MANUFACTURED HOUSING?

A few years ago, Don O. Carlson, editor and publisher of *Automated Builder* magazine, wrote what turned out to be a very popular and enduring article, titled "Exploding 10 Myths About Factory-Built Homes." Although this article is included in its entirety in Appendix A, some of his key points, as well as parallel characteristics suggested by Manufactured Housing Institute publications and others, point out the positive characteristics of manufactured housing:

- *Versatile:* There is no more versatile housing than manufactured homes. Because of the self-contained, transportable nature of their design and construction (i.e., fabrication), manufactured homes can be temporarily or permanently sited in a variety of environments: on scattered building sites, in landlease communities, in subdivisions, and in condominium and cooperatively owned communities.

[6] Don Carlson, "The 1991 U.S. Housing Pie," *Automated Builder,* (December 1992): 21.

- *Affordable:* Data show that owning a manufactured home is considerably less expensive than owning a site-built home. The average cost of a manufactured home in 1990 was $27,800 (without land), whereas the price of a new site-built home was $149,000 (with land) and $118,000 for older site-built homes. The median monthly housing cost for a manufactured home owner in 1990 was $257, as compared with $398 for site-built owners, and $424 for site-built or manufactured home renters. The size of manufactured homes has also increased, giving consumers greater flexibility and more living space for their money. In 1990 the average square footage for a multisection manufactured home was 1200 square feet, an increase from 1060 square feet in 1985. Multisection homes accounted for 48% of the homes shipped in 1990.[7] See Figs. 1.1 and 1.2 for additional statistics comparing manufactured homes with site-built homes. A direct side-by-side comparison of site-built and manufactured housing, without land considerations, usually demonstrates a direct savings of 25% to 30% with the latter type of housing.

- *Built to national construction standards:* The federal government's preemptive building code for manufactured housing (NMHCSS, 1976, mentioned earlier), though initially resisted by the industry, has turned out to be a positive marketing tool. It helped eliminate producers of inferior product, and facilitated the upgrading of building materials, fabrication quality, and even design standards and options.

- *Readily financed:* There are two ways to finance a manufactured home: as real property, when permanently sited on usually privately owned real estate; and as personal property, when sited in a landlease community. (See Chapter 10 for a full discussion.)

- *Easily maintained:* The home design, layout, room and utility configuration emphasize simplicity, which makes it easy to clean and maintain the home, and to preserve its value year after year. Most plumbing and electrical services are readily accessible to the home owner or service repairman.

- *Innovative:* Just about every modern feature one expects to find in a site-built home can be included with the design and fabrication of a manufactured home. Such features include the latest styles of kitchen appliances, every variant of HVAC, thick carpeting, large garden tubs, paneled or wallpapered Sheetrock walls, textured cathedral ceilings, ceiling fans, home security devices, and washers and dryers. Manufactured homes are also designed for the physically disabled. On top of all this, manufactured homes are among the most energy-efficient residential structures built today.

- *Readily insured:* Manufactured homes are just as easy to insure as conventional homes, and generally at a lower premium cost.

- *Quality housing that appreciates in value:* When a manufactured home receives the conscientious, regular care that every home deserves, and is properly sited in an attractive, consumer-desired environment, it generally appreciates in value over time.

---

[7] Bruce Savage. Used by permission.

Manufactured Homes	1985	1986	1987	1988	1989	1990
Average Sales Price	$21,800	$22,400	$23,700	$25,100	$26,600	$27,800
(All lengths and widths)						
Cost per sq. foot	$20.57	$20.18	$20.79	$21.36	$22.26	$23.07
Average sq. footage	1,060	1,110	1,140	1,175	1,195	1,205
Single Section						
Average Sales Price	$17,800	$17,800	$18,400	$18,600	$19,200	$19,800
Cost per sq. foot	$18.84	$18.84	$19.07	$19.18	$19.79	$20.20
Average sq. footage	945	945	965	970	970	980
Multisection						
Average Sales Price	$30,100	$30,800	$32,400	$33,600	$34,800	$36,600
Cost per sq. foot	$21.97	$22.08	$22.82	$23.41	$24.17	$25.42
Average sq. footage	1,370	1,395	1,420	1,435	1,440	1,440
Site-Built Homes						
Average Sales Price	$100,800	$111,900	$127,000	$138,200	$148,800	$149,800
Land Price*	$20,160	$22,380	$25,440	$37,314	$42,300	$41,048
Price of structure	$80,640	$89,520	$101,760	$100,886	$106,500	$108,752
Cost per sq. foot**	$45.18	$49.05	$53.42	$50.57	$53.25	$53.05
Average sq. footage (Living space)	1,785	1,825	1,905	1,995	2,000	2,050

Source: U.S. Department of Commerce

* National Association of Home Builders

** Without land cost

FIG. 1.1 Cost and size comparisons of new manufactured homes and site-built homes sold.

The case for manufactured homes is a convincing one. In fact, when prospective home buyers inspect a contemporary manufactured home, it is common to hear them exclaim that the home and its multitude of features surpass their expectations. It is thus easy to see why close to 14 million Americans already live in more than 6.7 million manufactured homes.[8]

A comprehensive history of the manufactured housing industry in general, and manufactured home communities in particular, Allan D. Wallis's *Wheel Estates* is informative and interesting reading. (See the Bibliography for details.)

[8] *American Demographics.* January 1993, quoted in NMNCs 'Washington Update' (January 1993), Washington, D.C.

Comparison of Manufactured Home Shipments to Sales of
New Single-Family Site-Built Homes
(in thousands)

	1985	1986	1987	1988	1989	1990
Site-Built						
Homes Sold	688	750	671	676	650	534
Percent of Total	71%	75%	74%	76%	77%	74%
Manufactured						
Homes Shipped	283	245	233	218	198	188
Percent of Total	29%	25%	26%	24%	23%	26%
Total New	972	995	904	894	848	722

Source: U.S. Department of Commerce, Bureau of Census Data Conventional Homes, C25 Construction Reports

Comparison of Manufactured Home Shipments to All
Privately Owned Site-Built Housing Starts
(in thousands)

	1985	1986	1987	1988	1989	1990
Site-Built Homes	1,742	1,805	1,621	1,488	1,376	1,192
Percent of Total	86%	88%	87%	87%	87%	86%
Manufactured						
Homes	283	245	233	218	198	188
Percent of Total	14%	12%	13%	13%	13%	14%
Total New	2,025	2,050	1,854	1,706	1,574	1,380

Source: U.S. Department of Commerce, Bureau of Census Data Conventional Homes, C25 Construction Reports

FIG. 1.2 Manufactured home shipments and site-built homes and housing starts compared.

MANUFACTURED HOME LANDLEASE AND SUBDIVISION COMMUNITIES

If any multifamily, income-producing property type has had an identity crisis, it has been the manufactured home landlease community. Over the years, at least eight different (but often related) terms have been used by consumers, regulators, the press, and even the industry itself, to describe this type of rental housing community. Past terms have included the following:

- Manufactured housing rental community
- Manufactured housing community

- Mobilehome community (term of choice with some Midwest and East Coast operators)
- Mobilehome park or mobile home park (still the preferred term among long-time property owners and managers and most West Coast operators)
- Home park or park home community
- Trailer park (the most archaic of variants)

Just what is a manufactured home landlease community? It is a developed parcel of real estate with in-ground utilities and other improvements such as paved streets, street lights, and homesites are landscape engineered and utility serviced. In cases where public utilities are not readily available, there are on-site fresh water and wastewater treatment facilities. Additional improvements usually include an office structure, clubhouse, one or more swimming pools, tennis and shuffleboard courts, playgrounds, basketball courts, fishing ponds, and other locally desirable features. Homesites are generally leased month to month or on an annual basis, depending upon local market conditions or mandate. A manufactured home sited on real estate owned by someone other than the homeowner (i.e., renter) remains a chattel, which in turn influences the type of mortgage available for financing the home purchase, and the basis for property tax computation.

Manufactured home subdivisions, although absorbing a minimum of the manufactured homes produced each year, are an increasingly popular investment option for homebuyers and homeowners. Variants of this ownership type are condominiums and cooperatives, collectively known as ROCs, or resident-owned communities. Although ROCs may start out as condominiums or cooperative ownership communities, they are frequently the result of conversions, through a homeowner or resident's purchase of ownership interest in the specific real estate upon which his or her home is sited, or investment in the corporation formed to purchase the property in toto. A manufactured home permanently sited on real estate owned by the homeowner (as in a subdivision or condominium, or on scattered building lots) becomes a fixture and, hence, part of the land. The permanent nature of such siting is usually characterized by the removal of wheels and axles from the home's steel undercarriage, affixing the home to a permanent foundation of some sort, and effecting permanent utility hookups or connections.

There are more than 50,000 manufactured home communities throughout the United States. Sometimes the figure of 24,000 manufactured home communities is quoted, but this generally accounts for those properties with more than 50 homesites. The 10 states with the largest census of manufactured home communities have a total of more than 24,000 properties among them.

What is the average size of landlease communities? Recent studies among owners and property managers of multiproperty portfolios indicate an average of 247 sites. These surveys, however, included few landlease communities of less than 100 homesites.[9]

---

[9] George Allen, "Community Corner," *Manufactured Home Merchandiser,* (January 1993): 25–29.

Monthly homesite rent ranges widely, from a low of $100 to an amount in excess of $500 per month. Rent amounts within a manufactured home landlease community may be the same for all homeowners, or may vary depending on desirability of homesites within the community. In addition, some property owners charge more for items such as having more than two individuals per home, pets, and washer/dryer hookups.

Average national physical occupancy among manufactured home landlease communities in 1989 was pegged at about 94%. In the same study, rural communities outnumbered urban communities 3 to 1, and 61% of landlease communities reported using written leases. Cable TV was the most common of 30 on-site features identified.[10]

TERMINOLOGY

Manufactured home landlease community is not the only manufactured housing industry term to evolve over the years. There are several other industry-specific terms that relate directly to real estate (i.e., property) management in general and landlease community operation in particular.

The difference between *manufactured home* (post-1976 factory-built homes) and *mobilehome* (pre-1976 mobilehome) should be clear by now. The only fine-tuning needed is to suggest that *mobilehome,* when spelled as one word, implies the relative permanence of the home, whereas the older two-word variant suggests mobility.

Resident is the preferred term to describe homeowners living in landlease communities. Although such people are technically lessees (as contrasted with landlords or lessors), or even tenants (this term is commonly associated with commercial properties), *resident* is an accurate and far better-sounding term.

Information Center and *office* are equally common parlance in manufactured home communities. Avoid *Rental Office* or *Park Office.* The use of *Information Center,* adopted from the apartment industry, is increasingly used in professionally managed communities.

Homesite or *site* has been used liberally to this point, because it does the best job describing what in the past has been variously referred to as lot, space, or pad. *Building* or *construction site* refers to the new manufactured home community while it is being developed.

Singlesection and *multisection* best describe manufactured homes and mobilehomes when they arrive at a homesite as a single house section, or two or more housing subsections that will be joined together at the homesite. *Singlewide* and *doublewide* are outdated terms, used in years past to describe similar housing configurations.

Retail or *Retail center* describe the manufactured housing sales center. One manufacturer has called it a "choice center," where manufactured homes are

---

[10] George Allen, "Community Corner," *Manufactured Home Merchandiser,* (November 1989): 32–34.

marketed and sold to consumers-at-large. Prospective homebuyers and homesite renters may also visit the retail center on-site at a manufactured home landlease community. Outdated terms include *dealer, sales lot,* and *street* or *boulevard dealer.*

A *property manager* is *not* the on-site, community resident manager of a rental property—whether it is a landlease or an apartment-type community. The property manager, in professional real estate management parlance, is the middle or executive-level manager with responsibility for and authority over two or more similar (or of different types) income-producing properties, usually within a given geographic region. In some lending institutions and investment houses, these professionals are referred to as *asset managers.*

A *resident manager,* in some circles or regions, is known variously as the community manager, resident administrator, on-site manager, owner-operator, or landlord. When the on-site "caretaker" (as some state regulatory bodies refer to the position) is not the property owner, then *resident manager, community manager,* or simply *manager,* is sufficient.

Transporter is the term that clearly describes the driver of the single-axle tractor designed and equipped to properly and safely move manufactured homes and mobilehomes. Earlier terms, in some parts of the country, were *toter* and *hauler.*

Rules and Regulations are specific and descriptive guidelines for personal and familial conduct, required in some states to be posted in a public place, outlining the do's and don'ts of living in a manufactured home landlease community. A relatively new term is *Guidelines for Living.* Either term is acceptable.

A *Rental Agreement* is the contemporary term referring to a homeowner's lease.

Skirting is an industry-specific term, which describes what some installers and suppliers variously refer to as foundation fascia or siding, curtain wall, even perimeter fascia. In any event, it is the vinyl or metal sheathing used to mask the air space between the bottom perimeter of the manufactured home and the ground below it. The skirting not only masks that area, to enhance the appearance of the home, but serves as a weather barrier as well.

Tiedowns and *earth anchors* serve the same basic purpose. Tiedowns are usually eyebolts inbedded in concrete slabs or runners, on a homesite, to which the home is secured with cable or steel strapping. Earth anchors are used in the absence of tiedowns, or to supplement them. Once sited, the home is affixed to the anchors or tiedown heads with bolts and steel straps affixed to the undercarriage of the home, or over the roof of the home.

Sales or *leasing consultant,* or *rental agent* is in current use. Like *Information Center, leasing consultant* is the term of choice among apartment management professionals and is enjoying increased use among landlease community managers. *Rental agent* too is descriptive, but like *lease,* is somewhat less desirable.

A *resale center* is where previously owned manufactured homes are sold. It may or may not be the same location as the retail center where new homes are marketed. A resale center, in the past, was referred to as a "repo lot" or *used home dealership.*

Trash removal and *refuse removal* are terms used interchangably to describe that common and needed on-site service.

Per capita charges are upcharges for additional individuals living in a manufactured home or mobilehome. Some owners and managers apply these charges, others do not.

Wastewater treatment facility or *plant* is the proper term for the operation. *Sewer plant* is not an acceptable alternative.

There is much more that can be said about manufactured home communities—and that is what will be presented in the chapters to follow. Although this is certainly one of the simplest income-properties to engineer and develop, because of the relatively few building improvements to plan and construct, it has its own unique peculiarities of operation and management. When properly researched, planned, constructed, marketed, and managed, the manufactured home community is difficult to surpass as a real estate investment.

CHAPTER 2

OVERVIEW OF THE LAND DEVELOPMENT PROCESS

The creation of a new manufactured home community, or the expansion of an existing site, is but another variation of the normal land development process. Heretofore, manufactured home community developments have been private enterprise ventures of a landlease nature, capitalizing on the positive characteristics of minimum building site improvements and easy management, along with potential for significant value appreciation. These rental communities varied in size, from four homesites (a minimum set by state statute, where regulated) to more than a thousand sites. Historically, most have been mom-and-pop operations, but over the years the majority of mid- to large-sized communities have been acquired by syndicates (during the 1970s to the mid-1980s) and, recently, by large portfolio companies, homeowners' associations (i.e., ROCs, described earlier in the text), public housing authorities, and private investors.

To an increasing degree, site-built housing developers are looking to manufactured housing and manufactured home communities as a unique "best of both worlds" opportunity. Not only do today's manufactured homes "look and feel" a lot like the builder's traditional product, but they offer the cost-saving and quicker response time benefits of factory-built production as well.

Even the federal government has expressed renewed interest in this housing and community type. In HUD's 1991 exhaustively researched and widely distributed so-called NIMBY Report (subtitled "Removing Barriers to Affordable Housing"), the president's blue ribbon commission makes 31 strongly and pointedly worded recommendations relative to removing said barriers. Here is a typical proposal:

Remove Regulatory Barriers to Certain Types of Affordable Housing Options
(#7-11)[1]

The Commission strongly recommends that States initiate actions to end discrimi-
nation against certain types of affordable housing options, such as amending their
zoning enabling act to: (1) authorize, under appropriate conditions and standards,
manufactured housing as a permitted dwelling unit under local zoning, and prohibit
local communities from enacting ordinances forbidding manufactured housing;
(2) direct that localities permit, under State standards, accessory apartments as of
right, not as a "conditional use," in any single-family residential zone within the
jurisdiction, subject to appropriate design, density, and other occupancy standards
set forth by the State; and (3) require localities to include a range of residential use
categories that permit, as of right, duplex, two-family, and triplex housing and adequate land within their jurisdictions for such use. The Commission also strongly
recommends that States require all local governments to review and modify their
housing and building codes and zoning ordinances to permit, under reasonable State
design, health, density, and safety standards, single-room-occupancy housing.

In many ways, manufactured housing and manufactured home communities
have indubitably rearrived on the American housing scene—not that they have
ever been gone, they have simply not been fully appreciated. Manufactured housing production is up, new manufactured home communities are being built
wherever land use regulations allow and market conditions permit, and would-be
investors literally clamor for the opportunity to corner a piece of the action.

There is no question that manufactured housing per se, and manufactured
home communities represent viable and affordable answers to this nation's much
ballyhooed "housing crisis." The challenge now is to learn and understand manufactured home community development in light of traditional real estate development and to fully appreciate the unique characteristics of manufactured housing
marketing and sales, and manufactured home community promotion, management, and operations.

REAL ESTATE DEVELOPMENT IN EIGHT STAGES[2]

In his 44-page report (#445), *Manufactured Housing Site Development Guide,* author Welford Sanders cites the Urban Land Institute's Eight-Stage Model of Real
Estate Development as an overall pattern for manufactured home community
planning and construction (see Fig. 2.1).

Whereas the eight-stage model is a comprehensive overview of the process,
the thrust of this text is oriented toward a ten-step iterative process—iterative
because each of the succeeding steps is dependent on the others, sometimes in

---

[1] U.S. Department of Housing and Urban Development, *"Not in My Back Yard": Removing Barriers to
Affordable Housing* (Washington, D.C.: Government Printing Office, 1991), p. 16.
[2] Welford Sanders, *Manufactured Housing Site Development Guide,* Report #445, (Chicago, Ill.:
American Planning Association, 1993).

Eight-Stage Model of Real Estate Development

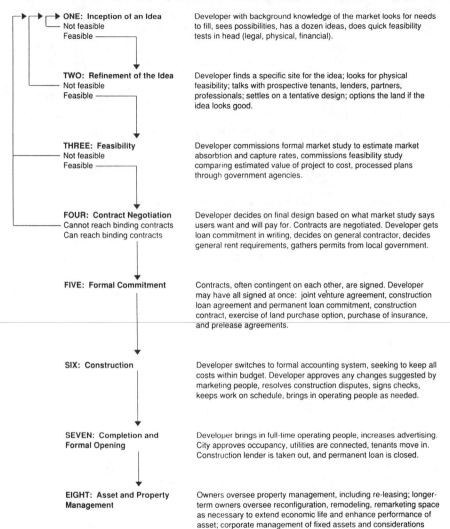

ONE: Inception of an Idea Not feasible Feasible	Developer with background knowledge of the market looks for needs to fill, sees possibilities, has a dozen ideas, does quick feasibility tests in head (legal, physical, financial).
TWO: Refinement of the Idea Not feasible Feasible	Developer finds a specific site for the idea; looks for physical feasibility; talks with prospective tenants, lenders, partners, professionals; settles on a tentative design; options the land if the idea looks good.
THREE: Feasibility Not feasible Feasible	Developer commissions formal market study to estimate market absorbtion and capture rates, commissions feasibility study comparing estimated value of project to cost, processed plans through government agencies.
FOUR: Contract Negotiation Cannot reach binding contracts Can reach binding contracts	Developer decides on final design based on what market study says users want and will pay for. Contracts are negotiated. Developer gets loan commitment in writing, decides on general contractor, decides general rent requirements, gathers permits from local government.
FIVE: Formal Commitment	Contracts, often contingent on each other, are signed. Developer may have all signed at once: joint venture agreement, construction loan agreement and permanent loan commitment, construction contract, exercise of land purchase option, purchase of insurance, and prelease agreements.
SIX: Construction	Developer switches to formal accounting system, seeking to keep all costs within budget. Developer approves any changes suggested by marketing people, resolves construction disputes, signs checks, keeps work on schedule, brings in operating people as needed.
SEVEN: Completion and Formal Opening	Developer brings in full-time operating people, increases advertising. City approves occupancy, utilities are connected, tenants move in. Construction lender is taken out, and permanent loan is closed.
EIGHT: Asset and Property Management	Owners oversee property management, including re-leasing; longer-term owners oversee reconfiguration, remodeling, remarketing space as necessary to extend economic life and enhance performance of asset; corporate management of fixed assets and considerations regarding investors' portfolios come into play.

Source: Mike E. Miles, et al., *Real Estate Development Principles and Process* (Washington, DC: ULI–the Urban Land Institute, 1991).

FIG. 2.1   Eight-stage model of real estate development.

sequence, often not. Research, planning, negotiating, marketing, and managing are but a few of the functions that are integral to one or more of the steps from start to finish. The following are the iterative ten steps:

1. Select and evaluate alternative building sites, and acquire or secure control of the land to be developed.
2. Research and prepare appropriate and comprehensive feasibility studies of the project and local market area.
3. Refine the concept by which the property will be developed, marketed, and operated.
4. Document and understand local land use, and regulatory and zoning measures.
5. Write, rewrite, and finalize a comprehensive business and marketing plan.
6. Proceed with appropriate project engineering.
7. Investigate and arrange for home buyer and project financing.
8. Effect construction of the manufactured home community and installation of homes.
9. Aggressively market the manufactured home community, ensuring effective sales and leasing efforts.
10. Professionally operate and manage the new manufactured home community.

This is certainly a complicated, but imminently manageable, process. Key decisions must be made all along the way, and this is what the following chapters are all about—how to make those decisions in an informed fashion. A closer review of the ten steps follows.

Select and Evaluate Alternative Building Sites, and Acquire or Secure Control of the Land to Be Developed

The ideal is to have a manufactured home community development concept well in mind, even researched and codified, before searching for building sites. However, with this type of multifamily property, the would-be developer may be in the position of either owning or controlling one of the few land parcels already zoned properly, in a favorable market area, or may be faced with the generally difficult prospect of rezoning an otherwise ideal piece of property. There is thus not always a clear-cut case of having to avoid "put the cart before the horse," but simply having to recognize circumstantial necessity.

In any event, guidance abounds as to what to look for when researching undeveloped land. In addition to the detailed information cited in Chapter 3, Robert DeHeer's *Realty Bluebook,* Volume 1, contains a comprehensive "Data Checklist for Undeveloped Land." He cites the following twelve key research categories, each with between three and fourteen subheadings.

- Ownership
- Size and Description
- Characteristics and Utilities
- Location
- Zoning
- Taxation
- Population
- Climate and Natural Hazards
- Local Building Trends
- Price
- Terms
- Important Exhibits, for example: survey report, plot plan, photographs, area map, inspection reports, statistical reports[3]

All this simply scratches the surface of building site research, evaluation, and decision making. Means of securing control of desirable land is also an integral part of this initial step of manufactured home community land development. As Allen Cymrot points out in his popular text, *Street Smart Real Estate Investing,* research—research—research, in the arena of real estate investing and development, is as crucial to success as location—location—location.[4]

Research and Prepare Appropriate and Comprehensive Feasibility Studies of the Project and Local Market Area

Feasible or not feasible? For anyone considering land development, this is a difficult but strategic question. There are several approaches to this subject, and Chapter 4 is a most comprehensive treatment.

An overview of the process is best couched in terms of demand, supply, and financial considerations. Typical feasibility *demand* items include matters relative to population (characteristics, current and projected growth); households (current and projected size and growth, housing unit types by group and demand); consumer buying power indicators; and a detailed buyer profile relative to family demographics, community features and preferences, number of first-time buyers, and number of retirees.

The feasibility *supply* items are associated with business and industry (employment by sector, current and projected growth); retail sales and bank deposits over several years; construction and real estate (e.g., building permit activity and manufactured home sales over several years); and the competition, by type, pricing, and historical rates of sale and leasing.

[3] Robert DeHeer, *Realty Bluebook,* 29th ed., (San Rafael, CA: Professional Publishing Corporation, 1993), pp. 55–58.
[4] Allen Cymrot, *Street Smart Real Estate Investing,* (Mountain View, CA: CR Publishing Company, 1993), p. 30.

Financial feasibility viewed as desirable and profitable from a landlease and/or subdivision perspective, covers, at a minimum, these bases:

- A consideration of whether the project (home sales and site leasing or leasing alone) will generate enough income to pay the interest on development loans and provide an early adequate return on investment. In other words, will the estimated absorption rate support the project's financing demands?
- Detailed and phased or time-laddered and workable pro forma cash flow projections, along with profit-and-loss statements for the same periods.
- Carefully prepared value appraisal, estimating the future value of the project (manufactured home community) when completed, filled, and operating smoothly.
- Availability and characteristics of project and homebuyer financing.

Do not shortcut this vital step in planning the development of a new manufactured home community; it is often the key to a project's success.

Refine the Concept by Which the Property Will Be Developed, Marketed, and Operated

The would-be developer's original ideas, plans, and concept of a new manufactured home community often undergo change and flux as the preceding steps are taken. At this point it is important that variables are literally nailed down, so that substantial development progress can be made. Decisions have been made, or must now be effected, in these, as well as other areas:

- Landlease or subdivision, or combination of both?
- Home sales and/or homesite leasing, land-and-home sales alone, or site leasing alone? What are the ancillary sources of income?
- Level of services to be provided, for example, refuse removal; private or public water and wastewater treatment; maintenance of streets, drains, and security lights. What is general practice in the area?
- Product (manufactured housing) selection by manufacturer, type, price range, and features.

A helpful way to evaluate these and other decision areas is to look at the proposed project through the eyes of prospective homebuyers and renters. A checklist for evaluating manufactured home communities is included as Fig. 2.2.

Document and Understand Local Land Use, and Regulatory and Zoning Measures

Land use and zoning regulations are such highly localized issues as to be difficult to consider in a general way. Suffice it to say, however, that the federal government is

1. Location
   a. Convenient to work, shopping, schools, medical facilities, and local transportation?
   b. Nearby areas acceptable? What type neighborhood?
   c. Desirable climate, including temperature range, amount of rain and snow, humidity, variations in seasons, etc.?
   d. Minimum potential for earthquake damage?
   e. Elevation above sea level?
2. Size of community
   a. Small (fewer than 50 homesites), medium (50 to 150 homesites)?
   b. Large (more than 150 homesites)? Larger communities generally have more and better features and amenities.
3. Appearance
   a. Attractive approach and entrance?
   b. Size and age of existing homes?
   c. Landscaping of individual homes and common areas?
   d. Width of streets?
   e. Well-maintained common areas and facilities?
   f. Well-lighted common areas at night?
4. Parking
   a. Adequate off-street parking for home owners?
   b. Adequate guest parking near clubhouse and throughout community?
   c. Secure storage area for RVs, trucks, boats, and travel trailers?
5. Utilities
   a. Gas and electric metered to each home? Natural gas available?
   b. Water metered or included in rent?
   c. Garbage, trash pickup and sewer included in rent or billed separately?
   d. Underground utility lines?
6. Noise levels
   a. Are any freeways, railroad tracks, or airfields a source of excessive noise?
   b. Do home location, orientation, and building materials minimize existing or potential noise?
7. Rents and rental agreements
   a. Ask manager for history of rent rates for past few years.
   b. Review all terms of any lease offered. Prospectus or rules available?
   c. Is property located in a city with rent control?
8. Resident-owned communities
   a. Cooperative type or co-op where residents own shares in corporation, which owns and manages property. Requires an investment in shares, but monthly fees are generally low.
   b. Condominium type, where homeowner also owns homesite.

(Continued)

FIG. 2.2   Checklist for evaluating manufactured home communities. Adapted from R. Hoffman, "Checklist for Evaluating Mobilehome Parks," Mobilehome Parks of Southern California (Mountain View, Calif.: Hoffman Books, 1993) p. 7.

9. Property management
    a. Ask a few residents about the management. Are the managers and staff friendly and helpful?
    b. Does the community appear to be well organized and well run? Rules enforced?
10. The following are amenities available in various communities:

Beauty salon	Movies
Bingo	Playgrounds
Bridge	Pool tables
Bus trips	Potlucks
Cable TV	Putting greens
Car-washing facilities	Saunas
Clubhouse	Shuffleboard
Craft classes	Social clubs
Dances	Spas
Exercise equipment	Storage area
Fishing ponds	Store on site
Health spa	Swimming pools
Horseshoe pits	Tennis courts
Laundry facilities	Vending machines
Lending library	

FIG. 2.2   *(Continued)*

eminently concerned with the widespread practices of local authorities erecting regulatory land use barriers to affordable housing. The aforementioned report of the HUD blue ribbon commission identified and described the wide variety of discriminating regulatory barriers and recommended many constructive measures to address the issue. To date, many states have indeed passed legislation to correct these inequities and abuses, and, in time, severe land use restrictions and stringent zoning barriers should be eased or removed.

In the meantime, would-be developers must research—research—research all there is to be learned about available parcels of land, land use regulations governing their development, and appropriate zoning ordinances. It is also a very good idea to learn the political power base of an area, and who can be counted on for support at critical stages of the plan approval, zoning, rezoning, and development process. After all, most new manufactured home communities have the very positive capability of bringing low- to midlevel-cost housing to areas that are not being considered by new industry owing to a lack of housing for the workers they would attract.

Write, Rewrite, and Finalize a Comprehensive Business and Marketing Plan

As with feasibility studies, there are a variety of formats relative to Business Plans, Marketing Plans and the like. Chapter 7 explores this very important topic in considerable depth. In simplest terms, the Business Plan package usually comprises two distinct items:

- A very well written, professional-looking cover letter, the content of which is accurate, brief, clear, concise, and complete.
- A binder containing the Business Plan proper, 20 to 40 pages in length. Copies are generally numbered consecutively and labeled "Confidential." Copies are usually bound, always professional looking and inviting to read.

What about the plan proper? It typically has about seven parts,[5] including, for example:

Executive Summary. Write a "hook" or attention-grabbing summary and convincing "snapshot" of the project's risks and rewards; the scope of the business opportunity is described subsequently in more detail.

General Company and Project Description. Give a complete physical description of the proposed project, the background of the firm and principals, a detailed description of the business type(s), and goals planned.

Market Plan. Much of the feasibility study research is reformatted here, as well as the advertising and sales strategy and a timetable with forecasts.

Management Plan. This section contains the organizational structure, staffing, and compensation matters.

Operational Plan. This section includes a chronology of planned actions, strengths and weaknesses of the project, policies and procedures, forms, and the like.

Financial Plan. Identify the capital requirements and describe how they are to be met—debt or equity? Give profit and loss projections for at least 2 years, plus pro forma cash-flow analysis and balance sheets. What is the break-even point?

Appendices. These may contain resumes of principals, a description of housing product alternatives and features, and other helpful information.

A tall order to be sure, but developing the business and marketing plan is another of those iterative steps that determine the level of success for a new manufactured home community development.

---

[5] G.F. Allen, "Creating Business Plans for Investors, Developers," *Merchandiser* (May 1992), pp. 23 & 24.

Proceed with Appropriate Engineering

One of the most creative steps in the 10-step development process is to proceed with appropriate engineering. By now preliminary site plans have been drafted, but adjustments may still have to be made. In any event, planning topography parameters, designing and engineering new manufactured home communities with curvilinear streets, homesites with comfortable density, and locally desirable common area features, are all an architect's dream.

Manufactured home community design, with its usual in-ground utilities and minimum above-grade building site improvements, offers numerous cost-saving possibilities to the efficient and experienced designer-engineer. It is also at this point that building permits are secured and bid documents prepared and distributed for contracting out various on-site construction tasks.

Investigate and Arrange for Homebuyer and Project Financing

Chapters 9 and 10 cover the timely and critical topic of financing in detail. Manufactured home financing itself is unique. Whether it is a new or resale manufactured home that is going into a landlease community or subdivision has a lot to do with the type of financing that is needed.

Project financing is one of the most critical of the 10 steps in the development process. Funds must often be obtained through taking on equity partners; through out-of-pocket (so to speak) resources during the expansion of an existing community—if local financing is not readily available; or through local sources when one is well-enough established and previously very successful in the market area where the new project is being built. In areas where affordable housing is desperately needed, it is increasingly common for public funds to be made available for this purpose.

Effect Construction of the Manufactured Home Community and Installation of Homes

The actual construction is one of those milestone stages that would-be developers welcome. Construction begins with the developer as general contractor—or this responsibility may be hired out—and continues in earnest. As underground utilities, streets, and homesite foundations are emplaced, new homes are sold and sites leased—or simply sold if they are part of a subdivision—and homes are installed and anchored to the sites. Landscaping is effected and on-site features and amenities erected. The project is well under way.

Aggressively Market the Manufactured Home Community, Ensuring Effective Sales and Leasing Efforts

Promotion and marketing usually begin before on-site improvements are complete. As soon as possible, a retail sales center is established nearby or on-site to provide a preview of the new community and its characteristic new homes. Sales and leasing staff are trained beforehand, and performance is evaluated and improved upon from day one. There is no room for any error in advertising or in phone or on-site handling of prospective buyers and renters. Owner, developer, and manager must be very sensitive to "what is selling and what is not," and insofar as possible, must adjust the product, features, and pricing to capitalize on those factors that enhance the initial and continued successful leasing-up of the new manufactured home community.

Professionally Operate and Manage the New Manufactured Home Community

Start-up operation and management of a new manufactured home community is one more step that adds to the confusion associated with construction, sales and leasing, and daily move-ins—all going on at the same time. A professional, planned start-up, however, is certainly necessary to ensure the smooth operation of the new income-property, even of a subdivision. The more planning that can be done beforehand the better. Forms and files design and setup, policies and procedures, rules and regulations (also known as Guidelines for Living), and financial accounts are all addressed very early on.

Ongoing operations and management of the new community take on the characteristics of conventional property management once most of the construction is complete, most homesites filled, and staff stabilized. Then the basics of professional property management play a major role in maximizing return on investment, good relations with residents, attractive curb appeal, and eventual property value appreciation over time.

SUMMARY

New manufactured home community development is a major undertaking, involving a wide variety of trade and professional skills, much planning, astute construction marketing, and general property management. Would-be developers should not only envision their concept early and seek out possible building sites, but recruit, select, and assemble a team that will be capable and supportive throughout this project. Reading and rereading this text, from start to finish, will go a long way toward enhancing one's likelihood of success in developing a new manufactured home community or expanding an existing one.

CHAPTER 3

SITE SELECTION AND LAND ACQUISITION

Before proceeding with site selection, developers must have a clear understanding of what they intend to develop and of their financial capabilities and goals. For example, one developer may want income property that generates depreciation benefits, and thus is more inclined toward a manufactured home landlease community. Another developer may not be interested in tax depreciation benefits, but may want a quick return of liquidity without the ongoing problems and responsibilities of property management; thus, a manufactured home condominium or subdivision would be the choice.

DEFINE CONCEPT

In order for developers to proceed with site selection, they must have a clear understanding of those elements that will define their project goals. To select a concept, the following elements must be well understood:

- Market
- Development site characteristics
- Economics
- Politics
- Product selection

Although concepts may be derived without input from the elements discussed in this chapter, proper concept development should at least consider the interrelationships of these five factors. For example, it would be an economic disaster to develop a $220 per month landlease community in a marketplace that supports only a $90 monthly rental rate. It is also unwise to construct a $90 per month landlease community in a marketplace that commands a $220 monthly rental rate, in terms of amenities and facilities to meet the market demands. There must be a proper balance between the five key elements. In a marketplace that supports only low rental rates, but in which land costs and construction costs are high, site selection demands economically favorable site characteristics. In other words, the land preparation and utility costs must be reduced to offset the high land costs and low rental structure. Therefore, the concept would not include wooded sites or steep topography. The extent or degree to which a particular element influences a concept varies with each particular situation.

LAND COST

There is no easy answer to what the developer can afford to spend per acre for raw land. In comparing costs between different properties, the net cost per acre must be calculated, as opposed to the gross cost per acre. In other words, it must be determined what percentage of the land is unusable as a result of the following factors:

- Floodplain
- Wetlands
- Easements
- Topography
- Proposed expansion of adjacent roadway right-of-way
- Acreage required for on-site wastewater treatment or domestic water supply, when needed
- Land losses owing to zoning ordinance or other regulations, such as open space requirements, soil erosion control and storm water management, buffer requirements, right-of-way requirements, or front yard, side yard, back yard, or density requirements.

For example, if 25% of the raw land will not be revenue producing, the full cost must be attributed to the remaining 75% of the land in order to calculate the true net acre purchase price.

The cost of servicing the site with access roads and utilities must be considered when comparing the land cost of one site versus another. One site may have municipal sewer and water services available at the site, whereas another may require the off-site costs of extending water, a sewer, or a storm sewer to the site. One site may require that an off-site roadway be constructed or paved, whereas another site may already have direct access to an adequate roadway.

Generally, the economics of manufactured home landlease communities require the developer to pay less for raw land than for multifamily or site-built residential properties. In metropolitan areas, this means the land search must take place on the fringes of the densely developed urban areas where land prices tend to decrease in proportion to the distance from the developable urban area. However, if the developer's concept includes the home and land package with simple interest and long-term financing favorable to single-family residential financing, there is the option of paying more for the property and selecting a property closer to the urban area and at prices comparable to single-family residential subdivisions.

However, the developer must be certain that the housing cost to the consumer is at least 20% less in the manufactured home community than for single-family residential homes in the market area (see Chapter 4 for further discussion).

SITE SEARCH PROCEDURE

General Evaluation

Assume that a market area has been selected, a major metropolitan area or a submarket within a particular metropolitan area. The task is to identify the areas of potential sites. At this point, developers are not identifying specific sites but, rather, general areas that satisfy the necessary criteria in which a specific site might exist.

The first thing a developer must do is become intimately familiar with the market area. Using a road map is a good starting point in becoming knowledgeable about the different municipalities, counties, and geographical features of the area. After this overview, search out, visit with, and collect all information available from regional planning, regional drainage district and/or floodplain agencies, and regional sanitary sewage districts, as well as all regional utility entities. Next, communicate with and collect all data available from the county branches of government and then from the smaller units of government, such as cities, towns, villages, or townships. At this point, many developers engage a professional planning and engineering firm to assist in the gathering, organizing, and interpretation of field data.

From the information and data collected, developers or their professional consultants prepare maps depicting the following:

1. Those locales being serviced with *existing sanitary sewage treatment facilities.* Maps can be collected from the sanitary sewage districts or municipalities, showing the service districts of the existing facilities or those areas that could be served within the sewage districts with trunk line extensions. It will, at this point, be necessary to evaluate those areas that fall within the probable economics of trunk line extension.

2. Those areas where *on-site private treatment facilities* can be developed. There are some states in which private sewage treatment facilities are all but

impossible to develop, and other states in which approval for private sewage treatment facilities is still not too difficult to obtain. Therefore, developers should be familiar with these state, metropolitan, or community regulations and policies. Where regulations permit, developers should focus on those areas that have approval potential.

3. Those areas capable of *supplying domestic water*. Such locales can be determined through conversations with existing water utility companies and through the engineer's investigation of the potential for operating a private water supply system.

4. Those areas with *soils favorable to development*. Most generally, soils maps of the area will be available from the Soil Conservation Service, which is an agency of the U.S. Department of Agriculture and generally located at the county courthouse. The Service will assist in identifying those areas that are in swamp or those soil types that would present developmental difficulties.

The Soil Conservation Service can also, on a preliminary basis, identify those areas where soil conditions will support on-site soil absorption systems for sanitary sewage treatment or disposal.

5. Those areas *in floodplains*. Once again, the Soil Conservation Service can be of assistance in the identification of floodplain areas. In addition, the county, regional planning, and drainage districts can supply floodplain maps.

6. Those areas *topographically suitable for developments*. U.S. Geological Survey (USGS) topographic maps are available at most local map stores and at most county and government planning and zoning agencies. A 10-foot contour interval USGS map will usually be adequate for identifying those general areas to be avoided relative to site selection.

7. Those areas desirable from a *transportation standpoint*. Developers may choose areas that are favorably located relative to the available transportation system. This information can be obtained from regional planning agencies and from existing road maps. Regional planning agencies can identify the types of roads, as well as provide traffic counts.

8. Those areas that have the *highest probability of obtaining favorable zoning or rezoning*. A composite of the areas previously discussed will narrow the land search considerably. At this time, these probable areas should be discussed with the zoning administrator or governmental body that approves zoning. The community zoning administrator or planner can then specify those areas for which the highest probability of obtaining favorable zoning is anticipated, as it relates to the planning and politics of the municipality. The developer should check the past zoning approval in the community.

9. Those areas that are *environmentally negative*. Again, through consultation with community agencies, those areas that are environmentally negative, as they apply to locations close to airports or industrial areas that may have odor, noise, or air pollution problems, can be eliminated. Developers should also physically

investigate the areas that have been determined to be probable sites as shown by the existing composite of the maps described earlier.

By developing a composite overlay of all the maps and area delineations discussed, the developers zero in on those areas that have potential relative to site selection and, more important, have eliminated a considerable amount of area.

Developers desiring assistance in the land search at this point may wish to enlist the services of a real estate broker. In this case, the developers should prepare a land search data sheet to present to the real estate broker with the composite map. The land search data sheet informs real estate agents of the size of the property and the terms that the developers will accept for an option or purchase agreement. On the other hand, developers not intending to use real estate brokers may obtain county plat maps to obtain the names of property owners. The developers are now ready to search out and evaluate specific sites.

Specific Evaluation

The task is to evaluate specific sites against the desired concept as defined by market, physical site characteristics, economics, politics, and product selection in order to make a site selection. Each potential site must be evaluated in regard to a number of factors, which are included in the following list. A detailed discussion of these elements is presented in Chapter 5.

Market Factors
- Location
- Demographics
- Project size
- Project staging
- Competition

Site Development Characteristics
- Topography
- Soils
- Vegetation
- Drainage
- Traffic
- Utilities
- Easements
- Surrounding vista and environment

Economics
- Sales price or rental rate of completed similar developments
- Land cost
- Development costs

Politics
- Adjacent land use
- Zoning
- Building codes

Product Selection
- Market determinants
- Site characteristic determinants

The sites selected must be reviewed and weighed against these parameters. At this point, specific sites can be identified with which to proceed. Proper evaluation of the listed factors requires expertise in development, land planning, and civil engineering. Developers lacking experience in these areas will find it necessary to expand the development team with qualified professional or developmental assistance.

No site will be perfect. If a particular site has grading or soil problems, but is found to have very positive characteristics, relative to the other parameters, the additional costs related to the soils or grading problems may be justified. To complete a thorough evaluation, it may be necessary for the developer to control a site for a short period of time. For example, the developer may negotiate a month's option in order to perform more investigative analysis, such as on-site soil borings or calculating the cost of off-site community sewage extension, prior to final site selection.

SOME ADDITIONAL CONSIDERATIONS IN CHOOSING A SPECIFIC SITE

Sites with topography slopes in the range of 0% to 6% are normally cost-effective, but sites with a slope of more than 10% will result in a considerable increase in development costs. However, sites with no positive slope may also present drainage problems.

The developer should be aware that the U.S. Army Corps of Engineers and the state Department of Environmental Regulation have jurisdiction over wetlands. The developer should consider wetlands as generally unbuildable. Detailed treatment of wetlands can be found in Chapter 8. In selecting a site, the total buildable acreage and net usable acreage should be analyzed.

Can the storm drainage be collected and drained from the site without adversely affecting the surrounding neighbors? What are the requirements of the storm water management regulations of the controlling governmental agencies? Many areas in the country now require that storm water be both detained and treated. The site should be analyzed for the practicality of meeting the appropriate regulations for management of storm water.

If the site is heavily wooded, the developer must determine whether the other site characteristics will allow trees to be cleared only in the roadways and left standing in the homesite areas. The tree ordinances of the community should be studied to determine whether trees can be cut down without a mitigation policy of replacement and whether they can be disposed of by burning, as opposed to chipping and hauling the tree chips off-site. The difference in cost between burning and hauling the trees off the site could be as high as $2,000 per acre. If the slope of the site is less than 6% and is positive relative to drainage, many of the trees can be saved, thus lowering the development cost and increasing the environmental and aesthetic quality of the proposed project.

The local utilities should be contacted to verify that the project can be provided with electrical, telephone, gas, and cable television services. The policies of the utility companies and the costs that would be required of the developer should be determined. The water utility should be consulted to determine whether adequate pressure is available to serve the project. The local development ordinance or a trip to the fire chief will alert the developer to the flows required by the fire department. Although 500 gallons per minute is adequate flow for fire protection, many communities require as much as 1,000 to 1,500 gallons per minute, which could have an effect both on the available pressure and the cost of the distribution system as it relates to water main sizing and water storage. The sanitary sewage utility or district should be contacted to verify not only that there is a trunk line or sewer line available, but also that the wastewater treatment plant is permitted to handle the additional flows from the proposed development.

Easements, too, may reduce the net usable number of acres of a development and may have a significant impact on the proposed concept plan. Therefore, all easements must be identified. This can be done by going to the Register of Deeds' office at the county seat and reading through the recorded deeds for the property in question. Although the seller of the property or the Realtor® should supply this information to the prospective buyer, experience has shown that all too often this information is not made available.

Both the local and state departments of transportation should be consulted. If the property is to be rezoned, one of the strongest arguments used by opponents to rezoning is that the roads in the area are not adequate for the increased traffic from the proposed development. The developer should have this information early in order to decide whether to proceed with zoning of a particular site. Moreover, if expensive acceleration and deceleration lanes are required, this will have an impact on the economics of the project.

Although it does not happen often, from time to time sites are purchased without the knowledge that the property had previously been used as a hazardous waste dump. If such a situation is suspected, through conversations with the Environmental Protection Agency or with local officials, the site should be investigated to verify that it is in fact not, and has never been, used as a hazardous waste dump. In addition, the developer should envision the site through the eyes of future residents in terms of noise, odor, view, and any other aspect that relates to the fill rate and marketing success of the project.

Generally, the manufactured home is not as adaptable to varied and steep topography as multifamily or single-family site-built housing, in which the structures can become retaining walls and grades can be transcended across a structure much more easily than across a manufactured home, in which the exterior walls cannot function as retaining walls. Thus, in site selection, topography, or the cost of grading, becomes a significant factor. However, manufactured housing, particularly where basements are not a part of the concept, has the advantage of being far more adaptable to properties with high groundwater elevations than single-family site-built houses designed with basements.

Zoning of manufactured housing developments has traditionally been more difficult than the rezoning of property for multifamily or single-family site-built developments. Therefore, in site selection, the developer must be more sensitive to surrounding land uses and the potential for community and political opposition.

ZONED LAND—UNZONED LAND

If the selected site is not zoned, developers should negotiate an option or purchase agreement giving them a minimum period of 12 months to implement rezoning. On the other hand, if the property is presently zoned, developers should seek a minimum of 3 months' option to prepare preliminary planning, engineering, and cost estimates in order to be assured of the project viability prior to closing on the property.

There are certainly exceptions to such time frames as these are only general guidelines. Each site must be carefully investigated and critical decisions made relative to the specifics of the particular site.

The major advantage of zoned land is that the developer can proceed much faster, with a shorter timetable. Moreover, the developer does not have the financial risk of preparing exhibits and paying for the professionals required in the rezoning process. However, the increase in value of the zoned property may be substantial, as opposed to its value as raw land. If the developer is successful in the rezoning process, significant additional value is created over the initial raw land purchase price. Prior to rezoning, it is essential that the developer closely scrutinize the concept definition to make sure it is compatible with the zoning ordinance and requirements.

SELECTING A REAL ESTATE BROKER

Buying property for development can be risky these days, owing to increasingly severe land use regulations. For a property to be legally buildable and mortgageable, it must not only meet topographical requirements and have the right soil types, but it must also meet hydrological standards and environmental contamination regulations and must be free of any archeological significance.

Exercising careful due diligence is of course, critical in evaluating a development site. An experienced real estate broker who is knowledgeable in development issues can be important to the developer, by acting as a "preselector" of possible building sites.

In most listing agreements, real estate brokers are paid by the seller. A developer is therefore buying property at a disadvantage, not knowing the true status of a given development site because of the broker's employment by, and loyalty to, the seller. Relying on representations of the seller's agent about a parcel can cost a developer much time and money during the site selection process.

Buyer's Broker

A "buyer's broker" relationship can help to overcome some of the disadvantages of working with a broker. In this type of agency, the real estate broker or agent represents the developer in acquisition of a site for development, not the seller. The buyer's broker works solely on behalf of the developer and is charged with the responsibility of assisting in the due diligence process to find a wholly acceptable site.

Although the buyer's broker commission is most often paid upon closing of the purchase and sale agreement, as it is in a "seller's broker" relationship, most developers will loyally stick with a broker through the long process of finding, reviewing, and selecting a viable development site from all those presented by sellers.

What to Expect from a Broker

Regardless of whom the real estate broker is working for, the developer can expect professional real estate expertise with regard to the proposed development site. The broker should be able to adequately assist the developer in determining the feasibility of site development, including revelation of any material facts that would negatively influence a decision to buy. In addition, the broker should be able to render an opinion regarding the value of the site, provide information on other possible sites, and review the price and terms of other similar properties that have recently sold.

TYPES OF AGREEMENTS

Land may be purchased in several ways, depending on the developer's financial objectives and the seller's desire to participate in the venture. Other than an outright cash purchase, the most common form is a purchase with partial release of land for the first phase of development. The balance of the development site is either optioned for purchase or remains subject to a time schedule for release. If a purchase money mortgage is negotiated at the time of sale, it will remain as an encumbrance on the land. Either this money will accrue interest or interest will be paid regularly. There is minimal risk to the seller of the land in such an arrangement.

Those sellers willing to earn more income for their land, and those who are not afraid to put it at risk, may be willing to sell a parcel and not release land for the first phase of development. They will, however, allow a subordination of their mortgage interests to an institutional development loan. Under this type of agreement, as the development fills, the seller is paid an accelerated, pro rata, partial payment and gives a release from the purchase money mortgage for each occupied site. Interest on the purchase money mortgage is frequently paid monthly in such an agreement.

Another type of purchase, at a higher rate of return on the land value but also at some risk to the seller, involves creating a limited partnership type of interest in the development entity by the developer as whole or partial payment of the land from the seller.

A third, also risky, method of land payment is the long-term lease with provisions for subordination of a recorded mortgage to an institutional lender for development financing. In such an arrangement, the lease payment is frequently determined to be a fixed percentage of the gross rental income to the project.

TAX CONSIDERATIONS

It is advisable to obtain good tax counsel when structuring a sale in which the seller retains some interest in the site by mortgage or partnership interest, inasmuch as tax law may imply a sale and therefore create a tax event upon completing a sale, regardless of the amount of actual cash flow at closing. Depending on the structure of the sale, the seller may be eligible for more favorable tax considerations, especially when capital gains taxes are lower than marginal rates. Depending on the tax laws in effect at the time, a seller may also be entitled to "installment income" rules, and thereby reduce any tax consequences.

MANUFACTURED HOME COMMUNITY DEVELOPMENT SITE ACQUISITION CHECKLIST

The checklist in Appendix B is to be used as a guide when performing the due diligence on a proposed development site. Although all information requested may not be available, its missing status may be a clue as to the acceptability or nonacceptability of the site for development purposes.

SUMMARY

There are many considerations in the selection of a site to be used for the development of a manufactured housing community. This chapter outlines numerous specific criteria to be considered in site selection. Although no site is perfect, the evaluation and comparison of sites will be greatly facilitated through the methodology presented here. The site search should start with an overall perspective of the market area and then proceed to a specific selection of sites. The developer must define financial capabilities and goals and, prior to site selection, must also determine the segment of the housing market to be targeted. If the developer selects a site that requires rezoning, careful analysis of the politics and evaluation of the potential for successfully rezoning the site are necessary before proceeding with control the property and beginning the rezoning process. Land is first controlled for a minimum period in order to perform due diligence evaluation. The land can then be optioned for a substantial period to give the developer time to rezone the property and to determine project feasibility prior to purchase. A local Realtor⊙ can often be of invaluable assistance during site selection.

CHAPTER 4

FEASIBILITY STUDIES

A good feasibility study is a thorough, arms-length, financial analysis of an economic model of a planned development project. The study describes and evaluates proposed housing products matched to the targeted buyer's needs, which fit the developer's timing and business strategy in the context of financial and management resources. The primary function of such a study is to provide a prospective developer with a method of estimating the market for and the economic feasibility of developing a manufactured home community. A feasibility study is often time-consuming and expensive and may seem like an unnecessary task to some, but it is a very important, even critical, step which must be taken—fully researched and evaluated—before proceeding with any major expenditure of capital.

A feasibility assessment is primarily a financial analysis, whereby a proposed manufactured home community development is evaluated for its financial viability according to a set of given data. These data include not only information that is peculiar to the targeted homebuyer and the local market area, but also information on the anticipated financial structure of the project, the limits of developer's capital, the available project management, and timing.

Data that must be collected regarding the buyer include targeted household composition and income levels, anticipated household funds allocated to housing, desired housing size and characteristics, utility costs, and so on. Market area information must include estimated project absorption rates, present market homesite pricing or rents, representative apartment rents, entry-level housing pricing, average manufactured home pricing, and so forth. The financial structure of the project must fit the developer's business strategy. For example, immediate cash flow requirements might suggest a subdivision or condominium project, or if long-term income is preferred, may suggest a landlease community. Debt or equity financing preference and availability must be established, and the developer's total capital resources must be estimated and assessed. In addition to the available capital, the developer's management strategy must be determined. Will a general contractor be used for construction or will the developer function as the general contractor? Is the project to be managed by a third party or directly by the developer or a salaried staff member? Will home sales be affected by the developer's using an on-site sales staff, or will home sales and placement be open to outside retailers?

Understanding the components of the data that must be collected and evaluated for a feasibility study requires knowledge of how manufactured homes fit various households' shelter needs. The data gathered must objectively evaluate market demographics, prospective buyer and renter income levels, and establish the implications of various home buyer financing programs. Preliminary cost estimates, project absorption rates, and operating budgets must be clearly understood prior to estimating and evaluating the developer's potential capital and management requirements and resources.

ASSESSING HOUSING DEMAND

It is important that the developer fully assess housing demand by type of home product, accessories, homesite characteristics, community type, amenities, and home price range, in the context of targeted buyer and renter demographics and available financing programs.

Information must be gathered on all other housing alternatives available for targeted buyers and renters. Then the developer must evaluate the impact and influence of these factors on the proposed manufactured home community development.

Manufactured homes are considered by many to be an alternative source of shelter; thus, as a general rule, affordability is an important feature of interest for prospective homeowners. An exception to this rule is the market in which communities are promoted as primary housing for retirees and empty nesters. Traditional examples of such areas are found in Florida, the Eastern Carolinas, Arizona, and California. In other isolated midwestern and eastern market areas—Boston, Massachusetts, for one—developers are finding success with "Florida-like" retirement communities.

The inexperienced developer must take care to select a housing "product" that is attractive and satisfying, but not overpriced for the targeted homebuyer. More than one project has failed because the developer overpriced the product by offering homes of too high quality, too many factory options, and requiring expensive on-site features. Although such upscale home products may be more attractive and stroke the developer's ego, they may be unaffordable for the marketplace and surpass the targeted homebuyer's purchasing ability.

EVALUATING PROJECT ABSORPTION RATES

One of the most important research aspects to be included in a feasibility study is the estimate of project absorption. The absorption rate is the rate at which a project is expected to lease or sell, usually expressed in number of homes sold and/or homesites leased per month. Estimating the absorption rate assumes the home product has been specified properly to match target market objectives. Under documented local market conditions, the new manufactured home community development project will fill at predictable rates.

According to the 1990 U.S. Census Reports, the average rate of population growth is approximately 1.1% per year. Households generally grow at a slightly higher rate, because the number of persons per household has been regularly declining. Unlike single-family site-built homes and multifamily housing, manufactured home communities, especially landlease communities, have a potential absorption rate frequently in excess of the area household growth rate.

Communities are generally family oriented, mixed family and empty nester or retiree, or all empty nester and retiree. The absorption rates will usually be different for each type of community. Historically, except in retirement areas of the country, the majority of manufactured home community residents have been smaller-sized, lower-income families, and there have been few if any empty nesters and retirees. Frequently, the percentage of the latter groups has been between 10% and 20%. Over the past 10 years, however, the percentage of empty nesters and retirees living outside traditional retirement areas has increased from less than 10% of a manufactured home community to today's 40% to 60%. This is particularly true in areas surrounding major metropolitan centers in eastern, western and midwestern states, but has not been characteristic of southwestern or southern states.

Overestimating an initial community absorption rate is one of the greatest mistakes a developer can make. Assuming the housing product has been correctly matched to the market needs, it is far safer to underestimate the fill rates for the first phases of development, and build the subsequent development phases sooner than expected, than to sit with large numbers of unsold or unoccupied homesites.

Typical absorption rates for projects with the number of recommended homesites per phase of development are as follows:

Monthly Rate	Number of Homesites
1 to 2	25 to 50
3 to 4	75 to 100
5 to 7	125 to 175
8 to 10	200 to 250
10 or more:	rate $\times$ 25

The majority of new manufactured home communities fill at rates of 2 to 5 per month, with an average rate of 4 for a well-planned project, under favorable market conditions. As a general rule, most builders build an inventory of homesites for 2 years of sales. Most new communities should not, therefore, build more than 100 to 125 homesites at a time, especially during the initial phase of marketing. Justifying absorption rates higher than these should be done only in the presence and context of very low vacancy rates in similar recently completed projects with documentable high absorption rates and well-documented continuing market demand.

In utilizing a computerized economic model template for cash flow and profit analysis, using a realistic monthly absorption rate is of the utmost importance, even if it seems to be too slow. Better to err on the conservative side than to doom the project to failure by promoting an unrealistic and, at worst, unachievable absorption rate.

BUYER PROFILE

There are four main sources of homebuyers for a manufactured home community: smaller-sized, lower-income-family homebuyers; converted apartment dwellers; empty nesters; and retirees. For community developments with a substantial percentage of smaller, lower-income-family homebuyers and conversions from apartments, local area household growth rates can be used to estimate absorption potential.

For upgraded projects, oriented to a larger percentage of empty nesters and retirees, household growth rates are not as reliable. Of more importance is the degree to which empty nesters and retirees in a local area sell their family homes to move into a retirement-oriented community. These residents may be local or, in retirement areas such as Florida, the Eastern Carolinas, Arizona, and California, may relocate from all parts of the United States and Canada.

Empty nesters are those who continue to work but have no children living with them at home. Like retirees, they tend to buy more expensive homes and live in nicer communities. Many are retired military personnel with a pension income, who must supplement it with local employment. Others wish to be near their children and choose not to move to retirement areas of the country.

The degree to which empty nesters will fill a community depends historically on several major factors:

- Sale of their site-built residences, at a good price, and in a timely fashion
- Availability of military facilities, such as hospitals, commissaries, and post and base exchanges
- Absence of children (or placement in another area of the project) in the manufactured home community, or
- Good community management and control of children

In evaluating empty nester and retiree residents, a good market survey, with detailed research into historical fill rates of other area similar projects, is the best indication of how well a new community will fill. As a part of the evaluation, it is important to compare amenities, location, home prices, homesite sizes, utility services, proximity to shopping, hospitals, and so on, among existing multifamily communities and the one being planned. Rent rates and homesite prices can be adjusted to offset deficiencies of a new development, to a degree. In major retirement areas, communities tend to prevail in specific geographic areas. For example, in Florida, the southern and central coastal areas do well with retirement communities, but central and northern panhandle projects do not. In those areas are the lower-quality, lower-rent, family-oriented communities.

The overall economic condition of an area is of major importance in determining project feasibility. As a rule, high unemployment or apartment vacancy rates above 10% in a given area are negative indications. Areas in which the local economy depends on a single, dominant economic employment resource, such as a military base or a large factory, must be evaluated carefully.

One apparent exception to the rule has been state capitals. In these areas, employment is generally more stable, and there are a relatively high number of households with medium-income wage earners, who cannot afford to purchase new single-family site-built homes and do not want to continue paying rent. They frequently have smaller families, their credit is usually good, and their employment has long-term stability.

To evaluate product pricing, a targeted buyer must be selected. The housing product type is matched to the targeted buyer in the context of a business strategy, and local market conditions are considered as well. If, for example, the targeted buyers are primarily retirees and empty nesters, a medium density, landlease community with amenities, primarily using multi-section homes may be indicated. If, on the other hand, the targeted buyers are primarily smaller families with blue-collar income levels, a medium to high-density landlease community with minimal amenities, using single-section homes in lower price ranges, may be indicated.

Manufactured homes in a subdivision are not perceived to be as favorable as site-built housing, so establishing the need for manufactured homes in new subdivisions and in projects where homesites are conveyed to the homebuyer along with the home as real property may be difficult. This type of development is usually indicated only when the developer has carefully evaluated the implications of possibly lower initial profit margins, stiff competition from the lower-priced end of site-built housing, and the possible difficulty of later selling off a partially developed community, if necessary, to another developer.

FEASIBILITY CHECKLIST

The following items are considered to be key indicators to evaluate in estimating project feasibility:

- Projected area household growth rate
- Median household size
- Estimated housing unit demand by type
- Anticipated employment growth rate
- Number and type of major employers
- Median household income
- Historical building permit activity

- Historical home resale rates
- Local apartment vacancy and rental rates
- Historical competitive sales history
- Competitive vacancy and rental rates or homesite pricing
- Competitive sales methodology
- Competitive marketing and advertising methodology
- Competitive home product pricing
- Competitive homebuyer sources
- Competitive homebuyer financing
- Pricing of "entry level" site-built housing
- Area retail sales history
- Area bank deposit history
- Historical area manufactured housing shipment rates
- Local buyer attitudes toward manufactured housing communities (which can substantially affect project feasibility)

In many parts of the country, manufactured homes are seen by the general public as a housing alternative, and not as a primary housing type. This attitude is prevalent in the Northeast and in parts of the West Coast. In large midwestern cities such as Detroit and Indianapolis, manufactured housing is relatively popular, as compared with other parts of the country, and is seen by many as a viable choice with many advantages over apartment or site-built home living. In sophisticated areas such as New York and San Francisco, manufactured housing is virtually unknown. However, manufactured home communities are quite popular in the suburban and "near rural" areas of these cities, such as the Santa Clara Valley in California and the Middletown area of New York.

HOMESITE CONFIGURATION

Generally, the more frontage a homesite has, the more attractive the community will be. For homesite configurations where the home is parallel to the street in a lateral or transverse installation, further expense must be added to the overall construction costs because of the additional homesite roadway frontage and longer utility service lines. All other things being equal in a comparable development, new manufactured home community projects with more frontage will cost more per homesite to develop and will, therefore, have a relatively higher price or rent.

To increase the number of homesites built on a residential street, thus keeping development costs and, therefore, prices and rents as low as practical, homesites are generally designed to be narrow and long. This is one of the most visible and easily identifiable characteristics of a manufactured home community. In this configuration, the home is sited perpendicular to the street, representing typical manufactured homesite installation.

HOME PRODUCTS

There are two basic types of home "products": manufactured homes on leased land, and manufactured homes on land fee simple, as in a subdivision, condominium, or cooperatively-owned community.

Because buyer perception is generally that manufactured homes, either on leased land or in a subdivision, are a housing alternative and not a primary housing type, it is necessary to offset this perception with a strong positive feature. The easiest and best approach is to initially reduce the targeted price of the home by a minimum 20% differential as compared with equivalent site-built housing. This differential may be reduced as the project proves its ability to meet housing needs and an adequate absorption rate is achieved. Home pricing (including land value) must initially be no more than 80% of comparable site-built homes and should meet buyer incomes qualifying at 60% to 80% of the median household income levels for the market. For homes sited in landlease communities, the home-only pricing should be at approximately 50% of comparable site-built homes. Note the following examples:

Site-built housing:	$79,000	Equivalent
Manufactured homes with		
fee simple land:	62,900	80% Maximum
Manufactured homes with		
leased homesite:	39,500	50% Maximum

A caution: Many first-time manufactured home community developers make the mistake of determining the home price by taking all their direct home or land-and-home costs, adding marketing costs, and adding a profit margin. This rarely works because the presumption is almost always that the home forms the basis for the acceptability of the product by the homebuyer and must therefore be as large and have as many houselike features as possible to be viable in the marketplace. Rarely does the resulting product price meet either the 80% of comparable site-built home test, or the 60% to 80% of median household income test.

The best method is to establish the initial sales price after a review of market conditions and buyer demographics. With the use of the calculated initial sales price, budgets for home invoice pricing from the factory can be established after deducting land, development, interest, and marketing costs. Simply determine the 80% (or 50%) sales price first, then deduct appropriate costs to arrive at a factory invoice target price.

Land Lease: An Income-Stream Investment

Generally, the placement or siting of manufactured homes on leased land results from a developer's desire to create an income-stream-producing investment. By leasing the land to the homeowner—after deducting operating expenses—the developer receives a regular cash flow, called net operating income, which after deducting debt service is the "return of" and "return on" the investment. In addition to this continuing net operating income flow, there is the possibility of a home sale to the initial resident and homebuyer within the community. However, it is important that this step be fully evaluated in the context of local and state laws, attitudes of other area retailers, and the depth of developer's financial and management resources.

The developer is usually able to raise rents annually by a modest amount, thus increasing the net operating income over time. When the project is subsequently sold, there is additional cash flow from the return of original equity (or investment). In a landlease community, the homeowner has no land ownership and is actually a "tenant," subject to management's enforcement of community rules and regulations. Depending on the jurisdiction, the home usually remains as chattel or personal property and is, in most states, not subject to real property taxes, but is taxed "ad valorem" through license fees and local personal property assessments. Methods of taxation vary from state to state. Owners of landlease communities pay real property taxes on the developed homesites as a part of their regular operating expense and pass this cost on to the homebuyer as a part of the total monthly rent.

Subdivisions

Manufactured homes sited in subdivisions as fee simple, condominium, or cooperatives, where the land is conveyed to the homeowner, are another consideration. In this type of community development, the developer often also sells the new home to the homebuyer and installs it on a permanent foundation as a "turnkey" land-and-home package.

In some cases, usually where community water and sewer services are not provided to the homesite, the developer may sell the lot only, leaving the responsibility for installing the well, septic system, and home to the homebuyer or to the home retailer.

CASH SALE COMPARISON

A comparison of similar homes, with price adjustments to the subdivision home for a permanent foundation system, larger homesites, and on-site amenities, for each of the two basic approaches would appear to the homebuyer as follows:

	Landlease	Subdivision
Home price:	$26,000	$28,500
Homesite price:	n/a	18,000
Total Price:	$26,000	$46,500

The homes are equivalent as fabricated by the manufacturer. The $2,500 price difference between the two is based on an average cost for the permanent foundation of the home sited in the subdivision. Without the permanent foundation, the land-and-home package will not qualify for 30-year real property financing programs. Although the land-and-home package appreciates in value at a higher rate, the lower monthly expense and greater liquidity of the landlease opportunity appeals to many prospective residents, especially retirees and empty nesters.

FINANCED COMPARISON

The following is a comparison of the costs for a typical financed purchase, assuming an FHA 207(b) loan for the subdivision home:

	Landlease	Subdivision
Down payment:	2,600	1,955
Closing costs and points:	0	2,425
Cost to close:	$ 2,600	4,380
Balance to mortgage:	23,400	46,545
Interest rate:	11.5%	9.0%
Loan amortization:	15 yrs	30 yrs

The first year estimated monthly costs would be:

	Landlease	Subdivision
Monthly payment:	270.76	371.72
Monthly rent:	200.00	n/a
Water fee:	n/a	18.00
Sewer fee:	n/a	12.00
Trash removal:	9.00	9.00
Electric:	75.00	75.00
Property taxes:	n/a	75.58
Ad valorem taxes:	5.45	0.00
Homeowners fee:	n/a	50.00
Insurance:	15.00	30.00
License fees:	7.08	0.00
Monthly Cost:	$582.29	$641.30

The down payment is 68% higher, and in this example, the monthly housing expenses for the subdivision home are 10% higher than for the landlease home.

INCOME QUALIFICATION: LEASED LAND VERSUS LAND AND HOME

For a financed sale, one lender's income qualification test is based on the total monthly housing expense as a percentage of gross income. Another leader includes monthly housing expense and long-term debt. For manufactured housing on leased land, the ratio of housing expense to gross income is typically 30%; the ratio for housing expense plus all long-term debt is typically 42%.

For the subdivision land and home product, the housing expense to gross income ratio is typically 28%; the ratio for housing expense plus all long-term debt is 35%. The ratios are higher for manufactured homes on leased land, because the homesite rent includes costs such as water, sewer, trash removal, and so on, expenses that are paid separately by subdivision homebuyers.

Minimum Qualifying Income

Using the ratios given for the preceding example, the minimum qualifying income for housing expense only, for each of the examples, is as follows:

	Landlease	Subdivision
Qualifying income:	$16,636	$21,987

In this example, the qualifying income is 32% higher for the subdivision land and home package than for the manufactured home in a landlease community.

Cash Buyer

For the cash purchaser, the homebuyer in the landlease community has the income from and the use of $18,000 for emergencies. This $18,000 invested at 5% per year yields $75.00 a month, more than the initial difference between the homesite rent and the homeowner's fees.

Comparison with Credit for Homesite Value

For a true comparison of expense, the landlease homebuyer should credit interest on the land value difference in purchase price. For this example, $18,000 + 2,500 for $20,500 was used for the land price, at an annual interest rate of 5.25%.

So for this example, the total monthly housing expense is almost equal between the two housing products, but the landlease homeowner has $20,500 in the bank for emergencies. Because of the high amount of up-front cash required, this analysis suggests the land and home purchase would generally be more attractive to the retiree or empty nester, and less attractive to the family buyer.

	Landlease	Subdivision
Monthly rent:	$200.00	n/a
Water fee:	n/a	18.00
Sewer fee:	n/a	12.00
Trash removal:	n/a	9.00
Electric:	75.00	75.00
Property taxes:	n/a	74.02
Ad valorem taxes:	5.45	0.00
Homeowners fee:	n/a	50.00
Insurance:	15.00	30.00
License fees:	7.08	0.00
Credit land:	−89.69	0.00
Monthly Cost:	$212.84	$218.02

LANDLEASE COMMUNITY ADVANTAGES AND DISADVANTAGES

Buyers of homes in landlease communities find advantages in the following features:

- Lower amount of cash required at closing
- Lower total monthly costs
- Professional management of the community
- Usually not directly subject to real property tax increases

The primary disadvantage is the homebuyer's fear of unconscionable increases in monthly rents.

SUBDIVISION ADVANTAGES AND DISADVANTAGES

Land sales programs such as subdivisions and condominium and cooperative communities may initially appeal more to homebuyers, especially because of the more favorable long-term financing programs. Costs may be higher owing to lower-density development and higher foundation and on-homesite costs. Cash flow is generally a little better in the early phases of development, and less reserve capital may be required. The developer makes only one sale per homebuyer. Once the project is sold out, except for fees for retained utility facilities, cable T.V. systems, and so forth, there is no more income.

Buyers of homes in subdivision communities perceive advantages in the following features:

- Equity in the land and home package remains with resident.
- The homeowners' association runs the community.
- Buyers are not subject to rent increases by a landlord.

Disadvantages are the higher prices, the homeowners association's control over community rules and regulations, and homeowners being subject to local real property taxes.

DEVELOPER'S VIEWPOINT

From the viewpoint of most developers and investors, given the right market conditions, there are more advantages to building and operating a landlease community. In fact, after careful analysis, most manufactured home projects are built as landlease communities.

Reasons vary, but as a general rule, landlease communities can be leveraged through a development loan, and, in the case of an internal community sales program, negative cash flows from initial operating and interest losses can be offset with home sales profits. The developer can also motivate homebuyers by offering lower rents during the early phases of fill-up. As the community occupancy increases, homesites that may have been rented at economically low rates, through regular rent increases, will produce positive cash flow.

When the community is eventually sold, these lots will contribute to a "return of" and "return on" the developer's investment, making up for the lower initial rental rates. Once a homesite has been sold to a resident in a subdivision, losses from below-market homesite prices cannot similarly be "made up."

TARGET PRICING: LANDLEASE COMMUNITY

Every analysis must start with a "targeted" sales price. This price should first be determined by ascertaining the income range of prospective buyers and applying a "discount" factor for manufactured housing.

For example, in attempting to qualify a homebuyer with a yearly income of $22,000, the analysis would be as follows:

Gross family income:	$18,000.00
Monthly housing + long-term debt (45%):	675.00
Long-term debt (car payments, etc.):	150.00
Balance to housing expense:	$ 525.00
Monthly homesite rent:	200.00
Water, sewer, and trash removal (inc. in rent):	0.00
Electric:	75.00
License:	6.51
Insurance:	8.50

Subtotal:	$ 290.01
Balance to home payment:	$ 234.99
Balance on 15-year loan at 11.5%:	$20,115.74
Price including down payment:	$22,350.82

The targeted price for the home is then determined by deducting sales taxes, transfer fees, installation costs, on-homesites costs, accessories, and so on.

TARGET PRICING: SUBDIVISION

To compute a "targeted price" for a subdivision with a land and home package, with 30-year financing, the analysis would be as follows:

Gross family income:	$23,810.00
Monthly housing + long-term debt (35%):	694.48
Long-term debt:	150.00
Balance to housing expense:	544.48
Homeowners association fee:	50.00
Property taxes:	62.88
Water:	18.00
Sewer:	12.00
Trash:	9.00
Electric:	75.00
Insurance:	12.00
Subtotal:	238.88
Balance to home payment:	305.60
Principal balance on 30-year loan at 9%:	$37,980.20
Purchase price including down payment (FHA 203b):	$40,350.00
Homesite price (example):	$18,000.00
Balance to home + foundation:	$22,350.00
Add cost for permanent foundation:	$ 2,500.00
Balance to home price:	$24,850.00

Note that this is nearly the same price for the home being sold in the landlease community at a qualifying family income of $18,000 per year.

By establishing a buyer income range and a product type, it is possible to determine the retail price of the home or of the home + foundation + land.

CASH VALUE OF LANDLEASE HOMESITES

An approximate method of estimating the cash value of landlease homesites is as follows:

Community Type	Conversion Factor
Very poor grade, high density	Rent × 50
Low grade, high density	Rent × 60
Low grade, medium density	Rent × 70
Medium grade, medium density	Rent × 80
High grade, medium density	Rent × 90
Very high grade, medium density	Rent × 100
Premium grade, high density	Rent × 105
Premium grade, medium density	Rent × 110

For example, an older community which can be described as low grade, high density, with a monthly rental rate of $85.00 per month, is estimated to have an equivalent value of $5,100 per homesite ($85.00 × 60). A new, higher-quality community, with a medium density and a monthly rental rate of $225.00, is estimated to have an equivalent homesite cash value of $22,500 ($225.00 × 100).

Other aspects of community desirability that influence conversion factors include the following:

- Occupancy (98% or better for highest factor)
- Proximity to area community services
- Physical: no deferred maintenance for high factor
- Popularity of retirement area (Florida, California, Arizona, coastal Carolinas, south coastal Texas, etc.)
- Communities with all adult or empty nester residents
- Majority of homes new or in good condition
- All homes showing "pride of ownership"
- Good natural, off-site amenities
- Good on-site community amenities
- Community located in a desirable neighborhood
- Waterfront or water view nearby
- Heavily treed property
- Mountain view property
- Located in a highly desirable neighborhood
- Golf course as an amenity
- Golf course adjacent

With regard to these aspects, the most highly desirable communities are obvious to the most casual observer. The presence or absence of other factors not as readily visible may positively or negatively affect a community's desirability and value, such as the following:

- Favorable attitudes of local residents
- Strong community rules and regulations that are consistently and regularly enforced
- Professional management attitudes and practices
- Stable local economy
- Good school district (for family projects)
- Not near schools (for all-adult or empty nesters)
- Favorable local employment levels
- Other similar, high-quality manufactured home communities
- Reputation and proximity of medical care facilities
- Availability of local cultural activities and centers

COST APPROXIMATIONS

Specific costs must be ascertained before proceeding with the construction of the project. The costs and factors used in Tables 4.1 and 4.2 are very general in scope and will vary somewhat in different market areas. They definitely should not be used in place of in-depth studies of specific parcels of land in the context of a specifically defined market.

These data enable the developer to make an informed decision about the practicality of proceeding. If, after this research and evaluation, the project seems feasible in the context of financial and management resources, the developer can begin working with engineers and consultants experienced in effecting the more detailed part of putting the project together.

Although it is important to research and compile market and site-specific cost information, certain planning data may not be readily available—thus the value of Tables 4.1 and 4.2. The data they provide has been derived from computerized, statistical analysis of several manufactured home developments across the United States. Much of the data are in the form of "interpolated" values that have been recreated from actual project costs. These general values do not take into account variables such as costs for removing or building around rock or hardpan, additional on-site requirements for storm water retention and detention, or extra costs incurred as a result of variations in topography. Prospective developers are cautioned to make every effort to refine costs by obtaining assistance from qualified professional engineers and consultants, who have reviewed local costs and are aware of specifics of the proposed development site, before making any final financial decisions.

"IN-COMMUNITY" SALES

Developer operation of an exclusive home-sales program within a community, as compared with reliance on local retailers or retail sales centers, is a sensitive

TABLE 4.1   Housing Cost Index by City

Albany	NY	0.93	Madison	WI	1.04
Albuquerque	NM	1.06	Memphis	TN	0.94
Allentown	PA	1.06	Miami	FL	0.93
Atlanta	GA	0.95	Milwaukee	WI	1.22
Augusta	GA	0.79	Minneapolis	MN	1.19
Austin	TX	0.94	Mobile	AL	0.95
Bakersfield	CA	1.29	Nashville	TN	0.85
Baltimore	MD	1.06	New Orleans	LA	1.07
Baton Rouge	LA	0.96	Newark	NJ	0.99
Birmingham	AL	0.94	Newport News	VA	1.07
Boise	ID	0.95	Norfolk	VA	0.88
Boston	MA	1.16	Oklahoma City	OK	0.88
Buffalo	NY	1.14	Omaha	NE	0.94
Charleston	SC	0.82	Orlando	FL	0.91
Charlotte	NC	0.78	Pensacola	FL	0.88
Chattanooga	TN	0.91	Peoria	IL	0.78
Chicago	IL	1.14	Philadelphia	PA	1.19
Cincinnati	OH	1.17	Phoenix	AZ	1.14
Cleveland	OH	1.35	Pittsburgh	PA	1.04
Columbia	SC	0.76	Portland	ME	1.10
Columbus	OH	1.12	Portland	OR	1.19
Dallas-Ft. Worth	TX	1.09	Providence	RI	1.10
Davenport	IA	1.06	Raleigh	NC	0.80
Dayton	OH	1.05	Richmond	VA	0.96
Denver	CO	1.14	Rochester	NY	1.02
Des Moines	IA	1.03	Sacramento	CA	1.36
Detroit	MI	1.33	St. Louis	MO	1.08
El Paso	TX	0.84	Salt Lake City	UT	0.96
Eugene-Springfield	OR	1.10	San Antonio	TX	0.86
Flint	MI	1.22	San Diego	CA	1.24
Fresno	CA	1.35	San Francisco	CA	1.49
Gary	IN	1.12	San Jose	CA	1.39
Grand Rapids	MI	1.01	Seattle	WA	1.28
Greensboro	NC	0.77	Shreveport	LA	1.39
Greenville	SC	0.82	Spokane	WA	1.15
Hartford	CN	1.04	Springfield	IL	0.98
Honolulu	HI	1.36	Stockton	CA	1.33
Houston	TX	1.01	Syracuse	NY	1.04
Huntsville	AL	0.85	Tacoma	WA	1.13
Indianapolis	IN	1.16	Tampa	FL	0.88
Jacksonville	FL	0.87	Toledo	OH	1.35
Kansas City	MO	1.06	Tucson	AZ	1.16
Knoxville	TN	0.84	Tulsa	OK	0.94
Lansing	MI	1.07	Washington	DC	1.12
Las Vegas	NV	1.11	Wichita	KS	0.88
Lexington	KY	1.00	Wilmington	DL	0.96
Little Rock	AR	0.91	Worchester	MA	1.00
Los Angeles	CA	1.35	Youngstown	OH	1.11
Louisville	KY	1.00			

decision. It should be made after reviewing local and state regulations for such operations and gauging local manufactured home retailer attitudes toward in-community sales programs. It is not uncommon for local retailers to go to their manufacturer suppliers and pressure them to refuse to sell homes to the in-community developer/retailer. The determination of whether this practice constitutes an illegal restraint of trade may call for the services of an attorney. At best, possible retailer hostility may be an irritant in the marketing of new homes to the public.

In some areas, land prices are so high that profits from home sales are necessary for new development to make financial sense. In these circumstances, it is important that the developer/retailer be especially sensitive when reviewing the implications and ramifications of an exclusive, in-community sales program.

One alternative frequently considered by developers is to allow local manufactured home retailers to operate within the community on a nonexclusive basis. Local area retailers may have a different agenda from that of the developer. The retailers in this case do not have the same risk of liability for development costs that the developer does and may be more interested in higher profits than in a fast fill rate. Care must be taken by the developer to assure, within legal boundaries, that retailer home pricing is not too high, severely slowing down the fill rate of the community.

If and when a sales program is started within the community, a vertical integration of pricing structure is recommended, starting with the targeted home product pricing, and modifying costs and profits to fit. Without such an approach, it is too easy for multiple profit entities to make the mistake of adding up all component pricing and overprice the home product for the market.

ESTIMATING TOTAL DEVELOPMENT COSTS FOR A SUBDIVISION

The following is an example of items to consider when establishing a budget for subdivision development costs, using the construction cost estimator from Table 4.2, as modified by the area index as shown in Table 4.1.

Targeted homesite price:	$18,000	
Developer's gross profit:	−4,500	25% of sales price
Balance:	13,500	
Construction interest:	−675	10% for 6 months
Marketing costs:	−1,800	10% of sales price
Land + construction:	11,025	
Hard construction costs:	8,385	Index = 1.20, 50' × 100' homesite
Value to land:	2,640	Adjusted for higher or lower construction costs

If construction costs are higher than shown here, and the market price for the homesite cannot be raised proportionately, then the land value must be decreased.

TABLE 4.2 Estimated Hard Development Costs

Shown in cost per lot for various lot sizes

Width	70	80	90	100	50	60	70	80	70	80	90	100
Length	80	80	80	80	100	100	100	100	120	120	120	120
Sq. Ft.	5,600	6,400	7,200	8,000	5,000	6,000	7,000	8,000	8,400	9,600	10,800	12,000
Density	6.2	5.4	4.8	4.4	7.3	6.1	5.2	4.5	4.7	4.1	3.7	3.3
Index												
0.76	6,068	6,641	7,214	7,787	5,311	5,884	6,456	7,029	6,844	7,417	7,990	8,563
0.78	6,228	6,816	7,404	7,992	5,451	6,038	6,626	7,214	7,025	7,613	8,201	8,789
0.80	6,388	6,991	7,594	8,197	5,590	6,193	6,796	7,399	7,205	7,808	8,411	9,014
0.82	6,548	7,165	7,783	8,401	5,730	6,348	6,966	7,584	7,385	8,003	8,621	9,239
0.84	6,707	7,340	7,973	8,606	5,870	6,503	7,136	7,769	7,565	8,198	8,831	9,465
0.86	6,867	7,515	8,163	8,811	6,010	6,658	7,306	7,954	7,745	8,393	9,042	9,690
0.88	7,027	7,690	8,353	9,016	6,149	6,813	7,476	8,139	7,925	8,589	9,252	9,915
0.90	7,186	7,865	8,543	9,221	6,289	6,967	7,646	8,324	8,105	8,784	9,462	10,141
0.92	7,346	8,039	8,733	9,426	6,429	7,122	7,816	8,509	8,285	8,979	9,673	10,366
0.94	7,506	8,214	8,922	9,631	6,569	7,277	7,986	8,694	8,466	9,174	9,883	10,591
0.96	7,665	8,389	9,112	9,836	6,708	7,432	8,156	8,879	8,646	9,369	10,093	10,817
0.98	7,825	8,564	9,302	10,041	6,848	7,587	8,325	9,064	8,826	9,565	10,303	11,042
1.00	7,985	8,738	9,492	10,246	6,988	7,742	8,495	9,249	9,006	9,760	10,514	11,267
1.02	8,144	8,913	9,682	10,451	7,128	7,896	8,665	9,434	9,186	9,955	10,724	11,493
1.04	8,304	9,088	9,872	10,655	7,267	8,051	8,835	9,619	9,366	10,150	10,934	11,718

Index	C1	C2	C3	C4	C5	C6	C7	C8	C9	C10	C11	C12
1.06	11,944	11,144	10,345	9,546	9,804	9,005	8,206	7,407	10,860	10,062	9,263	8,464
1.08	12,169	11,355	10,541	9,726	9,989	9,175	8,361	7,547	11,065	10,251	9,437	8,624
1.10	12,394	11,565	10,736	9,906	10,174	9,345	8,516	7,687	11,270	10,441	9,612	8,783
1.12	12,620	11,775	10,931	10,087	10,359	9,515	8,671	7,826	11,475	10,631	9,787	8,943
1.14	12,845	11,986	11,126	10,267	10,544	9,685	8,825	7,966	11,680	10,821	9,962	9,103
1.16	13,070	12,196	11,321	10,447	10,729	9,855	8,980	8,106	11,885	11,011	10,137	9,262
1.18	13,296	12,406	11,517	10,627	10,914	10,025	9,135	8,246	12,090	11,201	10,311	9,422
1.20	13,521	12,616	11,712	10,807	11,099	10,194	9,290	8,385	12,295	11,390	10,486	9,582
1.22	13,746	12,827	11,907	10,987	11,284	10,364	9,445	8,525	12,500	11,580	10,661	9,741
1.24	13,972	13,037	12,102	11,167	11,469	10,534	9,600	8,665	12,705	11,770	10,836	9,901
1.26	14,197	13,247	12,297	11,347	11,654	10,704	9,754	8,805	12,909	11,960	11,010	10,061
1.28	14,422	13,457	12,493	11,528	11,839	10,874	9,909	8,944	13,114	12,150	11,185	10,221
1.30	14,648	13,668	12,688	11,708	12,024	11,044	10,064	9,084	13,319	12,340	11,360	10,380
1.32	14,873	13,878	12,883	11,888	12,209	11,214	10,219	9,224	13,524	12,529	11,535	10,540
1.34	15,098	14,088	13,078	12,068	12,394	11,384	10,374	9,364	13,729	12,719	11,709	10,700
1.36	15,324	14,299	13,273	12,248	12,579	11,554	10,529	9,504	13,934	12,909	11,884	10,859
1.38	15,549	14,509	13,468	12,428	12,764	11,724	10,683	9,643	14,139	13,099	12,059	11,019
1.40	15,774	14,719	13,664	12,608	12,949	11,893	10,838	9,783	14,344	13,289	12,234	11,179
1.42	16,000	14,929	13,859	12,788	13,134	12,063	10,993	9,923	14,549	13,479	12,409	11,338
1.44	16,225	15,140	14,054	12,969	13,319	12,233	11,148	10,063	14,754	13,668	12,583	11,498
1.46	16,451	15,350	14,249	13,149	13,504	12,403	11,303	10,202	14,959	13,858	12,758	11,658
1.48	16,676	15,560	14,444	13,329	13,689	12,573	11,458	10,342	15,164	14,048	12,933	11,817
1.50	16,901	15,770	14,640	13,509	13,874	12,743	11,612	10,482	15,368	14,238	13,108	11,977

ESTIMATING TOTAL DEVELOPMENT COSTS FOR
A LANDLEASE COMMUNITY

The following is an example of items to consider when establishing a budget for landlease community development costs, using the construction cost estimator from Table 4.2, as modified by the area index as shown in Table 4.1.

Yearly lot rent:	$ 2,400	
Vacancy and collection:	−168	7% initially
Balance:	2,232	Adjusted gross income
Operating expenses:	−893	40% typical
Net operating income:	1,339	
Debt service:	1,071	1.25% ratio
Yearly cash flow:	$ 268	May be increased
Loan supported:	$10,108	25 years @ 9.5%
Developer's equity:	3,369	25% of development cost
Development cost:	13,477	Total cost
Construction interest:	−1,011	10% for 9 months
Marketing costs:	−1,200	50% of years rental
Land + construction:	11,266	
Hard construction costs:	8,385	Index = 1.20, 50' × 100' homesite
Value to land:	2,881	Adjusted for higher or lower construction costs
Cash flow:	$268/$ 3,369	8% initially (increases yearly with rental rates adjustments)

In this example, assuming the land development costs are the same, the developer building the landlease community can afford to pay considerably more for the land than for the subdivision.

ON-SITE COSTS

In this chapter (as shown in Table 4.2) on-site costs are based on typical manufactured home community construction experience. These costs will vary from location to location and may be increased or reduced for a particular development, as indicated by market conditions. Streets are presumed to be 22-foot-wide asphalt, with concrete curbs and gutters, and with no sidewalks. The cost factors are characteristic of underground, as opposed to overhead, electric service, and water distribution and wastewater collection systems are serviced by off-site utility companies. Costs for on-site utility services would have to be estimated individually and added to the estimated costs.

Normal and customary planning, engineering, and survey costs are included in the construction cost estimates. A general contractor's overhead, bond, and profit of 22% are also factored into Table 4.2; a developer operating as general contractor may reduce these cost estimates accordingly.

MARKETING COSTS

Marketing costs will vary from the conventional "real estate commission" approach, which is usually calculated as a percentage of the total sales price of the home or land and home. For a subdivision, 10% of the homesite sales price is used as the fee structure. This fee includes commissions and advertising expense. For a landlease community, 50% of the lot revenue for the first year is used. In lieu of the marketing costs for a landlease community, it is not unusual for the developer to offer a reduced monthly rental rate for the first 6 to 12 months to enhance the absorption rate.

The range of sales commissions is as follows:

In-house staff: 1.5% to 3.0% of sales price
Outside broker: 6.0% to 8.0% of sales price

For a more traditional off-site retail sales center approach, the commission is usually a percentage of the "gross profit" (a commonly used misnomer), which is also called the "hold." This is computed by subtracting the direct sales costs of the home + accessories + an overhead factor called the "pack" from the retail sales price less sales taxes, license fees, and so forth.

An example of the typical retail sales center commission structure is as follows:

Home sales price:	$25,000	before taxes, etc.
Home invoice:	−18,000	(inc. transport)
Pack:	−3,000	varies with home type
Hold:	4,000	(sales price less invoice and pack)
Commission:	800	% of the "hold" (20% in this example)

The range of percentages of the "gross profit" or "hold" is:

• 15% if there is a "fair to good" advertising program and an effective sales support organization

- 20% for some advertising and some sales staff support
- 25% if the salesperson is provided with virtually no advertising and no staff sales support

GROSS PROFITS

Based on business objectives, "gross profits" per homesite sold should be established as a function of the desired return on investment, and based on a cash flow analysis of the project under a given set of variables, such as fill rate, development loan interest rate, operating budgets, and so on. However much the developer wishes to maximize return on investment, an average gross margin is 25% of the homesite sales price. Assuming a 10% overhead factor, net profits (before taxes) usually average 15%.

A frequently successful strategy followed by many sophisticated developers provides for minimum profit margins during the first phase of development to achieve the fastest fill rate possible, raising the margins as subsequent phases are filled, to achieve desired targeted margins. For example:

Margin: 10%	5% of first ⅓ fill
	10% of next ⅓ fill
	15% of balance
Margin: 15%	10% of first ⅓ fill
	15% of next ⅓ fill
	20% of balance
Margin: 20%	15% of first ⅓ fill
	20% of next ⅓ fill
	25% of balance

DEVELOPER'S OVERHEAD ALLOWANCES

A developer's overhead allowances are typically 10% of the sales price. This amount is based on the average rate of sales. Typical costs include some or all of the following:

Project manager's salary	Sales manager's salary
Serviceman's salary	Payroll taxes
Health insurance premiums	Workmen's compensation
General liability insurance	Secretary/bookkeeper wages
General office supplies	License fees
Utility expenses	Leases on equipment
Telephone expense	Landlease for office
Postage and express	Printing and supplies

Ad valorem personal property tax   Computer supplies
Janitorial   Legal and accounting
Travel and entertainment

When the costs, as determined here, are subtracted from the targeted sales price, the remainder provides a "budget" from which the direct costs must be allocated.

COST INDEX

Table 4.1 shows a list of major cities across the United States with various cost indexes. These are representative of the relative cost differences for building the manufactured home community infrastructure. The index should not be used as a substitute for obtaining actual costs from a qualified professional engineer, architect, or general contractor.

To use the table, find the city that is closest to the location of the proposed development and select the corresponding index. For example: Tampa, Florida, has an index of 0.88; Detroit, Michigan, has an index of 1.33.

HARD DEVELOPMENT COSTS

The costs shown in Table 4.2 are created as estimates for typical "turnkey" construction of completed homesites, including but not limited to concept design, engineering, permits, supervision, and include a general contractor's gross profit margin of 15%. If the developer is acting as the general contractor, these costs may be used at 85% of those shown.

To use the table, identify the relative cost index as found in Table 4.1 and follow it down the page to the corresponding value. Across the top of Table 4.2 are various typical homesite sizes and densities. The conjunction of the two is the estimated hard development costs.

For example, for a homesite size of 50' × 100' to be built in Tampa, the cost would be estimated to be $6,149; for a homesite to be built in Detroit, with 60' × 100' dimensions, the estimated cost would be $10,297. Note that these costs do not include interest, marketing expense, amenities, or off-site improvements.

Off-Site Costs

Those costs which may be either off-site or on-site but are incremental to normal site development costs are considered to be on-site costs, which include the following:

Wastewater treatment plant   Water treatment system
Major drainage retention   Major drainage detention
Traffic lights   Roadway widening
Utility impact fees   Park and recreation fees

Amenities

Amenities are not included in the development costs shown in Table 4.2 and, therefore, must be added before establishing feasibility. On-site constructed features that are designed to enhance the attractiveness, life-style, and livability of the community include the following:

Playground	Park area
Tennis courts	Par course
Jogging trail	Clubhouse
Swimming pool	Jacuzzi
Barbecue area	Horseshoe area
Putting green	Golf course
Shuffleboard	Sauna and dressing rooms

Projects that are oriented to retirees and empty nesters frequently have a larger percentage of the development costs allocated to on-site amenities. For example:

Minimal on-site amenities:	$ 150 to $250 per homesite
Modest on-site amenities:	$ 500 to $750 per homesite
Substantial amenities:	$1,000 to $1,500 per homesite
Extensive amenities:	$2,000 and up per homesite

Amenities allocations must be carefully evaluated in the context of competitive projects in the area. If, for example, a neighboring project with 500 homesites has a $500,000 clubhouse, swimming pool, saunas, and so forth, the cost allocation is $1,000 per homesite. A competitive project with only 300 homesites adjacent or in the same market area would have to spend $1,667 per homesite ($500,000 divided by 300 homesites); otherwise it might not be competitive with the larger project.

HOMESITE CONFIGURATION CONSIDERATIONS

If the possible range of homesites that can be built on a parcel of land varies greatly in size, a developer may elect to use a site size that takes into account lower costs by virtue of reduced frontage. For example, a typical minimum homesite may be established by zoning at 5,000 square feet per lot. This may be configured as lots that are 50 feet wide by 100 feet long, or 60 feet wide by 83.33 feet long, or 70 feet wide by 71.43 feet long, and so on. At a cost of $400 per front foot, the 50' × 100' lots may have a cost of $10,000 each, whereas the cost of the 70 foot wide lots will be 40% higher, at $14,000 each. Although the wider lots may produce a better community appearance, the $4,000 higher costs may work against affordability.

Higher Initial Per Homesite Costs

In estimating costs, the initial cost per homesite may be higher for a phased development, inasmuch as the first phase of development usually includes off-site or major on-site costs that are amortized over the entire project. For the most accurate estimates, it may be necessary to increase the cost per homesite for the first phase of development and, except for inflationary factors, make a corresponding reduction in the per homesite costs for subsequent phases.

First phase premium: 115% to 120% of average costs
Subsequent phases: 80% to 85% (without inflation)

CONSTRUCTION INTEREST EXPENSE

The construction interest expense can be estimated by taking the maximum principal balance for the development loan (based on a time-phased development), at the loan interest rate for the estimated term of sales (including 6 months construction).

HOME INVOICE COSTS

Home invoice costs vary widely from manufacturer to manufacturer, of course, but when all features and factory support programs are taken into account, there is relatively little variation. Rather, the cost differences are in the minimum standard features the manufacturers have selected to include in their line of homes. Other features may be added, but may be considered "options" to the basic home.

For example, Manufacturer A may offer a standard 16' × 80' 3-bedroom home with a factory base price of $18,000. Manufacturer B may sell the same sized home for $16,000. A further analysis shows the following:

	Manufacturer A	Manufacturer B
Basic home:	$18,300	$16,000
Add second bath:	included	450
Upgrade carpet:	included	600
7.5' ceiling height:	included	900
Set and putty staples:	included	150
Perimeter heat ducts:	included	500
Total	$18,300	$18,600

In addition to a comparison of physical features on a home-by-home basis, there are series of services and factory policies that may be difficult to put a price tag on, but which represent value to the developer. Such items may include:

Volume rebate programs	Model home interest
Trip incentives	Advertising allowances
Points for financing	30-day invoicing
Reduced transport cost	National advertising

The home units used in this example are constructed to the Federal Manufactured Home Construction Standards, HUD Title VI. However, the old name *mobile home* is still used in many states and local jurisdictions and should refer to pre-1976 manufactured homes.

TRIAL SALES PRICE AND HOME INVOICE PRICE EVALUATION

A trial sales price can be determined by adding all the estimated costs as the first pricing effort. It is not unusual for developers to find that the resulting "residual" home invoice price is not high enough to purchase the quality home they had anticipated using. Many builders and developers of site-built housing, inexperienced with manufactured homes, seem to prefer to use the more expensive "site-built, home-like appearing" factory-built modular homes.

Most jurisdictions still limit to specifically zoned areas the siting of homes that are built according to HUD codes. Modulars may usually be sited in any location zoned for single-family residential construction. Except for the fact that they sometimes (but not always) appear more like site-built housing, the only advantage of so-called modular homes may be one of greater latitude in land use, owing to relaxed zoning requirements.

When factory-built home costs are not high enough for the desired product, it is necessary to return to the various costs and see where adjustments might be made. Selecting a product through this system, starting from a targeted price and selecting the home after all costs have been accounted for, may not allow for the homes to have an appearance more like expensive site-built homes.

In 1992 there were more than 217,000 HUD-code homes in the United States. This figure represents more than 20% of all single-family homes built. In spite of the fact that their appearance is not that of site-built homes, the lower priced product appeals to at least 1 buyer in 5. Current estimates are that 1 in 16 Americans lives in a manufactured home.

There are two possible paths to consider if the residual home product meets the financial objectives but does not have the appearance, size, or function a developer wants:

1. Do not build the project, because if the higher priced product is used, there will not be enough price differential to offset common public perceptions, and consumers will choose the site-built home product over the manufactured home.

2. Build the project, using homes based on the residual price analysis; meet the targeted price objectives; and accept the fact that the homes are still going to appeal to at least one happy homebuyer in five.

Factory upgrades and/or site-added features, although aesthetically desirable, very often add cost without adding safety, comfort, livability, or value to the shelter. These added features frequently cancel many of the inherent cost advantages of manufactured homes over site-built competition.

FINAL FEASIBILITY

Determining the feasibility of a proposed manufactured home community takes a great amount of time and resources, along with objective, accurate market research. With careful planning, however, and adequate financing, virtually all risk can be taken out of a well conceived and planned development opportunity.

Correctly matching the housing product to the targeted buyer is perhaps the most important part of the feasibility process. Establishing a retirement community, with its associated higher rents, home prices, and construction costs, in a market where there is no previous track record for such communities and there is a demonstrated need for family-oriented communities, would be a serious mistake. On the other hand, through careful evaluation of buyer income, household growth rates, histories of other area projects, and competitive analysis of similar communities, a developer can structure a project that is at little or no risk of unanticipated slow rate of absorption.

Times change, and building a project in an area the way it was done in the past may no longer be a formula for success. Prospective residents have new wants and needs. Areas of the country change in popularity, and higher-quality communities may work well in some older traditional markets.

Most important of all, in cases where research finds data that will not support the proposed development, it may be necessary to make adjustments to the home product, homesite pricing, or resident mix. This is the only way to establish project budgets for marketing, home invoices, setup costs, project amenities, and so forth.

FINAL ANALYSIS

A project's economic feasibility must be determined by estimating costs, determining profit objectives, and evaluating cash flow and return on investment in the context of realistically determined absorption rates.

The availability and relative ease of today's personal computer systems give the developer a new tool for evaluating a project's feasibility. By building an economic model on a template for a proposed project, using one of the many spread-sheet programs available, allows a developer to simulate cash flow based on best and worst anticipated case rates of absorption. With this tool, a developer can anticipate capital needs under worst-case circumstances. Without it, the project may be doomed before it is started, without the developer's knowing it until it is too late.

CHAPTER 5

CONCEPT DEVELOPMENT

The design of a manufactured home community begins by conceptualizing the relationships between various requirements. Some choices place constraints on the feasibility of alternative layouts. Other requirements allow unique opportunities for development and design. This chapter outlines the factors required for developing a concept. The developer has a selection of manufactured homes that can meet any market. Affordability is relative; in parts of California, home price and setup costs of $100,000, with rents of $500 per month, are affordable as compared with alternate housing choices. The high cost of land in California requires the kind of innovative designs which can increase densities as high as 10 units per acre, with homesite sizes as small as 3,500 square feet. Almost all of these creative designs include the zero lotline concept, in which a larger amount of usable space is created by putting all such space to one side of the homesite and creating a yard-patio combination that blends the inside living area and the outside living area. This creates a private courtyard which blends in with the rest of the home. This concept does increase the cost of both the landscaping and the structure itself, but in order to facilitate the architectural effect, extra cost is necessary to meet that particular market's needs. The majority of manufactured homes are built to suit a market (often lower-middle income) whose primary concern is affordability. Consider, for example, a young married working couple purchasing their first home, with little money available for a down payment and able to afford a home in the $20,000 to $30,000 range in an area where landlease community rents are approximately $160 per month. The challenge to the development team is to create the best possible environment for the residents and to enhance the marketability of the community while still maintaining the required affordability.

This chapter includes a comparison of the differences and similarities between a landlease community and a subdivision.

ELEMENTS OF CONCEPT

In order to prepare a concept, the following elements must be fully understood: *market, development site characteristics, economics, politics,* and *product selection.*

In a market that will support only low rental rates, but in which land cost and construction costs are high, site selection demands economically favorable development site characteristics. In other words, the land preparation and utility costs must be reduced to offset the high land costs and low rental structure mentioned earlier. Therefore, the concept could not include wooded homesites or steep topography. The extent or degree to which a particular element influences a concept varies with each particular situation. For example, given a property with a 10% to 15% grade, site characteristics will have a greater impact on the concept determination than the other four elements.

Market Development

The following items do not constitute a market study, but are those which must be extracted from the market study for conceptual consideration.

Location. There is much truth to the old saying that the three most important factors in real estate marketing are location—location—location. If a project is in a primary location, it may not require as many amenities to be successfully marketed as would an alternate site in a secondary location. The higher cost of land in a primary location is offset by the additional amenities and marketing costs necessary for the secondary location to be competitive. For example, an adult retirement community may require a golf course to overcome the inconvenience of its not being close to a shopping center and medical facilities, which are both very important to retirees.

Demographics. The market study presents the demographics of the population for whom the community is being designed. For example, a retirement community in the South will be very different in terms of life-style and amenities than a blue-collar community in the North.

The market study indicates the average take-home pay of the prospective residents of a blue-collar working community. From these data, the designer can assume that approximately 30% of a resident's income will be devoted to housing costs. If one subtracts the average monthly mortgage payments on the home that the prospective resident is purchasing and deducts other associated housing costs, the result is the amount per month the resident can afford to pay for rent. Knowing the anticipated rental rate of the community, the development costs (which must be considered in the formulation of concept) can then be calculated.

Project Size. The size of the project determines the traffic patterns and street designs. The size of the project also influences the type and amount of central and recreational facilities, as well as open space and pedestrian ways.

For example, if a 600-unit community is to be developed in three stages of 200 homesites each, the concept plan should be designed so that future construction phases are not disruptive to the residents living in earlier-built homes. The concept should allow construction traffic to have ingress and egress to future stages without using existing roadways through earlier stages. These roadways are generally not designed to carry heavy construction traffic. In a large retirement community where the central facilities need to be fully constructed with a partial first phase of development, staging should be properly coordinated so that future phases of development properly access the community facilities yet do not interfere with the previous stages of development.

Competition. The engineer or planner developing the concept must be properly directed by the market study regarding the desirable size of homesites, recreational and central facilities, and other design amenities that must be included in the concept in order for the project to be competitive in the marketplace. The costs to develop these matching facilities must also allow the property to be financially competitive in the marketplace.

Site Characteristics

The physical properties and characteristics of the property have an impact on the conceptual development of the lotting plan. The following paragraphs discuss various site characteristics and their impact on the conceptual planning.

Topography. Land slope can be adjusted more easily across the short dimension of the home as opposed across the long dimension of the home. It is not difficult to drop as much as 5 feet in elevation across a 50-foot homesite where the long dimension of the home parallels the contours of the ground. On the other hand, it is very difficult to accomplish a grade differential where the contour lines of the earth are parallel to the short dimension or the front of the home. If the property has a slope of 0% to 3%, grade has little conceptual dominance. When the slope of a property is between 4% and 8%, topography will begin to influence home layout and location. If topography includes a slope of more than 10%, grades have a profound effect from an economical perspective. Grading costs can sometimes be minimized by using steps or retaining walls; however, there must be an economic balance between earthwork and retaining wall construction.

Soils. Peat bogs and hydric soils are normally associated with wetlands, as defined and regulated by the U.S. Army Corps of Engineers and many local and state agencies. Developers are restricted in the destruction of wetlands. The concept plan can turn these areas into desirable natural amenities, thus avoiding the expense of excavating and filling the areas with suitable fill material or going through the jurisdictional requirements that permit the developer to use these areas.

Vegetation. Vegetation that offers advantageous natural landscaping should be used. Even the disadvantage of marsh or swampland may be turned into a desirable amenity by proper incorporation into the total community concept. Generally, economic densities can be maintained while preserving natural amenities.

If a property is heavily wooded, rather than totally clearing it a better option might be to lower the roads so that the homesites can be swale drained to the roadway system. Drainage can then be carried away without massive grading and clearing of the homesites. If a property is wooded and has a greater than 10% slope, it will be extremely difficult to save the trees and properly prepare the property for the placement of homes.

Drainage. If a property is low relative to the surrounding land area and there is no positive outlet for drainage, a man-made lake may become a very important part of the concept. The lake will receive the storm water runoff and stabilize the water elevation through absorption into the natural water table.

The concept plan will have to make provisions to maintain and not interrupt the flow of off-site drainage. This may require the realignment of the natural drainage regime, or it may mean developing a drainage system within the concept plan, which feeds into and uses the existing drainage regime.

Many regulatory agencies throughout the country require storm water management in the form of storm water detention or treatment. Storm water detention requirements typically allow for a rate of water, measured in cubic feet per second, to be discharged off the site at the predevelopment rate based on a 25-year rainfall event.* The site must retain the difference in flow between that predevelopment rate and the rate of water associated with the runoff of a 25-year event after development of the site. The first inch of runoff from a site contains most of the pollutants in the form of oils, sediment, and fertilizers. Therefore, many jurisdictions require that this first inch of runoff be treated either by retention or by a filtration system prior to discharge from the site. The amount of area set aside to accomplish the requirements of storm water management will vary significantly from one property to another, depending on the characteristics of the property and the depth that a lake or dry retention pond can facilitate. However, a rough estimate for initial planning would provide 7% of the total land area for the storm water management regime. The challenge to the designer is to incorporate these facilities into the concept plan in such a way that they are architectural benefits in the form of lake amenities or recreational facilities, as opposed to unsightly, unmanicured holes in the ground. In the central facility area a lake could be developed where water is pumped through a fountain, cascades over a rock outlet, and is then recycled back into the lake to form an attractive water amenity.

---

* Rainfall event is described in detail in Chapter 8.

Traffic. The roadway system in the community must be designed to properly handle the traffic it generates. Depending on the highway which the community accesses, it may be necessary to provide turn lanes, acceleration lanes, and/or deceleration lanes to facilitate traffic leaving and entering the community. There should also be adequate stacking facilities for traffic leaving the community. Most jurisdictions require a minimum of two entrances to the community for fire protection and emergency vehicles. Landlease community owners frequently want the security and control afforded by having only one main entrance, local authorities will often accept a single entrance if there is also an entrance with a gate available only to emergency vehicles.

Utilities. There is a direct correlation between the cost of utilities (sewer, water, storm sewer, electric, gas) and the street and lotting plan. The grid pattern is the least expensive but also the least aesthetically desirable. The planner must be sensitive to the relationship between utility placement and concept configuration versus development cost.

Easements. It is frequently found that a property has utility easements running through it, which must be preserved. In this situation it is necessary to design the roadway and lotting plan around existing easements. Most often the easements can be incorporated into the concept plan to satisfy the need for recreational space, open space in the form of pedestrian ways, recreational vehicle storage, and even storm water management facilities.

Surrounding Vista and the Environment. A site analysis map should indicate predominant wind direction and solar orientation. Solar orientation should be considered in the layout of such recreational facilities as tennis courts and baseball or softball fields, and the orientation of vistas relative to home placement and the central facility building. There have been studies prepared discussing the energy savings to manufactured homes and their placement relative to solar orientation. Wind direction also influences the orientation of structures and facilities.

The site analysis map should show the analysis of a vista survey achieved by standing on the site and categorizing the view in all directions. This information is used to plan views from patios and other vantage points. If a neighboring land use is offensive to the proposed manufactured housing community, the concept plan may use a buffer area of recreational vehicle storage or open space and landscaping to screen the adjacent property.

Economics

The following discussion is based on the assumption that a manufactured home landlease community justifies its own economics as an income-producing property, without considering the potential merchandising profit of home sales. This discussion does not apply to manufactured home condominiums or subdivisions where, in fact, the sale of the homes generally becomes an integral part of the project's economic feasibility. However, there are certain market areas and conditions in which merchandising is an integral part of the feasibility of a landlease community.

A community concept cannot be developed intelligently unless the engineer, planner, or architect has an understanding of these economic factors: *rent, land cost, development cost* and *in-fill rate.*

The market study determines the anticipated lease rate and in-fill rate. Land cost is easily obtained and, upon site analysis and conversation with local contractors, the design professional, through past experience, can approximate area construction costs. A preliminary economic feasibility analysis considers such items as the developer's equity, capital potential, and desired rate of return, and with these facts an estimated development cost can be projected.

Keeping these development costs in mind, the designer proceeds to the first step of concept development: a *lotting plan.* The projected cost influences density, street layout, open space allocation and central facilities. As the design professional proceeds in greater detail with the concept, cost projections are double-checked.

Sometimes a project can conceptually meet economic requirements but miss the market requirements. For example, a particular site characteristic may drive development costs up to the point where required high densities and lack of amenities make the project less competitive. A successful manufactured home community concept must meet both market and economic requirements. Many times, it can be recognized prior to concept development that a project is not feasible and should not be commenced; at other times preliminary engineering is completed before feasibility can be determined.

Politics

Local politics, planning guidelines, and zoning ordinances must all be considered in order to develop a viable manufactured home community. Even model zoning will not guarantee a quality residential development. On the other hand, there are many ordinances which, in fact, make it very difficult for the developer to construct a quality project. Generally, three political factors influence the conceptualization of manufactured home communities: *adjacent land use, zoning,* and *building and development codes.*

The developer should not blindly accept existing building codes or zoning ordinances. Instead, community leaders should be convinced that requirements that drive up construction costs must be eliminated—such as a total concrete slab under homes or sewer and water mains run exclusively under streets. Savings from avoiding these unnecessary costs can be reapplied to creating a better place to live with desirable amenities, attractive landscaping, and enhanced environmental development.

Product Selection

Traditionally, manufactured home communities have been designed to accommodate homes from a variety of manufacturers. Utilities are placed in such a way as to accommodate the majority of manufactured homes. Patios, driveways, and walkways are constructed prior to home placement. This procedure, however, does not optimize the potential of integrating home and site into a harmonious environmental relationship in which each complements the other.

When product selection becomes an integral part of concept development, home placement can be controlled as to the relationship of homes to each other and the integration of each home to its site. Parking and garage arrangement, patio construction, and land use can be integrated into floor plans and home access when product selection becomes part of concept development. The developer has the option of a zero-lotline community in which the relationship of structures is the predominant control factor. Zero lotlines achieve benefits in terms of increased density and useful lawn areas. Where it is not possible to determine product selection at the concept development stage, some of the environmental benefits discussed earlier can be achieved by constructing the homesite improvements after the home has been selected.

Concept encompasses much more than lotting and street arrangements. It includes consideration of the type of central facilities, the amount and type of landscaping, the percentage of open space, and signage. People relate to and preserve their environment from a vertical position at ground level, not from an airplane 3,000 feet above the ground. In other words, all too often a lotting plan and street layout are conceived by planners looking down on a scale layout, as if viewing the development from an airplane, without being sensitive to the homeowner's view of the environment at ground level.

THE SITE PLAN

The site plan must consider, weave together, and balance all the input derived from the elements of concept. The development site plan should not be looked at as just an arrangement of a group of buildings into a pattern pleasing in its two-dimensional view.

Comparison of Community Designs

Roadway and Homesite Configuration. The majority of manufactured home communities range in density from five to seven homes per acre, and homesite areas are approximately 4,500 to 5,000 square feet. With these densities, it is in many cases virtually impossible to have a staggered front offset to break up the monotonous streetscape of homes all uniformly set back from the roadway. If the homesite and street patterns are laid out in a grid system with long, straight streets, and negative and unpleasant resulting streetscape is further aggravated. It is not necessary to design a community on a grid pattern.

In many retirement communities in the South and in California, the regimented appearance of a community is often softened through innovative home placement and the use of screened porches, patios, aluminum work, carports, and other appurtenances in such a manner as to give variety and interest to the streetscape.

Subdivisions can also lend themselves to a more diverse streetscape by the use of larger homesites, alternating garage offsets and house-line variations in front offsets, diverse and individual landscaping between homesites, and variety in the location of roof lines and extensions.

The challenge remains to achieve the best living environment possible for the high-density, low-cost, affordable community. This challenge can be met through creative engineering that also saves money, particularly in areas not readily visible such as utilities, methods of grading, drainage, and storm water management. These cost savings can be applied to attractive landscape architecture and creative home placement so that each home can be more suitably integrated into its setting.

Alternatives to Grid Pattern Developments

Too often, manufactured home landlease communities are laid out in a simple rectangular grid pattern of similarly shaped homesites, all set the same distance from the street. This pattern of homes arranged in long, straight rows creates an unpleasant, monotonous landscape.

If this grid system is so unappealing, why are so many communities designed that way? The best explanation is that this pattern follows the path of least resistance. It is the easiest for the planner or engineer to draw; it is the easiest for the surveyor to calculate and lay out; and it is perceived by the developer as the most economical to build. This pattern requires the least imaginative effort by all those involved.

Fortunately, there is an alternative to the basic grid pattern, known as the modified grid or neighborhood concept. The neighborhood concept offers a different perspective, an interesting and appealing alternative to grid pattern development.

Figure 5.1 shows how the two designs differ. The neighborhood concept incorporates a landscaped boulevard separating different sections of the community, a vast contrast to the long, tedious stretches of streets and monotonously aligned homes common in the basic grid. Contrary to the cramped closeness of the grid pattern, the neighborhood concept promotes a sense of openness.

Comparing Costs

To determine how the basic grid, neighborhood concept, and other designs compare in housing density and costs, a prototype was developed for a hypothetical 40-acre community, ideal in terms of slope and soil conditions. Models were then created, based on four design concepts. Three were designs for a landlease community: basic grid, neighborhood, and curvilinear; and the fourth was for a subdivision.

The following parameters apply to the 40-acre model:

1. The topography slopes from the northwest corner to the southeast corner at a 3% grade.

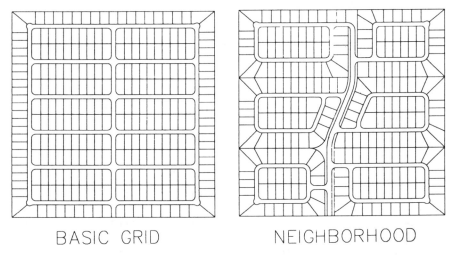

BASIC GRID   NEIGHBORHOOD

FIG. 5.1 In the basic grid pattern, the most common layout for manufactured housing rental communities, homes are arranged in even rows along tediously straight streets, creating an unpleasantly monotonous landscape. In the neighborhood concept, however, a curving landscaped boulevard separates the adult from the family sections and makes the whole community more visually appealing.

2. The frost penetration is 48 inches.
3. In the landlease community, the basic homesite is 5,000 square feet; the home is set back 15 feet from the street. Minor streets are 26 feet wide, and major streets are 30 feet wide with all parking provided off-street.
4. In the subdivision, the basic homesite is 7,500 square feet; the home is set back 25 feet from the street; streets are 30 feet wide with a 60-foot right-of-way.

The hypothetical models assume optimum conditions and densities with no allowance for central facilities or other amenities.

The comparisons shown in Fig. 5.2 are based on costs typical in the Midwest, assuming ideal conditions. Therefore, undesirable site characteristics, such as poor soil conditions, excessive grading, and a need for deep sewer lines, are not considered factors. Instead, the variables such as sewer collection, water distribution, roadways, curbs, and gutters were taken into consideration for each of the four designs. Quantities were assigned to these variables for each design, and unit prices were applied to the quantities to develop total cost comparisons.

Because the basic grid pattern proved to be lowest in cost, it was assigned a cost-comparison figure of 100%. The other cost-comparison percentiles are calculated by dividing the total cost of the design by the cost of the basic grid pattern.

For the subdivision model, a homesite area of 7,500 square feet and a street right-of-way 60-feet wide is used. It is not suggested that all manufactured home

	40-Acre Concept			
	Basic Grid	Neighborhood	Curvilinear	Subdivision
Number of units	281	256	222	160
Gross density per acre	7.0	6.4	5.6	4.0
Roadways in square yards	30,400	28,650	27,350	24,685
Curb in linear feet	18,020	18,160	14,125	13,220
6" Water main in linear feet	4,910	5,700	7,070	6,740
2" Water main in linear feet	11,175	12,470	7,770	660
¾" Water service in linear feet	825	1,080	2,000	12,800
8" Sewer main in linear feet	14,905	13,880	11,635	6,396
4" Sewer service in linear feet	450	700	4,020	14,440
Manholes—each	53	55	42	31
Cost Comparison	100%	105%	116%	160%

FIG. 5.2   Cost comparisons for development of various lotting plans.

subdivisions should have these measurements, but they do represent the norm, and such requirements are most generally found in the ordinances of manufactured home subdivisions across the United States. Generally, a 50-foot right-of-way and homesite sizes between 5,000 and 6,000 square feet are adequate. There are exceptions to these criteria, and each development must be analyzed individually.

If a manufactured home landlease community is converted to condominiums, it will not have to adhere to city subdivision ordinances if the project is zoned *mobile home park*. The streets and utilities will not be dedicated to the municipality, and the homesites are not platted. In this instance the developer could take advantage of basic landlease community planning economics and sell a land-and-home package at a greater profit as a condominium.

As shown in Figure 5.2, the basic grid offers the highest density of 7.0, as compared with 6.4 for the neighborhood concept. Zoning regulations in most cities, however, do not permit a density greater than six homes per acre, and market requirements in many areas also dictate fewer than seven homes per acre.

Although the basic grid is more economical in terms of sewer and water requirements, the neighborhood concept requires less area for roadways. The cost difference between the basic grid and the neighborhood concept is only 5%, a small price to pay for creating a much more marketable community that will command higher rents and is ultimately the more economically feasible choice.

The curvilinear concept consists of curved streets and a mixture of cul-de-sacs. Though not as cost and space efficient as other designs, some situations are tailor-made for this concept. For example, the topography of the ground may not allow a modified grid to work properly with existing land contours, whereas the curvilinear concept may fit well.

The subdivision is the most expensive concept to develop and yields the lowest density because subdivision ordinances normally require wider roadways and larger homesites. Because subdivisions are required to run utilities under the streets, development costs are also higher. In a landlease community, on the other hand, utilities may be routed in the manner most advantageous to the developer.

In light of these considerations, therefore, should a neighborhood pattern, a curvilinear design, or a combination of both be used? Should the development be a subdivision, as opposed to a landlease community?

For the developer to answer these questions, the local market, site characteristics and area economics, political factors, and product selection must be thoroughly researched and understood. Although it may save a few dollars in initial costs, it may not be to the developer's long-term advantage to lay out the community in a simple grid pattern.

THE HOMESITE

The manner in which homes are placed and integrated into the property contributes, to a very large extent, to the environmental quality of the entire project. The following discussion explores those elements normally included or associated with the property development. See Figure 5.3 for examples of lotting configurations.

Typical Homesite Details

Home Placement. The home may be placed perpendicular to the street or parallel to it. Marketers prefer a home's being placed parallel to the street, particularly in the case of multisection homes, as they prefer the "house" look given by this setting. However, the hard development costs related to this kind of placement are approximately 75% of the front footage of the homesite, and by increasing the front footage of the homesite, the cost of the development is increased. There are manufacturers who build homes that have an architectural front entry to permit the home to be placed perpendicular to the street, maintaining the residential subdivision appearance but with lower development costs.

Parking. Although there are a great number and variety of possible parking arrangements, most residents prefer to have their cars parked close to their homes. The lotting concepts using open space and homesites that require remote parking have not been well received in the marketplace. Carports are popular in the southern latitudes where the summers are hot, because they keep cars shaded. Most carports are extended on the side of the home opposite to the entrance and are normally 10 to 13 feet wide. Many communities in the North provide parallel parking in front of the home. There are an increasing number of

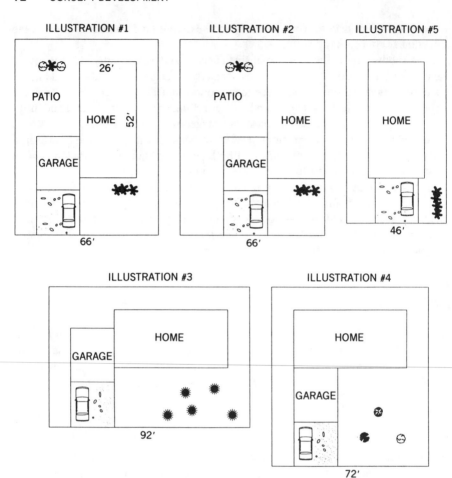

FIG. 5.3 The five illustrations demonstrate lotting configurations to accommodate 26 × 52 foot homes with side and rear setbacks of ten feet and a front setback of 20 feet. Illustrations 1, 2, 3, and 4 also incorporate a two car garage and illustration 5 uses no garage. Front footage of homesites vary from 46 feet to 92 feet. The construction cost per homesite is directly related to the front footage and therefore the cost to develop a homesite in accordance with illustration 3 using a 92 foot frontage is considerably greater than the cost of developing the homesite demonstrated in illustration 1 which has a width of only 66 feet.

Illustrations 1 and 2 are exactly the same arrangement of home and garage. However, illustration 2 is a zero lotline concept and it can be seen that additional usable patio space is created by use of the zero lotline as shown in illustration number 2.

garages incorporated into the site plan for parking automobiles. Many subdivisions in high-end market areas incorporate garages with the home structure.

Open Space and Patios. The open space or patio area can be developed in a variety of ways. The zero-lotline concept is well suited to developing maximum open space inasmuch as the entire area is usable, as opposed to the more conventional homesite where open space is separated into two smaller areas. As previously mentioned, the zero-lotline concept does not fit the open-space needs nor, particularly, the economic or affordability requirements in many areas. Most communities feature additional open space outside the homesite area in the form of pedestrian corridors, active and passive recreational areas, and central facilities.

Screened Porches, Carports, and Garages. Screened porches, carports, and garages can be combined in a variety of ways to make each homesite appear to be unique and independent from other homesites. Screened porches are particularly popular in the retirement communities of the South and in other areas of moderate climate.

Setbacks & Site Size. The regulations for setback requirements vary from municipality to municipality, and each produces its own zoning requirements and development ordinances. The issues relative to setbacks, other than the requirements of specific ordinances, are market considerations. This discussion of setbacks is based on the setback's being measured from the edge of pavement in the landlease community, and from the edge of the right-of-way in the subdivision. Developers must read the regulations carefully, as some communities require a right-of-way in a landlease community even though the roads and utilities will not be dedicated back to the community. The offset is often measured from an imaginary right-of-way line that is dictated by the regulations. The developer should be clear as to whether the offset is to the main structure or whether it applies to patios, garages, or carports.

In a landlease community, common setback requirements in a northern or midwestern community require 10-foot side setbacks, 10-foot rear setbacks, and 15 to 25-foot front setbacks, with a distance of 20 to 25 feet required between homes. If parking is required in the front of the home, a minimum of a 25-foot setback is desirable. In areas where snowplowing is required, adequate setback is important to provide areas for snow storage adjacent to the roadway. In moderate climates, particularly in the Southwest, lesser setbacks are used because of the difference in landscaping and other architectural amenities not prevalent in the North. In these areas, setbacks of as little as 5 to 10 feet from the edge of the pavement have been used successfully. Side and rear setbacks have also been successfully reduced owing to architectural treatment and landscaping.

Homesites generally range from 4,500 square feet to 6,000 square feet, with smaller homesites of about 3,500 square feet being used where special structural or zero-lotline techniques are implemented.

Subdivision regulations vary from community to community. Setbacks include: side setbacks of 10 feet, rear setbacks of 20 feet, and front setbacks of 25 feet from the right-of-way line. Most subdivision regulations require between 7,500 and 15,000 square feet for manufactured home subdivision homesites. With proper product selection and innovative design, attractive communities could be developed with subdivision homesites of less than 7,500 square feet.

There are examples of successful subdivisions that were developed on land zoned for landlease communities, where the economic advantage of the lease ordinance allowing private streets, smaller homesites, no right-of-way, and lesser offsets resulted in a more economic homesite package.

CENTRAL FACILITIES

Facilities for a community vary, depending on the market considerations and the economics of the development.

Entrance

Marketing professionals indicate that the prospective customer's first impression upon entering a project is formed within a matter of minutes and becomes a lasting impression. Therefore, the entrance must be nicely and appropriately landscaped. In retirement communities the marketer generally prefers a design whereby the entrance unfolds into the central facilities. Thus the money spent for the central facilities becomes part of the marketing plan and enhances a customer's first impression of the community. In a blue-collar working community a well landscaped entrance gives the resident the feeling that he or she resides in a desirable community.

Recreation Building

Family Landlease Community. If affordability is a key factor and if the competition has minimal central facilities in the form of recreational buildings, swimming pools, and so on, the developer may opt to minimize the central facilities. On the other hand, in some market areas it is necessary for the developer to include central facility buildings and recreational facilities to compete successfully with other communities.

Adult or Retirement Landlease Communities

Often a retirement community is attractive to prospective residents not only because of the economics but also because of the life-style available to them in this environment. In this case it is common to construct a 10,000 to 20,000-square-foot recreational facility building that has a 5,000-square-foot great hall for dances, plays, general gatherings of residents, hobby rooms, exercise rooms, pool tables, a park office, and a fitness center. A number of other recreational facilities are often included.

Recreational Facilities
- Pool
- Tennis
- Golf course
- Basketball
- Shuffleboard
- Walking, running paths
- Playground
- Tot lot
- Equestrian facility
- Fitness circuit
- Other

Feasibility Test

When the developer has completed the definition of concept, it is time once again to develop corresponding cost estimates and recheck the economic feasibility of the project. It may be necessary for the developer to eliminate some cost elements of the development, or it may happen that the economics of the situation will allow the increase of some of the facilities associated with the concept, thus making the project more marketable.

CHAPTER 6

ZONING

This chapter is presented to assist individuals who are seeking zoning changes, or the approval of conditional use permits or planned unit developments (PUDs), to allow the construction and operation of a manufactured home community. Despite the many changes and improvements within the manufactured housing industry, rezoning continues to be a major obstacle to the development of manufactured home communities.

Planning and zoning officials who sit in judgment of a requested zoning change are interested in many aspects of the proposed development. These officials have a genuine concern for the community. The developer must address their fears and doubts on issues such as:

- Are manufactured homes taxed sufficiently to pay for services provided by the community?
- Will new residents overcrowd the schools without paying a fair share of the cost of education?
- Will the moral conduct of manufactured home residents be of credit or a detriment to the community?
- Will new traffic from the manufactured home community create problems, congest and deteriorate the streets?
- Because manufactured homes do not look like site-built homes, will they be aesthetically suitable?
- How will the presence of manufactured homes affect the value of surrounding properties?

This chapter will help to answer concerns and questions of community leaders, and assist the developer in presenting the rezoning request in a professional and dignified manner.

SITE CONTROL

If the intent of the developer is to build a specific development, rather than speculate on or warehouse real estate, then the land should not be bought outright. There are many contingencies aside from zoning that must be addressed prior to a particular property's being substantiated as a feasible development.

Moreover, if the land sale is contingent upon rezoning approval, the property owner may be of assistance to the developer in the zoning process. The landowner can often provide political leverage and have a calming effect on the neighbors.

FEASIBILITY SITE ANALYSIS

Once a specific site has been identified and the developer decides to proceed with zoning, then a point has been reached where major expenditures of money are required for options, zoning, and planning. The developer must undertake an objective evaluation of the local housing market and development site characteristics and analysis and make an estimate of the potential for economic success. See Chapter Four for a complete discussion.

REZONING STRATEGY

Consult Community Staff

The first step in a rezoning strategy is to contact the following local staff: city manager or administrator, planner, engineer, and zoning administrator. The developer should have discussions with the community staff people, notifying them of the development plans and providing a profile of the development company and its experience with other projects. Because the developer's goal is to obtain information, not solve disputes, there are a number of guidelines to be followed: Make no commitments and do not argue. Obtain as much information as possible about the voting records of the planning commission and of the city board. Ascertain the nature of disputes, policies, or issues that are presently before the community.

Impress upon these people the professionalism, desire, and intent to proceed to develop a quality community that will be both beneficial and acceptable to the community. Bring the planner, architect, and engineer to this first meeting, to develop rapport with the community's professional staff.

Although there will be further visits with community staff members for more detailed information, it is important to find out, at least on a preliminary basis, as much information as possible about the existing zoning of the proposed site, as well as the zoning and plans for adjacent lands. Discuss staff's recommendations relative to sewage collection and treatment, water distribution, water supply, storm water runoff, solid waste collection and disposal, ingress and egress to the proposed development and its impact on existing and future traffic, and other pertinent facts.

The community staff will be able to provide additional information regarding other agencies that will be involved at some point in the approval of the proposed project and most likely will provide not only the name of the agency but the name of the person to contact, addresses, and telephone numbers. Although a straight rezoning of a zoned district to allow manufactured housing should consider only land use issues and the compatibility of that rezoning to the surrounding area, the developer must be prepared to address other non-land-use issues as well.

Consult Other Agencies

Other agencies to be contacted include regional planning, drainage districts (floodplain), U.S. Soil Conservation Service, water utilities and sanitary districts, state and county offices in regard to the obtaining of permits, regulations and statutes, and utility companies for telephone, electric, and natural gas services.

Inventory

Figure 6.1 shows an inventory of materials that should be gathered during meetings with community staff and other agencies. The developer will use this material to become familiar with the site and its advantages, disadvantages, and potential

A list of materials to gather from meetings with local officials includes the following:

1. Local, county, and state *zoning ordinances*
2. *Zoning maps*
3. *Areawide maps* that show the relationship of the site not only to the immediate area, but to the community as a whole
4. *Subdivision ordinances or regulations* that indicate specifications and standards the community requires in other types of developments
5. *Sewer and water maps*
6. *Drainage requirements or ordinances*
7. *Community Comprehensive Plan 701* or other plan
8. *Topographic maps*
9. *Floodplain maps,* ordinances, and regulations
10. *Aerial maps,* usually available from county government
11. *Soil maps*
12. All information that can be collected relative to the school situation in the area.

FIG. 6.1   Research and review checklist.

problems, prior to meeting with local politicians. The materials outlined in Fig. 6.1 will also be used in formulating and producing the zoning presentation.

Meet Local Politicians

Determine the power structure of the community at all levels: staff, planning commission, and board. What are the concerns of the community, neighborhood, planning commission, and board? If at first there is a strong negative reaction, the plan may have to be revised. However, do not be discouraged by a less than enthusiastic response. Ask for suggestions and be prepared to listen and observe. Do not take a hard stand and do not engage in argument.

Review the voting record of the board as it relates to planning commission recommendations.

In many areas the successful rezoning of land is as much or more a political issue as it is an academic exercise in proper land use control and comprehensive planning issues. Even if the developer has the favor of local politicians, it will be necessary to make a thorough presentation, building a strong enough case that a politician can take a stand against a crowded zoning hearing full of remonstrators.

FORMULATE ZONING PROCEDURE

Determine who will lead or monitor the zoning team, and decide who will be involved as expert witnesses. Possibilities include the engineer, architect, attorney, real estate appraiser, accountant, market feasibility specialist, and a manufactured housing trade association representative.

Most zoning ordinances allow manufactured home communities under three separate zoning classifications: zoned district, conditional or special use, or PUD (planned unit development). The PUD is in some jurisdictional areas referred to as a planned residential development (PRD).

Zoned District

Under the zoned district provisions of most ordinances, the manufactured home community is permitted within the zoning classification or zoned district. Under this procedure the ordinance also has a section called the *mobilehome ordinance,* * which regulates the density, street width, buffers, and all other development standards to which a manufactured home community, built within the zoned district, must adhere. The advantage of the zoned district to the developer is that, theoretically, the rezoning issue deals only with land use. The developer, technically, is not required to develop timely and expensive zoning presentation

---

* *Mobilehome ordinance* and *mobilehome park ordinance* are still common parlance with local land use planners and zoning boards. In time, *manufactured home community* will become the term of choice among enlightened planners and board members—Ed.

materials demonstrating the type of community to be built, as this is controlled by the mobilehome park ordinance. However, very few zoning bodies either understand this concept or are willing to rezone a property without additional detailed information.

The major disadvantage of a zoned district to the city or community acting on the rezoning is that after the property is zoned, the developer is controlled only by the mobilehome park ordinance. Virtually no mobilehome park ordinances are written in a manner that will guarantee a quality community. The city or community staff have little flexibility in approving the community's concept or controlling the community's quality, particularly as it relates to streetscape, landscaping, and other aspects that the typical mobilehome ordinance is not structured to control.

Conditional Use or Special Use

Conditional use or *special use* allows a manufactured home community to be developed in a zoned district that is not specifically set aside for manufactured housing. For example, a manufactured home community may be allowed in a commercial zoning, agricultural zoning, or apartment zoning, but requires the rezoning procedure in order for it to follow the regulations set forth in the conditional or special use requirements of the zoning ordinance. Although some ordinances or regulations also have a mobilehome park ordinance that dictates the requirements under the conditional use provisions, other ordinances sometimes require submittal of concept or engineering plans, which must be approved and which are not governed by a specific set of guidelines within the mobilehome ordinance. Securing approval for a manufactured home community through the conditional use procedure normally requires more submittal information than rezoning a present classification. The advantage however, is that the community or city has more control over the type of manufactured home community being developed and might look more favorably upon the project.

Planned Unit Development

Properties that are rezoned through the PUD procedure give both the developer and the community the most flexibility in terms of shaping requirements for the new community. Essentially, the PUD procedure consists of developing a zoning ordinance to fit specifically the project being approved. The disadvantage to the developer is that considerably more detail and information must be developed, submitted, and approved. However, if the community can be convinced that the concept is acceptable, this alternative gives the developer the flexibility of exercising an innovative design based on feasibility and marketability. For example, the developer could increase density and decrease development costs by improving upon antiquated zoning requirements that would have been mandatory under the zoned district or conditional use requirements.

The developer must decide what plans, color renderings, studies, reports, models, and visual aids will be used. Future meeting dates and specific presentation procedures must be determined as well. It is also important to obtain profiles on planning commission and board members, and determine with whom and how to make contact.

The procedure outlined for most communities requires one or two public hearings. Generally, the first public hearing is before the planning commission. The commission, a body appointed by local elected officials, is only an advisory group. The planning commission will send the project to the county or city board with its recommendations. The county or city board is composed of the elected officials, and their vote will be the official zoning act approving or denying the zoning change. Sometimes there is a public hearing at both the planning commission and board levels. At other times the public hearing may be held only once, at either the planning commission or the board level.

ZONING PRESENTATION—COMMUNITY STAFF

At meetings with community staff during the preliminary development of concept, it may be necessary to adopt a give-and-take attitude in order to develop a compromise solution to the proposal. The developer's professional staff must, therefore, know which items may be compromised. The developer should not try to do the job of the engineer and planner, as the community's professional staff will have difficulty communicating and relating—unless, in fact, the developer is disciplined and experienced in the staff's areas of expertise. Therefore, it is imperative at this point that professionals be engaged for the planning and engineering of the development.

It is crucial that the developer receive staff approval if at all possible. It is a major setback at a public hearing for the community's professional staff to recommend denial of the project prior to its formal presentation.

Both community engineers and planners encourage and welcome properly conceived developments. These are professional, rational, and experienced people, and if the developer does not have the ability to sell them on the project, it will be most difficult to sell angry, biased citizens. Few professional engineers and planners are prejudiced or biased against properly planned and designed manufactured home projects located in proper land use areas. Even if it takes several meetings, the developer should obtain general agreement and, if possible, positive staff ideas and recommendations relative to the preliminary concept before proceeding with the development of the final concept and preparation of formal presentation materials.

A community staff that recommends denial of a project is in a safe position and will not have to worry about future problems that may arise with a new community or with the political flack that may result from opposition to a project. On the other hand, if staff approves the project and it does not turn out well or problems arise, staff members may fall into disfavor with the community board. Therefore, it is important that the developer's professional staff help the community staff to feel comfortable in approving the project, with the knowledge that it is properly planned and conceived.

The first actual presentation of the project to community staff should include a number of items, as discussed in the paragraphs that follow.

Location Map Showing Site and Surrounding Area

As part of the first actual presentation, there should be a location map, showing the land use and the existing zoning of the surrounding area.

Site Analysis

The importance of the development site analysis plan (described in detail in Chapter 5) in dealing with community staff is that it provides the degree of comfort mentioned earlier and shows that the development is not taking place within the 100-year floodplain, floodway, or wetlands. The site analysis plan would also show future widening of rights-of-way along adjacent roadways, which assures the community staff that the plan being approved and built will not cause future embarrassment to the staff.

Picture Index of Property

A map is prepared with graphic arrows showing where specific photographs are taken at the site. This map should show the entrance road and demonstrate proper sight distances for the entrance to and exit from the property, as well as drainage and other physical features having an impact on the concept or of importance to the community staff. Large color, or black and white photographs, keyed to the map, are displayed.

Preliminary Concept

The preliminary concept plan is normally hand-drawn or sketched at a scale of $1" = 100'$. Little money should be spent in preparing the first preliminary concept plan, as it will likely change upon review and with input from the community staff. The plan should be detailed enough to indicate issues of concern such as density, homesite size, open space requirements, road patterns, and the manner in which the concept plan deals with the physical aspects of the site as presented in the site analysis map.

ZONING PRESENTATION—PLANNING COMMISSION

The developer should meet with the planning commission on two occasions. The first should be an informal meeting with the planning commission, and the second should be a formal meeting or public hearing at the planning commission level.

Preliminary Informal Meeting with Planning Commission

There are some communities that will not allow an applicant to make informal presentations prior to a public hearing. If the developer is not restricted by this requirement, it is a good idea to meet with and discuss the project at an informal nonpublic hearing with the planning commission prior to the public hearing.

The main goal in the informal meeting is to have an opportunity to promote the project to the planning commission and ascertain the members' attitudes and concerns prior to finalizing the formal presentation. It is also a definite advantage to satisfy the fears, questions, and doubts of the planning commission prior to the public hearing. The developer who can do a good job of selling the planning commission or at least softening its members prior to the public hearing, is in a much better position than if he or she were to walk into a public hearing cold, having to sell the planning commission as well as the citizens of the community.

Impress the planning commission with past developments and successes of the development team. Show slide presentations of the type of development intended for the community. Explain the advantages and disadvantages of the property involved, and suggest how the disadvantages or problems will be resolved. Show the *preliminary concept plan* and stress the fact that in working with local staff, only a preliminary plan has been developed and that the planning commission is invited to offer input and suggestions prior to proceeding with *final concept development.*

FORMAL PLANNING COMMISSION MEETING AND PUBLIC HEARING

The next step is the zoning presentation at a formal planning commission meeting and public hearing. Figure 6.2 is a list of recommended presentation materials.

The developer's objective is for the planning commission to approve the project and send it on to the board for official action. Typically, in most zoning cases, the planning commission is only an advisory body, and official zoning action can take place only at the council or board level. In some communities the board's action is always to vote in accordance with the recommendation of the planning commission. However, there are other communities in which the board or council pays very little attention to the planning commission's recommendations. By now there may be some politics in favor of the project, but do not forget that these allies can lend support only if the presentation will allow endorsement without fear or concern that its supporters look bad or appear to be bought.

Normally, the public hearing procedure begins when the chairperson calls the public hearing to order. Then the project is identified and the actions under consideration are explained. Next, the community staff, which normally includes the city planners, will give their presentation of the project and related recommendations. The chairperson then asks who in the audience is in favor of the project and wishes to speak in that behalf. At this time the developer or the developer's representative

Presentation materials for formal planning commission meeting and public hearing include the following:

1. Areawide map showing site location as it relates to total community
2. Site location map showing site and immediately adjacent properties and roadways
3. Zoning map showing existing zoning of proposed development, adjacent zoning and property owners
4. Picture index map and accompanying photographs
5. Site analysis map
6. Overall concept plan, generally a color rendering at a scale of 1" = 100'
7. Isolated slides or rendering of concept plan showing details of open space, recreational areas, entrances, etc.
8. Landscape plan showing size, number, and species of plantings
9. Individual site details showing home placement and amenities
10. Individual site details showing offsets
11. Lot plan showing dimensions
12. Architectural renderings of buildings and signage
13. Traffic map
14. Streetlight plan
15. Solid waste plan
16. Chart or slides showing ordinance requirements compared with actual project standards
17. Engineering drawings: preliminary engineering drawings at a scale of 1" = 100'—not to be confused with construction drawings that are part of the final engineering drawings
    a. Grading plan
    b. Sewage collection plan
    c. Water distribution plan
    d. Storm water or drainage plan
    e. Roadway details
    f. Water supply
    g. Sewage treatment
18. Zoning handout booklets, to be given only to commission or board members. The handout booklet should be given to the board members and staff prior to the public hearing. It is extremely prudent to give the city accountant or attorney time to read and validate the tax and school impact analysis in order to substantiate these documents prior to the public hearing.

FIG. 6.2   Minimum presentation material checklist.

will give the zoning presentation. After completion of the presentation, the planning commission chair will invite questions from other board members and from the audience. Generally, members of the audience must give their names and addresses, and if they are not local residents, a strong planning commission chair may strike their comments or testimony from the record.

After the question-and-answer session, the chair will ask who in the audience objects to the project and will open the floor to that viewpoint. Generally, the development team will be given a chance to rebut or respond to the opposition's comments prior to the chair's opening the discussion with other planning commission members before the zoning is approved or denied.

When a motion is made, the chair will ask for a vote on that motion. This can be a very critical time in the zoning effort. If it is obvious that there is too much public opposition for the board to vote in favor, or if it is apparent that the board is not prepared to approve the zoning, then it may be wise to ask for a continuation of the public hearing. This will give additional time to resolve the problems or develop answers to points of opposition.

ZONING PRESENTATION—BOARD LEVEL

The procedure of the zoning board has essentially the same format as that of the planning commission. If the planning commission recommends denial of the zoning, the development team should be prepared to counter those points upon which the denial was based. On the other hand, if the planning commission recommends approval of the zoning, then their recommendation should be communicated as one of the reasons that the board should approve the zoning. The board is usually more concerned than the planning commission with impact of the proposed project on schools and taxes, and the development team should be prepared to respond.

The presentation materials and the formal presentation itself are essentially the same as those introduced to the planning commission, but are modified in accordance with the suggestions and recommendations of the planning commission and in accordance with the concerns of the board, as ascertained through the political research.

The presentation should be summarized by emphasizing that the project is the highest and best use of the property, that the land use requested is compatible with surrounding land use and the comprehensive plan of the community, and that the project will be an asset to the community in terms of tax revenues and increased local commerce.

At a public hearing, the developer should:

- Assume that the members of the board are intelligent, unselfish, and have a genuine concern for the future of the community.
- Maintain dignity and decorum even when opposing factions become raucous, irrational, or discourteous.
- Point out the benefits of the proposal to the community, but do not be afraid to admit that the principal reason for the development is to make a profit.
- Be professional. The development team's ability to carry out the proposal will be measured by the character of the presentation. Make use of professional assistance wherever possible.
- Make the presentation brief but thorough. Be prepared to counter charges concerning taxes, schoolchildren, and effect on adjacent property values.

- Supplement the presentation with maps, charts, and pictures, large enough to be easily seen and understood by the entire assembly as well as zoning board members.
- Use the best of sales techniques to *sell* the idea, the concept, and, above all, the developer him- or herself.

Samples of Most Frequently Asked Questions at a Public Hearing

Schoolchildren

Question: What is the anticipated impact on schools as the result of additional children living in a manufactured home community?

Answer: Because most manufactured homeowners are newly married or adult empty nesters, the number of school-age children per manufactured home is normally much lower than the number in a comparable single-family subdivision home. This, of course, will vary from area to area, but generally the per pupil unit (number of children per home) for the manufactured home is .25 pupil units versus 1.5 or 2 pupil units for the residential subdivision. In a comparison of tax revenues generated per pupil unit for the school district, the manufactured home community's contribution is quite often larger.

Do not try to make the argument that the manufactured housing community pays all the costs required per pupil unit, because this is seldom the case. Do compare the cost for per pupil unit between the manufactured housing community and the residential subdivision; the winning argument is that the manufactured home community pays more per pupil unit as compared with the single-family residential subdivision.

Point out that the national average number of school-age children per manufactured home unit is .25. Generally, this is significantly lower than the average in any area for site-built housing. The average for local site-built housing should be available from the school board or administration.

Impact on City Services

Question: Won't this new community require additional police and fire protection?

Answer: No more so than a site-built community, and perhaps less. Residents of a landlease community tend to turn first to on-site management to handle minor police problems, and many incidents are resolved without calling for assistance.

Explain that landlease community residents and homeowners in manufactured housing subdivisions are subject to rules and regulations, the violation of which may result in eviction from the community. This permits tighter control over problem individuals than is available where the land is owned by the homeowner. Be prepared to offer a copy of the proposed rules and regulations.

Be armed with studies indicating that manufactured homes have fewer problems and fire fatalities than other types of communities. Be prepared also to point out that the plan has adequate fire protection, in terms of the water distribution system, and that roadways and cul-de-sacs are adequate for access by fire fighting equipment.

Impact on Surrounding Land Values

Question: Will the land around the manufactured home community increase or decrease in value?

Answer: The proposed use is the highest and best use to which the land may be put.

In addition, point out the screening, natural or man-made, around the project, along with other desirable amenities. Finally, suggest that the addition of consumers to the area will increase revenues for local businesses. Together, these increased revenues and an attractive community add value to neighboring properties.

Taxes

Question: Will the manufactured home community pay its way in the community at large?

Answer: Absolutely. Services normally provided and maintained by the municipality, such as streets, lighting, signs, and recreational facilities, are provided and maintained at the expense of the developer. These improvements, along with other site improvements, substantially increase the land value. The developer pays taxes based on the income generated, and property taxes based on the value of the improved real estate.

Finally, describe the method of taxation of manufactured home communities within the state. Prepare a comparison between revenues generated by manufactured housing communities and site-built single-family detached housing; add all taxes and subtract city maintenance costs.

Explain, if applicable, that sewer treatment and water distribution are privately financed and maintained.

THE ZONING ORDINANCE

Most mobilehome park zoning ordinances are outdated, and a development built strictly to those standards would not be of the high quality necessary to be competitive in the marketplace. Some ordinances are intentionally written in a way that makes it all but impossible for manufactured home communities to be developed successfully. Such ordinances may require densities or homesite sizes that are prohibitive or may specify a number of requirements that would prohibit use of manufactured housing.

ZONING THROUGH THE COURTS

Zoning through the courts is a time-consuming and expensive method of obtaining manufactured home community zoning. However, there are some situations where the prejudice of the community or political officials force this alternative.

REZONING IS POSSIBLE

Many successful rezonings have resulted from using the approach and methodology described in this chapter. Each rezoning case must be reviewed and developed in accordance with its unique and particular circumstances. There may indeed be situations that do not require as elaborate an approach as presented here. However, the general overall philosophy and attitude toward successful rezoning should follow the same basic approach:

- Appreciate and understand the concerns of the community staff, politicians, and citizens.
- Be prepared to address these concerns to whatever detail and extent is required.
- Use the sales techniques necessary to sell the development team and the project to the community, illustrating that it is an asset.

CHAPTER 7

BUSINESS AND MARKETING PLAN

The creation of a written business and marketing plan is critical to any new construction project. Business and marketing plans are useful not only for the developer, but also for lenders or investors, who will evaluate the project's likelihood of success, and for those who will actually implement such plans. Unfortunately, business and marketing plans are not always prepared prior to the actual start of a new development. If they were always in place at the beginning, there would probably be fewer marginal and failed developments.

The primary purpose of a business and marketing plan is to provide associates, subordinates, lenders, partners, and others with a clear understanding of the business opportunity involved in the proposed venture. In addition, the business and marketing plan should provide an estimate of financial resources required, the proposed method of finding, presenting, and selling the product to qualified prospective buyers, and an evaluation of the possible fruits of the venture, including targeted buyer characteristics, area competition, and market conditions, under anticipated (nominal case) and unanticipated (worst expected case) rates of absorption.

Above all, the business and marketing plan must be realistic and should be based on the best available information. Accurate budgets, absorption rates, and matching the product to market wants and needs are extremely important.

A carefully prepared business and marketing plan will result in a project that is minimally influenced by high rates of inflation, economic recession, unusually high interest rates, or high unemployment.

STRUCTURE AND STYLE

The business and marketing plan should be well organized and easily understood by the intended reader. Preparing written descriptions of financial plans and operations is at best an extremely difficult job. They must be written to the reading level of the general public, not over their heads. For example, each page should be easy to read, and sequentially numbered, and there should be a table of contents at the front or an index at the back. Key sections of the plan should be tabbed for easy reference. Additional guidelines include the following:

- A simple statement of the business opportunity being presented, with an executive conclusion, should be included in the beginning of the plan. Significant financial parameters and conclusions should be clearly stated early in the report (e.g., "loan size is estimated to be . . . ," "projected return on investment is . . . ," "a yearly estimated operating budget proposed is . . . .")
- Type style should be simple and consistent throughout the plan. Italics and bold type should be used when highlighting a point, when quoting someone, and when referencing a publication. Bold lettering should be used for section or paragraph titles. Use pica size or 10-point type for ease of reading.
- Each new section of the plan should begin at the top of an odd-numbered page on the right. Important subjects should not be split between succeeding pages. Tables and reference charts, questions and answers, and stand-alone illustrations should be displayed on the same page as the describing or associated text.
- Graphics should be clearly identified, and specific information referenced from within the plan should be highlighted with arrows or captioned in bold letters.
- Maps and site plans are a necessity. These should be shown early in the plan and include appropriate local, county, and state information.

When dealing with readers who are not familiar with manufactured housing, it is always a good idea to include a section that describes its role in the overall housing market. Give a description of the advantages of manufactured housing, including product features, price, function, financing, and low down payment. Another way to organize such data is to provide a section in the appendix, describing manufactured home products, financing, siting, and other features.

Attach a copy of recent news stories about affordability and high housing costs, to illustrate the key role of manufactured housing as a solution to affordable housing needs.

PLAN SECTION I: SCOPE

The first section of the plan should define the scope or range of the business and marketing plan and answer the following typical questions:

- For whom is the plan written?
- What is the function of the plan?
- What is the purpose of the plan?
- What questions is the plan intended to answer?

This section of the plan should also address questions about the developer's plans, local market conditions, operating budgets, cash requirements, development loan requirements, targeted homebuyer, home product, homebuyer's loan financing, and anticipated profits under best and worst performance conditions.

PLAN SECTION II: BUSINESS OPPORTUNITY DESCRIPTION

The statement of financial objectives, including a statement of the business philosophy for the entity, is the most important lead into this section of the plan. Include reasons for the business's existence (e.g., to provide low-cost housing or create an income-property opportunity).

Stating the financial objectives for the business entity is important, for example:

- We are creating a long-term income property investment opportunity.
- We are creating a short-term income property to sell soon after completion.
- We are rezoning land and intend to resell or "flip" it, without developing it, to another builder/developer.
- We are building single-family home and land packages (or condominium communities) with provisions for long-term buyer financing.

Include a description of current and projected market conditions that provide the basic business opportunity. Also include an analysis of how the proposed product fits into these market conditions. Review available homebuyer financing programs. Estimate the percentage of market that is expected to be captured.

Provide a description of the targeted homebuyer and community resident, including but not limited to:

- Family type (family, empty nester, retiree)
- Average income
- Educational level
- Employment characteristics
- Family size

This section should also include a description of the proposed housing product, anticipated down payments, and total monthly housing costs. Also calculate minimum family or gross income requirements and estimate the percentage of homes to be financed versus all cash purchases.

PLAN SECTION III: PHYSICAL DESCRIPTION

The third section of the plan is characterized by a review of information that adequately describes the location and condition of the project site. Include the following maps:

- State, showing the location of the county
- County, showing the location of the city, township, or town
- City, township, or town, showing the specific street location of the community

Also include:

- Photos of the selected site and adjacent relevant properties
- A copy of the development site plan, showing the location of on-site amenities, entrances and exits, and, if appropriate, phase lines
- Drawings showing typical homesite sizes and configurations, maximum home sizes, mandated lotline setbacks, and so on.

Copies of floor plans and exterior elevations of proposed homes, homesite price lists and rental rate estimates, and lists of available options are also useful.

PLAN SECTION IV: MARKET CONDITIONS

A description of local market conditions makes up the fourth section of the plan. Include demographics for targeted buyer groups, such as the following:

- Buyer age range and family characteristics
- Number of school-age children
- Average household income

Review competitive housing communities in the local market, including historical rates of absorption, comparison of home pricing and rent structure (or lot prices), on-site and off-site amenities, financing programs, and known marketing techniques.

This section of the plan should also present a financial analysis of other housing alternatives, including the following:

- New single-family housing prices and sales rates
- Condominium prices and sales rates
- Apartment rental rates, vacancies, and trends
- Home rentals and vacancies

When at all possible, include information on down payments and monthly expenses for multifamily, and entry-level single-family, site-built housing.

Estimate various absorption rates under varying market conditions. Include estimates for the best expected absorption rate case, the nominal case, and the worst expected case. Include a description of the assumptions underlying each type of case.

Summarize relevant community information that may have an impact on the success of the proposed project, including:

- Local household growth rate
- Unemployment rate, past and present
- Sources of community employment and economics
- Historical percentage of manufactured homes sold into nearby landlease communities
- Historical percentage of manufactured homes sold onto privately owned single-family homesites
- Number of persons entering preretirement (empty nesters) and retirement status over the next 5 years

Chart other manufactured housing project types, in terms of the following factors:

- Number of directly competitive local projects (landlease versus landlease, fee simple versus fee simple)
- Number of alternative projects (rental versus fee simple)
- Number of projects planned but not yet constructed
- Number of existing and filled manufactured home communities

Information on each project generally should include:

- Homesite sales price or rental rate
- Rate of community absorption
- Method of marketing and advertising
- Targeted market groups
- Samples of lease and rules and regulations for the community
- Monthly maintenance fees, if a condominium or cooperatively owned community
- Utility inclusions: normalize for water, sewer and trash removal
- On-site amenities (clubhouse, pool, tennis courts, etc.)
- Off-site amenities (lakefront, trees, close to schools, etc.)
- Home product description, including pricing, financing, accessories, landscaping, and so forth

Whenever possible, a brief narrative history of all recently filled or currently operational projects should be included. This history comprises start dates, methods of marketing, absorption rate histories, background of developers, sales incentives, sales commissions and management characteristics. If there have been some recent similar projects, an analysis of methods for success or causes of failure should also be presented.

PLAN SECTION V: HOME PRODUCT DESCRIPTION

In the fifth section, provide a complete description of the home product: the home, accessories, homesite, landscaping, and pricing, including available buyer financing programs. At minimum, include information on:

- Price lists
- Floor plans
- Options pricing
- Homesite sizes
- Rental rates
- Community rules and regulations (guidelines for living)
- Deed restrictions and covenants
- Available financing programs
- Seller's prepaid items (buy downs, FHA points, etc.)

Also include a description of the type of estate (e.g., leasehold, fee simple, condominium, or cooperative, etc.).

PLAN SECTION VI: SALES AND MARKETING

In the plan's sixth section, define the major marketing theme of the project, and estimate the advertising budget, and the projected marketing staff levels.

Describe the developer's plans to identify qualified prospective homebuyers and attract them to the sales center. Outline methods of tracking prospects once identified and qualified and follow-up procedures to be used with prospective homebuyers.

Elaborate on the sales team selected: whether it will consist of on-site commissioned sales staff, on-site sales coordinators, or outside brokers. Describe the amount of outside commissions anticipated and how outside advertising responsibilities will be handled. Illustrations for this section should include:

- Copies of proposed advertisements
- Copies of planned brochures

- A list of publications for placing advertising
- Advertising schedules and rate cards
- Outside broker or retailer commission structure

Also include a review of specific sales staff instructions for qualifying prospective homebuyers: properly greeting and conducting project tours, practice benefit selling, emphasis on benefits rather than features, and closing effectively. Describe procedures for keeping good, current mailing lists and tracking prospects regularly throughout the marketing process. Sales staff compensation structure, payment schedules, referral fees, and commission splits should also be described in this section.

Describe additional sales procedures, such as methods of deciding sales prospect "ups," or how sales staff will take turns greeting prospects as they come through the door, as well as sales staff performance and handling lost order (sales) reports.

Provide proposed staff job or position descriptions for all operational and sales staff in this section, including:

- Desired qualifications of employees
- Base salary levels and benefits packages
- Sales commission structure (draw schedule provisions, if any)
- Any additional sales incentives, spiffs or motivators, premium programs, and so on
- Sales management structure and organization chart
- List of primary staff responsibilities
- Order of authorities

If staff has already been selected, or is in place, copies of individual resumes and summaries of job experience are included in the appendix. Figure 7.1 shows a typical marketing and sales budget.

PLAN SECTION VII: OPERATING BUDGETS

The seventh section presents an evaluation of the estimated costs of the development including, but not limited to, land cost, hard construction costs, soft costs during construction, and soft costs during fill-in. Figure 7.2 shows typical construction cost factors for a multiphase development.

Also include a list of proposed operating costs for the project and marketing budgets for sales at various absorption rates. Contingency plans are described for unanticipated slow rates of sales, which may include making appropriate adjustments in the product, pricing, financing, or advertising programs. This section also discusses methods of using cash flow models to evaluate worst-case capital requirements.

	Monthly Home Sales	1	2	3	4	5	6	7	8	9	10	11	12
Estimated Sales Volume @	$28,500	28,500	57,000	85,500	114,000	142,500	171,000	199,500	228,000	256,500	285,000	313,500	342,000
Gross Margin	9,500	9,500	19,000	28,500	38,000	47,500	57,000	66,500	76,000	85,500	95,000	104,500	114,000
Setup, Transport, Skirt and Steps	2,500	(2,500)	(5,000)	(7,500)	(10,000)	(12,500)	(15,000)	(17,500)	(20,000)	(22,500)	(25,000)	(27,500)	(30,000)
Commissions and Overrides	950	(950)	(1,900)	(2,850)	(3,800)	(4,750)	(5,700)	(6,650)	(7,600)	(8,550)	(9,500)	(10,450)	(11,400)
Operating Income		6,050	12,100	18,150	24,200	30,250	36,300	42,350	48,400	54,450	60,500	66,550	72,600
Manager's base		750	750	750	750	1,000	1,000	1,250	1,250	1,500	1,500	1,750	1,750
Sales base		0	0	500	500	500	500	1,000	1,000	1,000	1,000	1,500	1,500
Secretarial		0	0	750	750	750	750	950	950	1,125	1,125	1,125	1,125
Service staff	1,200	1,200	1,200	1,200	1,500	1,500	2,250	2,250	2,250	2,250	2,250	2,250	2,250
Payroll taxes	18.0%	351	351	576	630	675	810	981	981	1,058	1,058	1,193	1,193
Workman's Compensation	3.5%	68	68	112	123	131	158	191	191	206	206	232	232
Wages and Benefits		2,369	2,369	3,888	4,253	4,556	5,468	6,622	6,622	7,138	7,138	8,049	8,049
Yellow pages		75	75	75	75	75	75	75	75	75	75	75	75
Billboards		0	0	600	600	600	600	1,200	1,200	1,200	1,200	1,200	1,200
Newspaper display		0	0	0	500	500	500	500	500	500	500	500	500
Newspaper classified	150	150	150	150	600	600	600	600	600	600	600	600	600
Floor plan interest	570	570	855	855	1,140	1,140	1,140	1,140	1,140	1,710	1,710	1,710	1,710
Liability insurance	250	250	250	250	250	250	250	250	250	250	250	250	250
Janitorial	50	50	50	140	175	175	175	175	175	245	245	245	245

Postage and express	175	175	175	175	175	175	175	175	175	175	175
Copying and printing	150	200	200	250	250	300	300	300	300	300	300
Business license	15	15	15	15	15	15	15	15	15	15	15
Computer lease	175	175	175	175	175	175	175	175	175	175	175
Office furniture lease	50	50	50	50	150	150	150	150	150	150	150
Model furniture lease	250	375	375	500	500	500	500	500	750	750	750
Telephone	196	268	339	410	481	553	624	695	766	838	909
Electric	225	300	300	375	375	375	375	375	525	525	525
Heating	75	100	100	125	125	125	125	125	175	175	175
Legal and accounting	150	150	150	150	150	150	150	150	150	150	150
Travel and entertainment	50	100	100	150	150	200	200	250	250	250	250
Dues and subscriptions	25	25	25	25	25	25	25	25	25	25	25
Tools and parts	29	57	86	114	143	171	200	228	257	285	314
Office supplies	45	45	65	65	85	85	105	105	125	125	150
Personal property taxes	100	100	100	100	100	100	100	100	100	100	100
Subtotal	2,805	3,515	4,324	6,019	6,239	6,439	7,158	7,308	8,518	8,618	8,742
Total Sales Budget	5,174	5,884	8,212	10,272	10,795	11,906	13,780	13,930	15,656	15,756	16,792
Estimated Net Cash Flow	876	6,216	9,938	13,929	19,455	24,394	28,570	34,470	38,794	44,744	49,758
Cash Flow per Home Sold	876	3,108	3,313	3,482	3,891	4,066	4,081	4,309	4,310	4,474	4,523
Number of salespersons	0	0	1	1	1	1	2	2	2	2	3
Number of model homes	2	3	3	4	4	4	4	4	6	6	6

FIG. 7.1 Marketing and sales budget.

	Unit	Unit Cost	Phase 1 Cost	75 Per Site	Unit	Unit Cost	100 Phase 2 of Cost	Per Site	Total Quantity	175 Total Lots Total	Per Site
Earthmoving	36,325 cu yd	2.10	76,283		0 cu yd	2.10	0		0	76,283	
Fine grading	9,400 sq yd	0.55	5,170		1,400 sq yd	0.55	770		1,400	5,940	
1 Rough Grading and Surface Shaping			81,453	1,086.03			770	7.70		82,223	469.84
10" PVC, SDR 35 pipe	1,968 ln ft	26.16	51,483		1,200 ln ft	26.16	31,392		1,200	82,875	
Wyes	53 ea	50.00	2,650		23 ea	50.00	1,150		23	3,800	
Standard manholes	8 ea	1,500.00	12,000		4 ea	1,500	6,000		4	18,000	
Lift station	1 l.s.	30,000.00	30,000		0 l.s.	30,000	0		0	30,000	
Force main and valves	400 ln ft	10.00	4,000		400 ln ft	10.00	4,000		400	8,000	
2 Sewer Collection and Conveyance System			100,133	1,335.11			42,542	425.42		142,675	815.29
6" PVC, CL200 pipe (on-site)	3,650 ln ft	10.00	36,500		3,650 ln ft	10.00	36,500		3,650	73,000	
Fittings	15 ea	150.00	2,250		15 ea	150.00	2,250		15	4,500	
Gate valve with box	6 ea	650.00	3,900		6 ea	650.00	3,900		6	7,800	
Fire hydrants w/valve	2 ea	1,200.00	2,400		2 ea	1,200.00	2,400		2	4,800	
Trace wire	3,650 ln ft	0.30	1,095		3,650 ln ft	0.30	1,095		3,650	2,190	
Granular backfill	250 cu yd	20.00	5,000		250 cu yd	20.00	5,000		250	10,000	
6" PVC, CL200 pipe (off-site)	900 ln ft	10.00	9,000		900 ln ft	10.00	9,000		900	18,000	
Fittings	5 ea	150.00	750		5 ea	150.00	750		5	1,500	
Gate valve with box	1 ea	650.00	650		1 ea	650.00	650		1	1,300	
Booster pump station	1 ea	18,500.00	18,500		1 ea	18,500.00	18,500		1	37,000	
Bore and casting	75 ea	161.76	12,132		0 ea	161.76	0		0	12,132	
Trace wire	900 ln ft	0.30	270		900 ln ft	0.30	270		900	540	
Tapping sleeve and valve	1 ea	1,200.00	1,200		1 ea	1,200.00	1,200		1	2,400	

3 Water Distribution and Fire Protection				93,647	1,248.63				81,515	815.15	175,162	1,000.93
Engineering Design	1	l.s.	37,910.00	37,910		0	l.s.	37,910.00	0		37,910	
Surveying and staking	1	l.s.	11,900.00	11,900		1	l.s.	8,925.00	8,925		20,825	
Building permits	1	l.s.	500.00	500		1	l.s.	300.00	300		800	
Easement preparation	1	l.s.	500.00	500		1	l.s.	500.00	500		1,000	
4 Engineering, Etc.				50,810	677.47				9,725	97.25	60,535	345.91
Clearing, grubbing		acres	1,500.00			0	acres	1,500.00	0		0	
Subgrade preparation	3,500	sq yd	1.50	5,250		3,500	sq yd	1.50	5,250		10,500	
Geotextile fabric	0	sq yd	1.00	0		0	sq yd	1.00	0		0	
Subbase stone (6")	0	sq yd	4.25	0		0	sq yd	4.25	0		0	
Curb and gutter	1,850	ln ft	10.50	19,425		1,387.5	ln ft	10.50	14,569		33,994	
PCC pavement	3,500	sq yd	14.00	49,000		2,625	sq yd	14.00	36,750		85,750	
5 Roadway Improvements				63,710	849.47				56,569	565.69	120,279	687.31
24" ADS pipe	560	ln ft	24.50	13,720		420	ln ft	24.50	10,290		24,010	
24" RCP	26	ln ft	26.00	676		19.5	ln ft	26.00	507		1,183	
15" ADS pipe	330	ln ft	15.50	5,115		247.5	ln ft	15.50	3,836		8,951	
15" RCP	45	ln ft	18.00	810		0	ln ft	18.00	0		810	
12" ADS pipe	43	ln ft	13.00	559		0	ln ft	13.00	0		559	
12" RCP		ln ft	16.00	0		0	ln ft	16.00	0		0	
Aggregate bedding	200	cu yd	20.00	4,000		100	cu yd	20.00	2,000		6,000	
Flared end section, 24"	1	ea	75.00	75		0	ea	75.00	0		75	
Flared end section, 15"		ea	60.00	0		0	ea	60.00	0		0	
Flared end section, 12"	1	ea	50.00	50		1	ea	50.00	50		100	
Inlet manholes	8	ea	1,000.00	8,000		1	ea	1,000.00	1,000		9,000	
Ditch shaping	2,170	ln ft	6.50	14,105		.25	ln ft	6.50			14,105	
Surface restoration	0	acre	1,500.00	0		0	acre	1,500.00	0		0	
Erosion protecton	0	sq yd	0.50	0		0	sq yd	0.50	0		0	
Head wall and flap valve	1	ea	1,500.00	1,500		0	ea	1,500.00	0		1,500	
6 Storm Water Retention and Conveyance				48,610	648.13				17,683	176.83	66,293	378.82
Underground allowance	1	l.s.	2,900.00	2,900		0	l.s.	2,900.00	0		2,900	

FIG. 7.2 Construction cost development.

Item	Unit	Unit Cost	Phase 1 Cost	75 Per Site	Unit	Unit Cost	100 Phase 2 of Cost	Per Site	Total Quantity	175 Total Lots Total	Per Site
Street lights 25', 175 watt lamp	4 ea	1,500.00	6,000		2 ea	1,500.00	3,000		2	9,000	
Gas main	9,100 ln ft	2.87	26,117		0 ln ft	2.87	0		0	26,117	
Railroad and highway jack and bore	180 ln ft	45.00	8,100		0 ln ft	45.00	0		0	8,100	
7 Gas, Electrical and Street Lighting			43,117	574.89			3,000	30.00		46,117	263.53
Fine Grading	1 l.s.	250	18,750		1 l.s.	250	25,000		1	43,750	
Permits	1 l.s.	35	2,625		1 l.s.	35	3,500		1	6,125	
Staking for piers	1 l.s.	75	5,625		1 l.s.	75	7,500		1	13,125	
6" Driveway	500 sq ft	1.75	65,625		500 sq ft	1.75	87,500		500	153,125	
4" Walkway	250 sq ft	1.75	32,813		250 sq ft	1.75	43,750		250	76,563	
4" Sidewalk	100 sq ft	1.75	13,125		100 sq ft	1.75	17,500		100	30,625	
30" × 24" Pier	32 ea	25.00	60,000		32 ea	25.00	80,000		32	140,000	
4" Aggregate base	1,000 sq ft	0.25	18,750		1,000 sq ft	0.25	25,000		1,000	43,750	
Electr meter base w/200 amp breaker	1 ea	550.00	41,250		1 ea	550.00	55,000		1	96,250	
Landscaping: seeding	0.1 /acre	1,200.00	9,000		0.1 /acre	1,200.00	12,000		0.1	21,000	
Landscaping: trees	2 ea	50.00	7,500		2 ea	50.00	10,000		2	17,500	
½ Water service	90 ln ft	6.00	40,500		90 ln ft	6.00	54,000		90	94,500	
Water service fee	1 l.s.	75	5,625		1 l.s.	75	7,500		1	13,125	
Water meter	1 l.s.	1,250	93,750		1 l.s.	1250	125,000		1	218,750	
Connection pit	1 ea	60.00	4,500		1 ea	60.00	6,000		1	10,500	
Valve	1 ea	23.00	1,725		1 ea	23.00	2,300		1	4,025	
Cable service	1 ea	0	0		1 ea	0	0		1	0	
Telephone service	1 ea	0	0		1 ea	0	0		1	0	
6" PVC sewer service	100 ln ft	12.50	93,750		100 ln ft	12.50	125,000		100	218,750	
Connection for home	1 ea	25.00	1,875		1 ea	25.00	2,500		1	4,375	

Item	Qty	Unit	Unit Cost	Amount (Phase 1)	Qty / Per-Lot	Amount (Phase 2)	Per-Lot	Total Amount	Per-Lot
8 Individual Lot Preparation	75		6,890.50	516,788	100	689,050	6,890.50	1,205,838	6,890.50
150' Water service	1	l.s.	8,000	8,000	0	0		8,000	
Sewer lift station	1	l.s.	50,000	50,000	0	0		50,000	
Water meter fee	1	l.s.	3,500	3,500	0	0		3,500	
Meter pit	1	l.s.	20,000	20,000	0	0		20,000	
Grinding station	1	l.s.	10,000	10,000	0	0		10,000	
Sewer fees	75	ea	45	3,375	0	0		3,375	
Engineering support	1	l.s.	15,000	15,000	1	5,000		20,000	
Traffic light at full cost	1	l.s.	30,000	30,000	0	0		30,000	
Street signs	35	ea	175	6,125	25	4,375		10,500	
Mailboxes	75	ea	35	2,625	175	6,125		8,750	
Road striping	1	l.s.	1,500	1,500	1	500		2,000	
Telephone system	1	l.s.	0	0	1	0		0	
Security gate	1	l.s.	0	0	1	0		0	
Acceleration/deceleration lane	1	l.s.	10,000	10,000	0	0		10,000	
Contingency			6.0%	83,403	0.06	960		84,363	
9 Other Costs			145,490	391,783	5,223.77	16,960		408,743	
10 Subtotal Infrastructure				1,390,050	18,534	917,814	9,178.14	2,307,864	13,187.80
Clubhouse and furnishings	1	ea	135,000	135,000	1	10,000		145,000	
Clubhouse lighting and landscaping	1	ea	25,000	25,000	1	2,500		27,500	
Front entrance	1	ea	15,000	15,000	0	0		15,000	
Pool and accessories	1	ea	35,000	35,000	0	0		35,000	
Day care center	1	ea	28,000	28,000	0	0		28,000	
Contingency at 10%			10.0%	23,800	0.1	1,250		25,050	
11 Subtotal Amenities				$261,800	1,424	13,750	137.50	275,550	1,574.57
12 Total Construction Cost Budget				1,651,850	19,958	931,564	9,315.64	2,583,414	14,762.37

FIG. 7.2 (Continued)

Specific budget information is structured to show various costs on a phase-by-phase basis for phased projects, then a total budget for all phases. Each successive phase states the basis for estimated inflated (future) costs. Projects without home sales may delete home-specific items, but overall, such budgets should generally include:

- Cost of raw, undeveloped land
- Hard construction costs, including the concrete "pad" (for midwestern states)
- Cost of actual home installation
- Costs of homes and accessories
- Estimated profit margins
- Sales and marketing budgets
- Community operations budgets
- Costs of models and sales center
- Advertising budgets

Each budget should include start-up costs and on-going expenses and should be adjusted over time for scheduled reductions. For example, advertising budgets may be expressed as a percentage of the entire project; however, costs are usually higher initially, and as the project fills up, they taper off to a lower expenditure level.

PLAN SECTION VIII: FINANCING

The eighth section of the plan is characterized by a comprehensive review of the proposed method of project financing, including possible sources of the developer's equity, seller financing, joint venture relationships, and institutional acquisition and development loan sources. In the case of debt financing, outline of the proposed loan structure is presented, which includes:

- Interest rate and structure (monthly or yearly, fixed or adjustable, etc.)
- Fees and estimated closing costs
- Repayment provisions
- Loan term, conversion rights to permanent financing
- Release clauses, draw schedule
- Collateral
- Personal guarantees
- Subordination clauses

In the case of equity financing, describe the characteristics of the investor's perfection of interest in the project, profit distributions, investor's liability, and other appropriate parameters.

Financing information for homebuyers should also be presented, covering the following items:

- Interest rates, adjustment period
- Loan amortization period
- Down payment, closing costs
- Method of determining amount (advance, appraisal, etc.)
- Buyer's income qualifications
- Required closing documentation
- Seller's incentives (buy downs, FHA points, etc.)
- Mortgage insurance requirements
- Loan structure (recorded mortgage, security agreement, chattel mortgage, trust deed, contract for deed, wraparound, all-inclusive trust deed, etc.)
- Eligibility for refinance upon resale
- Owner or non-owner occupancy permitted

A list of possible lenders is included, along with contact names, rates, and loan types.

PLAN SECTION IX: CASH FLOW ANALYSIS

The plan's ninth section describes methods for showing cash flow, profit/loss projections (based on a selected set of projections), operating budgets, home pricing, and homesite rent structure. The variables used must be listed, discussed, and shown at conservative levels. A set of typical project cash flow work sheets is shown in Fig. 7.3.

A good cash flow projection will include the following:

- Complete list of assumptions
- Variable fill rate
- Variable rents or price increases
- Variable operating budgets
- Yearly totals
- Phase and project totals
- Purchase money mortgages on land (if any)
- Lease payments (if any)

	TOTAL COST	YEAR 1	YEAR 2	YEAR 3	YEAR 4	YEAR 5	YEAR 6	YEAR 7	YEAR 8	YEAR 9	YEAR 10
LAND PURCHASE PRICE (inc comm)	595,000										
DEVELOPMENT COSTS	2,688,260										
TOTAL COST	3,283,260										
DEVELOPERS EQUITY	0										
CONSTRUCTION LOAN BALANCE	0	1,375,500	0	1,312,760	0	0	0	0	0	0	0
LAND PAYMENT (INC COMMISSIONS)	295,000	1,375,500	1,375,500	2,688,260	0	0	0	0	0	0	0
LAND LOAN BALANCE	300,000	300,000	300,000	300,000	0	0	0	0	0	0	0
LONG TERM LOAN BALANCE @	100.0%			2,977,269	2,946,996	2,913,696	2,877,065	2,836,772	2,792,449	2,743,694	

LOT RENTS PROJECTION 5.0% PER YEAR INCREASES

	YEAR	1	2	3	4	5	6	7	8	9	10
LOT RENT		$250.00	$262.50	$275.63	$289.41	$303.88	$319.07	$335.02	$351.78	$369.36	$387.83
CURRENT YEAR LOT RELEASE		24	44	52	50	24					
CUMULATIVE # OF UNITS		24	68	120	170	194	194	194	194	194	194

CASH FLOW ANALYSIS

REVENUE	YEAR	1	2	3	4	5	6	7	8	9	10
LOT RENT	$55.00	21,000	135,750	317,363	496,828	673,217	725,110	761,366	799,434	839,406	881,376
RENT CREDITS @		(7,920)	(9,372)	(16,236)	(18,810)	(17,292)	(7,920)	(38,068)	(39,972)	(41,970)	(44,069)
VACANCY / CREDIT (5%)		0	0	0	0	0	(36,256)	0	0	0	0
TOTAL		13,080	126,378	301,127	478,018	655,925	680,935	723,298	759,463	797,436	837,307
EXPENSES											
OPERATING EXPENSES (WHEN FULL)	30.0%	62,481	142,814	160,666	178,518	187,443	204,280	216,989	227,839	239,231	251,192
MANAGEMENT FEE (5%)		654	6,319	15,056	23,901	32,796	34,047	36,165	37,973	39,872	41,865
TOTAL EXPENSES		63,135	149,133	175,722	202,419	220,239	238,327	253,154	265,812	279,102	293,058
NET OPERATING INCOME		(50,055)	(22,755)	125,405	275,599	435,686	442,607	470,144	493,651	518,333	544,250
CONSTRUCTION LOAN INTEREST @	10.0%	82,530	82,530	161,296	0	0	0	0	0	0	0
DEBT SERVICE 25 YRS @ 1,2	10.0%	0	0	0	328,000	328,000	328,000	328,000	328,000	328,000	328,000
LAND CARRY INTEREST PAYMENT	8.75%	26,250	26,250	26,250	0	0	0	0	0	0	0
NET CASH FLOW		(158,835)	(131,535)	(62,141)	(52,401)	107,686	114,607	142,144	165,651	190,333	216,250
CAPITALIZED NEG CASH FLOW		158,835	131,535	62,141	52,401	0	0	0	0	0	0
EQUITY ON SALE		0	0	0	0	0	1,110,008	1,396,967	1,650,962	1,919,671	2,204,032
TOTAL CASH RETURN		0	0	0	0	107,686	1,224,616	1,539,110	1,816,612	2,110,004	2,420,282
CASH INVESTMENT	295,000	453,835	131,535	62,141	52,401	0	0	0	0	0	0
CONSTRUCTION - LONG TERM LOAN DIFFERENCE	0	0	0	10,991	0	0	0	0	0	0	0
CUMULATIVE INVESTMENT		453,835	585,370	658,502	710,903	710,903	710,903	710,903	710,903	710,903	710,903
CASH ON CASH		0	0	0	0	107,686	114,607	142,144	165,651	190,333	216,250
YEARLY RATE OF RETURN		0.0%	0.0%	0.0%	0.0%	15.1%	16.1%	20.0%	23.3%	26.8%	30.4%
YEARLY RATE OF RETURN WHEN SOLD		0.0%	0.0%	0.0%	0.0%	15.1%	172.3%	216.5%	255.5%	296.8%	340.5%
VALUE IF SOLD	0	0	0	0	0	3,960,780	4,023,704	4,274,032	4,487,733	4,712,120	4,947,726

FIG. 7.3 Sample cash flow worksheets.

08-Mar-93 04:43:10 PM

	TOTAL COST	YEAR 1	YEAR 2	YEAR 3	YEAR 4	YEAR 5	YEAR 6	YEAR 7	YEAR 8	YEAR 9	YEAR 10
LAND PURCHASE PRICE	595000										
DEVELOPMENT COSTS	2688260	1375500	0	1312760	0	0	0	0	0	0	0
TOTAL COST	3283260	1375500	0	1312760	0	0	0	0	0	0	0
DEVELOPERS EQUITY	0	0	0	0	0	0	0	0	0	0	0
CONSTRUCTION LOAN BALAN	0	1375500	1375500	2688260	0	0	0	0	0	0	0
LAND PAYMENT (INC COMMI	295000	300000	300000	300000	0	0	0	0	0	0	0
LAND LOAN BALANCE	300000	300000	300000	300000	0	0	0	0	0	0	0
LONG TERM LOAN BALANCE	100.0%	0	0	0	2572550	2501805	2423985	2338384	2244222	2140644	2026709

LOT RENTS PROJECTI — 5.0% PER YEAR INCREASES

YEAR	1	2	3	4	5	6	7	8	9	10
LOT RENT	$250.00	$262.50	$275.63	$289.41	$303.88	$319.07	$335.02	$351.78	$369.36	$387.83
CURRENT YEAR LOT RELEASE	36	68	78	12	0	0	0	0	0	0
CUMMULATIVE # OF UNITS	36	104	182	194	194	194	194	194	194	194

CASH FLOW ANALYSIS

REVENUE	YEAR	1	2	3	4	5	6	7	8	9	10
LOT RENT		31500	207750	482501	656053	690581	725110	761365.5	799433.8	839405.5	902873
RENT CREDITS @	$55.00	-11880	-34320	-48180	-29700	-3960	0	0	0	0	0
VACANCY / CREDIT (5X)		0	0	0	0	-34529.1	-36255.5	-38068.3	-39971.7	-41970.3	-45143.7
TOTAL		19620	173430	434321	626353	652092	688854.5	723297.2	759462.1	797435.2	857729.4

EXPENSES	YEAR	1	2	3	4	5	6	7	8	9	10
OPERATING EXPENSES (WHE	30.0%	62481	142814	160666	178518	195627.6	206656.4	216989.2	227838.6	239230.6	257318.8
MANAGEMENT FEE (5X)		981	8671.5	21716.05	31317.65	32604.6	33442.73	36164.86	37973.1	39871.76	42886.47
TOTAL EXPENSES		63462	151485.5	182382.1	209835.7	228232.2	241099.1	253154	265811.7	279102.3	300205.3
NET OPERATING INCOME		-43842	21944.5	251939	416517.4	423859.8	447755.4	470143.2	493650.4	518332.9	557524.1
CONSTRUCTION LOAN INTER	12.0%	99036	165060	322591.2							
DEBT SERVICE 25 YRS @ 1	12.0%				328000	328000	328000	328000	328000	328000	328000
LAND CARRY INTEREST PAY	10.00%	30000	30000	30000							
NET CASH FLOW		-172878	-173116	-100652	88517.35	95859.77	119755.4	142143.2	165650.4	190332.9	229524.1
CAPITALIZED NEG CASH FLOW		172878	173115.5	100652.3							
EQUITY ON SALE		0	0	0	0	1736793	2053569	1935646	2243509	2571473	3041692
TOTAL CASH RETURN		0	0	0	88517.35	1832653	2173325	2077789	2409159	2761806	3271216
CASH INVESTMENT	295000	467878	173115.5	100652.3	0	0	0	0	0	0	0
CONSTRUCTION - LONG TERM LOAN DIF		0	415710.4								
CUMULATIVE INVESTMENT		467878	640993.5	1157356	1157356	1157356	1157356	1157356	1157356	1157356	1157356
CASH ON CASH		0.0%	0.0%	0.0%	7.6%	8.3%	10.3%	12.3%	14.3%	16.4%	19.8%
YEARLY RATE OF RETURN		0.0%	0.0%	0.0%	7.6%	8.3%	10.3%	12.3%	14.3%	16.4%	19.8%
YEARLY RATE OF RETURN WHEN SOLD		0.0%	0.0%	0.0%	7.6%	158.3%	187.8%	179.5%	208.2%	238.6%	282.6%
VALUE IF SOLD		0	0	0	0	4238598	4477554	4274029	4487731	4712117	5068401

FIG. 7.3 (Continued)

105

	TOTAL COST	YEAR 1	YEAR 2	YEAR 3	YEAR 4	YEAR 5	YEAR 6	YEAR 7	YEAR 8	YEAR 9	YEAR 10
LAND PURCHASE PRICE	595000										
DEVELOPMENT COSTS	2688260	1375500	0	1312760	0	0	0	0	0	0	0
TOTAL COST	3283260	1375500		1312760							
DEVELOPERS EQUITY	0	0	0	0	0	0	0	0	0	0	0
CONSTRUCTION LOAN BALAN	0	1375500	1375500	2688260	0	0	0	0	0	0	0
LAND PAYMENT (INC COMMI	295000	300000	300000	300000	0	0	0	0	0	0	0
LAND LOAN BALANCE	300000	300000	300000	300000	0	0	0	0	0	0	0
LONG TERM LOAN BALANCE	100.0%				2977269	2946996	2913696	2877065	2836772	2792449	2743694

YEAR	1	2	3	4	5	6	7	8	9	10

LOT RENTS PROJECTI   5.0% PER YEAR INCREASES

	1	2	3	4	5	6	7	8	9	10
LOT RENT	$250.00	$262.50	$275.63	$289.41	$303.88	$319.07	$335.02	$351.78	$369.36	$387.83
CURRENT YEAR LOT RELEASE	36	68	78	12	0	0	0	0	0	0
CUMULATIVE # OF UNITS	36	104	182	194	194	194	194	194	194	194

CASH FLOW ANALYSIS

REVENUE / YEAR	1	2	3	4	5	6	7	8	9	10
LOT RENT	31500	207750	482501	656053	690581	725110	761365.5	799433.8	839405.5	902873
RENT CREDITS @ $55.00	-11880	-34320	-48180	-29700	-3960	0	0	0	0	0
VACANCY / CREDIT (5%)					-34529.1	-36255.5	-38068.3	-39971.7	-41970.3	-45143.7
TOTAL	19620	173430	434321	626353	652092	688854.5	723297.2	759462.1	797435.2	857729.4
EXPENSES										
OPERATING EXPENSES (WHE 30.0%)	62481	142814	160666	178518	195627.6	206656.4	216989.2	227838.6	239230.6	257318.8
MANAGEMENT FEE (5%)	981	8671.5	21716.05	31317.65	32604.6	34442.73	36164.86	37973.1	39871.76	42884.47
TOTAL EXPENSES	63462	151485.5	182382.1	209835.7	228232.2	241099.1	253154	265811.7	279102.3	300205.3
NET OPERATING INCOME	-43842	21944.5	251939	416517.4	423859.8	447755.4	470143.2	493650.4	518332.9	557524.1
CONSTRUCTION LOAN INTER 10.0%	82530	137550	268826							
DEBT SERVICE 25 YRS @ 1 10.0%				328000	328000	328000	328000	328000	328000	328000
LAND CARRY INTEREST PAY 8.75%	26250	26250	26250							
NET CASH FLOW	-152622	-141856	-43137	88517.35	95859.77	119755.4	142143.2	165650.4	190332.9	229524.1
CAPITALIZED NEG CASH FLOW	152622	141855.5	43137.05	0	0	0	0	0	0	0
EQUITY ON SALE					1291602	1563859	1396964	1650959	1919668	2324707
TOTAL CASH RETURN					1387461	1683614	1539107	1816609	2110001	2554231
CASH INVESTMENT 295000	447622	141855.5	43137.05	0	0	0	0	0	0	0
CONSTRUCTION - LONG TERM LOAN DIF			10990.87	0	0	0	0	0	0	0
CUMULATIVE INVESTMENT	447622	589477.5	643605.4	643605.4	643605.4	643605.4	643605.4	643605.4	643605.4	643605.4
CASH ON CASH	0	0	0	88517.35	95859.77	119755.4	142143.2	165650.4	190332.9	229524.1
YEARLY RATE OF RETURN	0.0%	0.0%	0.0%	13.8%	14.9%	18.6%	22.1%	25.7%	29.6%	35.7%
YEARLY RATE OF RETURN WHEN SOLD	0.0%	0.0%	0.0%	13.8%	215.6%	261.6%	239.1%	282.3%	327.8%	396.9%
VALUE IF SOLD	0	0	0	4238598	4477554	4477554	4274029	4487731	4712117	5068401

FIG. 7.3 (Continued)

08-Mar-93
04:45:01 PM

	TOTAL COST	YEAR 1	YEAR 2	YEAR 3	YEAR 4	YEAR 5	YEAR 6	YEAR 7	YEAR 8	YEAR 9	YEAR 10
LAND PURCHASE PRICE (inc comm)	595,000										
DEVELOPMENT COSTS	2,688,260	1,375,500	0	1,312,760	0	0	0	0	0	0	0
TOTAL COST	3,283,260	1,375,500	0	1,312,760	0	0	0	0	0	0	0
DEVELOPERS EQUITY	0	0	0	0	0	0	0	0	0	0	0
CONSTRUCTION LOAN BALANCE	0	1,375,500	1,375,500	2,688,260	0	0	0	0	0	0	0
LAND PAYMENT (INC COMMISSIONS)	295,000	0	0	300,000	0	0	0	0	0	0	0
LAND LOAN BALANCE	300,000	300,000	300,000	300,000	0	0	0	0	0	0	0
LONG TERM LOAN BALANCE @	100.0%	0	0	0	2,572,550	2,501,805	2,423,985	2,338,384	2,244,222	2,140,644	2,026,709

LOT RENTS PROJECTION — 5.0% PER YEAR INCREASES

YEAR	1	2	3	4	5	6	7	8	9	10
LOT RENT	$250.00	$262.50	$275.63	$289.41	$303.88	$319.07	$335.02	$351.78	$369.36	$387.83
CURRENT YEAR LOT RELEASE	24	44	52	50	24	0	0	0	0	0
CUMULATIVE # OF UNITS	24	68	120	170	194	194	194	194	194	194

CASH FLOW ANALYSIS

	YEAR	1	2	3	4	5	6	7	8	9	10
REVENUE											
LOT RENT @	$55.00	21,000	135,750	317,363	496,828	673,217	725,110	761,366	799,434	839,406	881,376
RENT CREDITS @		(7,920)	(9,372)	(16,236)	(18,810)	(17,292)	(7,920)	0	0	0	0
VACANCY / CREDIT (5%)		0	0	0	0	0	(36,256)	(38,068)	(39,972)	(41,970)	(44,069)
TOTAL		13,080	126,378	301,127	478,018	655,925	680,935	723,298	759,463	797,436	837,307
EXPENSES											
OPERATING EXPENSES (WHEN FULL)	30.0%	62,481	142,814	160,666	178,518	187,443	204,280	216,989	227,839	239,231	251,192
MANAGEMENT FEE (5%)		654	6,319	15,056	23,901	32,796	34,047	36,165	37,973	39,872	41,865
TOTAL EXPENSES		63,135	149,133	175,722	202,419	220,239	238,327	253,154	265,812	279,102	293,058
NET OPERATING INCOME		(50,055)	(22,755)	125,405	275,599	435,686	442,607	470,144	493,651	518,333	544,250
CONSTRUCTION LOAN INTEREST @	12.0%	99,036	99,036	193,555	0	0	0	0	0	0	0
DEBT SERVICE 25 YRS @ 1.2	12.0%	0	0	0	328,000	328,000	328,000	328,000	328,000	328,000	328,000
LAND CARRY INTEREST PAYMENT	10.00%	30,000	30,000	30,000	0	0	0	0	0	0	0
NET CASH FLOW		(179,091)	(151,791)	(98,150)	(52,401)	107,686	114,607	142,144	165,651	190,333	216,250
CAPITALIZED NEG CASH FLOW		179,091	151,791	98,150	52,401	0	0	0	0	0	0
TOTAL CASH RETURN		0	0	0	0	107,686	114,607	142,144	165,651	190,333	216,250
CASH INVESTMENT	295,000	474,091	151,791	98,150	52,401	0	0	0	0	0	0
CONSTRUCTION - LONG TERM LOAN DIFFERENCE		0	0	415,710	0	0	0	0	0	0	0
CUMULATIVE INVESTMENT		474,091	625,882	1,139,742	1,192,143	1,192,143	1,192,143	1,192,143	1,192,143	1,192,143	1,192,143
CASH ON CASH		0	0	0	0	107,686	114,607	142,144	165,651	190,333	216,250
YEARLY RATE OF RETURN		0.0%	0.0%	0.0%	0.0%	9.0%	9.6%	11.9%	13.9%	16.0%	18.1%
YEARLY RATE OF RETURN WHEN SOLD		0.0%	0.0%	0.0%	0.0%	9.0%	143.8%	174.3%	202.1%	231.7%	263.2%
VALUE IF SOLD		0	0	0	0	3,960,780	4,023,704	4,274,032	4,487,733	4,712,120	4,947,726

FIG. 7.3 (Continued)

The projection should be run over the anticipated range of expected rates of fill or sales rates and at various loan interest rates and various operating and sales budgets.

The reader must be able to determine easily, at any time during the project fill, the following information:

- Monthly, yearly, total cash flow
- Total development loan size
- Operating deficit reserves
- Interest payment reserves
- Net operating income
- Development and purchase money loan balances
- Cumulative cash flow

Also show a worst expected case of rate of sales or fill rate, so that the developer can prepare financially for future cash requirements under a variety of sales and operating circumstances.

PLAN SECTION X: CONCLUSIONS

The plan's tenth section is a summary evaluation of the financial viability of the project under present and anticipated conditions. The summary provides estimates of maximum venture or risk capital needs, equity capital and debt capital requirements, and projects a before-tax return on investment under best and worst expected case absorption rates.

The conclusions section also states the limitations on the analysis, including a review of the assumptions regarding the developer's capital and staffing resources.

PLAN SECTION XI: APPENDIX

As many as possible of the following items should be included in the appendix as reference materials:

- Developer's resume and qualifications
- Key staff members' resumes
- Qualifications of other key personnel
- Contractor's qualifications
- Demographic reference materials
- Floor plans of typical homes
- Home price lists and lot prices or rental rates
- Area sales history

- List of area major employers
- Utility company information and rates
- Employment rate history
- Apartment rental rate/occupancy report
- Historical area home sales report

CONCLUSION

Past project failures can be often traced to the fact that too few developers take the time to create a comprehensive business and marketing plan, and too few employees read and implement such a plan. It is as important as a good title insurance policy, property appraisal report, or boundary survey. A wise lender or investor should make it mandatory.

A good business and marketing plan is not created in the dark without regard for future implementation, but is written as the management "game plan" for the proposed community development. It is used as the basis for guiding management through the process of acquiring the development site, financing the development, building the project, and marketing the homesites. Like a hymnal at church, it ensures that everyone is singing the same harmonious song.

CHAPTER 8

ENGINEERING

This chapter is not a primer for the engineering of a manufactured home community, but rather a presentation of key information the developer should be aware of during the engineering of the project. It also provides information and insight for the land development professional who has not previously been involved in the planning and engineering of manufactured home communities. The engineering process is generally divided into three parts: (1) *conceptual determination,* (2) *preliminary engineering,* and (3) *final engineering.*

CONCEPTUAL DETERMINATION

Chapter 5, "Concept Development," points out that considerable information pertaining to the housing market, economics, development site characteristics, and local politics is required to formulate a viable concept. This is the phase in which projects that are not feasible should be terminated, or corrections for the plan should be proposed. The concept stage produces a development site plan or lotting plan that must be carefully scrutinized by both the design professional and the developer, as well as city, county, or other approving agencies. This ensures that all issues, such as homesite size, project density, and present and future rights-of-way, are resolved prior to proceeding with preliminary engineering.

PRELIMINARY ENGINEERING

After concept determination and development site planning have been completed, the design professional often proceeds to final engineering. However, there are definite advantages to completing an intermediate step, called preliminary engineering. Preliminary engineering, usually prepared at a scale of 1" = 100', includes the following plans and details:

- Concept plan
- Grading plan
- Sanitary sewer collection plan
- Water distribution plan
- Storm sewer plan
- Typical details

A bill of quantities can be generated from the preliminary engineering, and unit prices current in the area can be used to ascertain an accurate development cost for the project. This development cost can then be plugged into the feasibility study to ensure that the developer is still on track. If at this point the development costs are prohibitive, the developer can abandon the project prior to the expense of final engineering, or make the necessary adjustments to bring the project back to a financially feasible status.

FINAL ENGINEERING

Final engineering encompasses the design and preparation of construction drawings and specifications to implement the construction of sewage collection systems, treatment of sewage, water supply and distribution for domestic and fire protection, storm drainage and storm water management, site grading, roadways, utilities, central facilities, landscape architecture, and individual homesite improvements. Final engineering also encompasses all of the approvals necessary to construct the project, including permits from the appropriate local, state, and federal jurisdictions. Contract documents are also normally a part of and included in the definition of final engineering. The architecture of the manufactured home community follows the same planning procedure previously outlined. The final marketability and environmental quality of the project depends to a large extent on the type of architecture associated with central facilities, as well as entrance details, signage, and individual homesite development.

SELECTION OF ENGINEER OR ARCHITECT

A consulting engineer, architect, or planner is an independent professional who performs services for clients on a fee basis. Professional qualifications, integrity, and demonstrable experience are the warranty that best serves the interests of the client and the public when these services are retained.

Scope of Services

The first and probably most important step in negotiating an agreement for professional services is to define the scope of the services to be performed. Consulting services for the development of a manufactured home community are normally divided into environmental, surveying, geotechnical, engineering, and architectural functions. The developer may deal or negotiate with one firm that supplies all these services or, which is more generally the case, deal with several firms that supply a variety of expertise.

Selection Process

The selection of a consulting firm should be guided by one primary consideration: the qualifications of the firm in regard to the project to be undertaken. Selection of a consulting firm should be based on an informed judgment as to the specific qualifications for the task at hand. In determining these qualifications, the following parameters apply:

- Technical qualifications
- Reputation with existing clients
- Size and diversity of organization
- Experience with projects similar to the one under consideration
- Knowledge of the particular equipment and services to be specified
- Mobility and time availabilities

Above all, the developer should approach the selection of a consultant with the attitude that skill, reputation, experience, and motivation are the most important factors to consider. Professional integrity will assure that the compensation for services rendered will be both reasonable and equitable. The question should be not how much the consultant will cost but, rather, how much the consultant will save.

Company Structure

The size of a consulting firm is seldom a reliable single determinant. A relatively small organization of outstanding engineers may offer as wide a base of technical knowledge and experience as a larger firm. Conversely, large engineering organizations frequently have exceptional versatility in many fields of engineering and a history of completing many successful projects.

It is important for the developer to meet and interview the professional who will be in charge of the project and with whom he or she will be communicating. It would be unfortunate for the developer to be sold services by a top-notch principal of a firm only to find out that a less experienced individual in the company will be handling the project.

Compensation for Professional Services

The basis on which the professional will be compensated for his or her services will be determined by the wishes of the developer, the degree of definition of the scope of services, and the policies and practices of the professional. Normally, hazardous waste investigation, soil exploration, laboratory testing, wetlands delineation, and similar investigations are conducted under separate contract. The developer pays separately for these services even though they are specified and performed under the direction of the project engineer. Property boundary surveys and topographic surveys are usually paid for separately as well. Resident engineering services, including staking supplied by the engineer during construction, are normally furnished for a specified rate per day, month, or hour, plus mutually agreed-upon expenses. Recommended methods for compensating the engineer or architect for professional services are described in the following paragraphs.

Lump Sum. This method may be used when the scope of services can be precisely defined and the amount of time required of the engineer or architect can be predetermined.

Salary Cost Times a Multiplier. This method is usually used for special services that cannot be readily defined.

Percentage of Construction Costs. This method of establishing compensation is computed as a percentage of the construction costs exclusive of land, legal, financing, and developer administrative costs. The fees will normally be within a range of 4% to 15%, depending on the size and complexity of the project.

Per Diem Rates Plus Expenses. Per diem rates for personnel and out-of-pocket expenses required for the project are normally used for short-term engagements. These rates are used especially for personal services involving advice, reports, investigations, and similar types of activities for which little or no design, detail drafting, or other support services are required.

The decisions made by a consulting engineer affect the initial cost, the long-term operating costs, and the overall quality of a project. The savings in these terms to be derived from the proper handling of the project will often far exceed the total engineering fees. Therefore, it is in the best interests of the client to base the selection of an engineer on qualifications and references.

INVENTORY

Chapter 5 outlines the information necessary to develop a proper concept. The following paragraphs discuss additional information that the design professional will need prior to proceeding with the preparation of construction drawings and contract documents.

Boundary Survey

The boundary survey is performed by a licensed surveyor and includes all the encumbrances or easements associated with the property. The boundary survey should have an acceptable error of closure, with bearings, distances, and curve information given for the entire perimeter.

Topographic Survey

The topographic survey may be performed by a surveyor or engineer. Depending on the particulars of the specific site, the survey should extend an adequate distance into adjacent properties. This ensures that the engineer can properly assess and design a proposed grading plan that will not interfere or conflict with adjacent property owners' drainage or accessibility. The topographic survey should show all drainage features both on the site and off the site as required for the engineer to develop a proper drainage plan. There are many sites where the feasibility of development is directly related to the discharge elevation at which the storm sewer drainage can leave the site. In many cases it will be necessary to develop topography off the property, following the downstream drainage regime. Flat sites will require one-foot contour intervals with intermediate spot elevations, and steeper sites generally are adequately represented with two-foot contour intervals. Trees and other existing structures should also be included in the survey. If a topographic survey and map do not exist, the developer should counsel with the surveyor or engineer to determine whether an aerial survey is the best and most economical solution of whether the topography should be prepared by ground survey.

Wetlands Determination

The U.S. Army Corps of Engineers administers the rules and regulations pertaining to the classification and preservation of wetlands. In many cases a local jurisdiction will also have additional rules and regulations pertaining to the development of wetlands. The wetlands on a property should be delineated by a wetlands expert or consultant prior to the field survey or topographic survey so that the wetlands delineation can be incorporated into the topographic survey or mapping. There are different rules for the types and amounts of wetlands that can be disturbed. There is also a mitigation process that will allow the developer to disturb a wetland with proper mitigation. The rules are complex and constantly in flux, and if a property does have wetlands on it, a wetlands expert should be consulted.

Floodplain and Floodway

The Federal Emergency Management Agency (FEMA) prepares a Flood Insurance Rate Map (FIRM), a copy of which can usually be found at the local county seat or township or in the city planning office. This map will show both the 100-year floodway and floodplain. The developer will generally not be able to develop in the floodway, but may, however, be able to develop in the floodplain if individual homesites are above the 100-year floodplain elevation.

Soils Testing

The Soil Conservation Service, an agency of the U.S. Department of Agriculture, publishes soil maps that supply a great deal of information relative to the soils on a particular site. This information is very useful in the preliminary stages of feasibility and concept development. However, in the final engineering stage it is generally necessary for a geotechnical consulting firm to perform on-site soil testing. The soils report can be used by the architect in the designing of the building substructure and by the engineer in designing the roadways, storm water management, and grading plans. Too often a developer proceeds through concept, preliminary engineering, and final engineering only to find out that the project is not feasible, owing to subsurface rock that was not detected because soil borings were not taken earlier.

Environmental Factors

The following paragraphs discuss additional inventory items that should be researched and represented on a site analysis map. This information allows the engineer or planner to exercise judgment in how to deal with these factors in the preparation of the manufactured home community construction plans.

Wind Direction. The predominant wind rose (a graphic representation of the wind directions for a specific geographic location) of the site may have an impact on the landscape architecture as it relates to softening or buffering the wind against certain facilities or home placement. If the project is adjacent to an airport, a sewage treatment facility, or a land use that creates smoke, dust, or other kinds of residue, the wind rose or wind direction may influence the location of various land uses such as home placement versus open space, storm water management facilities, or recreational vehicle storage.

Noise. If a portion of the manufactured home community is adjacent to land uses that create noise, such as a freeway, commercial usage, or an industrial process, this should be clearly indicated on the site analysis inventory map. The designer may create a physical buffer by building an earthen berm with fill material if the site is adjacent to a noise source or a negative view.

Surrounding Area. The site analysis inventory map should show all land uses in the area so that any problems associated with wind direction, noise, and other environmental negatives may be compensated for in the design process.

View Analysis. The inventory should include a view analysis to be used as one of the considerations in the orientation of recreational and central facilities and home placement.

Ground Cover. The topographic map may be further supplemented by recommendations for ground cover. The engineer, walking through the site, can make specific notes as to ground cover, including sizes, types, and location of trees and other vegetation.

Hazardous Material. The developer is well advised to perform a Level 1 environmental audit. Unfortunately, there are too many projects that have been built that are later found to have been constructed on a site previously contaminated with hazardous waste. If it is determined prior to development that there are hazardous wastes on-site, it is usually more economical to resolve the situation before beginning the development.

Codes and Ordinances

The design professional will secure copies of all local, state, and federal codes and ordinances that apply to the project being designed and engineered. In most situations a manufactured home landlease community does not have to adhere to the subdivision regulations relating to rights-of-way, street design, or utility placement. The designer can take advantage of this freedom from the subdivision ordinance to be innovative and economically productive.

DESIGN CONSIDERATIONS

The following paragraphs discuss the design criteria used in the engineering of a manufactured home community.

Sewerage

Landlease communities discharge less wastewater to treatment facilities than do single-family residential subdivisions. However, most regulatory agencies across the country do not recognize this fact and require the landlease community to use the same design criteria as residential single-family subdivisions. Depending on the location and jurisdiction involved, design flow requirements can range from 150 gallons per day per manufactured home, to 400 gallons per day. Most jurisdictions arrive at their requirements based on a formula of 100 gallons per capita per day. Therefore, an adult retirement community with an average of two persons per home would use an estimated 200 gallons per unit per day. The family community, although the national average is approximately 2.5 persons per dwelling unit, is normally calculated as 3 persons per dwelling unit, thus resulting in a flow contribution per family home of 300 gallons per unit per day. The 100 gallons per capita per day was originally derived on the basis of a larger land mix of residential and commercial use. Years ago, when this number was generated, the infiltration standards of sewer mains were much higher than they are today. The average daily flow for design purposes in landlease communities should be 150 gallons per manufactured home per day. This design criterion is based on the assumption that there are not and would not be excessive infiltration and inflow problems associated with the collection system.

Manufactured home subdivisions, in many cases, not only look like residential site-built subdivisions, but the homes are also of the same size found in many single-family subdivisions. Therefore, it may be appropriate for the manufactured housing subdivision to use the same design criteria required for the residential site-built subdivision.

Pipe Sizing

The laterals in the sewage collection system must be designed to handle flows four times the daily average. Major collector lines must be designed to handle 2½ times the average daily flows, and lift stations are normally designed to handle 3 times the average daily flows.

In a landlease community, the smallest service line to a single home should be 4 inches in diameter and the smallest collector line should be 6 inches. Many ordinances and regulations require a minimum sanitary collector line to be 8 inches in diameter.

Manholes are recommended in lieu of cleanouts in order to facilitate cleaning and maintaining the system. Although a considerable amount of money can be saved initially by using cleanouts as opposed to manholes, over the course of time manholes are the best investment. The most common sewer main material used today is polyvinyl chloride (PVC) pipe manufactured in accordance with ASTM D3034, D1784, and SDR 35 specifications. It is the job of the developer's engineer to design and specify the sewage collection system so that it is cost-effective, requiring a minimum amount of maintenance and meeting the regulations of the approving agencies.

There are still some state agencies that require the antiquated regulation of venting and p-trapping as part of the individual home sewer service. This is an old regulation that is not applicable to today's manufactured home, which is properly trapped and vented internally, and has proper connections from the home to the sewer.

Arrangement of the Collection System

Where the sewer collection system is designed to municipal standards and will be maintained by the governmental entity, there is little flexibility in terms of how and where the sewer lines will be placed. However, in a manufactured home landlease community where the collection system will be privately owned and maintained, there is some flexibility in the layout of the collection system. Most service drops in manufactured homes are in the back third of the home, and there is a considerable cost savings by running the sewer line in back of the home and servicing two homes, as opposed to the subdivision standard of running lines in the street with much longer laterals to reach the back third of the home. There are many other cost savings beyond the scope of this text that the design engineer can implement, given the freedom of deviating from standard subdivision design.

Treatment of Sewage

It is not within the scope of this chapter to detail the design of sewage treatment facilities. The developer's engineer is responsible for the design, as sewage treatment is a specialized field requiring a design professional familiar with local jurisdictional requirements. However, it is important to point out to the design engineer that if the local jurisdictional code requires the design of a treatment plant to a subdivision standard (for example, 400 gallons per unit per day), it is necessary to know that the flows from a landlease community are considerably less. The design professional must take this into consideration, because a sewage treatment plant generally cannot produce an acceptable effluent unless it receives at least half of the design loading. As an example, an activated sludge plant will not function well if it is designed for 400 gallons per unit per day but is receiving only 150 gallons per unit per day. The characteristics of the influent to the treatment plant would be an average 5-day biological oxygen demand (BOD) loading of 200 milligrams per liter (mg/l) or, assuming 100 gallons per capita, .17 pounds per capita, and an average of 200 mg/l of total suspended solids. To determine the most efficient and cost-effective form of treatment for the manufactured home community, it will be necessary to determine from the appropriate regulatory agencies, the allowable discharge standards for that specific site. The sewage treatment plant discharge may be retained on-site using a percolation/evaporation pond, provided the soils on-site allow the use of these ponds. In many cases, it will be necessary to discharge off-site, which will require a higher level of treatment of the sewage.

Type of Treatment Facilities Common to Manufactured Home Communities

The majority of manufactured home landlease communities use prefabricated treatment plants produced by national manufacturers such as DAVCO, Smith & Lovelace, and Purestream or by small, local manufacturers. These plants are generally less expensive than engineer-designed plants, and most have the advantage of being produced in modular units that can easily be expanded as additional phases of the community are built. After determining the effluent requirements for the proposed site, the engineer will be able to determine which of the following levels of treatment must be designed.

1. *Primary treatment* consists of screening and clarification or settling tanks. The screening removes the larger debris that could enter the system, and the primary clarifiers or settling tanks remove the settleable solids.

2. *Secondary treatment* consists of an activated sludge treatment plant or a type of rotating biological contactor. For smaller treatment plants that are typical of manufactured home landlease communities, it is usually best to use an activated sludge process of the extended aeration type. This type of plant requires less operator attention and is also better able to handle wide variations in flow without a serious degradation in treatment efficiency. An activated sludge treatment plant using the contact stabilization process can be employed in cases where the average daily flows are greater than 50,000 gallons per day. This type of plant is more difficult to operate and cannot readily accommodate the shock loads fairly common to manufactured home landlease communities. Rotating biological contactors do not have as much difficulty with variations in loading and operate well across a wide range of flows. In addition, an advantage of both the activated sludge/contact stabilization plant and the biological contactor is that both are approximately half the size of the activated sludge/extended aeration treatment plant.

3. *Tertiary treatment* consists of filtering the effluent from a secondary treatment plant. This is done simply by installing a filter at the discharge end of the plant prior to discharging into a pond or off-site. The filter is normally a sand filter and usually provides for an automatic backwashing system to keep the sand clean and to prevent the filter from becoming blinded.

4. *Advanced treatment* is treatment that goes beyond the tertiary level and is usually associated with the removal of nutrients in the sewage.

Although there are many nutrients normally found in domestic sewage, the most objectionable in terms of harm to the environment are nitrogen and phosphorus. Both of these, along with carbon, stimulate plant growth. Removal of nitrogen can be done either biologically or chemically. Either way, additions to the treatment process are required, adding a significant increase in price to the treatment facility. Phosphorus is normally precipitated out in the clarifier, requiring only a relatively inexpensive chemical feed system.

Septic Tanks and Drainfields. Many jurisdictions allow septic tanks and drainfields to be used for the treatment of effluent from manufactured home developments. This type of treatment generally requires not only suitable soils but larger homesites, which results in lower densities. It is not uncommon for most regulatory agencies to require half-acre homesites if septic tanks and drainfields are used. However, many times higher densities can be achieved with smaller homesites in a cluster arrangement and the septic tank and drainfield treatment systems located in a larger open area adjacent to the clustered homes. The use of septic tanks and drainfields is not feasible for normally high-priced land in an urban setting, but is more feasible in rural settings with lower land costs.

Cost of Treatment Facilities

It is difficult to estimate the cost of sewage treatment facilities, even after it has been determined, on the basis of degree of treatment necessary, what type of facility is required. This is not only because of the normal increases in equipment cost caused by inflation, but also a result of increasingly stringent requirements imposed by the federal, state, and local regulatory agencies. In the 1970s the general rule of thumb was $1.00 per gallon pre day for a secondary-level sewage treatment plant installed. By the mid-1980s that number had doubled and since then has continued to rise. The best way to avoid overspending on the sewage treatment plant is to engage a design professional familiar with both the design and permitting of wastewater treatment facilities, to provide guidance in this area.

The cost of an individual septic tank and drainfield varies greatly, depending on the soils and the jurisdictional requirements. Again, the price of a septic tank and drainfield would have been estimated in the 1980s at approximately $1,000 per homesite, and has now grown to almost twice that.

In some jurisdictions lagoons or aerated lagoons are options. If the proposed site is in an area where land costs are low and a surplus of land is available, this economical option should be considered.

WATER SYSTEMS

The water systems discussed in this chapter pertain to community water systems, as opposed to individual wells used to service isolated sites or very small groups of manufactured homes.

Water Supply

Where a municipal water supply is available, it can normally offer the landlease community adequate pressure and storage to serve domestic and fire protection needs. If the developer is required to build a private water supply system, it usually comprises two or more water wells, a well house with a turbine pump and mechanical equipment, a standby power source, chlorination equipment, electric controls, and water storage in the form of a pneumatic, elevated, or ground storage tank. On the other hand, smaller, less sophisticated projects may include a well, a submersible pump, a pneumatic tank, and controls. The size of the required water storage is related to the size of the project, fire protection requirements, and the capacity of the well system. Many regulatory agencies require enough storage capacity to fight a 2-hour fire and to supply the peak daily domestic demand. Although a fire flow of 500 gallons per minute is adequate for a manufactured home landlease community, many municipalities require 1,000 gallons per minute. An average domestic flow of 150 gallons per day per home and an irrigation flow of 100 gallons per day per home provide a total average domestic and irrigation flow of 250 gallons per day per home. The irrigation requirements vary greatly from location to location, and the designer needs to use flows that are applicable to the particular location. Then, using a factor of four times the daily domestic average results in a peak daily demand of 1,000 gallons per day per home; this equates to .7 gallons per minute for peak daily domestic and irrigation flow. For a 200-site community, the storage requirements for a 2-hour, 1,000 gallon per minute fire flow is 137,000 gallons, and the storage requirements for a 2-hour, 500 gallon per minute fire flow is 77,000 gallons. A more economical solution is to use two high-capacity wells that generate 500 gallons per minute or more, using standby power, with a 10,000 gallon pneumatic storage tank. It is the role of the design engineer to explore the various options and corresponding costs to meet the needs of the development and the requirements of the regulating agencies.

Distribution

The distribution system should be capable of delivering the required fire flow and the peak daily domestic demand, including water used for irrigation, with the pressure in the system not dropping below 20 pounds per square inch (psi). The recommended method for designing the water distribution network system is to use the software developed by Dr. Don J. Wood at the University of Kentucky. The capacity of the system should allow individual homes 15 gallons per minute and small groups of homes to be supplied with a minimum of 6 gallons per minute, with pressure not dropping below 20 psi.

Pipe Sizing. Manufactured home subdivisions, for which the municipality takes over and maintains the utility, require the water distribution system to be designed in accordance with the municipality's or local utility's standards. This usually necessitates the size of the water main to be a minimum of 6 inches in diameter, and in some communities a minimum of 8 inches.

However, in the landlease community with private ownership of the water distribution, the system can be designed in accordance with state requirements for landlease communities. These normally allow much greater flexibility than local subdivision ordinances. In such situations, it is often possible to use 2 or 4-inch lines to serve the domestic requirements of the community, as opposed to the 6 and 8-inch lines required by the subdivision ordinances, thus substantially reducing the cost of the water distribution system. The commonly used pipe material for water mains is PVC pipe conforming to AWWA C-900, and the most commonly used service line material is ¾-inch copper or polyethylene tubing ASTM D2737.

Fire Hydrants. The fire hydrants in a landlease community should be within 300 feet of any structure and spaced not farther than 500 feet apart. The fire hydrants should be the type approved by the local fire department.

Gate Valves. Gate valves are used to shut off the water flow at specific points in the distribution system. In a properly designed and looped distribution system, a portion of the system can be shut down where repairs are needed without causing all the homes to be without water. It is important that the gate valving be adequately designed and located on the as-built drawings of the water distribution system so that the maintenance staff can locate and repair water main breaks or leaks with a minimum of inconvenience and disturbance to the rest of the community.

STORM DRAINAGE AND STORM WATER MANAGEMENT

Storm drainage and storm water management requirements vary a great deal among jurisdictions and locations across the country. The following paragraphs give an overview of commonly used and required practices. However, the developer and the engineer must become familiar with their project site characteristics and appropriate regulatory requirements.

Rainfall Events

As a simple example, a 5-year rainfall event, or frequency, indicates the maximum rainfall intensity that can be expected to occur once every 5 years. The internal storm drainage facilities for manufactured home communities are generally designed to handle 5- or 10-year rainfall events. However, the 100-year rainfall event must be considered relative to its impact on the homesite elevation for the manufactured home. Moreover, the design engineer must exercise judgment in selecting storm frequencies to design bridges and other structures, understanding their associated impact on the health, welfare, and safety of the residents, as well as the potential for costly future maintenance and repairs. There are parts of the country, particularly the Southwest, that receive only a few rainfall events per year, and in these areas it is often the design engineer's judgment that infrequent street flooding is acceptable, as opposed to designing a very expensive storm sewer system that is used only infrequently.

Surface Grades

Patios and Flatwork. Patios and flatwork should be constructed with a minimum drainage slope of ¼ inch per foot.

Lawn Areas. The lawn areas sloping away from the homes should have a positive grade of 2%, which is to say that the slope should fall at a rate of 2 feet vertically for every 100 feet horizontally. Once positive drainage has been established away from the structure, a minimum lawn grade of 1% is desirable. There are exceptions to the 1% lawn grade, particularly in areas that have very little rain and soil conditions with high permeability.

Roadways. Roadways should have a minimum cross-slope of ¼ inch per foot. Roadways with concrete curbs and gutters may be designed with a transverse grade of 0.3% minimum; however, a minimum transverse grade of 0.5% should be used where possible. Roadways that use asphaltic curbs should have a minimum transverse grade of 1%. There are situations in which a property does not lend itself to establishing positive road grades, and sometimes a solution may be a ditch system paralleling the edge of the roads, whereby the drainage is carried to the roadway edge and directly into the ditch in such a manner that water does not pond on the road surface.

Runoff Calculations

The rational method of calculating runoff is applicable for sizing internal catch basin and storm sewer facilities. However, the evaluation of the effects of off-site drainage as well as calculations associated with storm water management should use methods capable of generating hydrographs that can be used in hydrograph routing. Examples of these methods are the Soil Conservation Service TR-55 and TR-20, which are computer applications, and the Corps of Engineers HEC-1 computer model.

Offsite Drainage

The developer will be required to maintain the natural drainage regime as it affects the historical drainage of off-site areas that drain through the proposed project. The developer should enlist the services of a professional engineer very early in the evaluation of a proposed property, as off-site drainage through a proposed property can have a major impact on the cost and buildable area of the project.

Storm Water Management

Many areas in the country have enacted storm water management legislation and requirements, the purpose of which is to prevent downstream flooding as the upstream portion of a drainage basin is developed, thus increasing its runoff through the reduction of permeable surfaces such as fields and pasture lands into impermeable surfaces such as streets, parking lots, and structures. In many areas the increased quantity of water directed downstream is becoming a serious problem. The pollutants picked up by the storm water drainage associated with urban development are causing problems to the environment in the form of toxic chemicals, over-fertilization of waterways, and sedimentation. Regulations have been enacted requiring the treatment of storm water prior to its being discharged. In many cases an erosion problem develops during the construction phase before lawn areas are seeded or sodded and streets are paved. Erosion results in the transportation of materials, which are carried downstream and thus cause problems to downstream properties or to the quality of downstream watersheds, lakes, or wetlands. As a result, methods and plans for control of soil erosion are often required.

Quantity of Storm Water Runoff. The requirements for storm water detention vary greatly from one regulatory agency to another. The following is a typical example of such requirements: The developer is allowed to discharge the peak flow that leaves the property in its predevelopment condition during a 25-year rainfall event. The developer must detain on the property the amount of water resulting from a 25-year event after development until it is totally discharged, based on a maximum allowable discharge rate equal to the peak 25-year event predevelopment rate. The developer may choose any of several methods to detain the postdevelopment runoff on-site, including the use of dry ponds and swales. Wet ponds can be made into an architectural feature and retain the water through percolation into the ground.

Quality of Storm Water Runoff. The majority of all pollutants are carried off in the first inch of runoff, and therefore the first inch of runoff is usually retained on-site until it is treated. Various methods of treatment are used; for instance, one method is to pass the first inch of runoff through a filter media and then to a drainpipe prior to discharging from the site. Another method is to create a lake with wetland vegetation or a littoral zone where the storm water is biologically treated prior to allowing it to be discharged from the lake. Runoff may be treated by percolating it into the ground and not allowing it to leave the site via surface runoff. The challenge to the engineer is to incorporate the storm water management facilities into the project in such a manner that they become an environmental asset to the project, rather than unsightly wasted acreage.

SOIL AND EROSION CONTROL

The engineer should prepare a soil erosion control plan that prevents erosion and transportation of materials from the site during the construction phase. This can be accomplished by the proper development of sedimentation traps or basins that collect the storm water runoff and remove the settleable materials before the storm water leaves the site. Proper use of silt fences, hay bales, check dams, erosion control matting, and diversion swales also help to prevent the problems of soil erosion.

ROADWAYS

Type

Roadways are constructed in the standard crown or inverted crown form. A standard crown form is one in which the highest elevation of the roadway cross section is at the centerline and which slopes at a minimum of ¼ inch per foot from each side of the centerline to the edge of the pavement. An inverted crown is shown by a roadway section in which the lowest elevation of the roadway is at the centerline and which slopes up each side of the centerline at a minimum slope of ¼ inch per foot to the edge of the pavement. There are advantages and disadvantages to both the standard crown and the inverted crown. The inverted crown has some cost advantages, as the curbing along the edge of the pavement may be eliminated and the cost of storm sewer catch basins may also be reduced by collecting the water at the middle of an intersection with one structure, as opposed to the standard crown, which would require several structures to receive the drainage at intersections. However, the inverted crown does not function well in the northern climates where there is ice and snow. It is difficult to keep the streets properly plowed and to maintain adequate drainage during the slush periods when the ice and snow begin to melt. During heavy rainfalls the water tends to accumulate more deeply in the streets, making it less convenient for pedestrians to cross. The standard crown has an advantage in the North, in regard to snowplowing and drainage during thawing periods, and there is normally less ponding of water. Moreover, in many cases, the standard crown creates a more aesthetically pleasing architectural streetscape than the inverted crown.

Most manufactured home communities, owing to either regulations or market requirements, have paved streets. There has been an ongoing debate in the engineering community for years as to which is better: a concrete street or an asphalt street. An asphalt street in most areas is less expensive than a concrete street. However, there are situations or locations where concrete is competitive with asphalt. The proper design for the structural section of the streets can be made only after the engineer has accomplished adequate soil testing of the existing subgrade material and has analyzed the traffic conditions, including the amount and frequency of loading that will be taking place on the street being designed. The majority of manufactured home communities have used a roadway design for asphaltic streets consisting of subgrade correction, 6 to 8 inches of aggregate base course, and 1½ to 3 inches of asphaltic concrete. The base course can vary between aggregate, soil cement, asphaltic base course, and many other types, depending on the location of the project. Concrete streets quite often consist of subgrade correction with a base course and a 5 or 6-inch pour of concrete cement.

Most structural failures in roadways occur because of improper preparation of the subgrade (existing material) prior to construction of the base course. A warning to the developer: The engineer should be on the project full-time, supervising proper soil testing, and particularly during preparation of the subgrade.

Curbs and Gutters

There are many types of curbs and gutters. There is an advantage to the mountable curb and gutter, in that driveway returns are not required as they are in the standard curb. By not requiring driveway returns, the developer can lower the cost of the curb construction, and the streetscape or architectural look is much improved. In landlease communities that have high densities and smaller homesites, a driveway return at each site tends to emphasize the higher density. Most curbs and gutters are constructed of concrete because this material holds up particularly well where snowplowing is required.

Road Width

In landlease communities the paved road width, where there is no parking allowed on the street, is normally between 20 to 26 feet. Where parking is allowed on one side of the street, minimum paved road width should be expanded to 30 feet, and where parking is allowed on both sides of the street the paved road width should be a minimum of 36 feet.

Manufactured home subdivision streets must be built to local jurisdictional standards, and generally a paved road width of 36 feet is required.

Parking

Each manufactured homesite should have parking available for two cars, with additional parking available in the community for guests. Off-street parking has two important advantages. It looks cleaner and less cluttered than on-street parking. It also avoids the problem associated with on-street parking, whereby children can dash out between two parked cars without being seen.

UTILITIES

The electrical distribution system should be capable of delivering a minimum of 200 amps to all homesites. The electric company will usually design and install the primary and secondary distribution systems. There are situations in which the power company requires the developer to install the secondary system, and sometimes the entire electrical distribution system. The modern manufactured home community has all-underground electrical service. Overhead electric service lines are unsightly and usually require more maintenance.

Natural gas and propane gas systems are used in the colder northern climates. Gas systems are seldom used in southern Sunbelt developments.

Underground cable television is used in most all communities, inasmuch as individual television antennas give a ragtag look to the community.

The telephone company normally installs its utility underground at no cost to the developer and in some situations will share its trenching with the cable television utility.

EARTHWORKS

Single-family residential subdivisions with large homesites normally require only that the grading or earthwork take place within the right-of-way, establishing street grades and drainage all within the right-of-way. Site-built homes use foundations or stemwalls that can function as retaining walls, solving grading problems at the time the home is placed. This is not the case with manufactured home landlease communities, which have densities of up to seven units per acre and homesite sizes as small as 4,500 square feet. The manufactured home does not have a foundation system that can function as a retaining wall, and the densities in the community will not allow one homesite to be graded independently from those adjacent to it. Therefore, the drainage and grading regime must be planned for the entire acreage of the development, not just the areas within a right-of-way as is often typical in a standard single-family subdivision. The earthworks should be designed with the cut and fill balancing, so that it is not necessary to incur the cost of hauling additional fill onto the site or hauling fill off the site. The cost for moving dirt from a cut to a fill location on-site would be in the neighborhood of $1.50 per cubic yard, and the cost of hauling fill off the site or to elsewhere on the site could be in the range of $8.00 per cubic yard. Special care and attention must be taken by the design engineer when working with sites that are wooded if trees are to be saved. The task of saving trees becomes increasingly difficult as the steepness of the site increases, thus causing additional grading. As mentioned in the discussion of concept in Chapter 5, the planner must be sensitive to the topography when developing the plan to minimize the required earthwork. In addition, vertical relief adds interest and environmental quality to the community. Before the common excavation takes place at a site, the topsoil should be stripped and stockpiled, so that when the project is nearing completion the topsoil can be returned to those areas where turf is to be established. Two benefits of replacing the topsoil are the quicker establishment of a lawn, thus decreasing erosion, and a substantial reduction in the amount of irrigation necessary to maintain the lawn.

OFFSITE IMPROVEMENTS

It may be necessary for the developer to work with the local municipality and utility companies to extend sewer, water, storm sewer, or other utilities onto the property. Most municipalities require the developer to pay the costs of these off-site improvements. For sewage treatment and water supply the developer must weigh the cost of developing these facilities on-site versus the cost of extending the off-site facilities. The developer must consider more than just the initial costs, as the on-going costs of a private water supply or sewage treatment system can be significant.

Quite often it is necessary for the developer to improve the off-site roadway leading to the entrance of the manufactured home community. If the road is adequate, the developer may still be required to construct turn lanes, acceleration lanes, and/or deceleration lanes. This allows the traffic entering and leaving the development to minimize its interference with the existing through traffic on the city street or highway.

PERMITS AND APPROVALS

Prior to the developer's starting construction, all required permits must be obtained, including proper zoning for the land. The following paragraphs describe the permits typically required by local, state, and federal governments.

Local Government (County, Township, or City)

Prior to a local government's issuing a construction permit, all the required state and federal permits must be in place. In addition, before issuing a construction permit the local government will require all engineering and architectural plans to be reviewed and approved by community staff. Most local governments have a tree ordinance that requires a special permit for clearing trees on-site. The fire department will most likely be involved in the review of plans and require the approval of the fire chief before the building permit is issued.

A separate permit required for soil and erosion control may be issued at the local government level or at the county or state level.

State Permits

The state board of health, in most states, issues an overall development permit for the manufactured home landlease community and reviews the plan to ensure that it is in conformity with appropriate state regulations.

A separate department of the state board of health usually requires a separate permit for the water supply system and the water distribution system. However, in some states this review and permitting process is handled by the state department of environmental regulation (DER).

The state DER will review the engineering plans and issue a permit if the plans conform to its requirements. This review is normally limited to sewer and water facilities.

The U.S. Army Corps of Engineers requirements pertaining to wetlands may also be administered by the state government. Archeological and historical evaluation of the site is generally a function of the state government. The DER will review and issue permits relative to the requirements dealing with storm water management and treatment.

Federal Government

If the development impacts upon a floodway, it will be necessary to receive approval from the Federal Emergency Management Agency (FEMA). Moreover, if the development impacts upon navigable waters of the United States, a permit will be required from the U.S. Coast Guard. Navigable waters are defined as waters tied to coastal waters of the United States in which a canoe can be floated. If the project impacts the environment, particularly wetlands, the Corps of Engineers may become involved in the permitting process. The Environmental Protection Agency may also become involved if hazardous wastes are found on the site.

CONSTRUCTION DRAWINGS AND CONTRACT DOCUMENTS

Contract documents are discussed in Chapter 11. Figure 8.1 is a list of the typical engineering plans needed for the approvals and construction of a manufactured

Sheet No.	Sheet Title
1	Title Sheet
2	Grading Plan No. 1
3	Grading Plan No. 2
4	Road Profiles No. 1
5	Road Profiles No. 2
6	Road Profiles No. 3
7	Layout Plan No. 1
8	Layout Plan No. 2
9	Lotting Plan No. 1
10	Lotting Plan No. 2
11	Utility Plan No. 1
12	Utility Plan No. 2
13	Sanitary Profiles No. 1
14	Sanitary Profiles No. 2
15	Storm Sewer Profiles
16	Intersection Details
17	Details
18	Details
19	Lift Station Details
20	Soil Erosion Control Plan
21	Storm Water Management Plan

FIG. 8.1   Index to drawings.

home community that is tying into a municipality for its water supply and sewage treatment. For a 200-homesite development there would be approximately 20 plan sheets. The index of drawings in Fig. 8.1 indicates the number and type of plan sheets.

CHAPTER 9

HOMEBUYER FINANCING

It may seem redundant to talk about financing when talking about housing. The two are generally an inseparable transaction. However, there are nuances to home financing that slip past even the experts. This is especially true of manufactured home financing, which is unique because the product is unique. To understand this, one must look back into the history of the manufactured housing industry.

EVOLUTION OF MANUFACTURED HOME FINANCING

Some people see the beginning of the manufactured housing industry in covered wagons—the temporary and mobile homes of early western settlers. That may be stretching things a little, but the analogy is not a bad one. Manufactured homes built today have evolved from the travel trailers that became popular in the 1920s as America's love affair with the automobile began. These early trailers were designed to satisfy the desires of the adventurous who wanted not only to travel in their automobiles, but also to camp in it, or at least adjacent to it. Over time these travel trailers became larger, with more sophisticated kitchens, bathrooms, and sleeping areas that closely resembled the comforts of home. As the evolution proceeded, trailer homes developed, then mobile homes—too large to pull behind the family vehicle, but still small enough to be moved relatively easily by professional haulers. With the advent of larger and larger homes, and particularly of the multisection homes, came the final evolution from trailers to houses—from mobilehomes to manufactured homes. Long-term financing for the early travel trailers was almost nonexistent, and what terms did exist carried high down payment requirements and very short terms. As the product grew in size and sophistication, so did financing. Until recently, however, virtually all manufactured (or mobile, in those days) homes were financed much like vehicles—with a personal property loan, often referred to as a retail installment sales contract.

PERSONAL PROPERTY (CHATTEL) FINANCING

Because of its origins in the vehicle industry, financing for manufactured housing is still largely similar to automobile financing. In other words, the home does not become a permanent improvement to the real estate on which it is located. Rather, it remains a separate titled piece of personal property. Personal property financing of manufactured homes has remained the norm through the years because, historically, a majority of manufactured homes have been placed on property not owned by the homeowner, either in a manufactured home landlease community or on private land owned by someone other than the homeowner. Therefore, acquiring a real estate title to the home and land is not possible, nor is acquiring a mortgage. This practice is slowly changing, with some manufactured homes being made a permanent part of the land on which they are located and financed as real estate, just as site-built houses are. Nevertheless, because manufactured homes are not always legally tied to the land on which they are located, it is likely that there will always be some personal property financing of manufactured housing.

Naturally, there are pros and cons to the personal property financing that has evolved with the manufactured housing industry. On the positive side, as manufactured homes have become larger, more sophisticated, and therefore more expensive, personal property lenders have reacted by extending the length of their loans. A typical maturity for a loan to finance a new manufactured home today ranges from 15 to 25 years. On the negative side are interest rates. Typically, the interest rate on a personal property loan secured by a manufactured home is 2 to 3 points higher than on a mortgage loan secured on a site-built home and the land on which it was built. The interest rate differential also can be traced to the industry's evolution. As an extraordinarily affordable form of shelter, manufactured housing has attracted a large number of low and middle-income families. Because these families have squeezed budgets, little savings, and no one to turn to in hard times, they are at greater risk in economic slumps. They are, by virtue of their economic status, greater credit risks. Lenders who grant credit to a large number of such families can suffer greater losses than were they to lend money to families with higher incomes. These lenders' costs of doing business is higher, and to compensate they raise their prices to cover their costs. Because a lender's price is the interest rate it charges for a loan, raising prices amounts to charging higher interest rates.

Another somewhat more technical reason for higher interest rates on personal property versus real estate loans on manufactured homes is the size of the loan balance. Because manufactured housing has historically been the housing of choice for nongovernment-subsidized affordable housing, the average loan balance on a manufactured home has been well below the average loan balance on a real estate mortgage. Therefore, a lending institution with manufactured home loans, each at an average balance of $20,000, would have three times as many loans as a lender with mortgage loans, each with an average balance of $60,000, assuming both institutions had lent the same amount of money. A $10 million portfolio of $20,000 manufactured home loans would have 500 loans, whereas a $10 million portfolio of $60,000 mortgage loans would have 167 loans. It takes at least as much labor and materials to service a single manufactured home loan as it does to service a mortgage loan, and sometimes even more because collection activities for low-income customers must be stepped up.

Other positive aspects of the personal property loan are its ease of processing, as compared with the typical mortgage loan. A manufactured homebuyer can usually expect an answer to his or her credit application for a manufactured home loan within a few days, as compared with several weeks for a typical mortgage loan. Moreover, although interest rates may be higher, terms are usually a little shorter, which lowers the total interest paid. The interest saved by paying off a loan in 15 versus 30 years can be substantial.

As the industry has matured, and now builds manufactured homes to meet an ever wider range of income levels—homes that range from a basic 700 to 800-square-foot, two-bedroom home to a luxurious multisection home of 3,000 or more square feet—the financial services industry is reacting with a much wider range of financing options. Lenders are offering longer terms, up to 20 or 25 years. Some financing programs offer lower interest rates to borrowers making higher down payments. Others have "land-in-lieu" programs whereby borrowers who own their own land can offer it as security on the loan instead of making a down payment. There are adjustable rate programs, biweekly payment programs—an entire array of personal property manufactured home loan programs designed to meet a wide range of home and homebuyer needs.

REAL PROPERTY FINANCING

A trend that is gaining momentum is the financing of manufactured homes as real property, that is, placing the home on land owned by the homebuyer, making it a permanent fixture of the land, and acquiring a single real estate title to the land and home. This kind of financing has a number of advantages for the homebuyer and for the locality where the home is sited.

When the home becomes real estate, it is eligible for mortgage financing. For the homebuyer, the interest rate will almost always be lower for a mortgage loan than for a personal property loan, for the reasons discussed earlier. The tax base on real estate is generally higher than on personal property, so the local government collects more revenues to fund schools, roads, police, and other necessary services.

There also are some disadvantages. To gain acceptance in local communities and achieve favorable zoning, almost universally, manufactured homes that qualify for real estate treatment are larger, more expensive multisection homes. The homebuyer must purchase not only the home but also the land on which the home is to be located. The communities containing these homes will generally have to be developed as subdivisions rather than landlease communities, which usually carry higher development costs. These considerations combine to make the transaction more expensive, mitigating some of the affordability that is often associated with manufactured housing. Lower interest rates can offset some of the higher costs. Nevertheless, developing a manufactured home subdivision, or putting manufactured homes on scattered lots and financing them with land as real estate, usually results in a less affordable housing transaction for the homebuyer than building a manufactured home landlease community. On the positive side, however, the manufactured home communities or scattered lot sites that are developed as real estate usually result in a more upscale home and community for the homebuyer. As in most decisions involving money, buyers must balance home features, community size and location, and other considerations against what they can afford.

An interesting new concept involves developing manufactured home landlease communities, allowing long-term leases to the homeowners (40 years or more), and designing the leases so that there are homeowner protections built in. In California, where state law allows a manufactured home to be titled as real estate whether or not the homeowner owns the land on which the home is located, several of these communities have been developed and lenders are financing the homes with real estate mortgages. In some of the communities, the Federal National Mortgage Association (FNMA) is allowing mortgage lenders who are FNMA approved to pool these loans with their other residential real estate mortgages, creating a secondary market for such loans. This concept combines the affordability of a landlease situation, whereby the purchaser does not have to borrow additional funds to purchase land, with the savings of the lower interest rate mortgage loan. The participation of FNMA in communities that meet its guidelines gives access to a huge source of funds from institutional investors through the secondary market.

EXAMPLES OF MANUFACTURED HOME FINANCING PROGRAMS

Not only can manufactured homes be financed either as personal or as real property, but within both categories there are a number of different types of programs from which to choose.

Personal Property Programs

Personal property programs are typically carried out on a retail installment sales contract basis. Lenders operate what are known as indirect lending programs. That is, the retailer who sells the manufactured home acts on behalf of the lender in taking the customer's credit application and implementing some of the other administrative procedures involved with the lender's granting of credit to the customer to purchase the home. In simple terms, the retailer agrees to take installment payments from the purchaser at a stated rate of interest for a stated period of time; that is, the retailer executes a retail installment sales contract. Then the lending institution purchases this contract from the retailer.

There are two basic types of personal property financing programs for manufactured homebuyers: conventional and government-sponsored.

Conventional Personal Property Financing Programs

Conventional programs are the most common type of personal property financing for buyers of manufactured homes. Until the early 1970s the government-sponsored programs of the Federal Housing Administration (FHA) and the Department of Veterans Affairs (VA) were not available to the manufactured housing industry. Even after these programs became available, they never became as popular with the manufactured housing industry as they did with the site-built industry. Historically, the combination of new homes with FHA or VA financing has been between 10% and 20% of new manufactured homes shipped annually. Most retailers and lenders cite the amount of paperwork, delays in loan approvals, and difficulty in having claims paid in the event of a default as reasons they shy away from the government-sponsored programs.

There are a number of conventional programs available to manufactured homebuyers. Adjustable rates, various maturities, and land-in-lieu of down payment are a few examples. A typical manufactured home financing transaction might have the following characteristics: The maximum loan amount that the lender will allow is equal to 125% of the manufacturer's wholesale invoice price, including freight from the factory to the retailer's site, plus retailer-supplied extras such as air conditioning and a washer and dryer. The purchaser is required to make a cash down payment of 10% of the purchase price of the home, plus other closing costs not allowed to be financed, such as prepaid interest at settlement, taxes, and various filing fees. The loan term is 15 years, and the interest rate is 2 to 3 percentage points above the prevailing single-family, residential real estate mortgage interest rate. The calculations for such a loan are as follows:

Steps to Calculating Maximum Loan Amount:

Manufacturer's wholesale invoice	$19,500
Freight to retailer's salescenter	+ 500
	$20,000
	×125%
Maximum loan amount (subtotal)	$25,000
Sales price of home	$26,000
Central air	+ 1,000
Washer and dryer	+ 750
Total sales price	$27,750
10% down payment	− 2,775
Financing required (max loan amt)	$24,975

This transaction fits the lender's maximum loan amount guidelines of 125%. If the retailer needed to charge more for the home, the purchaser would be required to make a higher down payment.

The manufacturer's invoice plays a significant role in determining the maximum loan amount that a lender will allow on the purchase of a new manufactured home. Here again, this practice can be traced to the evolution of the industry from a vehicular product. In a sense, the manufacturer's invoice replaces the appraisal in a lender's determination of value of a new manufactured home in a personal property finance transaction.

Given the importance of a manufacturer's invoice for the lender in determining value, manufacturers, through the industry's trade association, the Manufactured Housing Institute (MHI) in Arlington, Virginia, have voluntarily adopted an invoice certification that says, in effect, that everything revealed on the invoice is true and correct, that there are no hidden charges or discounts, and that all financial aspects of the transaction are present in the invoice document. A similar certification was adopted by the FHA and VA and has been credited by lenders as adding a great deal of consistency to manufacturer's invoices. It has also given the lending community a much higher level of comfort with the information contained in the invoice documents.

Government-Sponsored Personal Property Programs

There are two primary government-sponsored financing programs for personal property loans for manufactured homes—the FHA loan coinsurance program of the Department of Housing and Urban Development (HUD) and the VA loan guaranty program. Both programs operate similarly to, but not exactly like, their site-built mortgage counterparts.

Everyone has heard of FHA and VA loans. Most of us have probably had one or will have one in our lifetime. Yet until the early 1970s neither of these agencies operated programs for manufactured housing. Since that time both agencies will insure or guarantee a loan secured by a manufactured home. They will do this both on a personal property transaction and on a real property transaction involving a manufactured home.

FHA Title I Manufactured Home Loan Insurance Program

The FHA program for personal property manufactured home loans is known as the Title I program, so called because Title I is the title in the National Housing Act that authorizes HUD to conduct an insurance program for manufactured home loans.

The FHA Title I program operates on the same theory of the FHA's regular home loan insurance programs. The government can promote home ownership by facilitating home lending, and it can facilitate home lending by operating a home loan insurance program that will allow the lender to insure some of its risk.

In the case of the FHA Title I program for manufactured housing, the FHA operates a coinsurance program. FHA insures 90% of the loan. Thus, if a borrower defaults on a Title I manufactured home loan, the FHA will pay the lender 90% of the unpaid loan balance. HUD regulations limit the amount lenders may recover from the FHA on a defaulted Title I loan, so as a practical matter, lenders seldom, if ever, recover 90% of their losses on a default through FHA Title I insurance.

The Title I program works much like conventional programs. On new homes, the maximum loan amount is determined by a percentage of the invoice plus certain items supplied by the retailer. FHA also applies an absolute limit of $40,500 on a loan to purchase a manufactured home, $54,000 for a loan to purchase a manufactured home and site on which to permanently place[1] the home, and $13,500 to purchase a site on which to permanently place a manufactured home. FHA has guidelines for both new and previously owned homes. They are listed in part in the following paragraphs, as paraphrased from the Code of Federal Regulations, Title 24, Part 201.

Loans on New Homes. The total principal obligation for a loan to purchase a new manufactured home may not exceed the sum of the following itemized amounts, up to a maximum of $40,500:

1. 125% of the sum of the wholesale (base) prices of the home and any itemized options, and the charge for freight, as detailed in the manufacturer's invoice;
2. The charge for any sales taxes to be paid by the retailer, as detailed in the manufacturer's invoice;
3. Transportation, including the rental of wheels and axles, to the homesite (if not included in freight charges), setup and anchoring charges, not to exceed $750 per module;
4. Foundation fascia costs, not to exceed $500;
5. Actual retailer's cost of garage, carport, patio, or other comparable appurtenance as approved by the secretary of HUD;
6. Actual retailer's cost of purchasing and installing a central air-conditioning system or heat pump, if not installed by the manufacturer;
7. State and local sales taxes paid by the borrower;
8. Premiums paid by the borrower for comprehensive and extended hazard insurance and vendor's single-interest coverage for the first year, including premiums for flood insurance, where applicable;
9. Credit report costs; and

---

[1] The words *permanently place* as they are used here in describing the FHA Title I program are intended to mean that the home is placed on the site and is intended to be used as a permanent residence. Permanently placing the home on the site for this purpose does not require that the home be permanently attached to a site-built foundation.

10. A fee for inspection of the property by the lender or its agent, to verify that:
    a. The terms and conditions of the purchase contract have been met,
    b. The manufactured home and options, if any, included in the price of the home, or to be financed with loan proceeds, have been delivered and completed,
    c. The certification required to be completed by the retailer and seller is correct. This certification stipulates that the manufactured home and any options (appliances, built-in items and equipment) included in the price of the home or to be financed with loan proceeds have been delivered to and properly installed or erected on the site, and that any other work to be accomplished at the site and financed with loan proceeds has been completed.

The lender may also require the borrower to pay certain fees and charges that may not be financed. These fees must be collected in the borrower's initial payment, prior to loan disbursement. These are as follows:

1. An origination fee, not to exceed 1% of the loan amount, excluding any amount to refinance the outstanding balance of an existing Title I loan made or held by the lender;
2. Any discount points to be paid by the borrower to the lender;
3. Recording fees, recording taxes, and filing fees;
4. Documentary stamp taxes;
5. Title insurance costs;
6. Payments into a tax and insurance escrow account for the current year;
7. Other fees necessary to establish the validity of a lien;
8. Appraisal fees;
9. Survey costs;
10. Handling charges to refinance or modify an existing loan, not to exceed $100;
11. Other such items as may be specified by the secretary of HUD; and
12. A fee for approving an assumptor and preparing the assumption agreement not to exceed 1% of the principal balance.

Lenders are prohibited from charging the borrower or paying themselves any referral fee to any retailer, home manufacturer, loan broker, or any other party in connection with the origination of a loan.

Loans on Previously Owned Homes. The guidelines for a Title I loan on a previously owned home are almost the same as those for a new home, except that a previously owned home's value must be appraised. Instead of determining the maximum loan amount based on 125% of the manufacturer's invoice, HUD requires that the home be appraised by a HUD-approved appraiser. The Title I loan amount allowed then is the lesser of the 90% total appraised value or the purchase price of the home as equipped and furnished. The absolute maximum loan amount of $40,500 applies here as well. Items eligible for financing on a new home are also eligible for financing on a previously owned home, and the same prohibitions apply to items that may be charged but not financed and charges that may not be a part of the transaction.

Loan Maturities and Interest Rates. Maximum terms for a manufactured home loan vary with the collateral, as follows:

- 20 years, 32 days for a home-only loan
- 25 years, 32 days for a combination multisection home and site loan
- 15 years, 32 days for a site on which to permanently place a manufactured home

The interest rate is negotiated and agreed to by the borrower and the lender and must be fixed for the full term of the loan. The lender and the borrower may negotiate the amount of discount points to be paid by the borrower. The lender also may negotiate with the retailer the amount of discount points to be paid by the retailer from its own resources for the benefit of the borrower, before or at the time of the borrower's initial payment to the lender. The retailer must not accept reimbursement for any such payment of discount points from the borrower, manufacturer, or any other party. The lender cannot require or allow any parties, other than the borrower or the retailer, to pay any discount points or other financing charges in connection with approving or disbursing proceeds of the loan transaction. The lender and retailer need not disclose to the borrower the amount of any discount points to be paid by the retailer to the lender, but they must comply with any federal or state requirements for disclosure to the borrower of financing charges to be paid by the borrower, including the interest rate and any discount points. Interest on the loan accrues from the date of the loan and must be calculated according to the actuarial method.

Down Payment Requirements. If purchasing a new manufactured home or a new manufactured home and site, the borrower must make a minimum cash down payment of at least 5% of the first $5,000 and 10% of the balance of the purchase price of the home. In purchasing a site on which to permanently place a manufactured home, the minimum down payment is 10% of the purchase price and development costs for the site.

Nothing other than the borrower's equity in an existing manufactured home, and any attached appurtenances, may be traded in on a new home and accepted in lieu of a cash down payment. In the case of a combination home and site loan, where the borrower already owns a site, the borrower's equity in the site may be accepted in lieu of the cash down payment.

The borrower is responsible for payment in cash of any costs, other than eligible discount points paid by the retailer, that will not be paid or are not eligible to be paid from the proceeds of the loan. These costs may include a loan origination fee, discount points, or costs in excess of the maximum loan amount. None of the cash payment required from the borrower may be borrowed from or paid by the retailer, the manufacturer, or other party to the loan transaction. If the borrower obtains any part of the required cash payment through a gift or loan, the source of the gift or loan must be disclosed and cannot be secured by the manufactured home for which the Title I loan is being made.

Borrower Eligibility and Eligible Use of Loan Proceeds. To be eligible for a manufactured home loan, the borrower must become the owner of the particular property that is to be financed with such a loan. When the loan involves a manufactured home that is classified as realty, ownership of the home must be fee simple. Where the loan involves a manufactured homesite, ownership of the site must be fee simple, except where the site consists of a share in a cooperative association that owns and operates a manufactured homes landlease community.

The manufactured home must be certified by the manufacturer to have been constructed in compliance with the National Manufactured Housing Construction and Safety Standards Act of 1974 (the HUD Code), as evidenced by a label or tag affixed to the manufactured home. The lender must obtain from the retailer a copy of the manufacturer's invoice for retention in the loan file. The home's installation or erection on the homesite must comply with the manufacturer's requirements for its anchoring, support, stability, and maintenance. Thereafter the retailer must inspect the manufactured home and its components for structural damage and must test the performance of its plumbing, mechanical, and electrical systems.

The home manufacturer must provide the purchaser of a new manufactured home a written warranty, duly executed by an authorized representative of the manufacturer on a HUD-approved form. The warranty must be provided without cost to the borrower. The effective date of the warranty is the date of delivery of the manufactured home to the borrower. The warranty obligates the home manufacturer to take appropriate action to correct any nonconformity with standards prescribed in the HUD Code. A copy of the warranty must be retained in the lender's loan file.

Credit Underwriting Guidelines. The lender must determine that the borrower[2] is solvent and an acceptable credit risk, with a reasonable ability to make payments on the loan obligation. The lender must obtain a separate dated credit application on a HUD-approved form from the borrower and any comaker or cosigner. The lender must conduct a credit investigation based on the credit application and must obtain written verification of the current employment and current income of the borrower. If the borrower has changed employment within the past 2 years, the lender must obtain written verification of the person's prior

[2] When used in this context, *borrower* includes also any coborrower or cosigner on the note.

employment and prior income during the 2-year period. The lender must also determine the total amount of the borrower's existing and proposed Title I loans to ensure that the maximum Title I loan amounts are not exceeded.

As part of its credit investigation, the lender must obtain a consumer credit report stating the credit accounts and payment history of the borrower. The lender must check with the inquirers concerning all credit inquiries reported within the preceding 90 days to determine whether the borrower has incurred debts not listed on the credit application. If a consumer credit report is not available or is incomplete, the loan file must contain other documentation of the lender's diligent investigation of the credit of the borrower or of the comaker or cosigner. The lender must obtain written verification of the existence of all funds of the borrower required for the borrower's initial payment.

For a borrower's income to be considered adequate, the borrower's total housing expenses[3] (including payments on the manufactured home loan) must not exceed 29% of the effective gross income,[4] and the borrower's total fixed expenses[5] (including payments on the manufactured home loan) must not exceed 41% of effective gross income.

If the maximum expense-to-income ratios are exceeded, a borrower's income may be considered adequate to qualify for a loan only if the lender determines and documents in the loan file the existence of compensating factors concerning the borrower's creditworthiness that support approval of the loan. Examples of such factors include, but are not limited to, the following:

1. The borrower receives benefits not included in effective gross income, but which directly affect the borrower's ability to meet financial obligations (e.g., a company automobile that is available for personal use).
2. A considerable portion of the borrower's effective gross income is from nontaxable sources.
3. The borrower has substantial cash reserves available for contingencies (e.g., a savings account with the equivalent of several month's income).
4. The borrower's total fixed expenses have been at the same or higher levels for the past 2 years, without any evidence of delinquency.

If the lender has any doubt about whether a particular compensating factor is acceptable, a specific ruling should be requested from HUD.

---

[3] *Housing expenses* includes all payment for principal, interest, loan or mortgage insurance charges, ground rent or leasehold charges, real estate taxes, hazard insurance, and home owners association or condominium fees, but does not include utility costs.

[4] *Effective gross income* is defined as continuing income from all sources that is reasonably expected to be available during the first 2 years of the loan obligation, without any deduction for income taxes or other items.

[5] *Total fixed expenses* is the sum of the borrower's housing expenses and payments on automobile loans, furniture loans, student loans, installment loans, revolving charge accounts, alimony or child support, child care, and any other debt where the obligation is expected to continue for 6 months or more.

Requirements for a Manufactured Homesite. HUD has a number of other guidelines for the FHA Title I program, including rules for home and site loans and site-only loans. For any FHA Title I loan, the home must be placed on a site that is:

1. Served by adequate public or community water and sewage systems, unless appropriate local officials certify that either or both such systems are unavailable to provide an adequate level of service to the manufactured homesite. If either or both such systems are not available, the manufactured homesite must comply with local or state minimum lot area requirements for the provision of on-site water supply and sewage disposal;

2. Where the manufactured home is to be placed on a leased site in a manufactured home community, the lender must obtain directly or through the borrower a certification from the state or local authority which licenses such landlease communities that the property complies with minimum standards relating to site location, vehicular access, water supply, sewage disposal, utility connections, storm drainage, site development, and landscaping. Where no state or local licensing authority exists, or where the licensing authority does not establish or enforce minimum standards for landlease development, the lender must similarly obtain a certification from a registered civil engineer that the landlease community meets minimum design and construction standards prescribed by the secretary of HUD;

3. Where the manufactured home is to be placed on an individual manufactured homesite or other site owned or leased by the borrower, the lender must obtain certifications from the appropriate local government officials directly or through the borrower that:

   a. The site is zoned to permit the placement of the manufactured home,

   b. Adequate public access from a public right-of-way is available to the site,

   c. Adequate water supply, sewage disposal, and storm drainage facilities are available on the site, and

   d. Other minimum local standards for site suitability are met.

Where there are no appropriate local officials, or where minimum local standards for vehicular access, water supply, sewage disposal, storm drainage, and site suitability are not established or enforced, the lender must similarly obtain a certification from a registered civil engineer that the site meets minimum design and construction standards prescribed by the secretary of HUD.

Requirements for Securing the Loan. All Title I loans must be secured by a recorded first lien that is superior to any other lien on the property. The lien must be evidenced by a properly recorded financing statement, a properly recorded security instrument executed by the borrower, or another acceptable instrument such as a certificate of title issued by the state and containing a recitation of the lender's lien interest in the manufactured home.

Approving Retailers. Lenders may approve only retailers they consider to be reliable, financially responsible, and qualified to satisfactorily perform their contractual obligations to borrowers. The lender's approval of the retailer must be documented on a HUD-approved retailer approval form, signed and dated by the retailer and the lender. The approval form must contain information supplied by the retailer on its trade name or names, place or places of business, type of ownership, type of business, and the names and employment history of the principal individuals and other parties who control or manage the business. Each retailer must be reapproved annually. The lender must require a current financial statement and credit report from the retailer and may require other documentation it deems necessary to support its approval.

Lenders must supervise and monitor each approved retailer's activities with visits to the retailer's place of business periodically during the year. Lenders must maintain a file on each approved retailer that contains the executed retailer approval form with supporting information and documentation of the lender's experience with loans originated for the retailer. This information must include information about borrower defaults, records of completion of site-of-placement inspections, and records of borrower complaints and their resolution.

Requirements for Flood and Hazard Insurance. If the property securing the loan is located in an area that has been identified by the Federal Emergency Management Agency (FEMA) as having special flood hazards, then the community in which the property is located must be participating in the Nation Flood Insurance Program and flood insurance must be obtained on the property by the borrower, naming the lender as the loss payee. This insurance must be maintained for the full term of the loan.

Hazard insurance in an amount at least equal to the unpaid loan balance must be obtained by the borrower, naming the lender as loss payee for the full term of the loan. If the borrower fails to maintain such insurance, the lender must obtain coverage at the borrower's expense.

No loan may be insured on property located within the Coastal Barriers Resources System.

Mortgage Insurance Premium. The lender must pay a fee for Title I insurance equal to .50% of the loan amount, multiplied by the number of years of the term of the loan. This fee is payable in annual installments that vary according to the term of the loan as follows:

Loan Term 2–12 Years	Loan Term 12–16 Years	Loan Term 16+ Years
1.00% first 3 years	1.00% first 4 years	1.00% first 5 years
0.75% next 2 years	0.75% next 3 years	0.75% next 4 years
0.50% until full fee is paid	0.50% until full fee is paid	0.50% until full fee is paid

All percentages are applied to the original loan amount in computing the mortgage insurance premium.

Foreclosure and Repossession on a Defaulted Loan. A lender may undertake foreclosure of repossession of the property securing a Title I loan that is in default only after it has timely serviced the loan with diligence in accordance with the regulatory requirements and has taken all reasonable and prudent measures to induce the borrower to bring the loan account current. Before taking action to accelerate the maturity of the loan in the event of default, the lender or its agent must arrange a face-to-face meeting with the borrower, or make a reasonable effort to do so, in order to assist the borrower to avoid the default. If the lender is unable to arrange a face-to-face meeting, it may discuss the default with the borrower by telephone and attempt to secure the borrower's agreement to curing the default.

Unless the borrower cures the default or agrees to a modification agreement or repayment plan, the lender must provide the borrower with written notice that the loan is in default and that the loan maturity is to be accelerated. In addition to complying with applicable state and local notice requirements, the notice must be sent by certified mail and contain the following:

1. A description of the obligation or security interest held by the lender;
2. A statement of the nature of the default and of the amount due to the lender as unpaid principal and earned interest on the note as of the date 30 days from the date of the notice;
3. A demand upon the borrower either to cure the default by bringing the loan current or by refinancing the loan or to agree to a modification agreement or a repayment plan by not later than the date 30 days from the date of the notice;
4. A statement that if the borrower fails either to cure the default or to agree to a modification agreement or a repayment plan by the date 30 days from the date of the notice, then, as of the date 30 days from the date of the notice, the maturity of the loan is accelerated and full payment of all amounts due under the loan is required;
5. A statement that if the default persists, the lender will report the default to an appropriate credit reporting agency; and
6. Any other requirements prescribed by the secretary of HUD.

The lender must report the default to an appropriate credit reporting agency if the loan maturity is accelerated and the loan is not reinstated.

When a manufactured home loan is in default and the lender cannot contact the borrower within the prescribed notice period, it must make a visual inspection of the property, determine whether the property is vacant or abandoned, and prepare a report on its condition for placement in the loan file. In any case of vacancy or abandonment, the lender must take reasonable steps to preserve and maintain the property, including any items of removable personal property covered by the loan.

After acceleration of maturity on a defaulted manufactured home loan, the lender must proceed against the loan security by foreclosure or repossession in compliance with all applicable state and local laws and acquire good, marketable title to the property securing the loan. The lender must also take all actions necessary under state and local law to preserve its rights to obtain a valid and enforceable deficiency judgment against the borrower.

The lender must obtain a HUD-approved appraisal of the property as soon after repossession as possible, or earlier with the permission of the borrower. The appraisal should reflect the retail value of comparable manufactured homes in similar condition and in the same geographic area, as listed in a current value rating publication acceptable to the secretary of HUD. Where the manufactured home is without hazard insurance and has sustained at any time prior to the sale of disposition of the home, damage that would normally be covered by hazard insurance, the lender shall report its situation in submitting a Title I insurance claim, and will assure that the appraised value is based upon the retail value of comparable homes in good condition and in the same geographic area, without any deduction for such damage.

Where the lender obtains title to property securing a manufactured home loan by repossession or foreclosure, the property must be sold for the best price obtainable before making an insurance claim to HUD. In the case of a combination loan, the manufactured home and site must be sold in a single transaction and the manufactured home may not be removed from the site unless the prior approval of the secretary of HUD is obtained. The best price obtainable is the greater of (1) the actual sales price of the property, less the cost of repairs to make the property marketable, or (2) the appraised value of the property before repairs.

Insurance Claim Procedure. A claim for reimbursement for any loss on any eligible Title I loan must be made on a HUD-approved form executed by a duly qualified officer of the lender. The claim must be fully documented and itemized and accompanied by the complete loan file pertaining to the transaction. If state or local law requires retention of the original note, security instrument, and related documents, the lender may submit copies. The claim application must be supported by the following:

1. Documentation of the lender's efforts to effect recourse against any retailer in accordance with any recourse agreement if such an agreement was entered into;
2. Certification under applicable criminal and civil penalties for fraud and misrepresentation that the lender has complied with all applicable state and local laws in carrying out any foreclosure or repossession, including copies of all notices served upon the borrower or published in connection with such foreclosure or repossession; and

3. Where a borrower has declared bankruptcy or insolvency, or is deceased, the notice of bankruptcy and evidence that the lender has filed a proof of claim with the court having jurisdiction.

A claim may be filed no later than 12 months after the date of default for manufactured home-only loans, and 18 months after the date of default for combination manufactured home and site loans.

The secretary of HUD may deny a claim for insurance in whole or in part based upon a violation of the regulations unless a waiver of compliance with the regulations is granted.

Calculation of Insurance Claim Payment. The lender will be reimbursed up to 90% of its loss on any eligible loan up to the amount of insurance coverage in the lender's insurance reserve account. The amount of the claim payment is 90% of the sum of the following amounts:

1. The unpaid amount of the loan obligation (net unpaid principal and the uncollected interest earned to the date of default) after deducting the following amounts:
   a. The best price obtainable for the property;
   b. All amounts to which the lender is entitled after the date of default from any source relating to the property, such as rent, other income, recourse recovery against the retailer, hazard insurance benefits, and rebates paid on insurance premiums; and
   c. Amounts retained by the lender after the date of default, including amounts held or deposited to the account of the borrower or to which the lender is entitled under the loan transaction, and which have not been applied in the reduction of the borrower's indebtedness.
2. The unpaid amount of interest on the unpaid amount of the loan obligation from the date of default to the date of the claim's initial submission for payment plus 15 calender days, calculated at the rate of 7% per annum. On a manufactured home-only loan, interest will not be paid for any period greater than 9 months from the date of default, unless with such period the lender requests in writing an extension not to exceed an additional 3 months and the request is approved. The maximum period for combination loans is 18 months.
3. For a manufactured home-only loan, the amount of costs paid to the retailer or other third-party to repossess and preserve the manufactured home and other property securing repayment of the loan, such as including hazard insurance premiums, personal property taxes, and site rental, plus actual costs not to exceed $750 per module for removing and transporting the home to a retailer's lot or other off-site location.
4. The amount of a sales commission paid to a retailer, real estate agent, or other third party for the resale of the home or site. Where the home is resold

on-site, the commission may not exceed 10% of the sales price. Where the home is sold off-site, the commission may not exceed 7% of the sales price.

5. For manufactured homesite loans, and for combination loans where both the foreclosed manufactured home and site are classified as realty, the amount of:

   a. State and local real estate taxes, ground rents, and municipal water and sewer fees or liens, prorated to the date of disposition of the property;

   b. Special assessments that are noted on the loan application or that become liens after the insurance is issued, prorated to the date of disposition of the property; and

   c. Transfer taxes imposed upon any deeds or other instruments by which the property was acquired by the lender.

6. The amount of uncollected court costs, including fees paid for issuing, serving, and filing a summons.

7. The amount of attorney's fees on an hourly or other basis for time actually expended and billed, not to exceed $500.

8. The amount of expenses for recording the assignment of the security to the United States and for costs of repossession or foreclosure other than attorney's fees, but not to exceed costs that are customary and reasonable in the jurisdiction where the repossession or foreclosure takes place, as determined by the secretary of HUD.

Other FHA Title I Guidelines. The preceding guidelines are a fairly detailed sample of the rules one must follow when using the HUD FHA Title I insurance program for manufactured home loans. Nevertheless, they are only a sample. There are many more rules in the actual regulations than are paraphrased here. Anyone interested in using the FHA Title I program should consult the Code of Federal Regulations, Title 24, Part 201, a HUD approved Title I lender, or the FHA Title I staff at HUD.

Department of Veterans Affairs Manufactured Home Loan Guaranty Program

The Department of Veterans Affairs (VA) program for manufactured home loans operates on the same theory as the FHA Title I program. This program facilitates manufactured home lending by allowing the lender to mitigate some of its risk. In the case of the VA program, the government supplies a guarantee to the lender that it will pay some or all of a lender's loss resulting from a default on a VA-guaranteed loan. In the case of a personal property loan for a manufactured home, the maximum guaranty is 40% of the loan, not to exceed $20,000. For example, a lender could get a $20,000 VA guarantee on a $50,000 or greater loan secured by a manufactured home. On a $40,000 loan the guarantee would be limited to $16,000, or 40% of $40,000.

In general, VA-guaranteed loans on manufactured homes are available to individuals who have served or are serving in the armed forces of the United States or the U.S. Coast Guard.

Like the FHA Title I program, the VA program has formulas for determining how much a lender may finance with a VA-guaranteed loan. Here again, the amount is based on a percentage of the manufacturer's wholesale invoice price plus certain items supplied by the retailer.

A partial summary of the VA manufactured home loan guaranty program guidelines follows, as paraphrased from the Code of Federal Regulations, Title 38, Part 36.

Loans on New Homes. The loan amount to purchase a new manufactured home, in an individual case, may not exceed the sum of the following:

1. 120% of the figure produced by the following computation: Subtract from the manufacturer's invoice cost the manufacturer's invoice cost of any components (furnishings, accessories, equipment) removed from the home by the retailer. To the remainder add the retailer's cost for any components added by the retailer. The sum obtained is the figure to be multiplied by the percentage specified above;
2. Actual fees or charges for required recordation of documents;
3. The amount of any documentary stamp taxes levied on the transaction;
4. The amount of state and local taxes levied on the transaction;
5. The premium for customary physical damage insurance and vendor's single interest coverage on the manufactured home for an initial policy term of not to exceed 5 years;
6. The actual cost of transportation or freight not to exceed $400 for a single-section or $600 for a multisection home;
7. Setup charges for installing the home on-site not to exceed $400 for a singlesection or $800 for a multisection home;
8. A guaranty fee of 1% of the total loan amount (not including the guaranty fee).

No other fees may be charged to a veteran borrower without the prior approval of the secretary of the Department of Veterans Affairs. If any of the fees authorized by the secretary exceed the maximum amounts prescribed, the excess must be paid from the veteran borrower's own resources without borrowing.

Loans on Previously Owned Homes. Guidelines for a VA-guaranteed loan for a previously owned manufactured home are virtually the same as those for a new home, except that the loan may not exceed the reasonable value as established by the secretary of Veterans Affairs; that is, the home must be appraised by a VA-approved appraiser. The loan amount may also include:

1. Actual fees or charges for required recordation of documents;
2. The amount of any documentary stamp tax levied on the transaction;
3. The amount of state and local taxes levied on the transaction; and
4. The premium for customary physical damage insurance and vendor's single interest coverage on the manufactured home for an initial policy term not to exceed 5 years.

Loan Maturities and Interest Rates. Maximum loan terms for a manufactured home loan vary with the collateral, as follows:

- 20 years, 32 days for a singlesection home-only or singlesection home and site loan;
- 23 years, 32 days for a multisection home-only loan;
- 25 years, 32 days for a multisection home and site loan;
- 15 years, 32 days for a site on which to place a manufactured home.

For a loan to purchase a previously owned manufactured home, the same maximum terms apply unless the secretary of the Veterans Affairs determines (through a VA-approved appraisal) that the remaining useful life of the home is less than the maximum terms for new homes. In that case, the remaining useful life would be the maximum term of the loan.

The VA periodically sets maximum interest rates for manufactured home loans and publishes them in the *Federal Register*. Rates on loans may not exceed these rates.

Down Payment Requirements. The VA requires that the veteran purchaser of a manufactured home make a minimum 5% down payment based on the purchase price of the home and accessories.

Borrower Eligibility and Eligible Use of Loan Proceeds. The VA has an elaborate system for determining the creditworthiness of a borrower. The borrower must meet a two-part test, one a debt-to-income ratio test—generally not to exceed 41%—the other a residual income test, which is described in detail in the Code of Federal Regulations, Title 24, Part 36.4337.

To qualify for purchase with a VA-guaranteed loan, a manufactured home must:

1. If a singlesection home, a minimum of 10 feet wide and have a minimum floor area of 400 square feet;
2. If a multisection home, be a minimum of 20 feet wide and have a minimum floor area of 700 square feet;
3. Be so constructed as to be towed on its own chassis and undercarriage or independent undercarriage;

4. Contain living facilities for year-round occupancy by one family, including permanent provisions for heat, sleeping, cooking, and sanitation; and
5. Comply with the specifications in effect at the time the loan is made that are prescribed by the secretary of Veterans Affairs.

The manufacturer must supply the veteran purchaser with a written warranty in the form and content prescribed by the secretary of Veterans Affairs, and the warranty must be in addition to and not in derogation of all other rights and privileges that the purchaser or owner may have under any other law or instrument. The warranty must be submitted with the loan papers prior to loan guaranty approval. In the case of a previously owned manufactured home, the retailer selling the home must supply the veteran purchaser a written warranty as prescribed by the secretary of Veterans Affairs with provisions the same as those required for a new home.

Credit Underwriting Guidelines. There are two primary underwriting tools that will be used in determining the adequacy of the veteran's present and anticipated income. They are debt-to-income ratio and residual income. Ordinarily, to qualify for a loan, the veteran must meet both standards. However, there are instances in which meeting one or the other of the tests will qualify the veteran, as well as instances in which meeting both tests will not qualify a veteran.

The debt-to-income ratio is computed by taking the sum of the monthly principal, interest, taxes, and insurance (PITI) for the loan being applied for, homeowner's and other assessments such as special assessments, condominium fees, homeowners' association fees, and so on, and any long-term obligations divided by the total of gross salary or earnings and other compensation or income. A veteran usually must have a ratio of less than 41%, although lenders may use other compensating factors to approve the loan of a veteran whose debt-to-income ratio exceeds 41%. The compensating factors must be fully documented in writing.

Residual income is what the veteran has left to meet living expenses after estimated monthly shelter expenses have been paid and other monthly obligations have been met. The VA uses guidelines for residual income that are based on data supplied in the Consumer Expenditure Survey (CES) published by the Department of Labor's Bureau of Labor Statistics. Regional minimum residual incomes have been developed for loan amounts under and over $70,000. The regulations stress, however, that no single factor is a final determinant in any applicant's qualification for a VA-guaranteed loan.

The borrower's income and employment must be verified, and that of the spouse if it is needed to qualify for the loan. Income that has not or cannot be verified cannot be given consideration when analyzing the loan. If the veteran or spouse has been employed for less than 2 years, a 2-year history covering prior employment, schooling, or other training must be secured. Any periods of unemployment must be explained. Employment verifications must be no more than 90 days old.

Requirements for a Manufactured Homesite. Any rental site on which a manufactured home to be purchased, with a guaranteed loan, will be placed, must qualify as an acceptable rental site as follows:

1. The site must be located within a manufactured home landlease community or subdivision that is acceptable to the VA; or

2. The site can be one that is not within a manufactured home landlease community or subdivision, provided that it is determined by the VA to be an acceptable rental site, or the manufactured home purchaser and retailer has certified to the secretary of VA that:

   a. Placement of the manufactured home on the site is not a violation of zoning laws or other local requirements applicable to manufactured home;

   b. The site is served by water and sanitary facilities that are approved by the local public authority and are acceptable to the VA;

   c. The site is served by an all-weather street or road;

   d. The site is not known to be subject to conditions that may be hazardous to the health or safety of the manufactured home occupants or that may endanger the manufactured home; and

   e. The site is free from, and the location of the manufactured home thereon will not substantially contribute to, adverse scenic or environmental conditions.

3. No manufactured home purchased with a guaranteed loan may be placed on a site owned by an eligible veteran or on a site to be purchased or improved with the proceeds of a guaranteed manufactured home loan, unless the site owned or to be so purchased or improved is determined by the VA to be an acceptable manufactured homesite.

4. A manufactured home landlease community or subdivision that is not approved by the FHA will be acceptable to the VA if it:

   a. Is designed to encourage the maintenance and development of manufactured homesites that will be free from, and not substantially contribute to, adverse scenic and environmental conditions, and

   b. Complies otherwise with the applicable standards for planning, construction, and general acceptability prescribed by the secretary of the VA.

Requirements for Securing the Loan. The interest in the manufactured home acquired by the veteran at the time of purchase shall be either:

1. Legal title evidenced by such document as is customarily issued to the purchaser of a manufactured home in the jurisdiction in which the manufactured home is initially sited; or

2. A full possessory interest convertible into a legal title conforming to the paragraph above (Item 1) upon payment in full of the guaranteed loan.

The loan must be secured by a properly recorded financing statement and security agreement or other security instrument that creates a first lien on or equivalent security interest in the manufactured home and all of the furnishings, equipment, and accessories paid for in whole or in part out of the loan proceeds.

Approving Retailers. Unlike the FHA, the VA has no guidelines for approving retailers. However, there are guidelines for suspending a retailer, manufacturer, or landlease community operator. The secretary of the VA may refuse to guarantee loans for veterans to purchase manufactured homes offered for sale by any retailer if substantial deficiencies have been discovered in such homes. If the secretary determines that there has been a failure or indicated inability of the retailer to discharge contractual liabilities to veterans, or that the type of contract of sale or methods, procedures, or practices pursued by the retailer in the marketing of such properties have been unfair or prejudicial to veteran purchasers, the VA may refuse to guarantee such loans.

The secretary of the VA may refuse to approve as acceptable any site in a manufactured home landlease community owned or operated by any person whose rental or sale methods, procedures, requirements, or practices are determined by the secretary to be unfair or prejudicial to veterans renting or purchasing such sites.

The secretary of the VA may refuse to guarantee loans to be secured by manufactured homes constructed by manufacturers that:

1. Refuse to permit the periodic inspections of their facilities by the VA provided for in the regulations;
2. Manufactured homes not in conformity to the structural standards prescribed in the regulations; or
3. Fail or are unable to discharge their warranty obligations.

In every case, a suspended community owner or operator, manufacturer or retailer has an appeal process available.

Requirements for Flood and Hazard Insurance. The lender must require the borrower to maintain insurance policies sufficient to protect the security against the risks or hazards to which it may be subjected to the extent customary in the locality. Flood insurance will be required, including coverage of the contents to the extent that such contents are security for the loan if the security is located in an area identified by FEMA as having special flood hazards and in which the sale of flood insurance is available under the national flood insurance program. The amount of flood insurance required will be equal to the outstanding balance of the loan or the maximum limit of coverage available for the particular type of property under the national flood insurance program, whichever is less. All moneys received under such policies covering payment of insured losses shall be applied to restoration of the security or to the loan balance.

Loan Guaranty Fee. A fee of 1% of the total loan amount must be paid to the secretary by the lender within 15 days after loan closing.

Foreclosure and Repossession on a Defaulted Loan. A lender may not begin proceedings in court or give notice of sale under power of sale, repossess the security or accelerate the loan, or otherwise take steps to terminate the debtor's rights in the security until the expiration of 30 days after delivery by certified mail to the secretary of a notice of intention to take such action, except that immediate action may be taken if the property to be affected has been abandoned by the debtor or has been subjected to extraordinary waste or hazard.

Upon receiving notice of default, the secretary may require the holder to assign the loan and collateral to the VA, although this seldom happens with a manufactured home loan.

After the lender has notified the VA that it intends to repossess and sell the loan collateral, the VA assigns a minimum amount that will be credited against the borrower's indebtedness—an appraised value for the collateral. The lender is required to resell its repossessed collateral within a reasonable period of time. If the lender is unable to resell the collateral for the appraised value after a reasonable period of time, it may submit a written notice of the price, terms, and conditions under which it can sell the collateral. VA then may agree to let the lender resell the collateral at the terms and conditions specified, or it may lower its appraisal and require the lender to reoffer the collateral at the lower appraised value.

If the lender is unable to resell the repossessed collateral within 6 months, it may submit a claim and the VA will pay the difference between the appraised value of the collateral and the indebtedness, including the following costs:

1. Any reasonable amount necessary and proper for the maintenance or repair of the security;
2. Payment of accrued taxes, special assessments, or other charges that constitute prior liens;
3. Premiums on fire or other hazard insurance against loss of or damage to the collateral;
4. Court costs in a foreclosure or other proper judicial proceeding involving the collateral;
5. Other expenses reasonably necessary for collecting the debt or repossession or liquidation of the security, including a reasonable sales commission to the retailer or sales broker for resale of the collateral;
6. Reasonable trustee's fees or commissions paid incident to the sale of real property;
7. Reasonable amount of legal services actually performed to exceed 10% of the unpaid indebtedness as of the date of the first uncured default up to $700;[6]

[6] The sum of items 6 and 7 may not exceed $700.

8. The cost of a credit report on the debtor;

9. Any other expense or fee that is approved in advance by the VA.

The lender must notify the VA within 10 days after it has repossessed a property and then proceed within a reasonable time to terminate the debtor's rights in that property.

If a lender fails to take appropriate action within 30 days after a default, after being requested in writing to do so by the VA, or does not prosecute such action with reasonable diligence, the VA may intervene to bring the claim to a conclusion. The VA also may fix a date beyond which no further charges may be included in the computation of the guaranty claim.

Calculation of Guaranty Claim Payment. The amount payable on a claim for the guaranty is the percentage of the loan originally guaranteed times the indebtedness as of the date of the claim but not later than:

1. The date of judgment or of decree of foreclosure; or

2. In nonjudicial foreclosures, the date of publication of the first notice of sale; or

3. In cases in which the security is repossessed without a judgment, decree or foreclosure, the date the lender repossesses the security; or

4. If no security is available, the date of claim but not more than 6 months after the first uncured default.[7]

The claim may also include accrued and unpaid interest up to the date of the claim as determined by the preceding guidelines. For loans guaranteed on or after May 4, 1984, the holder may include accrued interest from the cutoff date to the date of resale or other liquidation. The rate of interest is 4.75% below the contract rate, and the period may not exceed 90 days.

Other Department of Veterans Affairs Guidelines. As with the FHA Title I guidelines, we have attempted to give a fairly detailed explanation of the VA's rules for a guaranteed loan on a manufactured home. However, because we have only paraphrased the regulations, this presentation should be used only as a guide to how the VA's manufactured home loan guaranty program works. One should consult the regulations themselves as well as applicable guidebooks and VA personnel.

Real Property Programs

As noted earlier, when a manufactured home is permanently attached to a foundation, it generally may be financed with a real estate mortgage. Real estate loan

---

[7] Deposits, credits, and escrowed or earmarked funds legally applicable to the indebtedness must be deducted from the loan balance upon which the claim is based.

maturities typically run 30 years, as opposed to the customary 15 to 20 year maturities for personal property manufactured home loans.

Manufactured homes that are financed as real estate are eligible for all of the same programs of the FHA, the VA, the Farmers Home Administration (FmHA), the Government National Mortgage Association (GNMA), the Federal National Mortgage Association (FNMA), and the Federal Home Loan Mortgage Corporation (FHLMC).

Conventional Programs

Conventional real estate mortgage programs are available to purchase manufactured homes that are permanently affixed to a site. Generally, there are requirements that the home be built to the Manufactured Home Construction and Safety Standard, wheels, axles, and trailer hitches are removed, and the home and land are treated as a single real estate entity under state law.

Government-Sponsored Programs

As in a personal property transaction, the FHA, VA, and FmHA will insure/guarantee real property transactions involving manufactured homes. Three such programs are described in the following paragraphs.

FHA Title II Program. Manufactured homes placed on permanent foundations have been eligible for FHA Title II financing since April 6, 1983. To be eligible for Title II mortgage insurance, the mortgage must cover both the manufactured home and its site, the mortgage must have a term of not more than 30 years, and the home must be classified and taxed as real estate.

The FHA requires that the manufactured home be permanently attached to a site-built permanent foundation that meets HUD's Minimum Property Standards. All features of the mortgaged property not addressed by the Manufactured Home Construction and Safety Standards must meet or exceed the applicable requirements of HUD's Minimum Property Standards.

Department of Veterans Affairs Program. On January 24, 1985, the VA amended its regulations to allow the guaranty of permanently sited manufactured home loans. It is the lender's responsibility to obtain the required lien on the property and to ensure that any loan guaranteed by the VA conforms with the applicable regulations. Lenders are also advised to consult VA regulations for general loan provisions and authorized loan purposes.

VA regulations do not specify how the home must be affixed to the land, nor do they give guidelines on foundations. The VA looks to state law as the determinant of whether the manufactured home and the land on which it is installed together constitute a real estate entity.

Farmers Home Loan Program. The FmHA recognizes manufactured homes as eligible for its Section 502 Rural Housing and Section 515 Rural

Rental Housing programs. Homes must be permanently sited on suitable foundations and meet FmHA energy standards, and the home and land must be treated as real estate. The seller of the home must be approved by the FmHA county supervisor and is responsible for installation of the manufactured home and the site development.

The FmHA Rural Housing loan program is intended as a credit source for low- and moderate-income persons who need housing in designated rural areas. Borrowers must have incomes that do not exceed limits set by FmHA and be unable to secure the necessary credit for a home purchase from other sources upon terms and conditions that the applicant could reasonably be expected to fulfill.

Loans may be made for up to the full market value or appraised value of the home and site, although in some cases a minimum 10% down payment is required. Loan maturities cannot exceed 30 years.

FmHA Section 515, Rural Rental Housing Loans, authorizes loans to provide for economically designed and constructed rental and related facilities for eligible occupants, suited to their living requirements. To be eligible, applicants must be unable to obtain the necessary credit from private or cooperative sources on terms and conditions that would enable them to rent the homes for amounts that are within the payment ability of eligible low- and moderate-income, senior citizen, or disabled occupants.

Loan applicants are required to submit site development and foundation installation drawings and specifications to the FmHA. The project must have two or more contiguous sites and homes. The project owner/borrower must be the first owner purchasing the manufactured homes for purposes other than resale. Borrowers may be eligible to receive interest credits if they constitute a nonprofit corporation, consumer cooperative, state or local public agency, or if the borrower is an individual or organization operating on a limited-profit basis.

Secondary Markets for Manufactured Home Loans

Government National Mortgage Association. GNMA has a secondary market program for traditional manufactured home personal property loans. There also are private sales between lenders and brokers and public and privately placed securitizations backed by manufactured home installment sales contracts.

Under the GNMA program, lenders pool loans that are either guaranteed by the VA or insured by the FHA, secure a guarantee from GNMA, then issue GNMA securities. The GNMA program is a modified pass-through program; that is, the lender must pass through to the investor all principal and interest due each month regardless of whether the borrower has made the scheduled payment. Lenders need to remember that only the manufactured home loans that are guaranteed by the VA or insured under the FHA Title I program are eligible for this GNMA program.

FNMA and FHLMC Secondary Market Programs. The FNMA and the FHLMC also recognize manufactured homes treated as real estate as eligible for their secondary market programs. As with the FHA Title II and VA real estate programs for manufactured housing, the manufactured home must be permanently affixed to a suitable foundation and the home and land must be considered real estate under state law. Standard FNMA or FHLMC underwriting guidelines apply as well. Lenders should consult the FNMA and FHLMC seller/servicer guidebooks and regional office for specific guidelines in their area.

FNMA and FHLMC requirements are quite similar. Both require that the homes be built in accordance with the Federal Manufactured Home Construction and Safety Standards. FNMA further stipulates that it will accept loans on multi-section homes located on individual sites, in subdivisions, condominium projects, or planned unit developments (PUDs). A mortgage on a singlesection manufactured home is eligible only if the home is located in a subdivision, condominium project, or PUD. FHLMC makes no distinction between requirements for single-section and multisection home loan eligibility.

The following requirements apply in general to both FNMA and FHLMC programs. To be eligible, the land and home must represent a single real estate transaction under state law, and the financing must be evidenced by a mortgage or deed of trust recorded on the land records. The home and land package must be taxed as real property. In jurisdictions that prohibit real estate taxation of manufactured homes, the lender must notify FNMA before selling them the loan. There must be a title insurance policy that identifies the home as part of the real property, and the policy must insure against any loss that might be incurred if the home were later determined not to be part of the real property.

The mortgage cannot include the financing of furniture, mortgage life insurance, property damage insurance, or any other form of insurance. Financing of kitchen and laundry appliances and carpeting may be included in the mortgage. All foundations, both perimeter and piers, must have footings that are located below the frost line. If piers are used, they should be placed where recommended by the home manufacturer. The foundation system must have been designed by an engineer to meet the soil conditions of the site. Wooden foundations must have been designed and installed in accordance with nationally recommended trade association procedures.

FNMA requires that lenders take into account in their underwriting considerations the marketability and comparability of the individual housing units. In general, each property should be comparable to site-built housing in the local marketplace.

SUMMARY

The information presented in this chapter is an attempt to familiarize anyone who is interested in manufactured housing with how the product is financed. It relies heavily on the FHA and VA programs as examples of such financing, but not because these programs are heavily used by the manufactured housing industry. Actually, they are not. However, these government-sponsored programs are designed with features similar to the more popular conventional programs. Because the rules and procedures are codified in federal regulations, the government-sponsored programs are more easily researched and summarized than the many conventional programs available today from leaders active in the manufactured housing industry.

Manufactured housing is a shelter product with unique origins. As a result of these origins, financing and other considerations involved in purchasing a manufactured home are often different from those encountered in purchasing a site-built home. As manufactured housing evolves and becomes a more widely accepted housing choice, as it continues to do, these differences will begin to evaporate. In the meantime, they should not be used as a barrier to letting manufactured homes fulfill their part of the housing mix that makes up the U.S. housing industry.

CHAPTER 10

ACQUISITION AND DEVELOPMENT FINANCING

Capital must come from somewhere to acquire the land, construct the homesites and amenities, and market the project. With an adequate amount of working capital and/or a good loan program, most well-designed projects will succeed, even survive most unexpected economic downturns. More projects fail as the result of inadequate financing than for any other single reason.

DEBT FINANCING

In most instances, the developer of a manufactured home community will use debt to finance the undertaking. Even if the developer possesses sufficient cash to complete a project without borrowing, the benefits of using other people's money are often greater than using one's own.

There are several approaches the developer can take to finance the land and improvements planned for the community. In addition, the land may be financed alone initially, or together with proposed improvements, on either a construction or permanent loan basis.

LAND ACQUISITION AND CONTROL

If the land is not already controlled by the developer, several methods may be used to gain control, which can be classified in two fundamental categories:

- An option to purchase the land, or
- A contract to purchase the land.

Choosing between an option or contract depends on the developer's objectives as well as the negotiating strength of the parties. In either situation, a developer needs to gain enough time to allow physical and financial plans to materialize. This often requires as much as a year, and perhaps longer if extensive government regulations must be satisfied.

Option

An option to purchase the land gives the prospective buyer, or optionee, the right to buy the land at the negotiated price at any time before the option expiration date.

If the optionee decides later that the site cannot be developed as anticipated, the option can be allowed to expire, and the cost of the option is forfeited. With an assignability provision, the option contract may be sold or assigned to another developer.

Closing on the purchase and sale of the property and starting construction will require the developer to seek additional sources of purchase money. These include (1) cash purchase, (2) seller financing, and (3) various types of joint ventures.

Cash Purchase. The purchase price for unimproved land is generally less when it is purchased for cash. This is because the seller receives the total sales price at the time of the sale and can reinvest it immediately. If the seller's reinvestment opportunities are attractive, the seller will value cash in hand more highly than the promise of a greater amount of cash to be paid over a period of time or at some future date. On the other hand, the purchaser must part with all the cash at the time of the sale. Because the buyer must commit a large amount of cash in such a transaction and cannot use it for other purposes, the "all cash" sale price is frequently negotiated lower than when seller financing is effected. Many sophisticated developers seek financial leverage and rarely purchase raw land for cash.

Seller Financing. A second method for purchasing raw land is the use of financing provided by the seller. The seller takes a down payment on the land, with the balance due over a period of perhaps 5 to 10 years. In virtually all cases, the seller retains title to the land until the balance of the note is paid. If the terms of this type of financing are structured properly, the developer can minimize the amount of up-front capital.

Terms. The terms of seller financing are variable. For instance, the terms of the note could provide for interest-only payments until the landlease community or subdivision is complete and generating revenue. Principal payments could then commence and continue for a period of several years, with a balloon payment coming after the community is in operation for 5 to 7 years. Or the note could be amortized in a series of level payments.

Subordination. Of particular importance to the buyer is the fact that it may be necessary for the seller to subordinate his or her interests to those of the lender providing the development financing. If this cannot be agreed to, it is unlikely that a financial institution will make a development loan on the property.

Installment Sale. A sale financed by the seller will be treated as an installment sale for income tax purposes. Such treatment may reduce the seller's tax bite in the year of the sale, unlike the all-cash sale. This often affects the price the seller is willing to accept for the land, and the price may be raised to accommodate these terms.

Joint Venture. In the case of a joint venture, there may not be an actual sale of the land; rather, the developer and the landowner become partners in a joint venture. The landowner contributes the land and the developer contributes the expertise and development effort; their agreement provides for ownership of the land by their joint venture, with a negotiated division of the profits.

A particularly important aspect of the joint venture is that it eliminates the need for the developer to commit money for land acquisition at the onset of the project and for principal and interest payments during early stages of the project.

A joint venture requires the negotiation of several points between the developer and the landowner, which may include the following:

- *Allocation of the ownership between the two.* Often each takes a 50% ownership position.
- *Development fees.* How much and when will they be paid?
- *Return of the landowner's contribution.* Will the return be based on full value of the land? Will the landowner be allocated the benefit of land appreciation during the development period? Will the funds to pay the landowner come from operating profits or from the sale of the property?
- *Expenses during the development period.* Will the landowner share in them?
- *Form of business organization.* Will the joint venture be a limited or general partnership, or a corporation? How will management decisions be made, and by whom?
- Who will sign on the development loan, if any? the developer and the landowner? or just the developer?

LEASING

Leasing is an approach that eliminates the need for a substantial up-front expenditure for land and the associated interest costs, and may eliminate the need for taking an investor or partner into the venture.

A long-term lease will probably result in a smaller annual cash outflow for the developer than would be the case with seller financing. It is quite likely that operating profits will be greater if the land is leased, but the developer of a community on leased land will not enjoy the anticipated benefits of land appreciation.

FINANCING DEVELOPMENT COSTS

In most instances, the land and the proposed improvements are financed together. The best approach is to tie up the land by using an option or a contract with a contingency clause. Unless the required financing can be arranged, the land is not acquired and little money is lost.

Commercial Lender

The most common source for a development loan is an institutional lender, such as a local commercial bank or savings and loan association. Either type of interim lender is likely to require a commitment letter from another institution to be assured of quick repayment of the principal loaned when construction is completed. The commitment letter also describes the terms of the permanent financing, frequently referred to as a "take out loan."

Consequently, financial arrangements typically are planned in reverse of the development's sequence. That is, a permanent financing commitment is secured first, then construction financing, then land acquisition, and then construction may proceed.

If, however, the land has been financed under a subordinated contract of sale, or contributed to a joint venture, the developer may not want to refinance the land. Instead, the developer might seek intermediate term financing for 5 to 7 years from a third-party lender. This period allows sufficient time for construction and operations to get on stream, which may result in better terms when permanent financing is sought.

HUD FHA 207(M) Loan Guarantee Program

The most active of all government finance programs is the Federal Housing Administration (FHA) 207(m) loan guarantee program.[1] The purpose of the program is to provide good quality housing that will serve the needs of a broad cross section of the rental housing market. Its further purpose is to facilitate the rehabilitation and modernization of existing manufactured home landlease communities.

HUD/FHA insures approved private lenders against losses on mortgages made for the purposes described earlier. Insured mortgages may be used to finance the construction or rehabilitation of manufactured home communities and must be developed on the entire financed site. Funding will not be provided for land for future development. This program is authorized under the National Housing Act as amended October 12, 1976.

[1] Edward Hicks, "How to Get an FHA 207(m) Loan Guarantee." Consultants Resource Group, Inc., Portland, ME, 1993.

Borrowers may be investors, trusts, builders, cooperatives, and others who meet HUD requirements as sponsors. The eligible property must be a community of eight or more homesites, located in an area approved by HUD in which market conditions demonstrate a need for such housing.

The use and design of the development site for an intended manufactured home landlease community should not adversely affect adjacent properties. The site should be reasonably accessible to shopping centers or neighborhood stores and sources of employment, and to parks and schools if families with children are anticipated as residents.

The property must be held fee simple or on a leasehold basis for 99 years or more as specified by HUD. The mortgage accepted for insurance must cover a property or project that is economically sound. A project may consist either of homesites to be built or an existing community to be rehabilitated.

Projects may vary widely in layout, size, and design, depending on the type of market to be served. They must be built in conformity with Minimum Design Standards for Mobile Home Parks (HUD Handbook 4940.5). All other local, state, and federal regulations and guidelines must be met, such as zoning regulations.

The mortgage amount cannot exceed the lesser of (1) 90% of HUD's estimate of the value of the community after the construction of improvements or completion of substantial rehabilitation, or (2) an amount equal to $9,000 per homesite (this sum may be increased to 210% in high-cost areas).

The maximum term for a HUD loan is 3 years for construction, plus 40 years or 75% of the remaining economic life of the project for the permanent portion of the loan. If the community does not conform to anticipated future development of the area, the term cannot exceed 20 years.

The maximum interest rate is as determined at the time of the loan by HUD, usually reflecting the Government National Mortgage Association (GNMA) bond rates, plus mortgage insurance and service fees.

The developer's minimum equity is usually 10%, with exceptions for sponsors showing a substantial equity in the land value.

Equal monthly payments toward principal and interest are made, with an amortization schedule of up to 40 years for a new development and not more than 75% of the remaining life for rehabilitation projects.

The loan security is the land and improvements. Except for attesting to the truthfulness of the application, the borrower does not have to sign personally on the note; and in the case of a default on the terms of the associated note and financing agreement, there is no borrower liability.

Mortgagee Sources.   With the guarantee of the U.S. government on the loan, a large number of lenders and investors are willing to provide funding through a HUD-approved mortgagee. All approved loan guarantees are fundable. Loans under $750,000 are more difficult to place and may result in higher mortgagee and broker fees. Larger loans, those over $3,000,000 may be eligible for lower points and interest rates through direct negotiation with the mortgagee and lender or investor.

Staff Support. It may be difficult to obtain information from the local HUD field office serving the area in which the property or project is to be located, because the staff may not be equipped to teach the program details. It is suggested that a mortgagee or mortgage broker who is experienced in HUD multifamily loan guarantee programs be consulted for program details. The 207(m) program is not currently available for the delegated processing program as are the majority of other multifamily programs, such as the 221(d4), the 223f, and the 232 programs. As a result, the local HUD staff provides a direct endorsement of all 207(m) applications for site appraisal and market analysis (SAMA) letters, applications for conditional commitment, or applications for firm commitment. Except for an occasional congressionally mandated program that may take priority, the HUD staff will process applications when received, in a timely manner, under statutory scheduling.

Application Fee. The application fee is $3.00 per $1,000 of the loan amount, paid to HUD in three increments, over a nominal 4 to 6-month period. During the SAMA letter process, primarily used for new projects, the market rents, land value, project absorption rate, and estimated rate of return will be evaluated by HUD. The conditional commitment application contains virtually everything required for a loan closing, with the exception of completed engineering drawings and the negotiated agreement with contractors. The firm commitment application is essentially the same as the conditional, with the addition of the completed engineering drawings and the signed contractor's agreement.

Because of the complexity of the program and the length of processing, mortgage brokers assisting a developer with a loan commitment application and mortgagees frequently also charge consulting fees associated with preparation of feasibility studies and compilation of required documentation. The broker and the mortgagee may reimburse the developer these fees from allowable expenses that may be included in the funded loan amount.

In years past, HUD required approvals for any rent rate increases. As of 1984, although a yearly rent roll must be submitted to HUD, this preapproval requirement has been eliminated from the program. A technical requirement still exists for the sponsor to provide HUD with rent rolls on an annual basis.

Leased Land. If the land is held under a 99-year lease, a development project may be eligible for mortgage guarantee insurance. Special provisions are made for leases of shorter duration when the land is owned by a legally constituted American Indian tribe.

Loan Terms. The terms of FHA 207(m) loans are as follows:

- Up to 3 years construction period
- Up to 40 years permanent loan amortization
- Fixed rate for the loan term
- 90% of replacement cost

- 80% of land value
- Funding on 10% builder's and sponsor's profit
- Fully assumable when the property is resold
- No personal guarantees required

Restrictions.   The restrictions on FHA 207(m) loans are as follows:

- Must not prohibit families, unless designated as an "elderly" project
- May not legally require home buyers to buy a home from a specific retailer
- Will not fund off-site improvements, or excess land
- Must comply with Davis-Bacon Act
- Limited to $9,000 per site, unless in an approved "high cost" area, where up to 210% additional funding may be approved
- Must provide HUD with annual rent roll
- May not subordinate the HUD mortgage to other debt
- Must use HUD-approved contractors, and must pay prevailing wages, under provisions of the federal Davis-Bacon Act.

LOAN PACKAGING

To get a permanent lender interested, a developer must prepare a loan package. Preparing the loan request is an extremely important aspect of putting together the financial arrangements.

Although the information supplied to the lender must convey the factual and truthful financial and economic details of the manufactured home community and the proposed borrower, the information should be packaged in an appealing way. In other words, the developer must sell the project, and a properly prepared loan proposal does just that. The developer should bear in mind, as the request package is prepared, that it will pass through the hands of several different persons—the lending officer, the credit analyst, the loan committee, and perhaps even the financial institution's executive committee. Providing appropriate information to all these persons in a single report requires that the package contain complete information that is easily read and understood. One way of accomplishing this is to provide summary pages followed by more detailed information, so that the report progresses from the general to the specific. Some of the loan reviewers will want to study the proposal in detail; others will be content with a summary presentation.

Loan Request

A typical loan request might follow this outline:

- Executive summary of the project
- Table of contents of the request

- Evidence of site control
- Evidence of utility availability
- Evidence of site zoning and land use controls
- Project design and economic analysis
- Project and site description
- Details of financing request
- Payment and draw schedule
- Area vacancy factors
- Area competitive projects
- Rent rate, and sales price surveys
- Absorption rate analysis
- Buyer income/expense analysis
- Developer's experience and credentials
- Overall site plan
- State, county, and local area maps
- Review of environmental status
- Review of archeological status
- Neighborhood map
- Land value appraisal (R-41C for S & Ls)
- Personal financial statements and last 2 years' personal income tax returns for sponsors or investors and partners with more than 10% interest in sponsor entity

A properly prepared proposal begins with an artist's rendering of the proposed community; the lender wants to know how the development will look. A quality rendering conveys the desired positive image of the new community. On the page facing the rendering, it is a good idea to place a one-page executive summary of the development and financing request. The page should contain several two or three-sentence paragraphs that emphasize the highlights of the proposed community:

- *Project:* A brief description of the size, number of homesites, and amenities
- *Demand:* The level of demand for homesites in the area
- *Proximity:* Ease with which lender can monitor progress of investment
- *Financial:* Expected financial characteristics of interest to the lender, such as anticipated debt coverage ratio and break-even occupancy percentage the first year
- *Amount:* The total amount of financing requested
- *Location:* Relative to major highways, employment centers, schools, shopping, and so forth.
- *Highlights:* Unique and particularly desirable features, if any, of the proposed community

Pro-Forma Operating Statement

- Projected gross income
- Vacancy and collection factors
- Ancillary income projections
- Adjusted gross income
- Operating expenses
- Net operating income
- Debt service (as projected, based on the requested loan)
- Cash flow (before taxes)

Project Cost. The entire hard cost, based on an engineer's estimate or contractor's bid, should be detailed. A phased development schedule, if applicable, should be shown.

Land Ownership or Control. Describe the status of land ownership or control, with particular attention to details if the land has been acquired by sales contract or contributed by a joint-venture partner.

Scheduling Information. Projected scheduling at a nominal rate for construction and sell out or fill-up should be described.

Information on Sales Programs. If homes are to be sold in conjunction with the community fill-up operations, a complete projected operating statement and sales operating budget should also be included in the loan request, including:

- Source of and amount of inventory (floor plan) financing
- Number and description of model homes and pricing
- Sales-related operating expenses
- Marketing budgets
- Commission schedules
- Projected sales rates

Homebuyer Financing. Homebuyer home-financing programs that are currently available in the market should be described here. Also include a summary of financing terms and conditions, as well as names of current lenders.

The information should be presented in a logical order. The preceding outline is described more fully in the following paragraphs. When preparing a report, however, the sequence is not as important as providing a complete report that is easy to read and understand.

Detailed Project Description. A reasonably detailed project description follows the summary page. The type of community, acreage, topography, description of homesite improvements, streets, gutters, sewer system, water distribution system, common area facilities, and amenities are included in this description.

Finance Request. The specific financing request is next. This request should be straightforward, the amount of the loan desired and the minimum acceptable maturity of the loan stated clearly.

Of course, the rate of interest and the term of the loan are subject to negotiation, but a minimum amortization period and maximum periodic payment will be critical to the financial success of the community. Any other requirements that are essential, such as the duration of the financing commitment, prepayment options, right of assumption, and maximum occupancy levels for fully funding the loan, should be clearly set forth.

Long-Term Cash Flow Pro Forma. Include a summarized pro forma operating statement for a 5- to 10-year period. The principal purpose of this statement is to convince the lender that the repayment of the loan is scheduled and assured. The pro forma operating statement should forecast realistic increases in rent and operating expenses during the term of the loan so that the lender can compare net operating income during the life of the loan with the planned loan payment.

If the net operating income is forecasted to increase during this period, the lender's increasing security can be demonstrated. A break-even occupancy ratio calculation also can be used to demonstrate improving loan security over time.

Project Cost. The next section of the proposal presents a detailed statement of the anticipated project's cost. The cost of the raw land, common-area improvements such as laundry rooms and game rooms, streets, gutters, the sewer and water distribution system, design and planning fees, legal fees, closing costs and financing fees must all be set forth clearly. A lender will know what items should appear on the list, as well as appropriate cost levels. Leaving out items or providing artificially low cost estimates will raise unnecessary questions and stimulate doubt. Present the brightest and most realistic, comprehensive picture as possible. Do not try to be too conservative. If the lender applies reduction factors to sales rates, profit margins, or pricing, let the lender be the one who does so. Trying to make the proposal too conservative will result in the lender's applying reduction factors to an already reduced pro forma cash flow analysis. Such manipulations will not help a developer obtain the desired loan size or terms.

Market Survey. The developer introduces the results of a thorough local market survey. The case must be made that demand for a manufactured home community exists, and that the projected rents are reasonable and collectable. The lender needs information about the level of occupancy in other similar communities, as well as accurate information about growth of the targeted population segment. In many cases, there may be little or no net household growth. In these instances, it will be necessary to demonstrate targeted market segments that do not rely on household growth, for example, empty nesters, conversions from apartment dwellers, retirees, and so on. If the developer is approaching a lender outside the immediate area in which the new community is to be located, a description of the local area's economy must be included. A brief summary will suffice for a local lender.

Developer's Credentials.   The proposal generally concludes with a recitation of the developer's credentials to undertake the development project. This section includes all relevant previous development and construction experience, other significant business experience, and personal financial statements. The financial statements show the lender that there are sufficient working capital resources to carry any negative cash flows from community operations until it reaches a break-even and satisfactory level of occupancy.

APPRAISAL OR FEASIBILITY STUDY

An "as built" appraisal or feasibility study of the project is a valuable tool to assist the lender in making a favorable decision regarding the viability of the marketplace and the ability of the project to meet market needs. Additional credibility is frequently given to the study if it is performed by an outside appraiser or consulting firm with proven experience in manufactured home community development. The more professional in appearance and thorough in content, the greater value the lender will give to the study. Gone are the days of presenting a development plan on the back of the famous cocktail napkin. The massive failures of developments in the 1990s have taught lenders not to be as inclined to reply only on a developer's past reputation, but to look much more carefully than ever before to current and anticipated market conditions and how the proposed project is structured to meet them.

LOAN COMMITMENT

The goal of an application for development financing is to receive a lender's commitment. This usually comes in the form of a letter, with attached and sometimes lengthy conditions. The lender agrees to lend a certain sum of money at a specified variable rate of interest for a particular period, based on the presentation at the closing of specific documentation. Typical conventional loan terms may provide for up to 70% or 80% of the raw land, plus hard construction costs. Unless there is a unusually low loan-to-vale ratio or the borrower has a relatively high land equity, and excepting certain engineering costs, soft costs such as interest, operating expenses, marketing, and so on are not usually funded by institutional lenders.

The loan term is virtually always less than 3 years and usually requires some kind of construction loan "take out" or permanent loan commitment before funding. Construction lenders need assurance that they will be "taken out" on their loans once construction is complete. Many construction lenders are not interested in becoming long-term lenders. In the case of a subdivision or condominium type of project, evidence of substantial presales may be required. Often, the commitment will also include a commitment for permanent or construction loan "take out" financing, based on a predetermined level of occupancy or percentage of homesite sales. Typically, the lender charges 1 to 2 points of the commited loan amount as an origination fee, at 2% over the prime rate. Construction loan interest rates are almost always floating rates, whereas permanent or construction loan "take out" loan rates may be fixed for 5 to 7 years or longer, with a 25 or 30-year payment amortization schedule.

Some items in the commitment letter will concern important but routine legal matters, such as title insurance and zoning compliance. In addition, there are other important points, such as the terms of prepaying the loan, assumption of the loan, duration of commitment, and the fee for issuing the commitment letter.

The developer may insist on some provisions for negotiating an extension of the commitment in case of unforeseen circumstances. When the community is complete, the development loan will probably be replaced by permanent financing.

LOAN DRAW SCHEDULE

The lender will specify when funds will be advanced to the developer during the development period and the details of any required property inspections during this time. Typically, money advances will follow the completion of certain construction stages. Retentions of up to 10% of the completed work may be required for various contractors and subcontractors, to assure the quality and timeliness of their work and materials. Usually, the lender requires that development begin by a certain date and be completed by a certain date. Before agreeing to the terms of the commitment on this point, the developer should be sure that this requirement can be fulfilled.

PERMANENT FINANCING

Although permanent loans are negotiable, terms for manufactured home communities typically correspond to those of other income property developments such as shopping centers and multifamily housing projects. Long-term interest rates are usually higher than for single-family housing by about .5 to 1%. The rate may be variable or may be fixed for shorter 5 to 7 year term loans. Because the amount borrowed will be limited to some percentage of the estimated market value as of completion, an "as built" appraisal as of completion (to R-41c standards), showing the discounted "wholesale" value, is almost always required.

The loan usually requires some amortization of the principal, from 20 to 30 years, most often 25 years. It is important to negotiate the availability of money from that lender when the loan matures, so that the loan really becomes a roll-over, without a foreclosure-threatening balloon payment.

If personal liability is of concern to the borrower, it is crucial to negotiate the amount of liability or an exculpation agreement at the outset.

INVENTORY FINANCING (FLOOR PLAN)

As manufactured homes are generally financed as personal property, the lender making the inventory or wholesale "floor plan" financing (sometimes referred to as "flooring" of inventory), must assure an adequate security interest in the new homes. Floor plan financing may be provided by a lender to assure the first right of refusal to retailer-originated homebuyer financing loans. Other lenders may provide only floor plan financing and are not interested in obtaining homebuyer loans.

At the time of home shipment from the factory, the lender is issued the manufacturer's certificate of origin (MSO) or (C of O), even though the retailer is named thereon as purchaser. In most states, a home may not be registered to the homebuyer or conveyed as an improvement to real property by the tax assessor without the endorsement of the MSO over to the retailer. The MSO is held by the floor plan lender until the retailer pays off the home, either through sale to a purchaser or through flooring reductions. The lender may also secure an interest in the inventories home by filing a UCC-1 form with the county in which the home is located.

The retailer usually signs a "flooring agreement," which specifies a maximum line of credit for purchases. Some floor plan lenders will allow the retailer to exceed this line if the unit being ordered from the factory is for a specific prequalified customer, and was ordered to the customer's specifications. This is referred to as a "factory order" and is frequently differentiated from the retailer's normal stock order.

The flooring agreement also specifies the interest rate for the line of credit and includes a provision for modification if the interest rate is to be adjusted up or down in the future.

CURTAILMENTS

A provision for the "curtailment" of principal is also agreed upon, whereby the retailer agrees to a scheduled reduction in principal over a predetermined time period. This is designed to reduce the lender's risk of a devalued short term loan due to inherent depreciation in a manufactured home not yet sold. Of course, this has not been the case for many years, and except for exceptional wear and tear, the retail value of a retailer's stock is almost always higher than the amount for which it was purchased.

The floor plan lender performs a monthly "flooring check" by physically inspecting the inventory, so as to be assured that the home has not been sold or removed from the inventory without the lender's knowledge and consent. Such an illegal act on the part of the sales operation would put it "out of trust" with the lender, under the terms of a lender's originated, individual home or blanket trust agreement for the payoff of principal on the inventory when sold or conveyed to a homebuyer. Homesite accessories, such as skirting, awnings, porches, and sheds, are not usually floorable. Some lenders in some states will include the freight costs of shipping the home from the factory to the sales lot, if included in the invoice by the manufacturer.

If homes are being marketed within a new community, to protect the value of the model center beyond 1 year a developer must negotiate an extended curtailment schedule with the lender, taking the term through the projected sales of the model homes. Otherwise, it may be necessary to sell a model center each year and establish a new one with a new home. Under some circumstances, it may be possible to negotiate an agreement with a manufacturer, especially when the project uses one manufacturer exclusively, to provide floor plan financing for the model center.

FINANCING IMPORTANCE

Assuring an adequately flexible financing program is critical to a development. All manufactured home communities depend on financing of one kind or another, from financing land acquisition and homesite development costs through floor plan financing and homebuyer loans. Manufactured home community developers with previous track records with a lender will have it easiest; those with little or no previous experience will have a difficult time obtaining good financing. Previous experience as a business person, with a well-presented, accurate, thoroughly documented business plan and feasibility study, will go a long way to ensuring an acceptable loan program for the new manufactured housing community developer.

CHAPTER 11

CONSTRUCTION PHASE

Prior to the start of construction of a manufactured home community, the developer should have all required approvals in place and be cognizant of all assessments and impact fees associated with the project. The contract documents and scheduling of the project completion time should be clearly understood and agreed to by both developer and contractor. The developer should see that adequate construction inspection will be available to ensure that the work will be properly performed and that adequate testing of workmanship and materials will be implemented.

After the contractors' bids have been received and analyzed, a final feasibility review should be performed. This is the last step before beginning construction of the manufactured home community.

PERMITS AND APPROVALS

Verification of all permits and approvals must be obtained prior to the start of construction. The necessary permits and approvals for a project are discussed in Chapter 8, and the following is a list of those that are normally required.

- Soil erosion control
- Storm water management
- Tree clearing permit
- Environmental Protection Agency (EPA)
- Department of Environmental Regulation (DER)
- Health department

- Mining permit (excavation)
- Building permit (city, county)
- Coast Guard
- Corps of Engineers

IMPACT FEES AND CONCURRENCY

It is necessary for the developer to thoroughly understand and account for information on impact fees and concurrency early in the project and to accurately assess the influence on project feasibility. If impact and concurrency fees[1] have not been paid prior to construction, and if the developer does not have the option of paying these fees as homes are placed, then this payment may be required prior to starting construction.

CONTRACT DOCUMENTS

Following is a list of the most commonly required contract documents:

- Instruction to Bidders
- Bid Form
- General Conditions
- Special Conditions
- Technical Specifications
- Forms
- Contract

The contract documents outline and clarify what is expected of the developer and the contractor during the construction of a manufactured home community. The contract documents are referenced in the contract between the developer and contractor and serve as the guidebook or instructions for resolving misunderstandings and disputes that may arise during the construction process. The following paragraphs discuss the sections contained within the contract documents.

Instruction to Bidders

The Instruction to Bidders outlines for the contractor how the bids are to be prepared and how the developer intends to award the contract. It conveys to the contractor when the bids are due; whether a bid bond is required; whether the bids,

---

[1] Impact fee is charged to a development to pay its share of an existing community infrastructure. Concurrency fee is the cost of new community infrastructure needed to support a new development.

when received, will be opened privately or publicly; the cost, method of submission, and address where specifications and plans may be obtained; the completion date or how the amount of time the contractor has to complete the job will be determined; and what penalties or liquidated damages will be assessed against the contractor if the job is not completed on time. Additional information includes whether the bid will be a unit price, a lump sum, or a combination of both.

Bid Form or Proposal Form

The Bid Form allows each contractor to submit cost estimates for developing the project in exactly the same manner as his or her competitors, so that the developer can assess and compare the proposals of a number of contractors fairly and on an equal basis.

Lump Sum Bid. In submitting a lump sum bid, a contractor states an amount of money that he or she is proposing as compensation to perform all work outlined or described in the plans and specifications, without regard to quantity or measurement. An entire manufactured home community could be bid on a lump sum basis for completing it in accordance with plans and specifications.

Unit Price Bid. In a unit price bid, the contractor bids an amount per unit price, such as per linea foot, square yard, or cubic yard. The contractor's total bid price for each item is the product of the unit price times the estimated quantity, and the total price is a summation of all the extensions of the unit price times the quantity.

The proposal form can be set up so that the entire manufactured home community is bid by one general contractor, or it can be set up to be bid by a number of subcontractors. The proposal form is divided into the different construction disciplines, and a large construction company functioning as a general contractor may have the capabilities in-house to perform all the various sections of work or may subcontract some work sections to other contractors. There is usually an advantage to having a general contractor do all the work, as this requires less coordination effort by the developer. There are times when the developer can get considerably lower cost bids by awarding the work to numerous smaller subcontractors. The savings should be enough to compensate the developer for the additional costs of coordination and liability incurred by functioning as a general contractor.

The contract documents often specify a completion date. However, it is sometimes prudent to let the contractor specify a completion date or a total number of working days as part of the bid.

General Conditions

General Conditions usually consist of 20 to 40 pages of boilerplate material. This verbiage describes the legal relationship between the contractor and the developer and spells out the responsibilities of both parties. Following are some specific items of General Conditions that merit explanation.

Bid Bond. The bid bond is supplied to the developer by the contractor, guaranteeing that if chosen as low bidder, the contractor will enter the site and perform the work as agreed to and stipulated in the contract documents.

Payment Performance Bond. The payment performance bond is supplied by the contractor to the developer, guaranteeing that the project will be completed and all materials and subcontractors will be properly and fully paid. This provision is designed to minimize the opportunity for mechanics' liens to be filed against the property.

Special Conditions

The Special Conditions outline and describe specific conditions and requirements peculiar to the project. The Special Conditions modify and clarify both the General Conditions and Technical Specifications. For example, the Technical Specifications would have material or pipe specifications for all pipes to be used on a project. The Special Conditions, however, would refer to the exact pipe material to be used on the project. More explicitly, the Special Conditions could specify that a particular governmental agency with jurisdiction over the project does not allow the burning of the cleared and grubbed material for tree removal. This section could state that the cleared material must be hauled off-site and not allowed to be burned on-site.

Technical Specifications

Technical Specifications are generally boilerplate, describing all the materials and methods that may be used in the construction process. As mentioned earlier, Special Conditions specify which particular materials or construction methods described in the Technical Specifications are to be used.

Forms

A number of forms are used to control the construction process. The Notice of Award (Fig. 11.1) informs the contractor that he or she has been selected and awarded the contract. The Notice to Proceed (Fig. 11.2) puts the contractor on notice to enter the site and start construction by a specified date. The Change Order (Fig. 11.3) is used to decrease or increase the dollar amount of the contract, based on unexpected changes that arise during the construction period or on the developer's decision to modify the scope of the project. Approval of Payment (Fig. 11.4) is used by the contractor to request periodic payment, usually on a monthly basis. The Certificate of Substantial Completion (Fig. 11.5) is used to substantiate the point at which the contractor has met all obligations to the developer and has completed the project. The Lien Waiver is a form completed by the contractor and submitted to the developer or construction lender, stipulating that all subcontractors and material suppliers have been paid. This ensures that after the contractor receives final payment, the developer will not be obligated

NOTICE OF AWARD

Dated _____, 19____

TO: _____
(BIDDER)

ADDRESS: _____

_____

_____

PROJECT _____

OWNER's CONTRACT NO. _____

CONTRACT FOR _____
(Insert name of Contract as it appears in the Bidding Documents)

You are notified that your Bid dated _____, 19____ for the above Contract has been considered. You are the apparent Successful Bidder and have been awarded a contract for_____

_____

_____
(Indicate total Work, alternates or sections or Work awarded)

The Contract Price of your contract is_____

_____Dollars ($).

[Insert appropriate data in re Unit Prices. Change language for Cost-Plus contracts.]

_____ copies of each of the proposed Contract Documents (except Drawings) accompany this Notice of Award. ____ sets of the Drawings will be delivered separately or otherwise made available to you immediately.

You must comply with the following conditions precedent within fifteen days of the date of this Notice of Award, that is by

_____, 199____.

1. You must deliver to the OWNER ____ fully executed counterparts of the Agreement including all the Contract Documents. This includes the triplicate sets of Drawings. Each of the Contract Documents must bear your signature on (the cover) (every) page (pages _____).

2. You must deliver with the executed Agreement the Contract Security (Bonds) as specified in the Instructions to Bidders (paragraph 18), General Conditions (paragraph 5.1) and Supplementary Conditions (paragraph SC-5.1).

EJCDC No. 1910–22 (1990 Edition)
Prepared by the Engineers Joint Contract Documents Committee and endorsed by The Associated General Contractors of America.

FIG. 11.1 Reprinted with permission of the National Society of Professional Engineers.

3. (List other conditions precedents)

_____

_____

_____

_____

_____

_____

_____

_____

_____

_____

_____

Failure to comply with these conditions within the time specified will entitle OWNER to consider your bid in default, to annul this Notice of Award and to declare your Bid Security forfeited.

Within ten days after you comply with the above conditions, OWNER will return to you one fully signed counterpart of the Agreement with the Contract Documents attached.

_____

(OWNER)

By: _____

(AUTHORIZED SIGNATURE)

_____

(TITLE)

ACCEPTANCE OF AWARD

_____

(CONTRACTOR)

By: _____

(AUTHORIZED SIGNATURE)

_____

(TITLE)

_____

(DATE)

COPY to ENGINEER
(Use Certified Mail,
Return Receipt Requested)

FIG. 11.1 *(Continued)*

NOTICE TO PROCEED

Dated _____ , 19 _____

TO: _____
(CONTRACTOR)

ADDRESS: _____

_____

PROJECT _____

OWNER's CONTRACT NO. _____

CONTRACT FOR _____

_____
(Insert name of Contract as it appears in the Bidding Documents)

You are notified that the Contract Times under the above contract will commence to run on _____ , 19 _____ . By that date, you are to start performing your obligations under the Contract Documents. In accordance with Article 3 of the Agreement the dates of Substantial Completion and completion and readiness for final payment are _____ , 19 _____ and _____ , 19 _____ .

Before you may start any Work at the site, paragraph 2.7 of the General Conditions provides that you and Owner must each deliver to the other (with copies to ENGINEER and other identified additional insureds) certificates of insurance which each is required to purchase and maintain in accordance with the Contract Documents.

Also before you may start any Work at the site, you must _____
(add other requirements)

_____

_____

_____

_____
(OWNER)

By: _____
(AUTHORIZED SIGNATURE)

_____
(TITLE)

ACCEPTANCE OF AWARD

By: _____
(CONTRACTOR)

_____
(AUTHORIZED SIGNATURE)

_____
(TITLE)

_____
(DATE)

Copy to ENGINEER
(Use Certified Mail,
Return Receipt Requested)

EJCDC No. 1910-23 (1990 Edition)
Prepared by the Engineers Joint Contract Documents Committee and endorsed by The Associated General Contractors of America.

FIG. 11.2   Reprinted with permission of the National Society of Professional Engineers.

CHANGE ORDER

(Instructions on reverse side)   No._____

PROJECT ....

DATE OF ISSUANCE .... EFFECTIVE DATE ....

OWNER ....

OWNER's Contract No. ....

CONTRACTOR .... ENGINEER ....

You are directed to make the following changes in the Contract Documents.

Description:

Reason for Change Order:

Attachments: (List documents supporting change)

CHANGE IN CONTRACT PRICE:	CHANGE IN CONTRACT TIMES:
Original Contract Price	Original Contract Times
$ _____	Substantial Completion: _____ Ready for final payment: _____ _{days or dates}
Net changes from previous Change Orders No. ____ to No. ____	Net change from previous Change Orders No. ____ to No. ____
$ _____	_____ _{days}
Contract Price prior to this Change Order	Contract Times prior to this Change Order
$ _____	Substantial Completion: _____ Ready for final payment: _____ _{days or dates}
Net Increase (decrease) of this Change Order	Net Increase (decrease) of this Change Order
$ _____	_____ _{days}
Contract Price with all approved Change Orders	Contract Times with all approved Change Orders
$ _____	Substantial Completion: _____ Ready for final payment: _____ _{days or dates}

RECOMMENDED: APPROVED: ACCEPTED:

By: _____   By: _____   By: _____
     Engineer (Authorized Signature)   Owner (Authorized Signature)   Contractor (Authorized Signature)

Date: _____   Date: _____   Date: _____

EJCDC No. 1910-8-B (1990 Edition)
Prepared by the Engineers Joint Contract Documents Committee and endorsed by The Associated General Contractors of America.

FIG. 11.3 Reprinted with permission of the National Society of Professional Engineers.

APPLICATION FOR PAYMENT NO. _____

To _____ (OWNER)

Contract for _____ .

OWNER's Contract No. _____ . ENGINEER's Project No. _____ .

For Work accomplished through the date of _____ .

ITEM	CONTRACTOR's Schedule of Values			Work Completed	
	Unit Price	Quantity	Amount	Quantity	Amount
	$		$		$
Total (Orig. Contract) C.O. No. 1 C.O. No. 2			$		$

Accompanying Documentation:

_____

_____

_____

_____

GROSS AMOUNT DUE .... $ _____
LESS ____ % RETAINAGE .... $ _____
AMOUNT DUE TO DATE .... $ _____
LESS PREVIOUS PAYMENTS .... $ _____
AMOUNT DUE THIS APPLICATION .... $ _____

CONTRACTOR'S Certification:

The undersigned CONTRACTOR certifies that: (1) all previous progress payments received from OWNER on account of Work done under the Contract referred to above have been applied to discharge in full all obligations of CONTRACTOR incurred in connection with Work covered by prior Applications for Payment numbered 1 through _____ inclusive; (2) title to all Work, materials and equipment incorporated in said Work or otherwise listed in or covered by this Application for Payment will pass to OWNER at time of payment free and clear of all liens, claims, security interest and encumbrances (except such as are covered by Bond acceptable to OWNER indemnifying OWNER against any such lien, claim, security interest or encumbrance); and (3) all Work covered by this Application for Payment is in accordance with the Contract Documents and not *defective* as that term is defined in the Contract Documents.

Dated _____ , 19 _____   _____

                                                        CONTRACTOR

                                    By _____
                                              (Authorized Signature)

Payment of the above AMOUNT DUE THIS APPLICATION is recommended.

Dated _____ , 19 _____   _____

                                                        ENGINEER

                                    By _____
                                              (Authorized Signature)

EJCDC No. 1910–8-E (1990 Edition)
Prepared by the Engineers Joint Contract Documents Committee and endorsed by The Associated General Contractors of America.

FIG. 11.4   Reprinted with permission of the National Society of Professional Engineers.

CERTIFICATE OF SUBSTANTIAL COMPLETION

PROJECT ....

DATE OF ISSUANCE ....

OWNER ....

OWNER's Contract No. ....

CONTRACTOR ....   ENGINEER ....

This Certificate of Substantial Completion applies to all Work under the Contract Documents or to the following specified parts thereof:

TO ....
OWNER

And To ....
CONTRACTOR

The Work to which this Certificate applies has been inspected by authorized representatives of OWNER, CONTRACTOR and ENGINEER, and that Work is hereby declared to be substantially complete in accordance with the Contract Documents on

....
DATE OF SUBSTANTIAL COMPLETION

A tentative list of items to be completed or corrected is attached hereto. This list may not be all-inclusive, and the failure to include an item in it does not alter the responsibility of CONTRACTOR to complete all the Work in accordance with the Contract Documents. The items in the tentative list shall be completed or corrected by CONTRACTOR within _____ days of the above date of Substantial Completion.

EJCDC No. 1910–8-D (1990 Edition)
Prepared by the Engineers Joint Contract Documents Committee and endorsed by The Associated General Contractors of America.

FIG. 11.5   Reprinted with permission of the National Society of Professional Engineers.

From the date of Substantial Completion the responsibilities between OWNER and CONTRACTOR for security, operation, safety, maintenance, heat, utilities, insurance and warranties and guarantees shall be as follows:

RESPONSIBILITIES:

OWNER: _____

              _____

              _____

CONTRACTOR: _____

                      _____

                      _____

The following documents are attached to and made a part of this Certificate:

[For items to be attached see definition of Substantial Completion as supplemented and other specifically noted conditions precedent to achieving Substantial Completion as required by Contract Documents.]

This certificate does not constitute an acceptance of Work not in accordance with the Contract Documents nor is it a release of CONTRACTOR's obligation to complete the Work in accordance with the Contract Documents.

Executed by ENGINEER on   .... , 19 .....

                 ....
                          ENGINEER

        By: ....
                       (Authorized Signature)

CONTRACTOR accepts this Certificate of Substantial Completion on .... , 19 .....

                 ....
                       CONTRACTOR

        By: ....

OWNER accepts this Certificate of Substantial Completion on .... , 19 .....

                 ....
                        OWNER

        By: ....
                       (Authorized Signature)

FIG. 11.5 *(Continued)*

to a subcontractor to pay for work or materials that were supplied to the general contractor.

Contract

The developer should consult an attorney to draft a contract between the developer and each contractor. In addition to price, it should include reference to the plans, contract documents, and specifications, clearly making them part of the contract.

THE BIDDING PROCESS AND CONTRACTOR SELECTION

The Bidding Process

The bidding process varies, depending on the availability and qualifications of contractors and the developer's knowledge and relationship with the contractors in the area. If the developer is not negotiating directly with a specific contractor but, rather, is asking for bids from various contractors, it is recommended that the developer receive a minimum of three bids. Developers often use local construction trade publications, inserting an advertisement for bids or Instruction to Bidders so that all contractors in the area learn of the project. Alternately, specific contractors may be asked to submit bids. The Instruction to Bidders will state the time, place, and other information necessary for a contractor to properly submit a qualifying bid. The contractor should also be advised through the Instruction to bidders whether the bid will be sealed, opened only by the developer, or opened publicly and read aloud. The contractors should be given sufficient time to prepare bids; a minimum of 1 month is normally adequate. During the bidding process, the contractors often find discrepancies between the plans and the contract documents or may suggest changes to the plans that would save the developer money. Where obvious changes are needed, an addendum is submitted to all bidders, outlining the changes so that all bids received will be on an equal basis.

Contractor Selection

The developer normally selects the lowest qualified bid submitted by a contractor able to complete the project in the required time. It is not always to the developer's benefit to select the lowest bidder. If low bidder is not qualified or has made an obvious mistake and the developer suspects that the contractor cannot complete the project based on the bid submitted, it would be prudent of the developer to select another contractor. The fact that a contractor can supply a performance payment bond to the developer is not in itself a guarantee that the project will be finished properly and in a timely manner. There are many situations in which contractors have gone broke on a project and a year or two passes before the developer can get the bonding company to complete the project. In many cases expensive legal action is required to make the bonding company honor its obligations. The developer should also receive an engineer's estimate to provide a guide in evaluating the contractors' bids.

UTILITIES

The utility companies generally involved in the construction process are electric, gas, telephone, and cable television. All too often construction is delayed owing to poor coordination with one of the utility companies because it has not scheduled construction crews to enter the site at the proper time or has not preordered materials. Many such delays can be avoided if the utility companies are contacted during the engineering phase and continuous liaison is maintained throughout the engineering and bidding processes.

The utility companies normally would not enter the site to start work until the sewer, water system, storm sewer, and grading have been completed. However, these companies should enter the site and complete their work prior to the completion of fine grading or turf establishment. Utility companies are notoriously poor at restoration of the site after their trenching and backfill. By getting them on-site to complete work prior to the fine grading and turf establishment, additional costs and disagreements can be avoided.

SCHEDULING

The project manager coordinates the scheduling of all entities involved in the construction phase, including the contractor, the surveyor, the inspectors, the utilities, and the lender. Total project scheduling can then be converted to a bar chart or, better yet, a project evaluation and review technique (PERT) or critical path method (CPM) chart that shows the interrelationships and timing of all entities involved in the project. The CPM or PERT chart will give the developer and project manager control over the timing of the project's completion. CPM provides a graphic depiction and analysis showing whether the project is being completed on time and, if not, where the responsibility lies. The CPM also provides a graphic identification of tasks that are critical to the completion time and thus deserve the most attention or effort. An example of a PERT chart for the development of a manufactured home landlease community is included in Appendix E.

PRECONSTRUCTION CONFERENCE

Prior to the preconstruction conference, the following should have taken place:

- Approval of all development permits as presented in Chapter 8
- Contractors selected and contracts executed

- Agreements and contracts with utility companies executed and utility plans completed
- Agreements and contracts executed with the developers, engineers, surveyors, and architects relative to their involvement in the construction phase
- Financing arranged and set up as outlined in Chapter 10
- Selection of the construction manager for the project

The role of construction manager may be filled in a variety of ways. For example, the developer may be the construction manager, or a general contractor, professional engineer, or architect may take on the responsibilities of construction management. Alternatively, the developer may hire an individual with construction management experience and capabilities for that position.

The purpose of the preconstruction conference is to have everyone involved in the project together to clarify the functions and expectations, and to coordinate the members of the construction team. If there are problems with coordination or understanding the work effort, this is the time for clarification. This is also when the PERT chart is posted and the entire process reviewed in detail with all individuals involved in the development or construction phase. The engineer and inspector make very clear what is expected of the contractors. The project manager develops a clear understanding among contractors and utility companies relative to scheduling, the point at which the utility companies can and are willing to move onto the site, and the amount of restoration work that is expected from the utility companies and contractors. If there are potential on-site conflicts between the sewer, water, and storm sewer systems, or the electrical, telephone, gas, and cable television systems, these issues must be discussed and solutions determined prior to a contractor's start of work. It is beneficial to have existing utilities located and marked by the utility companies and reviewed by the contractor prior to the preconstruction conference. In this way, conflicts with existing utilities are discussed and resolved at the preconstruction conference.

CONSTRUCTION INSPECTION

It is important that the project be constructed with the correct materials and infrastructure functioning properly. This ensures that the developer will have a minimum amount of the maintenance and repairs that are often associated with poor construction techniques. Therefore, the construction work must be monitored and inspected by qualified persons independent of the contractor. The inspector is most generally a technician who is put on the job full-time and supervised by an engineer or architect. In many locations it is a requirement of the approving agencies that inspections take place and be certified by a registered professional. The inspector is required to keep a daily log, documenting everything taking place on the site, noting particularly the amount of equipment, the weather, and the number of working days. Monitoring all of these factors is important to ensure that the project is completed in a timely manner in accordance with the original contract documents. If for some reason the developer ends up taking the contractor to court, these daily records will be invaluable.

Periodic Inspection

If the developer contracts with an engineer for periodic inspection, the engineer is obligated to visit the site on a weekly or monthly basis, or when the developer requests his or her presence on-site. Periodic inspection provides the developer with input and observations from the engineer as to the progress and general condition of the project. It does not guarantee the developer that the project is being built in strict accordance with the plans and specifications.

Resident Inspection

If the developer contracts with an engineer for resident inspection, this gives the developer a much higher degree of confidence that the project is being constructed properly and in accordance with the plans and specifications. If the engineer has a contract for resident inspection, full-time personnel will be at the site, observing all aspects of the construction. This is particularly important with underground work such as construction of water distribution, sanitary sewage collection, and storm sewer systems. The inspector observes these installations, confirming that pipes are properly laid and bedded and that all backfill is properly compacted. If utilities are not properly bedded and installed, the developer may have to make costly repairs, owing to the necessity to excavate the utilities. This action could then require the expensive restoration and replacement of lawns, driveways, roadways, and other facilities in areas where the construction has been completed.

SUMMARY

Following the procedures outlined in this chapter, the developer will go a long way to ensuring that the project will be properly built on time and on budget. By starting the project with good, comprehensive engineering plans and contract documents and with a carefully orchestrated preconstruction conference, the developer will substantially reduce misunderstandings and miscommunication with the contractor, which will work to everyone's benefit.

CHAPTER 12

INSTALLATION OF HOMES

A manufactured home is normally installed on a homesite that has been stabilized and improved to provide adequate support for the home and anchoring system. The types of homesite improvements vary widely across the United States and Canada and may include simple ground stabilization, application of gravel, parallel concrete runners or solid rectangular slab, concrete block piers, or more elaborate foundation design and construction.

Home installation must allow clearance for the home's transport wheels and axles and for utility service connections; therefore, the manufactured home is generally placed 24 to 36 inches above grade. Because the steel frame or undercarriage and floor joists measure 14 to 20 inches in depth, the finished floor of the manufactured home may be as much as 56 inches above grade.

PERMANENT VERSUS NONPERMANENT FOUNDATIONS

A home may be installed on a homesite in one of 2 basic ways: the installation may be qualified as a permanent foundation system, or nonqualified. Nonqualified installation is found primarily in landlease communities and on some privately owned homesites.

To qualify for 30-year home and land financing programs, homes must be installed on qualified permanent foundation systems.[1] Although homes are designed to and built to HUD specifications, regulation of the home installation is

[1] U.S. Department of Housing and Urban Development, *Permanent Foundations Guide for Manufactured Housing,* HUD Handbook 4930.3. (Washington, D.C.: Government Printing Office, 1989).

enforced by local building authorities. Local regulations usually take into account the manufacturer's recommended installation instructions and often exceed such requirements.

HUD BUILDING CODE

The Manufactured Home Construction and Safety Standards (MHCSS) (24 CFR, Part 3280) establish performance requirements for the design of manufactured homes and are sometimes referred to as the HUD building codes. A manufactured home designed and constructed in accordance with these standards will have a 2- by 4-inch aluminum plate label attached to the lower left side of the back end (farthest end from the street in a normal installation) of the manufactured home.

Undercarriage

HUD code-built manufactured homes are designed to be transported over road-ways, using a permanent steel frame undercarriage. Some homes built to so-called modular codes may have reusable chassis systems or may use caissons of wheel assemblies that are returned to the factory for use on other homes. Figure 12.1 shows the basic configuration of a singlesection chassis and frame system.

Siting and installation requirements for manufactured homes, generally a state or local regulatory responsibility, are outside the scope of the MHCSS. The MHCSS do, however, require that installation instructions be incorporated into an owner's manual supplied with each new manufactured home. This is to ensure that the homebuyer receives instructions on the correct procedures for siting and installing the manufactured home. In addition, the American National Standards Institute's (ANSI) Standard A225.1-1982, "Manufactured Home Installations," provides installation criteria applicable to many areas of the country.

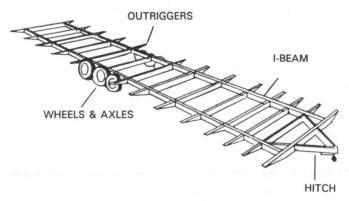

FIG. 12.1 Chassis and frame system.

High Wind and Flood-Prone Areas

It is important to recognize that installation procedures included in both the owner's manual and ANSI Standard A225.1-1982 are not considered adequate in locations where high winds or flood forces are anticipated.

Footing Placement

A typical manufactured home installation involves supporting the manufactured home on piers (concrete masonry blocks resting on concrete footings) placed every 8 to 10 feet beneath the two steel chassis I-beams of the undercarriage. Conventional installation is rarely adequate for resisting the flood forces that can be expected in areas prone to flooding. A manufactured home that is elevated a few feet above the ground and anchored to resist wind forces will still be vulnerable to the uplifting forces produced by flooding. Movement of the home from the foundation supports, inundation, or both can result in home damage.

Depending on the characteristics of anticipated flooding, the home may be elevated by using taller piers, posts, pilings, or fill. The use of an elevated foundation will differ from a normal siting technique in terms of the desired height above grade and the structural capacity of the elevating system to withstand anticipated flood and wind loads.

The primary load-bearing point on a home is under the I-beams, and not under the sidewalls. This is illustrated in Fig. 12.2. Foundation designs must incorporate the I-beams as the primary points of live and static load distribution from the home to the homesite.

Installation Responsibility

Although a limited number of modular home manufacturers install their homes for a retailer, virtually all HUD-Code manufactured homes are installed by the retailer or a qualified subcontractor. In some states, a specialty contractor's license is required. In others, a specialty subcontractor will perform the setup of the home on a nonpermanent or permanent basis.

Transportable Chassis Systems

Homes are built in the factory on a transportable chassis system for each home "subsection" (12, 14, or 16 feet wide), consisting of a set of parallel steel I-beams, with "outriggers" for sidewall support, and attached axles for attachment of the wheel and brake system. The spacing of the frame and the outriggers and the location of the axles are a function of the home floor plan and related weight distribution.

These parallel steel I-beams, for each home subsection, are the primary focus for weight distribution, or "load bearing," for the home. Foundation and installation support system components are located along an axis parallel to and directly

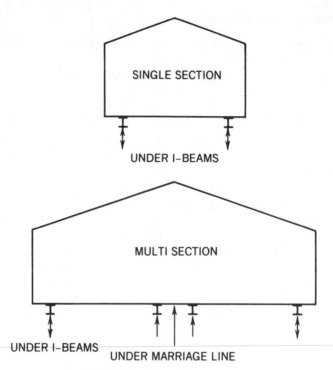

FIG. 12.2 Load bearing points.

under the I-beams. For multisection homes, additional supports are placed under the connection line, or "marriage line," of the subsections. Permanent foundation or home setup systems that distribute home's weight under the exterior walls must be redesigned to support the weight carried by the parallel steel beams.

HOME INSTALLATION

Local approval of design and construction of permanent foundations is required, and is not preempted by HUD construction codes.

Figure 12.3 shows a side-view schematic diagram of an installed manufactured home. For illustrative purposes, the door, usually placed on the front or left side of the home, is shown on the right side of the home. Home installation consists of four basic steps: preparation of the homesite for installation, transport of the home from factory to homesite, siting or installation of the home and attachment to utility services, and addition of accessory structures.

Homesite Preparation

The homesite should be finish-graded with 1% or more slope away from the "footprint" of the home. All utility services should be in place on the homesite,

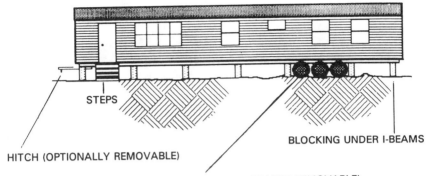

STEPS

BLOCKING UNDER I-BEAMS

HITCH (OPTIONALLY REMOVABLE)

WHEELS & AXLES (OPTIONALLY REMOVABLE)

FIG. 12.3   Home after installation and blocking.

ready for connection to the home. In the case of a landlease community, a "pedestal" is used for electrical service. The electric company will wire the pedestal to their service. Depending on the jurisdiction, an electrician may be required to hook up the home wiring to the pedestal, or a licensed manufactured home installer may perform this service.

The homesite should be dry and stable enough to support the heavy weight of the transport vehicle. A curb cut should have been made to ensure easy transition by the transporter of the home or home subsections from the street onto the homesite.

Foundations: Nonpermanent

Depending on local soil conditions and building regulations, homes are installed by placing a series of supports or piers between the longitudinal I-beams and the ground. A treated wood or concrete base is placed between the support and the ground. The size of the base and the spacing between supports depend on the soil conditions and the weight distribution of the home.

Manufacturers Recommendations. Manufacturers place a recommended support spacing diagram, for each floor plan, in the home at time of shipment from the factory. A copy of this document must be included in the application for installation or foundation system. Figure 12.4 shows a diagram of a typical multi-section home prior to installation on a foundation system.

Home Supports. Home supports are generally constructed by stacking two, two and a half, or three 8" × 8" × 16" concrete building blocks together. In western and southwestern states, steel "stands" or "jack stands" with "screw jack" bolts in the top, of varying preconstructed heights, are frequently used. In areas of high seismic activity, specially designed steel piers are available. Figure 12.5 shows a typical nonpermanent multisection home installation.

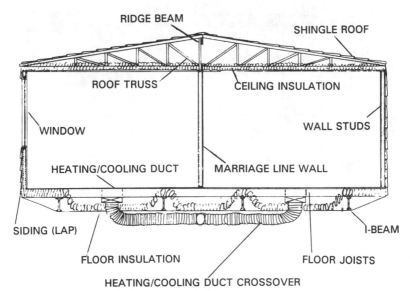

FIG. 12.4 Multisection home diagram.

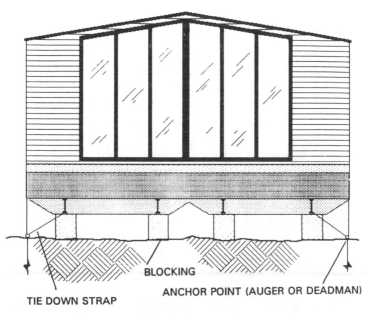

FIG. 12.5 Typical multisection installation.

Anchors. Where there is a high wind shear possibility, steel auger or other types of earth anchors are added to the installation, spaced at manufacturer's recommended intervals, to hold the home in place during high winds. The screw end is driven into normal soils by a manual or motorized "auger." In areas with harder soils or rock, specially designed hardened steel tip anchors are used.

Concrete Slabs. In many midwestern and some eastern states, it is common practice to pour a solid concrete slab for installation of the home supports and anchors. The thickness of the slab will depend on the soil conditions and the home floor plan. Although this type of installation provides an easy work surface for installers, it is very expensive and may have to be altered if a different-sized home is subsequently installed on the homesite. Figure 12.6 shows a typical singlesection home, installed on a concrete slab and secured to the anchor hardware or tiedown using under-home strapping procedures as specified by the manufacturer.

Concrete Piers. A recent and less expensive approach has been to pour a series of round concrete piers, on which the home supports are placed. The diameter and depth of the piers depend on the floor plan and the depth of the prevailing frost line for the area. In areas of minimal frost, the piers are usually 18 inches deep. In deep frost areas, the piers may be placed to a 42 to 48-foot depth or deeper. If

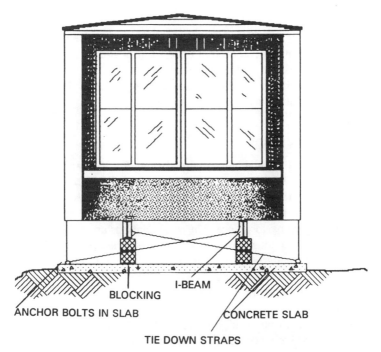

FIG. 12.6 Single section installed on concrete slab.

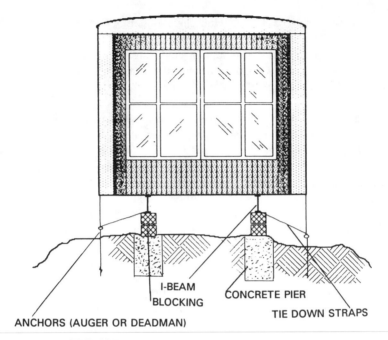

I-BEAM
BLOCKING
CONCRETE PIER
TIE DOWN STRAPS
ANCHORS (AUGER OR DEADMAN)

FIG. 12.7   Single section installed on concrete piers.

another home of different size is subsequently installed on the homesite, additional concrete piers may be poured at little additional cost. Figure 12.7 shows a singlesection home installed on concrete piers. Figure 12.8 shows the cross section of a typical skirting or foundation fascia system and interrelationships of a nonpermanent foundation and anchor strapping.

Foundations: Permanent

When a home is installed on a homesite qualifying for 30-year home and land financing, a permanent foundation system is required. An example of an approved permanent foundation system is described in detail in the FHA Handbook 4930.3.

Permanent foundations are those that have been engineered for safety and long-term satisfactory performance. These foundations are also designed specifically for use with HUD-code manufactured homes. The FHA Handbook contains construction recommendations to ensure that the home, the foundation, and the homesite are all compatible. Because these recommendations are based on estimated conditions, it is important to have complete design information for the manufactured home and appropriate site data.

To approve a permanent foundation for a manufactured home, the local building department must have a complete information package about the home and its site. Two basic pieces of information must be submitted:

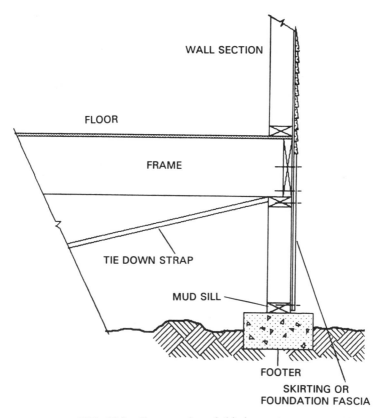

WALL SECTION

FLOOR

FRAME

TIE DOWN STRAP

MUD SILL

FOOTER

SKIRTING OR
FOUNDATION FASCIA

FIG. 12.8   Cross section of skirting system.

1. The homeowner's and manufacturer's installation information packages, and usually an Installation Manual tailored to the home design.
2. A design work sheet.

Using the information from these packages, the local building department can approve a foundation design. Information about the home and a design for the foundation of the home must be provided by the manufacturer. To simplify the approval process, the manufacturer prepares a work sheet for each standard foundation system and floor plan.

Information about the homesite is provided by the retailer, developer, or home-owner to the approving agency. The size of the foundation, the depth of the footings, and the anchoring requirement depend on the home and homesite characteristics.

Figures 12.9 and 12.10 show the placement of two of the most popular types of home anchors, the auger type and the deadman type.

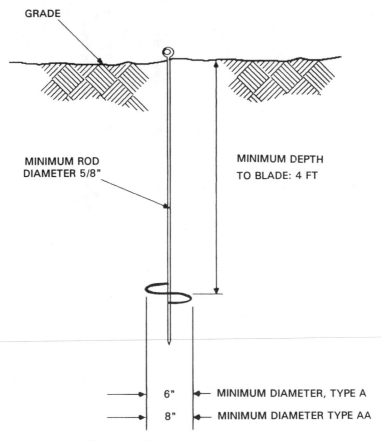

GRADE

MINIMUM ROD
DIAMETER 5/8"

MINIMUM DEPTH
TO BLADE: 4 FT

6"   MINIMUM DIAMETER, TYPE A

8"   MINIMUM DIAMETER TYPE AA

FIG. 12.9   Placement of auger type anchor.

FHA 30-Year. For their 30-year home and land financing programs, FHA requires installation of homes on a permanent foundation built to the MHCSS (Manufactured Home Construction and Safety Standards) as designed by a registered architect or engineer and in accordance with FHA Handbook 4145.1.

Farmers Home. Minimum Property Standards for Housing; Final Rule-24 CFR, Part 2C0 .926d, contains provisions that apply to installations recommended in FHA foundations. In addition, if adverse homesite conditions are encountered, specific design recommendations by a geotechnical engineer must be included with the application for approval. The FmHA (Farmers Home Administration) also has provisions for approval of permanent foundations for manufactured homes under its long-term financing programs. These loan provisions are contained in Subpart A of Part 1924 and Subpart A of Part 1944 of Chapter XVIII, Federal Register, Vol. 51, No. 12, January 17, 1986.

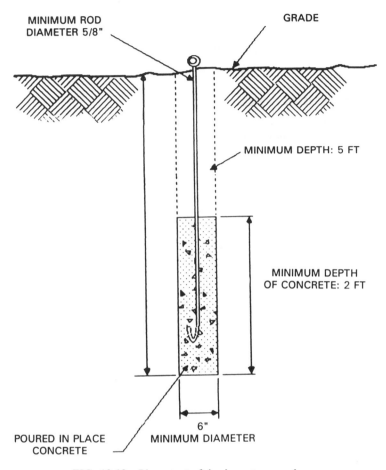

FIG. 12.10   Placement of deadman type anchor.

QUESTIONABLE SITE CONDITIONS

Specific site conditions determine whether a given permanent foundation design will be suitable for a manufactured home. Problem soils, flood-prone building sites, sloping sites, and high groundwater levels can affect decisions about foundation design. An investigation of a questionable homesite by a qualified geotechnical engineer is recommended to determine whether site conditions will adversely affect foundation performance.

Building sites near lakes, rivers, streams, and oceans are potential flood areas. Information about whether the homesite is flood prone may be obtained by examining FEMA (Federal Emergency Management Agency) flood maps, or from USGA quarter-section maps. If the adjoining homesite is within a flood zone, the finish grade of the building homesite must be located above the 100-year return frequency flood elevation and in accordance with HUD Handbooks 4135.1 and 4145.1 and Executive Order 1, 1988.

ELEVATED FOUNDATIONS

Homes within flood zones may be installed on elevated foundations. Refer to *Manufactured Home Installation in Flood-Hazard Areas,* FE.N4A-85/ September 1985. Homes built on elevated foundations must comply with the requirements of the National Flood Insurance Program (NFIP) to qualify for flood insurance. The base of the foundation footing must be below the maximum frost penetration depth. Because water table elevations vary from season to season or by location, all building structures, streets, paved areas, and utilities must be located and designed to minimize the adverse effects of a high water table.

Developed portions of a homesite that can be adversely affected by potentially high groundwater must be drained where possible, based on recommendations by a geotechnical engineer. For individually sited homes, the water table elevation may be based on local records if available; otherwise, it can be determined by subsurface investigation through the use of test wells, boring, or piezometer tubes.

Soil conditions typically vary with depth. Subsurface investigations to a minimum recommended depth below the footing depth, usually conducted by a geotechnical engineer, using appropriate laboratory tests, are recommended to identify soil type and estimate bearing capacity.

BEARING CAPACITY

Allowable soil-bearing pressures are based on various national model codes, such as the following:

   BOCA—Basic National Building Code
   SBCC—Standard Building Code
   ICBO—(Uniform Building Code)
   CABO—One- and Two-Family Dwelling Code

For individual homesites the bearing capacity may be estimated, based on local building codes, unless the homesite is located in an area of known or suspected adverse soil conditions, as defined in Section 203. Then a subsurface investigation may be advisable or required.

If any type of problem soil is identified at the proposed homesite, removal of the problem soil and replacement with an engineered fill is permitted if plans are submitted and approved by a geotechnical engineer. Typical problem soils include the following:

1. Loess: deposits of windblown organic silts, susceptible to moisture and frost action and excessive settlement
2. Peat: river or water deposits of organic matter and silts, susceptible to excessive settlement
3. Topsoil: top organic layer of soil, susceptible to excessive settlement

Other reasons for special consideration in foundation design include:

1. Unstable clays with potential for large movements
2. Soils with expansive characteristics
3. Soils with highly plastic characteristics
4. Soils with high compressibility
5. Areas of termite hazard

FOUNDATION DESIGN

In the early 1980s when 30-year home and land financing was first allowed for HUD-Code manufactured homes, local building codes were interpreted as requiring an exterior foundation wall similar to those characteristic of site-built homes. These foundations were designed to distribute the load from the home to an exterior "pony wall" under the exterior walls of the home. In addition, the normal piers and supports for the longitudinal frame members were installed under the steel I-beams, increasing the cost of the foundation system beyond reason.

As building codes evolved, foundation systems were designed to distribute home loads from the longitudinal frame members to the soil, and the exterior "pony wall" became a non-load-bearing foundation fascia or skirting system.

HOME TRANSPORTATION

Most home manufacturers transfer ownership of the home to the retailer or developer F.O.B. from the factory. Although some manufacturers have their own home transporters, as a general rule, once the home leaves the factory grounds, ownership passes to the retailer or developer. Technically, the only proof of ownership is the Manufacturer's Statement of Origin (MSO), which is sent to the floor plan lender or interim financing agent. If the home is purchased with cash, the MSO is sent directly to the retailer or developer. A retailer or developer may use his or her own state licensed transporter, or as is most common, a firm specializing in manufactured home transport. The retailer or developer, when possible, should inspect the home before transport to ensure that it was manufactured according to the sales order and that everything inside the home is adequately "tied down" for transport. A less desirable option is to assign the responsibility for inspection to the transport company driver.

Transport Insurance

Minimum insurance against home damage during transport is included within the fees charged by carriers under the various states' tariffs. This insurance coverage is minimal and may be insufficient for more expensive homes. In the case of damage to a subsection of a multisection home, the insurance policy, or an agreement with the manufacturer, should provide for payment of costs to return all subsections to the factory to facilitate the reconstruction or replacement of the damaged subsection.

Secondary Transport

When a home is being retransported from a retail sales center to a homesite, it is important that all items listed on the original factory invoice be included. The home must also be carefully and completely readied for transport from the sales center to the homesite.

Theft and Damage During Transport

Unfortunately, theft of appliances, thermostats, furniture, and so forth, plus damage from over-the-road transport of a home, does occur. Using a capable and responsible transporter will save a retailer or developer much time, effort, and expense in trying to resolve transport problems.

Transporter Time at Homesite

Once the home has arrived at the homesite, as a part of many state tariffs, a provision is made for a maximum of 1 hour per home subsection for "proximate" home placement on the homesite by the transporter. Although the setup crew will inch it along to its final position, gross movements of the home on the homesite are usually more easily performed by the transporter than by the setup crew.

SETUP

Setup of the home on the homesite consists of removing the transport materials, taillights, cables, and lamps, positioning the home in exact place, and leveling it for installation. Setup also includes the installation of supports on the piers or wood or concrete bases, securing of home subsections together, and the hookup of utility services between the subsections. If applicable, the setup crew also hooks up the utility services, where legal.

Setup Checklist

A checklist of setup services should include, but is not limited to the following:

- Obtain building permit
- Remove shipping materials

- Place home on homesite
- Level home for setup
- Install blocking under I-beams
- Install blocking under marriage line, if applicable
- Install anchors and strapping under and over the home
- Check shut-off valves
- Check electric water heater
- Check appliances
- Trim off roof (effecting minor repairs and adjustments)
- Trim out exterior (effecting minor repairs and adjustments)
- Hook up electrical service*
- Check and adjust doors
- Hook up cross-overs*
- Install options
- Hook up utilities*
- Install, seam, or patch carpet, if applicable
- Clean windows
- Clean interior
- Unders inspection
- Install light bulbs
- Adjust furnace, if applicable*
- Adjust water heater, if applicable*
- Check hot and cold water lines
- Obtain certificate of occupancy
- Remove shipping materials from homesite
- Install temporary or permanent steps
- Remove hitch, axles, and wheels from homesite

*These tasks may require a qualified, licensed subcontractor and additional permits.

ACCESSORIES

Once the home has been installed on the foundation, or supports and bases, accessory structures may be added, such as those listed here:

- Foundation fascia (skirting)
- Driveway, when not provided by community
- Walkways, when not provided by community
- Carport awning or garage

- Patio awning
- Screened patio
- Raised porch
- Storage shed
- Breezeway
- Fireplace (approved type)
- Gutters and downspouts
- Fireplace or barbecue area

REVIEW SETBACK LIMITATIONS

The retailer, developer, or property owner should review limitations on the size and location of various accessories. These may be stipulated by local zoning setback requirements and by community rules and regulations.

For aesthetic reasons and improved access, it may be desirable to employ a "low profile" siting, in which the homesite area is excavated below grade.

NATIONAL FLOOD INSURANCE PROGRAM

The National Flood Insurance Program (NFIP) is the federal government's principal administrative mechanism for reducing flood losses. Established by Congress in 1968 and broadened and modified since then, the NFIP is administered by the Federal Insurance Administration (FIA) of FEMA. The program offers property insurance for buildings and their contents in flood-prone areas where conventional insurance has been generally unavailable.

The NFIP provides insurance to communities that agree to implement comprehensive land use planning and management to reduce flood damage in their jurisdictions. This requirement generally involves an evaluation of zoning, building codes, and other government regulations that place various requirements on new construction and on substantial improvements to existing construction in identified flood hazard areas.[2]

Some communities, either in recognition of the benefits of a strong floodplain management program or in response to specific problems, adopt regulations that are considerably more restrictive than the minimum NFIP requirements.

Special Flood Hazard Areas

FEMA establishes "Special Flood Hazard Areas" that include those areas inundated by the 100-year flood.

[2] FEMA, *Manufactured Home Installation in Flood Hazard Areas.* 1985-529-684/31054. (Washington, DC: Government Printing Office, 1985.)

The 100-year flood standard is used by every federal agency in its administration of flood-related programs. This standard has also been adopted by many states and is used administratively in the operations of their own programs involving floodplain management.

The NFIP is administered in two parts: the Emergency Program and the Regular Program. The function of the Emergency Program is to make flood insurance readily available to property owners throughout a flood-prone community.

Notification of Status

The FIA notifies a community that it has been identified as flood prone by providing the community with a Flood Hazard Boundary Map (FHBM). This map is a preliminary delineation of flood hazard areas within the community.

A community receiving such a map may participate in the program by completing an application to the FIA. Upon approval of the application, that community becomes eligible for federal flood insurance.

FHBMs generally show flood-prone areas as either A-Zones or V-Zones. Riverine flood-prone areas and coastal flood-prone areas subject to storm surges with velocity waves of less than 3 feet during the 100-year flood are generally classed as A-Zones. "Coastal high hazard areas" are shown on FHBMs as V-Zones. The V-Zone is the portion of the floodplain subject to storm surges with velocity waves of 3 feet or more during the 100-year flood.

Based on this information, regulatory standards that are more detailed than Emergency Program requirements are adopted and enforced by the participating community. These standards include requirements that influence the location and type of installation of manufactured homes.

Manufactured Home Placement in Hazard Zones

Local community officials should be contacted to determine what NFIP regulations govern the placement of manufactured homes in flood hazard areas.

New Mexico, for example, requires manufactured home retailers to provide the homebuyer with a notice to check with the local government to determine installation requirements in a flood hazard area. In Texas, North Carolina, and several other states, when more than one-fourth of a manufactured home's frame members are more than 3 feet above grade, the foundation system must be designed by a registered professional engineer or architect.

The appropriate state government departments responsible for manufactured housing installation, floodplain management, water resources, building codes, or coastal zone management should be consulted prior to installation of a manufactured home in a flood hazard area.

Each state has also designated a state coordinating agency to assist in the implementation of the NFIP. This agency is a focal point for information on flood insurance, floodplain management, and coordination of the diverse state agencies with responsibilities for riverine and coastal floodplains.

The authority of each state's coordinating agency varies and can best be determined through direct contact. These agencies can be important sources of physical data, information on community eligibility for flood insurance, state regulations, references to other agencies, and, in some instances, technical assistance.

Floodplain Management

Local governments play the key role in floodplain management. Most local jurisdictions have limiting ordinances and regulations for manufactured homes and manufactured home developments. In addition, they can have sources of flood hazard data and other regulatory information. Local offices that may be of assistance include Departments or Offices of Public Works, Building, Engineering, Zoning, and Planning.

The Building Officials and Code Administrators' (BOCA) Basic/National Building Code, the International Conference of Building Officials' (ICBO) Uniform Building Code, and the Southern Building Code Congress International's (SBCCI) Standard Building Code all include sections requiring structural integrity of foundations, walls, floor slabs, and retaining walls that may be subjected to flooding.

These model codes are used in many parts of the country and are developed with technical data from many organizations and individuals through an annual code revision process. Some communities may have similar or more stringent requirements that specifically address manufactured homes. State and local guidance should be used to determine what flood-related codes are in effect for a particular area.

Wind Forces

Wind forces exert pressure on a manufactured home and its supporting foundation. Structural components, such as walls and roofs, are affected by winds and are designed to withstand certain wind forces. These forces also affect all connections within the manufactured home, as well as those securing it to the foundation system.

Wind is also of particular importance as it affects the loads imposed on the manufactured home itself. The MHCSS currently provide for structural integrity of manufactured homes under two conditions: lateral loads and uplift loads imposed by wind. In hurricane zones, the lateral and net uplift design loads are 25 pounds per square foot and 15 psf respectively; less in non-hurricane zones.

It is important in homesite considerations that wind and flood forces be reviewed in advance for possible additional costs to installing the structure, its foundation system, and anchoring mechanisms.

Proper Installation Importance

Careful community design in the context of anticipated unnatural weather conditions, soil types, floor plans, and weight distribution will provide the homebuyer with a stable and functional foundation system. Using the right procedures during home transport and installation on the foundation system will also go a long way toward assuring the residents of a safe, functional, and long-lived home.

Serious wind and flood hazards in the early 1990s made apparent the importance of proper home installation. In most cases, where manufactured homes have been installed to updated state anchor and foundation standards, home damage has not been any greater than for site-built housing. Although many jurisdictions will review a proposed development for natural environmental problems, it is the developer's responsibility to ensure that the project is not built in areas of flood or wind hazard. Failure to recognize and install homes to the highest installation and foundation standards can create the potential for loss of homes and lives in a community, and a loss of revenues to the developer.

CHAPTER 13

MARKETING THE NEW COMMUNITY

"Proper prior planning prevents poor performance." The 6-P Rule of Business Planning has no more apt application than with the four Traditional P's of Marketing:

Product
Price
Place
Promotion

Market planning begins before the first spade of earth is turned for a new investment property and continues as long as there is a homeowner or renter on-site.

The purpose of this chapter is to acquaint developers, property owners, and managers with general marketing basics, and then to demonstrate their application to manufactured housing and landlease communities. This will be accomplished in four steps:

1. Review of Marketing Basics
2. Marketing Manufactured Housing
3. Marketing Landlease Communities
4. Promotion and Advertising

MARKETING BASICS

Developing the Marketing Plan

At this point in the development of a new landlease community, a preliminary marketing plan has been formulated as part of earlier feasibility studies, concept statements, and the business plan prepared for investors, lending institutions, planning commissions, and zoning boards. The marketing plan is an in-depth analysis of

- What is to be sold or leased (i.e., manufactured housing and/or landlease homesites) to whom,
- At what price, rent level, or dollar spread,
- Where (location is virtually set at this point), and
- How to best promote and advertise.

There are key elements of a marketing plan that should be reviewed and, if necessary, adjusted.

- Study and update the original feasibility study. Time has passed and circumstances have likely changed since it was drafted. Is the original market forecast still valid, relative to its assumptions and conclusions?
- Update earlier market studies. Depending on the format used earlier, this is a good time to introduce the market survey form commonly encountered on-site at mature landlease communities (see Fig. 13.1).

How to Use the Market Survey Form

- Insert name of subject property, (even if not ready for move-ins) on line 1.
- On lines 2–11, list nearest landlease community competitors, with closest or strongest competitor listed on line 2, and the next closest competitor on line 3.
- Column 2 is self-explanatory. *Note:* Print all entries and retype data later, if desired.
- Column 3 asks for total number of homesites per property surveyed. Make a personal, physical count the first time this form is used. Then periodically verify the count with subsequent surveys.
- Column 4, Estimated Occupancy. The formula is shown at bottom of the page (e.g., number of occupied homesites ÷ total number of homesites = physical occupancy percentage). See later in this text how physical occupancy compares with economic occupancy as a management performance indicator.
- Column 5 is self-explanatory; it simply includes items used for further comparison of properties and their relative desirability to homeowners or renters.
- Column 6—other information can be included, depending on dynamics of the market. It might be noted, for example, whether water and sewer charges are part of the monthly rent. Encode swimming pool (SP), clubhouse (CH), playground (PG), and other amenities appropriate for market comparsion purposes.

| MARKET SURVEY |
| - Rental Community - |

Market Area Surveyed

Preparer

Type Properties: _____

Year _____

Use this form to conduct market survey once each quarter or four years in succession.

Name & Address of Property	Phone # Manager Name	Total # of Rental Un.	Estimated Occupancy %*	$ Deposit / Lease Term	Other Info	AVERAGE RENT RATE PER UNIT			
						Date ____ $	Date ____ $	Date ____ $	Date ____ $
1.									
2.									
3.									
4.									
5.									
6.									
7.									
8.									
9.									
10.									
11.									
MARKET AVERAGE	N/A	____	____ %*	N/A	N/A	$____	$____	$____	$____

*Formula = # of occupied units + # available, for physical occupancy%.

This form available for purchase in tablet format.
Property Management Form #101
Copyright Jan 1989

G·FA
MANAGEMENT
P.O. Box 47024
Indianapolis, IN 46247

FIG. 13.1   A standard real estate management form.

• Columns 7, 8, 9, and 10 are rent rate comparsion columns. Use only Column 7 the first time a new market survey form is used; use Column 8 the next time, and so on. Did the survey encounter different site rental rates for single and multisection homes? If so, use two market survey forms, one for single-section and one for multisection homes. Did the survey encounter a rent range, owing to a premium charged for corner sites, for example? In most cases, compute a mathematical or weighted average rent and put it in parenthesis, for example, $200–220 ($210).

Finally, on the bottom line of each market survey form used, calculate the indicated totals and averages. Once these data are tabulated, it is possible to estimate or adjust the in-fill or ongoing homesite rental rate or rates, keeping in mind the developer or owner's rent rate philosophy, how much is needed to meet financial commitments, and what will ensure the landlease community's competitive marketability and desirability to prospective homebuyers and renters.

How do the results of the market survey compare with plans set forth in earlier planning documents? Are there any adjustments needed or desirable at this point?

In mature, close-to-full landlease communities, it is usually a good idea to distribute copies of the completed market survey form to all properties listed on it. Property owners and managers on the low end of the rent range may thereby be motivated to bring their homesite rents into line with the market average.

Planning Market Strategy

Is the targeted market the same as proposed in earlier studies and plans? Has the market changed over the past 6 to 12 months, or does the targeted market need to be broadened—or narrowed? These are all timely and strategic questions to answer as landlease community fill-in begins, and certainly as it is in progress. It is also a very good idea to redo the market survey at least every 6 months until the property is near maximum physical occupancy. Hence the reason for additional columns in Fig. 13.1, which make it easy to track specific rent rate adjustments and the market average over a period of time.

What is the best access to the targeted market or markets? What are competitors doing? What type of promotion and advertising is being employed? Identify the local tried and proven avenues and techniques as a base upon which to build, then implement creative approaches to

Get Attention!
Generate Interest!
Stimulate Desire!
Motivate to Action!

This well-known acronym, AIDA (Attention, Interest, Desire, Action), works well in the manufactured housing sales and community leasing arenas.

In a recent PMN Publishing national survey of manufactured home landlease community owners and property managers, respondents identified, and ranked in declining order, their top 10 marketing approaches used to stimulate consumer awareness of and interest in landlease communities:

1. Local image and reputation of the property in the market area
2. Overall curb appeal (i.e., how the property "looks" to the casual passerby)
3. Resident relations (tied with item 4)
4. Professional property management (tied with item 3)
5. Local retail salescenter relations
6. Advertising of all types
7. On-site signage
8. Skilled leasing and sales staff
9. Off-site signage
10. Direct mail effort[1]

Each and every marketing approach has its own distinct possibilities and pitfalls, so develop and adjust the marketing plan carefully and comprehensively.

Dual Marketing

Well before this point, the decision was probably made whether to sell new manufactured homes exclusively on-site, and lease homesites to the new homebuyers

or

to encourage local manufactured housing retailers to sell new manufactured homes on-site, and the landlease community management staff to concentrate on leasing homesites

or

to encourage local manufactured housing retailers to sell new and resale homes into the new landlease community, and management staff to simply lease homesites

or

one of several variations to these three dual marketing possibilities.

The point is that there is more than one way to effect the in-fill of a new landlease community, even the ongoing leasing effort of a mature property, and several important factors come into play, such as the following considerations:

- Is the local market strong enough (i.e., all neighboring landlease communities are full and consumers want to buy manufactured homes) to support the first option described above? This is certainly the most profitable way to proceed,

---

[1] G.F. Allen, "Ranking Your Marketing Tools," *Manufactured Home Merchandiser* (December) 1991, p. 26.

but depends heavily on the developer's being correct concerning the market assessment, having a reliable and timely source of quality product (i.e., new manufactured homes and ready homesites) when and where needed, adequate financing sources in place, and an effective sales staff. This is a big order, to be sure, but one with big profit potential too.

- The second option will be popular with local manufactured housing retailers, given the market conditions described earlier. The landlease community ownership, however, foregoes the extra income stream available from the sale of new homes and related accessories. It is possible, in some locales, to recoup a portion of this lost profit by collecting an entrance fee from either the homebuyer or the retail salescenter. In addition, if more than one local manufactured housing retailer is actively selling homes into the community, in-fill could proceed more quickly than if community management wore home sales and site leasing hats. It is prudent, however, to be careful about favoring one retailer over another without good cause. For if one retailer opens a sales center on-site and others do not, the latter may be reluctant to send qualified prospective home-buying customers to the property to select a homesite if there is any chance of their being attracted to a competitor's on-site sales operation.
- The third option, theoretically, will ensure the fastest in-fill of all, when new, resale, and transferring homes are encouraged to move in. The downside is less up-front profit from the sale of new homes and a heterogenous collection of older and new homes.

There is yet more to this market mix complexity:

- What are the requirements, if any, concerning size, quality of home, or type of features in homes moving in? For example, is the developer or property owner mandating house-type siding, a pitched and shingled roof system, a required storage building, concrete steps, or a particular skirting specification?
- The point of sale. Is it off-site (e.g. local retail salescenter) or on-site (e.g. based at a retail salescenter or clubhouse), or possibly "spec" or speculation homes set-up on-site.

These are all key issues to be addressed and readdressed early in the planning process, during construction, and when the new landlease community is available for move-ins.

MARKETING MANUFACTURED HOUSING

Product-Related

There are many attractive product-related features characteristic of manufactured housing. These are features related directly to the housing product.

1. Homes are built to rigid national construction standards (HUD Code) that ensure their safety and durability.
2. Design flexibility allows consumers to specify a variety of floor plans, architectural designs, appliance options, exterior treatments (siding, roof, windows, and doors), and contemporary interior decor.
3. Energy efficiency is also ensured by the HUD Code, which establishes and monitors stringent thermal design standards.
4. Space is efficient. Every square foot of today's spacious manufactured home has a practical use.

Price-Related

1. Manufactured homes are affordable. The bulk purchasing and production efficiencies and the quality control characteristics of homes built in a controlled factory environment translate into lower home prices for the consumer.
2. The self-contained nature of the manufactured home, leaving the factory on its own steel frame, allows it to be sited on piers or concrete runners or slabs, saving the expense of excavated basements and crawl spaces.
3. Financing is readily available for new and resale homes, in the form of both chattel and real estate mortgages.
4. Heating bills are lower, because manufactured homes are energy efficient and have less space to heat.

Place-Related

1. Manufactured homes may be purchased on-site at manufactured home landlease communities, or at manufactured housing retail salescenters located across the United States and Canada.
2. Manufactured homes may be sited in manufactured home landlease communities, on private property, and in subdivisions. According to the Manufactured Housing Institute, in 1991, of the 174,000 home placements reported, 105,000 went on scattered building sites; 63,000 into landlease communities; and 6,000 into subdivisions.
3. When manufactured homes are placed in subdivisions and landlease communities, the homeowners have a variety of life-styles and locations to choose from: family communities, retirement communities; desert or seaside environments; rural or close to urban settings; and older "intimate" surroundings or wide open, spacious homesites.
4. Today's manufactured home, although still transportable, is far more permanent than it was in years past. It can be moved from one locale to another—when an economy sours, with job changes, or for any other reason. At the same time, the home is relatively easily anchored to the real estate on which it is sited and may become a permanent fixture to the land.

Promotion-Related

All of the foregoing product, price, and place features are promotion-related. Each consumer will prefer one or more market-related feature over another, whether it be affordability, energy or design efficiency, transportability, or performance.

MARKETING LANDLEASE COMMUNITIES

Product-Related

There are several key product-related (i.e. the physical homesite and rental community at large) features that make this type of property popular.

1. There is a wide variety of manufactured home landlease and subdivision—type communities: family and retirement; small and intimate or very large and spacious; lower-rent and few amenities; and every combination in between.
2. A sense of community generally develops in a manufactured home landlease community. Many extended families and groups of friends prefer this life-style.
3. Yards are usually just large enough for easy care, but not so large as to be a burden and detract from leisure activities.

Price-Related

1. Rents are considerably lower than for comparably sized apartments and townhouses.
2. Rent typically includes water, sewer, and refuse removal services. Cable TV, if not included in the rent, is billed separately, like electricity, natural gas, and heating fuels—and sometimes water and sewer charges.

Place-Related

1. Landlease communities are virtually everywhere—near cities, to ensure proximity to employment; in the suburbs and rural areas—to facilitate quiet country living; and in resort and highly desirable climates, such as retirement communities.
2. Rural landlease communities outnumber their urban counterparts 3 to 1.[2]

---

[2] G.F. Allen, 'Survey Reflects Community Development,' *Manufactured Home Merchandiser,* Chicago, Ill, Nov. '89, pp. 32–34.

Promotion-Related

1. Landlease communities provide a generally easier life-style, with an energy-efficient and near maintenance-free home and a smaller yard to mow.
2. Again, rent is lower, and there are a number of community types and locations with the same, if not more, amenities provided in apartments and subdivisions.
3. This is also the most affordable of all housing options. Homes are less expensive to purchase, insure, maintain, and to heat or cool.

PROMOTION AND ADVERTISING

There are a wide variety of promotion and advertising options available to support the marketing of manufactured home landlease communities. For the purpose of this chapter, *promotion* is defined as being "the futherance of the acceptance and sale of merchandise through advertising, publicity, or discounting."[3] *Advertising* is defined as "sales oriented mass communication through print or broadcast media."[4] It has also been suggested that "advertising is salesmanship in print."

In the PMN national survey cited earlier, manufactured home landlease community owners ranked "advertising of all types," as number 6 out of 10 marketing approaches. Interestingly, the first five marketing approaches are subjective in nature and highly dependent on perception and personal opinion:

1. Local image of the property (i.e., reputation)
2. Curb appeal (i.e., how the property looks to the casual passerby)
3. Resident relations (i.e., interpersonal relations)
4. Professional management (i.e., personal conduct)
5. Local retailer relations (i.e., personal contact)

The last five marketing approaches cited in the survey, headed by advertising, are more empirical in nature and readily measured via recording of responses to ads, who saw which off-site signs, sales and leasing conversion percentages calculated weekly, and recorded number of responses to direct mail solicitations.

Promotional Measures

Promotional measures are generally those actions taken that bring a landlease community, even a retail salescenter, to the positive attention of the public at large. There are several ways to do this:

[3] *Webster's Ninth New Collegiate Dictionary* (Springfield, MA: Merriam-Webster, 1984), p. 942.
[4] "The Glossary of Sales and Marketing Definitions," Henry Lavin Associates, Conn., 1974.

- Send regular, well-written press releases to the local media, describing newsworthy events and upcoming activities taking place on-site or at the salescenter.
- Invite representatives of the news media to visit the landlease community as judges for annual Home of the Month contests. Frame the best news articles and photos of Home of the Month winners and display them on information center walls.
- Encourage management and resident volunteers to be actively involved in altruistic social and community projects and endeavors.
- Use color and design-coordinated stationery, complete with a distinct logo, to promote the attractive life-style of the landlease community. Use the color scheme and design on premium gifts (e.g., coffee mugs, key fobs) and staff uniforms, in off-site and on-site signage, and in advertising.
- When required by state statute, produce a landlease community Property Prospectus that is image-building as well as informative.
- Produce a regular on-site newsletter for residents and mail copies to prospective renters and homebuyers. Sell advertising in the newsletter to offset its cost.
- Design and distribute an attractive license plate or bumper sticker featuring the community's name or logo.
- Give premium gifts to local manufactured housing retail sales consultants; use these as prizes for Home of the Month contest winners and even as "Welcome Aboard" gifts to new residents.
- Assemble photo collages featuring attractive views of the community. Placed at manufactured housing retail salescenters along with brochures, a collage is an effective promotion tool.

Advertising Measures

The PMN survey cited earlier ranked various forms of advertising, according to the responses of landlease community owners and managers:

1. Newspaper classified ads
2. Yellow Pages of telephone directories
3. Other local directories
4. Miscellaneous advertising, including:
   Referrals from retailers and residents
   Flyers and property brochures
   Billboards off-site
   Direct mail pieces

Interestingly, the PMN survey quoted statistics indicating that 30% of the typical landlease community's advertising budget goes for newspaper classified ads,

25% for Yellow Pages ads, and 15% for other advertising, such as radio and TV (minimal in each case) advertising. The remaining 30% of the ad budget is spread across the board for premium gifts, flyers, property brochures, and business cards.[5]

Here are guidelines for designing and implementing various types of print advertising:

• *Yellow Pages.* Ads in the Yellow Pages are particularly effective draws for landlease communities in outlying market areas. It is a good idea to include a small route map when the ad size permits. Ads are priority-positioned on the directory page by Yellow Pages copywriters according to size, ink color (red versus black) and alphabetical order.

• *Newspaper classified ads.* Once again, recall AIDA:

  • Get Reader's *A*ttention; for example, L(.)(.)K as an ad graphic. This simply uses typewriter graphics to create a lead that can grab reader's attention and direct their vision down to body of the ad.
  • Generate *I*nterest; for example, "Free Rent!"
  • Stimulate *D*esire; for example, "Quiet Country Living" or whatever appeals to prospects in the market area.
  • Motivate to *A*ction; for example, "Call Today!"

The following are the Small Business Administration's (SBA) four criteria for evaluating advertising effectiveness, once designed and placed:

  • Full coverage of local market area?
  • Enough repetition of message?
  • Right readership of message?
  • Cost per thousand exposures of message, when compared with other advertising options.

Here are some design tips:

  • Use an easily recognized logo, if available and permitted by the media. Use this on signs and stationery too. If this is not possible, try the well-known "happy face" logo or L(.)(.)K strategy described earlier.
  • Choose and promote a consistent, attractive advertising theme.
  • Use a bold or unique ad border; change the border from time to time to freshen the ad.
  • Change the ad design periodically (weekly or biweekly) to attract readers' attention.

[5] G.F. Allen, "Ranking Your Marketing Tools," *Mfd Home Merchandiser,* Chicago, Ill, Nov. '89, pp. 32–34.

- Be alert to new ad ideas when traveling; clip ad samples and mount them on 3 by 5-inch cards to preserve them.
- Use ad white space to advantage.
- Monitor every ad for accuracy and verify placement.
- Keep track of responses, saving the best-drawing ads for future reuse. Put these ads into a scrapbook or mount them on 3 by 5-inch cards and file.
- Apply the ABC Rule of Communication: Ads should be Accurate; Brief; Clear—Concise—Complete.

- *Yellow Pages of Telephone Directories.* Many of the same rules for newspaper classified ads apply to ads in the Yellow Pages. Keep in mind that the ad designed and contracted for will be unchanged in size and monthly cost for 1 year. Therefore, it is important to do it right the first time. Are there vacancies? Use a larger ad. No vacancies? Use a much smaller ad, but do maintain a presence.

- *Local Directories.* The placement of an ad in a local directory is usually a cheaper, one-shot affair; use the best-drawing ad from the newspaper classified ad scrapbook. Make sure that the soliciting directory has relevance and a good chance of drawing potential renters and homebuyers. If not, do not advertise unless there is a good reason to do so.

- *Miscellaneous Advertising.*
  - Referrals are word-of-mouth recommendations by local manufactured housing retail salescenters and satisfied landlease community residents. In a soft market, encourage both types of referrals with a modest referral or finder's fee, or with a desirable premium gift such as a coffee mug.
  - Flyers, property brochures, and handbills offer an opportunity for creative design. These often contain photos of the property's best features (e.g., pool, clubhouse), a map showing the property location, and, certainly, the name, address, and phone number of the landlease community. Distribute them to local manufactured housing retail salescenters (along with the manager's business card), chamber of commerce, area motels, and other usual gathering places such as laundromats and stores. Easiest to produce are tri-fold brochures, printed on 8½ by 11-inch stock, then folded in thirds for self-mailing or envelope stuffing.
  - Signage is an important advertising tool. Off-site signage is not very common for manufactured home landlease communities. It can be helpful, however, when vacancies exist and when a property is not easy to find. Use the property's color scheme, logo, and theme to facilitate recognition as prospects relate ads they have seen in the newspaper or Yellow Pages to the property itself. On-site signage, although not advertising per se, with one exception, enhances the image of a community. A really nice site sign welcoming prospects to the property, followed by a single 1 by 2-foot "Welcome Home" sign inside the entrance and an "Information Center" sign at the office, all

work to this end. Avoid using any negatively worded signs (e.g., warning off solicitors, prohibiting trucks parked on-site or dogs on the premises). Use a sign that announces: "This Choice Homesite for Lease, call (information center's phone number)". When placed on select, vacant, manicured homesites, this sign is a good response generator from after-hours drive-through rental prospects.

- Direct mail pieces are most often sent to apartment dwellers, and sometimes to residents of other manufactured home landlease communities. Creative, attractive, studio-type cards are effective in this application. Show apartment renters how to stop paying high rent and start building equity affordably, and they will generally respond.

The variety of promotion and advertising measures is limited only by one's imagination, creativity, and pocketbook. Use the preceeding ideas to get started, identify which work best, and concentrate on them.

SUMMARY

Preparing the marketing plan for a new, or even an ongoing, manufactured home landlease community is a formidable creative challenge. Once knowledgeable about the product, the developer, property owner, and management staff decide what combination of product, price, place, and promotion will best attract the targeted market to the salescenter and the landlease community.

CHAPTER 14

ON-SITE SALES AND LEASING

"Always Be Closing!" is another helpful ABC rule of business. Closing the sale or lease is not bad advice either, for the fill-up and ongoing success of a manufactured home landlease community depends directly on how well the staff sells homes and leases homesites. Yet, as in other truisms in business and in life, there is a need for balance. Note, for instance, these two contrasting slogans:

"Never sell too soon!"
"It's never too soon to sell!"[1]

Be sensitive to the need for balance when planning what to market to whom, when and where to sell and lease, and why. This chapter describes the basics of selling and leasing in general, how these basics apply to new and resale manufactured home sales, and the leasing of homesites to homebuyers and homeowners.

SALES AND LEASING BASICS

The Six Levels of Any Sales or Leasing Effort

Before looking at the comprehensive six-level technique of sales and leasing, consider the popular but shorter, four-step variant.

    Introduction
    Qualification

[1] John Rothchild, *A Fool and His Money* (Viking Penguin, 1989) NY, NY: pp. 36, 37, 38.

Demonstration

Closing the sale[2]

These four quick steps are an easy memory aid for new sales or leasing consultants. They simply remember to:

- Make *Introductions* (setting a positive, friendly tone and conveying a supportive environment),
- *Qualify* prospects (Can they afford what they need or want?),
- *Demonstrate* the product or service ("Show, don't tell"), and
- *Close the sale* ("Ask for the Order [AFTO]" by asking prospects to complete the application).

Although these four steps constitute an easy-to-remember tool, they do not provide the complete picture. Some sales pros advocate a five-step selling process:

Attention

Interest

Conviction

Desire

Close[3]

- In the *Attention* step, the goal is to avoid buyer rejection and strive for acceptance;
- In the *Interest* step, overcome indifference and motivate the buyer to be anxious to purchase or lease;
- In the *Conviction* step, eliminate skepticism and achieve belief;
- In the *Desire* step, discourage delay and stimulate buyer to action; and
- In the *Close* step, allay fears, inspire confidence, and "make the sale."[4] This system is a bit more complete, but still one step away from the best approach for selling and leasing in the manufactured housing and landlease community environments.

Now look at the Six Levels of a Manufactured Home Sale or Homesite Lease.[5]

1. *Announcement.* As in the five-step procedure, Announcement and Attention are synonymous. It is vital, through promotion and advertising, to see the fulfillment of the classic marketing acronym AIDA:

---

[2] "Friday's Miscellaneous," *A-1s Homes Newsletter,* Houston, Texas, December 20, 1991.

[3] D. Forbes Ley, *The Best Seller* Sales Success Press, CA: 1990), front cover.

[4] D. Forbes Ley, *The Best Seller,* front cover.

[5] G.F. Allen, "Six Levels of a Sale," *Management Wisdom Card Series* PMN Publishing, (Indianapolis, IN: 1985).

Get *A*ttention

Develop *I*nterest

Stimulate *D*esire and *D*ecision to Respond

Get Prospect to Take *A*ction by Calling or Visiting

This is where the fruit of successful marketing is found. It is when prospective buyers and sellers decide to respond. This is also where the failure to market properly becomes clearly evident. No "Attention" means no calls or visits.

2. *Telephone Contact.* This is not always the prospect's first contact with the hands-on sales and leasing effort, but many times it is. The two-fold goal of telephone contact is to qualify the prospect and get an appointment (Telephone sales are discussed again later.)

3. *Personal Contact.* Here the serious selling and leasing begins, especially if there has been no previous telephone contact. It is through personal contact that the customer's needs and wants are identified. Ask questions and listen to responses. Use the acronym FORM, a helpful conversation and networking guide, if time and circumstances allow:

F = ask about *F*amily (one of best icebreakers).

O = ask about *O*ccupation (helps qualify prospect).

R = ask about *R*ecreation (builds rapport).

M = Sales/leasing *M*essage—the "close" step, or set next *M*eeting, if necessary, especially if FORM is being used for networking purposes.

The key, however, is to ascertain what type, size, and configuration of home is needed or desired; and what type and size of homesite is sought, and when it is needed.

4. *Demonstration.* Show and listen! Do not talk away a sale. Use a cue card to keep remarks brief and to the point. Listen to what the prospect says, look for clues to a "closing hotbutton"—a particularly desired feature, price, and so on. As an old proverb suggests: "From listening comes wisdom." So show, listen, and learn, and all along the way, practice "benefit selling," whereby product or community features are described as benefits to the homebuyer and prospective resident.

5. *Agreement.* Answer objections, if any, and "close the sale." Recall the earlier ABC sales & leasing acronym: ABC = *A*lways *B*e *C*losing and do not wait until this step to begin. Keep a personal note card listing previous objections, and memorize effective responses that can be used to close convincingly when the time is right. When selling homes, be alert to desired options that will add value to the sale and increase profit margin.

6. *Renewal and Referrals.* It is difficult to understand why this step is not part of other sales and leasing success formulae. It seems quite a natural strategy to close on one sale or lease and immediately lay the foundation for the next. How? Upon the next opportunity, with same buyer or lessee,

Sale or Renewal; e.g. upgrade of product (e.g. home) or renew lease upon anniversary.

Generate Referrals; from satisfied homebuying customers and present and former residents; encourage same from new customers and residents.

The most effective way to do this is with superior product and service; exemplary customer and resident relations.

The six generic levels of a sale or lease can take a faithful practitioner a long way toward marketing success. In addition, there is a personal sales variation to the six-level approach.[6] Simply stated, it includes the following guidelines:

Know Beforehand What You Are Going to Say

Memorize Openings and Closings
Rehearse on Your Own and Practice with Someone

Introduce Yourself; Exchange Names

Be Cheerful and Positive; Avoid Artificiality
Use Prospect's Name During Presentation

Qualify the Prospect

Can You Supply What Is Needed or Wanted and When?
Serious or Looker? Prospect Capable of Purchase?

Demonstrate the Product, Service

Review and Stress Features
Answer Objections with Positive Counters

Close the Sale

"Ask for the Order!"
Perform Follow-up, Paperwork, Service

Earlier, telephone sales were given passing mention. The six-step telephone procedure here, mirrors, to some extent, the five steps of personal sales.[7]

Know Beforehand What You Are Going to Say

Memorize Openings and Closings
Rehearse on Your Own and Practice with Someone

---

[6] G.F. Allen, "Personal Sales," *Management Wisdom Card Series* PMN Publishing, (Indianapolis, IN: 1985).
[7] G.F. Allen, "Telephone Sales," *Management Wisdom Card Series* PMN Publishing, (Indianapolis, IN: 1984).

Answer on the *Second Ring* of the Telephone

Use the First Ring to Get Motivated—Smile!
Second Ring Shows You Are Not "Too Quick" or "Too Late"

Introduce Yourself by Name; Ask Prospect's Name

Be Cheerful and Avoid Artificiality
Use Prospect's Name During Conversation

Qualify the Prospect

Can You Supply What Is Needed or Wanted and When?
Is the Product or Service Affordable?

Describe the Product, Service Briefly

Accentuate Positive Features; Any Questions?
How Did Prospect Learn of the Product, Service?

Close the Sale or Schedule an Appointment

Perform Appropriate Followup; Give Directions
Record Sale Data on Appropriate Form(s)

This is as good a point as any to draw together all three ABC Rules of Business and Communication found throughout this text:

*A*lways *B*e *C*losing!—as in sales and leasing.
*A*lways *B*e *C*ourteous!—as in sales and leasing, and in resident and employee relations.
Be *A*ccurate, *B*rief, *C*lear—*C*oncise—*C*omplete in whatever is verbally communicated or written.

Sales Basics Applied to New Home Sales

When new manufactured homes are sold on-site, a parallel track to the leasing effort must be established. In many cases staff can fill two roles, working both sales and leasing. But when the market is strong and prospect traffic heavy, it is best to have skilled, experienced, and motivated staff working separately in both areas. The following is a brief outline of general steps for setting up a new manufactured home sales operation on-site at a landlease community.

1. *Establish Business.* Take all necessary steps to be in compliance with local, state, and federal regulatory statutes and practical guidelines regarding business

licenses to operate, sales tax reporting, separate bank accounts, bookkeeping system, insurance, staffing requirements, equipment and supply needs.

2. *Establish Relationships with Manufactured Home Source and Related Supplier.* Retail salescenters are generally inspected and approved by the manufacturer's representative and a state licensing agency. The initial inventory is carefully selected and ordered, the manufacturer's line of homes studied, options and pricing structure learned. Sales and floorplan literature is inventoried.

3. *Secure Floorplan (Wholesale) and Retail Financing Sources.* Described in Chapter 9.

4. *Implement Marketing Plan for New Home Sales.* Promote and advertise, via newspaper classified and display ads, radio, and cable TV, to targeted markets, such as:

Singles

Young marrieds

Families

Empty nesters

Seniors, retired individuals

5. *Display Homes.* Set up homes in the most visible and accessible fashion possible. Champion Homes has called theirs a "Freedom of Choice Display," where singlesection and multisection homes are placed side by side and connected at floor level with an attractive patio deck. The homes are landscaped, including foundation skirting or painted picket fencing, tastefully furnished, and attractively decorated inside.[8] Sales literature and floorplans are kept either readily available to prospective buyers or in possession of sales staff to ensure opportunity to talk with visitors. Another choice is whether to leave display homes unlocked during the daytime—to encourage casual visits by interested parties—or secured so that sales staff is assured the opportunity to properly and effectively "show" or demonstrate the homes.

6. *Make the Sales Effort Proper.* This step has been covered in detail earlier, but there are a few additional considerations.

- Emphasis should be on profitability when selling home, not simply price selling; that is, cutting the profit margin. In the final analysis, buyers should commit to what they can afford, but additional options do improve the value of the home, enhance the life-style of the homeowner, and produce a healthier profit picture for the retail salescenter.

- Be sensitive to unique desirable features of the home, and capitalize on these to draw and sell customers. Such a feature may be energy efficiency in frigid climates, name-brand appliances, or just plain affordability.

---

[8] Joe Morris, *Sales Success School,* Champion Homes, Michigan, 1987.

- Do not forget the value of prompt service and response to warranty claims as a source of future referrals, inquiring prospects, and repeat sales.

Sales Basics Applied to Resale Homes

The marketing and sale of resale homes in a landlease community is a common occurrence in mature properties, but not so frequent during in-fill, unless the developer is actively buying older homes wholesale and reselling on-site. In any event, there are quite a few things an on-site manager and staff can do to assist community residents in selling their own homes, and in preparing property-owned homes for resale.

"You don't get a second chance to make a good first impression" is good advice for anyone selling a manufactured home. Inside and out, there are many things homeowners and managers can do to enhance a home's marketability and increase its value and eventual sale price.

Start outside. Are the walkway and patio clear of distracting debris? Will the addition of shrubs, flowers, and inexpensive stepping stones dress up the front yard?

Is the exterior of the home clean and in good repair, with no rust stains, cracked windows, or weatherworn wood or metal trim? A fresh coat of paint on the front door always makes a good impression on visitors and prospective buyers. Make sure the storm and screen door combination is sturdy and in good condition.

What is the condition of the skirting? It should be continuous, well maintained, and enhance the appearance of the home. Replace plywood, chipboard, and dented metal skirting with attractive color-coordinated nonflammable vinyl skirting.

The entry steps should be sturdy, freshly painted if needed, and anchored in place. Apply caulking to all outside seams of the home. This improves fuel efficiency, reduces wind noise, and increases value.

Grass and shrubs must be neatly trimmed, and all outside storage items should be placed under the home or in an attractive storage shed. If the home is equipped with outside security lighting and a door bell, both need to work properly, as do any locks.

Apply fresh roof coating before showing the home, and mention it to prospects to increase their perceived value of the home.

Walking into any home that looks and smells clean is a desirable and pleasant experience. From one end of the home to the other, make sure the carpets are shampooed, floors waxed, walls and ceilings cleaned thoroughly. Effect major and minor repairs that are needed. Everything that is left undone—such as dripping faucets, worn carpets, spongy bathroom floors, and broken cabinet door hinges—decrease the value and eventual sale price of any home. Clean the oven and appliances; polish and scrub all fixtures.

Are the owners ready to show the home? They must let in plenty of daylight. Open curtains and drapes (make sure the windows are clean) throughout the home, and turn on most or all lights. Closets should be open and straightened to show how roomy they are. While the home is being shown, keep children and pets away; make sure the television, radio, and stereo are turned off.

There are additional items that should be addressed. Check outside. Does the home use fuel oil? The oil tank must be wire-brushed, freshly painted, and its support bracing strengthened if necessary. Are water lines properly heat-taped and insulated? Point this out to prospective buyers. Does the home have a storage building? Whether it is part of the sale or not, it should be made as sturdy-looking as possible and given a fresh coat of paint, color coordinated with the home. The same advice applies to mailboxes in front of the home. Is the home anchored and tied down properly? Are the wheels and axles still in place or stored under the home? Finally, the homeowners should have copies of utility bills on hand for prospective buyers to examine.

How much is the manufactured home worth? What are the appropriate retail, loan, and wholesale values of the home being sold? The best way to find out is for the owners to hire a qualified manufactured home appraiser. Names of appraisers are usually listed in the telephone directory Yellow Pages, and it is also possible to call a nearby manufactured home retailer and ask for recommendations.

Many appraisers will explain the significance and differences between the retail, loan, and wholesale values when a home is appraised. Once the values are known, they are compared with the principal balance of the outstanding mortgage, if there is one. The difference between the two amounts, assuming the appraised retail value is greater than the outstanding mortgage principal, is the amount of margin or potential profit with which to work during sales price negotiations with prospective buyers. If the services of a manufactured home broker are retained, the sales commission will come out of that margin as well.

What is the best way to market a resale manufactured home? There are several alternatives. Place ads in the real estate or classified ad section of local newspapers and in all "free" consumer newspapers. Take flattering photos of the home—reproductions of a good 35mm color photo taken in the spring are usually best. Put copies on bulletin boards in stores and laundromats. If the home is sited in a landlease community, help the homeowners by encouraging them to post photos and sale information sheets, complete with phone number and address, in the information center, or on a clubhouse bulletin board. If permitted, suggest that the homeowners put a "For Sale" sign in the street-facing front window of the home, not in the front yard. Finally, if the home is listed with a real estate or manufactured home broker, the owners should be cooperative about showing the home whenever possible. The more people visiting it, the greater the opportunity of selling the home at or near the desired sale price.

Selling a manufactured home the right way involves a lot of preparation, personal effort, and some expense. It is, however, usually worth the extra effort in the long run, because most homeowners do not do all the things that have been suggested here. When prospects look at a dozen homes and find one that is properly prepared, they are less liable or able to "beat down" a listed sale price, because the deferred maintenance (things that should have been done but were not) and other shortcomings have already been addressed by the homeowner. Prospective

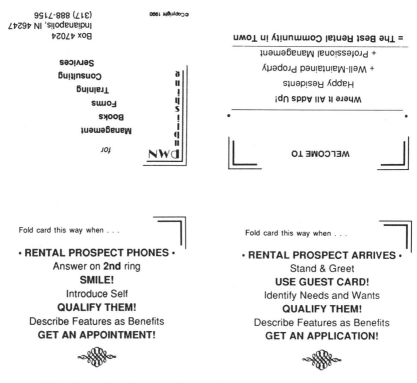

FIG. 14.1 Simplified telephone and in-person leasing procedure.

buyers will quickly recognize that they will be purchasing a better home with fewer problems.[9]

SALES AND LEASING TOOLS

There are a variety of helpful sales and leasing tools available to manufactured housing salespersons and leasing consultants. All of the following are adaptable to both sales and leasing.

1. *Desktop Card.* (See Fig. 14.1.) This foldable card has two sides and room for four messages. The card shown is tailored to landlease community leasing and summarizes the sales and telephone steps described earlier. It can be easily made with a 3- by 5-inch index card folded in half.

2. *Phone Sticker:* "Ask for an Appointment." This handy reminder, printed on an adhesive-backed tag or strip, is usually placed on the sales or leasing

---

[9] G.F. Allen, "Get a Better Price for Used Mobile/Manufactured Homes," *Manufactured Home Merchandiser,* (August) 1988 pp. 28–30.

LOAN AMORTIZATION CARD
MONTHLY PAYMENTS TO REPAY (AMORTIZE)
EACH $1,000 OF A LOAN

YEARS OF LOAN	PERCENT INTEREST							
	6%	7%	8%	9%	10%	11%	12%	15%
1	88.08	86.54	86.99	87.45	87.92	88.39	88.85	90.26
2	44.33	44.73	45.23	45.69	46.15	46.61	47.03	48.49
3	30.43	30.88	31.34	31.80	32.27	32.74	33.22	34.67
4	23.49	23.95	24.41	24.89	25.36	25.85	26.34	27.83
5	19.34	19.80	20.28	20.76	21.25	21.74	22.25	23.79
10	11.10	11.61	12.13	12.67	13.22	13.78	14.35	16.13
15	8.44	8.99	9.56	10.14	10.75	11.37	12.00	14.00
20	7.16	7.75	8.36	9.00	9.65	10.32	11.01	13.17
25	6.44	7.07	7.72	8.39	9.09	9.80	10.53	12.81
30	6.00	6.65	7.34	8.05	8.78	9.52	10.29	12.64

FIG. 14.2   Typical simplified loan amortization chart for handy reference.

consultant's desk phone. The "Telephone Doctor," Nancy J. Friedman of St. Louis, also recommends a "Smile (It might be the boss calling)" sticker. The same source also publishes a handy wallet card reminder of phrases for use on the phone and in person:

Five Forbidden Phrases	Recommended Responses
• I don't know . . .	"Let's find out."
• I can't . . .	"Let's try this—" (Offer the alternative.)
• You'll have to . . .	"What you'll need to do . . ."
• Just a second . . .	"Are you able to hold?"
• No . . .	Offer a positive alternative.[10]

3. *Map.* Keep a copy of a state map in a desk drawer, to assist with giving directions over the telephone. Best for this purpose are car rental agency maps available free at most airport-based car leasing counters.

4. *Booklet.* The Manufactured Housing Institute publishes a very helpful booklet (24 pages) titled *How to Buy a Manufactured Home.* Not only is it a good sales training tool, but when offered in ads for landlease communities, as a "Free Booklet, *How to Buy a Manufactured Home,* Call _____," the response is generally heavy. Staple a business card to the booklet's front cover, enclose a brochure describing the landlease community, and send it to the interested party.

5. *Business Cards.* The reverse side of a business card represents a super sales or leasing message opportunity. Many manufactured home salespersons print a loan amortization chart there (see Fig. 14.2) or a list of "10 good reasons to buy a manufactured home." Landlease communities often put a "Free Rent for 30 Days" coupon there or a sketch map showing how to locate the property. There are all sorts of result-producing possibilities. The front of the card includes the

[10] Nancy J. Friedman, "Telephone Doctor," wallet card. St. Louis, Missouri, (314) 291–1012.

FIG. 14.3 A standard real estate management form tailored to manufactured home community leasing.

name, address, and phone number of the salescenter or landlease community, and the contact person's name.

6. *Guest Card.* When a sales or leasing prospect walks in the door, after the initial greeting and introductions are made, he or she should be asked to complete a Guest Card. See Fig. 14.3 for a sample landlease community-tailored format. The card is easily designed for the retail sales center as well.

7. *Traffic Record.* After every telephone conversation and on-site interview or sales presentation, a traffic report is completed. Figure 14.4 is a Weekly Prospect Inquiry Report form in frequent use at landlease communities, and Fig. 14.5 is an Opportunities to Do Business form used by some retail sales centers.

There are more sales and leasing tools available. Those described here may suggest measures that can be adapted to enhance one's ability to sell and lease effectively at retail sales centers and on-site at landlease communities.

LEASING HOMESITES

There are four key steps to effective leasing of homesites in a landlease community.

1. *Personal Preparation.* Training is the vital activity here. One of the best training aids available is a two-cassette tape plus workbook package from the Institute of Real Estate Management in Chicago, entitled *How to Be a Successful Apartment Rental Consultant.* Memorizing "openings," "closings," and "responses to objections" and practicing role-playing with peers are good ways to prepare. Especially important are to learn and apply the tried and true sales-leasing ABC rules: "Always Be Courteous" and "Always Be Closing."

2. *Telephone Technique.* It is important to learn and use proper telephone technique. Using the desktop tent card described earlier is the easiest way to master

WEEKLY PROSPECT INQUIRY REPORT

FOR (Property)_____

Date	Time	Phone √	Visit √	Name of prospect	Address, Phone #	Newspaper Which?	Yellow Pages	Radio/ TV	Referral	Passtby	Other	Other	Followup: Call, letter, etc.
TOTAL #		___	___	N/A	N/A								N/A

CONVERSION %s = 1) # visits ÷ # calls per week = telephone call %. Good = 25%+
2) # applications ÷ # visits per week = visit call %. Good = 25%+

This form available for purchase in tablet format.
Property Management Form #103
Copyright Jan 1989

GEA
MANAGEMENT
P.O. Box 47024
Indianapolis, IN 46247

FIG. 14.4 A standard real estate management form.

$$\boxed{\text{STANDARD SHOPPING REPORT}}$$

I. GENERAL INFORMATION
A. Property _____
B. Address _____
C. Telephone No. (   ) _____ , Date: Phone _____ Visit _____
D. Person Shopped: Phone _____ , Visit _____ Shopper _____
E. Directions to Property _____

II. TELEPHONE SALES & LEASING EVALUATION (50 possible points)
A. Circle **Yes or No** and assign points appropriately   Possible Points/Points Given
1. Number of rings before being answered? (2=ideal)_____   2/_____
2. Was answering party SMILING & friendly? _____ Y or N _____ 5/_____
3. Exact greeting? '_____   ' _____ 5/_____
4. Asked for your name, address & telephone number? _____ Y or N _____ 3/_____
5. Asked about housing needs? (when, size)_____ Y or N _____ 5/_____
6. Told pricing information or did you have to ask? _____ _____ 2/_____
7. ASKED FOR A DEFINITE APPOINTMENT TO VISIT? _____ Y or N _____ 5/_____
8. Given directions to the community? _____ Y or N _____ 3/_____
9. Asked how you heard about community? _____ Y or N _____ 5/_____
10. Given undivided attention during conversation _____ Y or N _____ 2/_____
11. Thanked for calling? _____ Y or N _____ 5/_____
12. Length of conversation? _____ minutes _____ _____ 5/_____
13. How many times was your name used in conversation? ___ _____ 3/_____
14. Shopper's Comments & Suggestions for Improvement: _____
_____
_____ total = 50/_____

III. ON-SITE SHOPPING EVALUATION. 50 possible points.
A. Arrival and Curb Appeal (circle **Yes or No** & assign points appropriately)
1. Signage enroute?_____ Y or N _____ 1/_____
2. Signage in good condition? _____ Y or N _____ 2/_____
3. Entrance attractive, well-marked? _____ Y or N _____ 2/_____
4. Route to Information Center clearly identified? _____ Y or N _____ 1/_____
5. Grounds well-cared-for (e.g. no loose trash)? _____ Y or N _____ 2/_____
6. Building exteriors well maintained? _____ Y or N _____ 2/_____
7. Initial overall impression of the property: _____

B. Leasing Consultant or Resident Manager Evaluation.
1. Stood & introduced self? _____ Y or N _____ 2/_____
2. Greeted confidently & enthusiastically? _____ Y or N _____ 2/_____
3. Asked for name, address, phone#? _____ Y or N _____ 2/_____
4. Agent at ease & self confident? _____ Y or N _____ 2/_____
5. Shopper's name used during conversation? _____ Y or N _____ 2/_____
6. Information readily offered? _____ Y or N _____ 2/_____
7. Given undivided attention? _____ Y or N _____ 2/_____
8. Attire & grooming professional looking? _____ Y or N _____ 2/_____
9. Any distractions? (smoking, eating, noise,visitors)? _____ Y or N _____ 2/_____
10. Shopper's Comments & Suggestions for Improvement: _____

C. Rental/Sales Information Center Evaluation
1. Property brochures & business cards available? _____ Y or N _____ 1/_____
2. Convenient place for completing application? _____ Y or N _____ 1/_____
3. Office suitable for purpose? _____ Y or N _____ 1/_____
4. Parking convenient to office? _____ Y or N _____ 1/_____
5. Shopper's Comments & Suggestions for Improvement: _____

(over)

MANAGEMENT
P.O. Box 47024
Indianapolis, IN 46247

FIG. 14.5 A standard real estate management form.

D. Model & Vacant Apartment/Condominium Evaluation (if applicable)
   1. Initial Impression? _____
   2. Ready to rent? _____
   3. Shopper's Comments & Suggestions for Improvement: _____
      _____

E. Amenities shown and/or explained? _____
   _____
   _____

F. Leasing/Sales Presentation Evaluation:
   1. Asked to complete a Guest Card? _____ Y or N _____ 1/ _____
   2. Prospect "qualified" early? (income, family size)_____ Y or N _____ 2/ _____
   3. Housing "needs" identified? (size, when. . .) _____ Y or N _____ 2/ _____
   4. Good "product knowledge" by consultant? _____ Y or N _____ 1/ _____
   5. Good "community knowledge"? (schools, stores. . .) _____ Y or N _____ 1/ _____
   6. Practice "benefit selling"?_____ Y or N _____ 2/ _____
   7. Quoted prices before you had to ask? _____ Y or N _____ 1/ _____
   8. Prospect's objectives answered quickly? _____ Y or N _____ 1/ _____
   9. Lease & rules reviewed & explained? _____ Y or N _____ 1/ _____
   10. HOW MANY ATTEMPTS TO "CLOSE THE SALE"? _____ Y or N _____ 2/ _____
   11. Asked to complete an application? _____ Y or N _____ 2/ _____
   12. Asked to leave a deposit, if applicable? _____ Y or N _____ 0/ _____
   13. Asked about pets?_____ Y or N _____ 1/ _____
   14. Given a sales brochure and/or business card?_____ Y or N _____ 1/ _____
   15. Reviewed utility & related costs?_____ Y or N _____ 1/ _____
   16. Recommend another community? Name_____ Y or N _____ 1/ _____
   17. Shopper's Comments & Suggestions for Improvement _____
      _____

IV. **SHOPPING REPORT SUMMARY**
   A. Spotted as a 'shopper' _____ Y or N _____ 0/ _____
   B. Telephone Evaluation.   Total # points = _____
   C. On-Site Evaluation.   Total # points = _____
                                 TOTAL POINTS = _____ out of a possible 100

FOOTNOTES TO STANDARD SHOPPING REPORT:
-
-
-
-
-

PHOTOGRAPHS ATTACHED?   YES or NO

SUPPLEMENTAL CHECKLISTS:
1. Disabled and/or unlicensed vehicles?
2. Condition of Trash Dumpsters?
3. Storage Area Condition?
4. Mailboxes (NDCBU's)?
5. Condition of Streets?
6. Resident Relations Indicators?
7. Parking?
8. Lighting?

This form available for purchase in tablet format.
Property Management Form #106
Copyright Jan 1989

GFA
MANAGEMENT
P.O. Box 47024
Indianapolis, IN 46247

FIG. 14.5   *(Continued)*

this sequence. The "Smile" and "Ask for an Appointment" stickers can help too. Learn the basic steps and practice with someone.

3. *Professional Leasing Techniques.* Learn and use professional leasing techniques—again, the desktop tent card can help. Regular use of the Guest Card and the traffic report will also ensure effective leasing. Keep telephone and on-site interview and approved application conversion percentages above 25%. See the bottom of Fig. 14.4 for both formulae.

4. *Measure Performance.* Compute the conversion percentages (mentioned earlier) weekly. Report or record results over time, to evaluate performance and identify areas to improve. Engage a professional mystery-shopper service to visit the property, by phone and in person, every 6 months. Shopper service is described in Appendix H. Most important, keep in mind the maxim "Every visitor is a shopper"—because it is true. Figure 14.5 shows a standard shopping report format.

Once these basics of effective leasing have been mastered, it is important to learn to screen leasing applicants properly and carefully. Effective prospect screening is composed of five distinct and significant steps:

1. Initial Impression
2. Application Information
3. Tenant Record
4. Income Status
5. Credit History

Each step is critical in its own right, and all five must be taken to develop a complete picture of prospective renters.

Initial Impressions are obtained during the prospect's first telephone call and visit to the leasing or property information center. The leasing consultant must determine the housing needs of the prospect, and whether the community can, or desires to, meet them. For instance, what is the size and age of the prospect's manufactured home? Is it too large for the homesites found in many older manufactured home communities, or is the home too old (assuming poor-to-fair condition of home as well) or too small to fit in favorably (i.e., enhance or detract from curb appeal) with homes already sited? Furthermore, how long has the prospect been employed, and how much does he or she make each week or month? In effect, the person can afford to live in the manufactured home community? Every community should have set guidelines pertaining to such qualifiers, as well to such topics as whether pets are permitted and the maximum number of people allowed to reside in a two- or three-bedroom home.

When prospects arrive at the information office, take note of the condition of their car, their personal attire, and overall cleanliness. These observations give some indication of what management can reasonably expect once the prospects move into the community. Be especially careful and diligent not ever to discriminate on the basis of age, sex, race, religion, or family status.

Application Information is very important. Every part of a community application should be fully and legibly completed. The areas pertaining to past landlords, whom to contact in an emergency, and who actually owns the manufactured home being moved into the community are especially significant. The information on past landlords will be important for the next screening step. The emergency data are obviously critical in the event of an actual emergency and can be equally important as a collections aid if a manufactured home is abandoned for one reason or another. Who really holds title or ownership of the home? This, too, is vital information if timely rent collection becomes a problem. Often, a lending institution will cooperate to encourage a homebuyer to stay current with the manufactured home community. Ask to see a copy of the manufactured home title (in titling states) or to see that a loan identification number and lending institution point-of-contact and phone number are listed on the application.

If the homeowners are moving the manufactured home in which they reside, a drive-by inspection of their present homesite is an important part of the screening process. However, many homes are located too far from the screening community to be easily visited. In these instances, insist that the prospects bring in (or if moving from out-of-state, mail in) at least two recent Polaroid-type photos of the home, each taken from a different exterior perspective. One photo should show one end and side of the home; the other photo should show the other end and side of the home. This is certainly not a foolproof method, but it does give management an additional piece of information to evaluate during screening. Naturally, management must make sure that the home actually moving into the community is the one photographed.

In cases where a photo shows a manufactured home with unpainted galvanized or particleboard foundation siding, and landlease community rules require a prefinished metal or vinyl type of skirting, this can be pointed out to the prospects as a condition that must be addressed to ensure move-in approval. The same can be done relative to roof coating, general cleanliness of the home, or even a need to have the home repainted.

Tenant Record verification is a laborious but very necessary step in the screening process. Use the information from the application and contact former landlords. Usually, within the manufactured home community fraternity, community managers will give candid information about departing homeowners. It is too easy for erroneous or misleading information to backfire on the people giving it, especially if the manufactured homeowners move within the same geographic area. Avoid accepting other communities' problem residents.

Income Status is another area that is important but not always vigorously pursued. Are the prospects employed? How long have they been on the job and what is the take-home pay? Be especially careful where self-employed individuals are concerned. If employers will not give the wage or salary amounts over the phone, simply verify whether the amount stated on the application is accurate.

Credit History is explored if the previous steps show the prospects in a favorable light. To know that good renters are moving into the manufactured home landlease community is well worth the amount charged by a credit bureau. When people are turned down, however, because of an unsatisfactory credit report, the community managers must give the prospects the name and address of the credit bureau.

Rental prospects cannot be turned down for reasons of race, religion, age, sex, or national origin (Title VIII of the Civil Rights Act of 1968), nor because of familial status (HUD 1988). It is important, therefore, to be careful with the selection process. Use the five steps listed earlier, and keep copies of rejected applications on file so that they are available if it becomes necessary to demonstrate consistency and fairness in rejecting prospects for reasons other than those mentioned.

Resident screening is a time-consuming but very important part of professional manufactured home community leasing management. Decide now what policies and criteria to use when screening prospects, and commit to using all five important steps: Initial Impression, Application Information, Tenant Record, Income Status, and Credit History.[11]

SUMMARY

With the development and establishment of a manufactured home landlease community being the substance of a new business venture, sales and leasing are the proverbial icing on the cake. Good marketing planning, effective advertising, and professional management procedures set the stage for interested homebuyers and prospective renters to be enticed to purchase and lease in the manufactured housing environment. Indeed, effective sales and leasing can be the key to success or failure at this stage of the development process.

[11] G.F. Allen, "How to Screen Possible Community Residents," *Manufactured Home Merchandiser,* Chicago, Illinois, Nov '88, pp. 48 & 49.

CHAPTER 15

START-UP AND ONGOING PROPERTY MANAGEMENT OPERATIONS

Manufactured home communities, of all the types of multifamily housing, have received least attention from national real estate trade associations and professional training and certifying agencies. The assumption seems to have been that if one successfully manages apartment or condominium communities, one can manage manufactured home landlease communities. Although many standard real estate management principles are indeed applicable, there are also peculiarities and differences that apply to the start-up and ongoing property management of the typical manufactured home community.

The unique aspects of manufactured home landlease community management are important to identify and describe. This chapter discusses issues pertaining to the property itself, the residents, the homes, marketing, rent collection, maintenance, terminology, industry issues, supplemental sources of income, and a property rating system.

It is also important for manufactured home landlease staff and portfolio property managers to be familiar with the basics and importance of property operations start-up, management office, personnel matters, resident relations, and financial and general management.

UNIQUE CHARACTERISTICS OF MANUFACTURED HOME LANDLEASE COMMUNITY PROPERTY MANAGEMENT

The Property

Rural manufactured home landlease communities outnumber their urban counterparts 3 to 1.[1] A manufactured home landlease community may have as few as

[1] G.F. Allen, "Survey Reflects Community Development," *Manufactured Home Merchandiser*, Chicago, November 1989, pp. 32–34.

2 to 4 homesites (when so mandated by a state regulatory agency) or well over 1,000 sites.[2] Regulated manufactured home landlease communities are inspected regularly, pay a periodic licensing fee, and receive formal authorization to operate. Some regulating agencies require that an on-site caretaker be named and the property owner clearly identified to residents. Some also require Guidelines for Living (rules and regulations) to be posted in public view, a Property Prospectus published, homes properly anchored in place, and electric cables buried between the service pedestal and entry into the home.

Manufactured home landlease communities enjoy a unique economy of scale. As with apartments and other forms of rental property, when income rises owing to improved occupancy or a rent increase, total operating expenses generally account for a smaller percentage of the gross income. With landlease communities this effect is compounded. As the property reaches maximum physical occupancy, there are generally less labor, equipment, and repair costs, because fewer vacant homesites require security and maintenance. Specifically, the only grass left to mow will be in common areas, as each resident usually cares for his or her own rental homesite, and few, if any, utility service risers remain exposed to weather and damage.

According to the Institute of Real Estate Management (IREM) 1991 Income/Expense Analysis Data for conventional apartments nationwide, the average OER (operations expense ratio) was 51.5% (54.3% when unit heating costs are included). The national average for manufactured home landlease communities in 1989 (the last year for which data are available) was only 37.8%.[3] It is not unusual to see this already low OER percentage drop from 37.8% to 25% and lower when a several-hundred homesite landlease community approaches 100% physical occupancy.

Finally, the real estate tax basis is usually less for a landlease community, because there are generally fewer "brick and mortar" types of improvements to value and tax. The individual homeowner-renters, however, pay annual personal property taxes on their homes, unless they live in a locale that treats all manufactured homes as real estate. Then they are taxed accordingly.

Residents

Manufactured home living, for many, is a desirable and preferred life-style. The homes are energy efficient, affordable, and easy to maintain. Landlease communities and manufactured housing subdivisions with moderate-sized homesites strike a balance with apartment living: they provide privacy, as opposed to the intimate proximity to neighbors, characteristic of apartment and condominium living; and they dispel the fear of living too far apart, a real concern of many seniors and retirees.

---

[2] G.F. Allen, "Managing the Manufactured Housing Community," *Journal of Property Management,* IREM, Chicago, 1988, pp. 42–45.

[3] G.F. Allen, "Mobilehome Communities Prove a Better Investment Than Apartments," *Manufactured Home Merchandiser,* Chicago, August 1992, pp. 26 & 27.

Who is the typical manufactured homebuyer? About 23% of homebuyers are under 30 years of age, 48% are 30 to 60 years old, and 29% are more than 60 years. Some 31% are blue-collar workers, 24% white-collar workers, 25% retired, and 20% fall in other categories.[4]

More than 90% of manufactured homes never leave the rental community in which they are first sited. Most are sold in place, some are subleased. The newer, larger, singlesection and multisection homes are difficult to transport, and the expense of such an effort is prohibitive.

The homeowner living in a landlease community has the dual identity of being a renter (i.e., landlease) and home equity owner, thus experiencing the benefits and shortcomings associated with each identity.

The Homes

Today's manufactured homes rival the most attractive contempory apartment decor. Garden tubs, cathedral ceilings, fireplaces, washer-dryer hookups, central air conditioning, and stereo-intercom systems are common features.

Since 1976 all manufactured homes have been required to comply with the federally mandated National Manufactured Housing Construction and Safety Standards (NMHCSS).

Manufactured homes, when sited in landlease communities, are most often taxed as personal property. When permanently anchored on the homeowner's property, however, they are usually taxed as real estate. Some states now tax all manufactured homes as real estate.

Marketing

Manufactured home landlease community homesites are advertised much like apartment rentals, through newspaper classified and, sometimes, display ads, plus telephone Yellow Pages and other local directories. Manufactured homes, however, usually have an added marketing opportunity via local manufactured housing retail salescenters.

Homes to be resold, once sited in a landlease community, are often advertised, even brokered, through the property's information center and staff. In any event, prospective homebuyers and renters are screened and preapproved by the community manager before the home sale is consumated. Additional marketing-related measures, characteristic of manufactured home landlease communities, are discussed in Chapter 13.

Rent

Manufactured home landlease community rent usually includes refuse (i.e., trash) removal and water and sewer charges. Sometimes the cable TV fee is absorbed in

[4] Allen, "Managing the Manufactured Housing Community," pp. 42–45.

the rent, as well as additional or per capita charges for pets or more than two people living in a home, to offset additional water usage. Just as often, however, water and sewer charges and cable TV fees are metered and billed separately.

Rent rates may vary within a manufactured home landlease community, depending on the homesite location, size (for singlesection or multisection homes), or other value-added characteristics. Monthly rents are usually due the first day of the month, with or without a grace period of 2, 5, or sometimes 10 working days. Most property owners prefer to have all rents due on the same day of the month, to avoid having payments made and deposited throughout the month. Property owner-levied penalties and NSF (nonsufficient funds) check fees may range from $10.00 to $25.00 per incident. *Note:* Everything in this paragraph may well be tempered by local and state rent control statutes.

Manufactured home landlease community homesite rent, as a rule of thumb, is usually one-third that of three-bedroom apartments or townhouses in the same market area. In other words, it takes three manufactured home landlease homesites to generate the same potential gross rental income as an apartment in a nearby apartment community.

Rental prospect screening includes the usual checks on creditworthiness, employment verification and apartment leasing history. Landlease community managers often visit a prospective renter's home for a visual check of the exterior, to assess the condition of the home and the renter's life-style. If the home is too distant, the prospective renter may be asked to provide two recent color photographs of the home, each taken of a different exterior view. Management should also request a copy of the homeowner's title or contract to purchase, to include with the application to lease.

Once again, depending on local rent control and landlord-tenant legislation, these characteristics will vary: ground leases are usually month-to-month; the majority of manufactured home landlease communities use written leases (61%); and notice requirements of rent increases and changes to property rules and regulations (i.e., guidelines for living) will range from a minimum period of 30 days to 6 months and longer.

What are the rent incentives characteristic of landlease communities? The scope is almost as broad as one's imagination: free site rent for 1 month after the home is sited and properly skirted (i.e., foundation fascia installed); reduced rent (i.e., one-half the usual rate) for 3 to 6, or even 12 months; "free" move or home setup, if the destination landlease community has the appropriate transport equipment and trained staff. Moreover, referral or finder's fees given to local manufactured home retailers and community residents are commonplace.

Management

Managing a manufactured home landlease community is often likened to being mayor of a small town. Most of the residents, even though they are tenants holding landleases on their homesites, do in fact own their homes. Many landlease communities have on-site convenience stores, beauty shops, and other such business services. Most often managers, usually couples working as a team, live on-site (many states require this) and interact with their residents just as a mayor does with the citizens of his or her community.

Why is a couple living on-site, working together, usually the desired staffing arrangement for a landlease community? Ideally, the two people complement each other in disposition, job skills, and experience. It is often the case that one party generally prefers to work outdoors, handling maintenance, grounds, and related tasks. The other party may handle site leasing and home sales and office-related responsibilities from within the property's information center, whether this office is in the couple's home or in a separate building. This arrangement is also valuable, in that manager couples are usually readily accessible in the event of an emergency. Finally, given a small to moderate-sized community, hiring a retired couple, wanting to supplement their income and stay active, is generally far more cost-effective than hiring two unrelated individuals to head up separate maintenance and office functions. In regard to compensation, community managers are paid salaries, which may be adjusted if rent and utility concessions are part of the compensation package. Opinions vary as to whether such concessions are fair and desirable, or confusing and "less than motivating."

What are the unique aspects of a manufactured home landlease community manager's job? To begin with, this job is unlike that of an apartment manager's, in that every move-in and move-out must be closely supervised by a responsible and knowledgeable person on the staff. When homes are moved onto or off homesites, there is always a real risk of damage to the home and site. It is management's responsibility to ensure that utility connections are disconnected and that proper precautions are taken to prevent compression or twisting of underground water and sewer lines. Furthermore, although on-site staff observe, and sometimes assist with utility hookups, especially water and sewer, it is not usually recommended that they effect electric, natural gas, or other fuel connections, as there is a far greater liability potential associated with these hookups.

Maintenance

Community maintenance staff, in northern climates, ensure that waterline hookups, and individual water meters if present, are properly protected from freezing, usually through installation of heat tapes and insulation wrap.

On-site staff often assist, sometimes even contract themselves out, to generate additional income for the property by installing foundation fascia (skirting) for new move-ins. They may also assist in the spotting and installation of earth anchors around the home, and possibly securing the home to the anchors and tiedowns, using steel straps secured to the undercarriage or over the top of the home. However, many property owners prefer to have home owners contract these services with a speciality firm.

A PMN Publishing-sponsored national survey identified waterline leaks and water riser problems, and street or pavement deterioration, as the two most common maintenance challenges in manufactured home landlease communities. It is, therefore, important that engineering design and construction supervision not only be cognizant of potentially troublesome areas, but plan and develop the community to lessen the likelihood of their occurrence. At a minimum, maintenance staff need to be skilled at effecting waterline and water riser repairs—and be willing to do so, even in inclement weather. In addition, prompt attention to early pavement deterioration prevents this concern from becoming a major problem over the long haul.[5]

Terminology

Most general terms characteristic of manufactured home landlease communities are covered in the Introduction to this text and in previous chapters. A few new and specific terms worth reviewing, however, include the following:

- *Utility risers:* Any underground utility or service line terminating at grade level; for example, water, sewer, electric pedestal, fuel oil, cable TV, and telephone terminal boxes.
- *Home sizes* depicted as 16×80 or 80×16; 24×60 or 60×24: nominal size of a singlesection home, for example, $16' \times 80'$ or $80' \times 16'$; and a multi-section home, for example, $24' \times 60'$ or $60' \times 24'$.
- *Hitch:* Permanent or removable frame-end device (welded or bolted to frame), used to transport or move a manufactured home.
- *Book value of home:* Refers to approximate wholesale and resale values of singlesection and multisection homes. Reference is usually to values computed using one of four or more trade data books or information sources (see Fig. 15.1).
- *Closed or open community:* Admittance to the former is restricted to home owners who buy a new home from the developer of a particular landlease community, which is akin to the practice of developers of upscale conventional housing subdivisions. Access to an open community is available to any new or used manufactured home meeting the property owner's standards (e.g., regarding the age, size, and condition of the home). All landlease communities in the United States are subject to Federal Fair Housing standards.

Issues

When manufactured home landlease community owners and managers were polled nationwide as to issues of most concern to them, the top three were:

- Rent control or threat thereof
- Restrictive zoning and rezoning practices
- Tenant rights or landlord-tenant legislation.[6]

---

[5] Allen, "Survey Reflects Community Development," pp. 32–34.
[6] Allen, "Survey Reflects Community Development," pp. 32–34.

Boeckh Building-Cost Manual
Box 664 (c/o American Appraisal Association)
Milwaukee, WI 53201-9813
(800) 558-8650

Datacomp Appraisal Systems
5250 Northland Drive, N.E.
Grand Rapids, MI 49505
(616) 363-8454

F.W. Dodge Division
McGraw-Hill Publishers
1221 Avenue of the Americas
New York, NY 10020
(212) 512-2000

Kelley Blue Book
5 Oldfield
Irvine, CA 92718
(800) 444-1743

Marshall & Swift's Valuation Services
1617 Beverly Boulevard
Los Angeles, CA 90026
(800) 526-2756

Mobile/Manufactured Home Blue Book
29 N. Wacker
Chicago, IL 60606
(800) 621-9907

N.A.D.A. Appraisal Guide
Box 7800
Costa Mesa, CA 92628
(800) 966-6232

FIG. 15.1 Sources of cost guides and value appraisal information relative to manufactured homes.

Manufactured Home Landlease Community Rating System

There is no contemporary, universally accepted, industry-wide property desirability rating system. Various federal agencies (e.g., FHA and VA) have published in-house standards in years past, and several insurance companies have in-house parameters. The last nationwide, formal rating system is the long-defunct Woodall STAR Mobile Home Park Rating System, which is described in Appendix F. Although this system is still loosely referenced by real estate brokers, bankers, and some landlease community owners, it has not been updated or published since the mid-1970s.

BASICS OF START-UP

Planning for property management start-up is a unique and creative business opportunity, which, effectively managed, can position and enhance a project's marketing and organize management resources from day one.

Research

Take time to research all appropriate information available relative to manufactured home landlease community development management, manufactured housing per se, and real estate management in general. Many good reference books and trade periodicals are listed in the Bibliography of this text. Read and take copious notes; highlight and underline liberally—these references become valuable tools. Broaden research to cover areas that may be new, for example, manual bookkeeping alternatives, various computer programs for bookkeeping and tenant relations, the state's labor laws, and "how to" guides on advertising, hiring and supervising, property finance controls, equipment repair and maintenance, and management methods and procedures.

Getting Organized

Compiling a property operations manual, also known as the SOP (standard operations procedures), is the best way to organize for start-up and ongoing operations. With start-up, the SOP forces the compiler to touch all bases relative to personnel, equipment, inventory, policies and procedures, budget and operating reports, marketing, and resident relations. Moreover, the SOP manual is just as important to the manager and staff of an ongoing property operation and must be updated from time to time. It can be used as a training tool for new hires and a model when other new landlease communities are developed or acquired.

There is more than one format for a property operations manual. The most common is a conventional-sized, three-ring binder (preferably with 1-inch, rather than 3-inch, rings, depending on the volume of material to be included) with a cover of any color but red. This is a relatively inexpensive product, and it makes future updates to the manual a snap. Each section of the binder is identified with a color-coded or clear, typed index tab. The operations manual usually sits on a bookshelf near the manager's desk for easy reference.

Another critical tool is a bright red three-ring binder for the property's "Emergency Procedures Manual." The emergency manual is simply a collection of property plot plans (i.e., construction "as-built prints" reduced to 8" × 10" sheets of paper) with color-coded utility lines and identified shutoffs, and step-by-step procedures for various emergencies. A copy of the emergency procedures should also be included in the operations manual. Keep the bright red emergency binder within plain view and easy reach on the resident manager's desk.

Update both the operations and emergency manuals periodically—on both an "as needed" basis, when company policies change or procedures are revised, and annually as a formal review by the property owner, community manager, and staff.

Writing Style

Operations manuals are actually about the easiest writing assignment a manager can have, because the ABC Rule of Good Communication should prevail with every paragraph written. That is, every sentence should be Accurate, Brief, Clear—Concise—and Complete. Write in the present tense and active voice (not past and passive), and with an easy conversational style. The goal is to produce an operations manual that is easy to read and helpful to all management staff.

Content

What should be included in an operations manual, and in what order?

1. Start with a title page that identifies the notebook as an operations manual. Identify the specific property for which it was prepared, and who complied it and when. Then include a page to list future amendments and dates.

2. The next page should be a table of contents, listing all the tabs and perhaps including a very brief subtopic list or description to help the reader quickly find the section needed at the time.

3. Next is the introduction to the manual. Try to keep it to one or two pages in length, double-spaced. Include the purpose of the manual (one sentence is all that is needed); an overview description of the company, along with its goals and a mission statement; a brief description of the landlease community served by the manual; and possibly, if applicable, company and property personnel organization charts.

4. As mentioned earlier, there are several ways to organize the researched data. One approach is described here—the "M's of Management." This is a handy tool for the property manager. For the purpose of assembling an operations manual, use nine M's of Management. Each rates a separate tab in the manual, and is described in the following paragraphs.

• *Manpower:* (Personnel.) This section includes appropriate job descriptions, hiring and interviewing guidelines, blank personnel-related forms, and company policies pertaining to personnel matters, such as vacations. All important manpower items are included in this section. Additional items might include job performance evaluation guidelines, and tips on how employees can help improve resident relations.

• *Machinery, equipment, tools:* Here include basic information about water—well size and pump capacity—wastewater treatment plant operating characteristics, heating fuel distribution system, cable television contacts, swimming pool basics, a tool and personal property inventory for the landlease community, and other information that pertains to property vehicles, tractors, and larger tools.

• *Materials and supplies:* This section includes materials that are purchased on a regular and seasonal (pool chemicals, ice melt) basis, the quantities ordered, and from whom. This is a good place to keep the property's annual purchasing calendar and previously researched Purchasing Comparsion Charts (see Fig. 15.9).

• *Methods:* This is usually the largest section in the operations manual. It contains the general policies and procedures for a property, as well as the materials of the separate and earlier described "Emergency Procedures Manual." Leasing, sales, and resident policies and procedures are also found in this section, plus a copy of the rules and regulations (Guidelines for Living).

• *Money:* In this section are the guidelines pertaining to accounts receivable, such as rent and supplemental income; accounts payable, operating expenses, and chart of accounts; rent collections guidelines; and the current operating budget for the landlease community.

• *Management:* Included here are the overall management policies and procedures that have to do with the landlease community. A suggested problem-solving procedure and a description of key management functions (e.g., plan, organize, lead, control) are helpful tools to include. A list of useful business contacts, complete with addresses and phone numbers, is another recommended feature.

• *Maintenance:* This is the place to include preventive maintenance schedules for various pumps and other equipment and vehicles at the community. It is also the place to put a reference list as to the location of shop manuals, property "as-built" plans, and a narrative describing any peculiarities of the property, such as the location of an emergency water valve that might connect the property to a nearby municipal water system when the on-site pump is down.

• *Marketing and sales:* In this section are samples of newspaper ads that have been successful in the past, brochures, and other marketing tools. A copy of the most recent market survey belongs here too (see Chapter 13 for format). Finally, step-by-step sales and leasing guidelines for telephone and personal interview contacts are placed here, along with a training outline for new sales and leasing consultants.

• *Miscellaneous:* Samples of forms referenced throughout the operations manual can be grouped here or made part of each appropriate section. If the community is not too large, the tenant rent roll can be included as a reference in this section.[7]

A final word about emergency procedures manuals. A vital part is a set of procedures, well thought out in advance, even tested where possible, covering such emergencies as fire in the home, explosion, fuel leak, tornado, earthquake, death in a common area, flooding, sewer backup, public disturbance, and so forth. For example, here is one possible set of steps to take when responding to a residence fire.

---

[7] G.F. Allen, "Operations Manuals Can Be Valuable to Community Owners/Managers," *Manufactured Home Merchandiser*, August 1987, pp. 34–36.

1. Life safety and preservation!
2. Call fire company; attempt to control fire until arrival (include phone number).
3. Notify affected resident.
4. Notify community manager, property manager, or owner, as appropriate (include phone numbers).
5. Call in necessary employees (e.g., maintenance).
6. Secure the premises, if necessary.
7. Comply with fire department requests.
8. Help resident relocate.
9. Notify insurance company (include phone number).
10. Prepare a cleanup schedule.
11. Complete an Incident-Accident Report (see Fig. 15.2).[8]

THE MANAGEMENT OFFICE

As the property operations manual is researched and compiled, be sensitive to items that serve double duty, as key items in the SOP and integral to the management office operations. There will also be materials and references germane to the office but not easily included in the SOP.

Generally, the information center or office contains the property management files; standard forms; bookkeeping records (manual or computerized); and a collection of appropriate management tools, text references, cassette tapes, and other materials. As pointed out earlier, the information center or management office may be in a stand-alone structure such as a clubhouse—or even a construction trailer, in the early days of a new development—or in the community manager's home, if sited in a small to mid-sized landlease community.

Files

In broad terms, there are at least three types of files needed at a manufactured home landlease community. There are resident files, property files, and pending files. Some would add to these "reference files," such as business cards, or a Rolodex categorized by name, product, or service.

Resident Files.   The resident files have three or more categories.

---

[8] G.F. Allen, "Emergency Procedures Manual," *Southeastern Manufactured Housing Journal,* Atlanta, Georgia, March '83, p 4.

INCIDENT / ACCIDENT REPORT

(Type or Print All Entries and Attach Photographs)

Date of this report: _____   Vehicular_____ Employee _____

Preparer's Name: _____   Personal Injury _____Fire _____

Rental Community: _____   Property Damage _____Theft_____

_____   Other_____(specify)

1. Date of incident/accident: _____

2. Exact location where this incident / accident occurred (address, intersection, etc.). (Attach a diagram if necessary.) _____

3. Describe in detail what occurred as you know it (use additional pages if necessary): _____
    _____
    _____

4. What police/fire unit(s) if any, were called to the scene? _____

5. Was a police investigation made and report prepared?_____(If you have a copy of the police report, attach a copy to this report.)

6. Was anyone transported to a hospital or physician's office from the scene of the incident/accident? If so, who? _____

7. Who/what (hospital, clinic) administered medical treatment? _____

8. If you know, what type of treatment was given to the patient? _____
    _____

9. Was anyone formally admitted to a hospital for injuries suffered as a result of this incident/accident? If so, who? _____

10. If an arrest was made, who was incarcerated and where? _____
    _____

11. If this was an accident involving a vehicle(s), who was driving? _____
    _____

12. What damage, if any, was done to the vehicle(s) involved? _____

13. Witnesses to this incident/accident (name, address, phone number): _____
    _____

14. Drivers license number(s) of all parties involved (including witnesses): _____
    _____

15. Name, address and phone number of insurance companies (also agents or representatives): _____
    _____

Footnotes:

This form available in tablet format.
Property Management Form #110
Copyright Jan. 1993

DMN Publishing
P.O. Box #47024
Indianapolis, Indiana 46247

FIG. 15.2   A standard real estate management form.

Active Resident File. This is a file maintained on every homesite lessee, and apartment (i.e., rental mobilehome)—if there are any, within the manufactured home landlease community. A typical Active Resident File contains the following:

- Original copy of a properly signed and dated rental agreement and appropriate addendums (see Fig. 15.3).
- Signed and dated Guidelines for Living (rules and regulations) (see Fig. 15.4).
- Copies of completed maintenance work orders, relative to that homesite or rental home (see Fig. 15.5a).
- Copies of all rules violations notices and late rent payment notices (see Fig. 15.5b).
- Original or copy of the application to rent, with its record of emergency contacts and, when possible, a copy of the ownership title or information pertaining to mortgagor (see Fig. 15.6).

The conscientious manager will "paper the files," when appropriate, to document negative behavior, rent payment history, and related matters that may become grounds for eviction in the future.

Closed Resident File. These are resident files on renters/homeowners who have moved out of the community. It is important to physically remove these files and place them in a separate, clearly identified file drawer or box. Keep these records on hand, however, for a reasonable period of time.

Rejected Applicant File. Keep rejected applications on file to prove, if necessary, that the landlease community is in compliance with Federal Fair Housing laws and is not discriminating.

Property Files. Property files are as simple or extensive as required or desired to properly manage a particular landlease community. Here are some recommended categories:

- Engineering drawings, as-built construction drawings, and street layout diagrams.
- Incident-Accident Reports (completed). See Fig. 15.2, cited earlier.
- Guidelines for Living, or rules and regulations.
- Past newsletters.
- Correspondence file.
- Swimming pool-related matters.
- Wasterwater treatment plant reports and maintenance records.
- Drinking water reports and test results, if applicable.
- Accounts receivable (A/R) records (e.g., Summary of Delinquent Accounts). See Fig. 15.7.

MANUFACTURED HOME COMMUNITY LEASE

Name _____

Address _____

Phone # _____

Lot # _____

THIS AGREEMENT made this _____ day of _____, 19_____ by and between _____,

having its principal place of business situated in _____ County, State of Indiana, and hereafter referred to as "OWNER/MANAGER"; and

_____ hereinafter referred to as "RESIDENT";

WITNESSETH:

That said OWNER/MANAGER in consideration of the Covenants of this Agreement and pursuant to the Rules and Regulations incorporated herein by reference, hereby leases to RESIDENT a certain manufactured home site/lot which lot is situated upon said real estate located in _____ County, State of Indiana, and more particularly described as follows, to-wit:

RESIDENT to have and to hold the same from the _____ day of _____, 19_____, and each month thereafter that the RESIDENT complies with the covenants and considerations set forth herein until termination of this Agreement. In consideration of OWNER/MANAGER agreeing to accept this lease, RESIDENT agrees as follows:

I.   **RENT**
   A. RESIDENT agrees to pay to the OWNER/MANAGER upon the execution of this Agreement and on or before the _____ day of each succeeding month the sum of $_____ (_____ and _____/100 Dollars), which payments shall be the monthly rental payment due and payable in advance. Such payments shall be made at the office of the OWNER/MANAGER, or at such other places that may be designated from time to time in writing by OWNER/MANAGER.
   B. In addition to any rent that is due as described in sub-paragraph A above, there shall be assessed a late charge of $_____
   (_____ and _____/100 Dollars) in the event that the RESIDENT should fail to pay the rent by the _____ day of any given month. If the _____ day of any given month falls on a Saturday, Sunday or a holiday, the said late charge shall not be assessed until the next following business day.
   C. Any monies paid following any period that a delinquency as described in sub-paragraph B above exists shall be applied by OWNER/MANAGER to first reduce any delinquency or arrearage.
   D. Residents shall receive thirty (30) days advanced notice of all proposed rent increases. No tenant shall be subject to a rental increase more than one time per year.
   However, Owner/Manager shall have the right to pass through the residents without notice at the same percentage rate increase received by Owner/Manager all unforseen or unpredictable increases in expenses directly related to the operation of the community which expenses shall include but not be limited to: water, sewage, electric, waste removal, state or local assessments, and real estate taxes for which the owner is not provided at least one years notice prior to increase.
II.   **SECURITY DEPOSIT**
   A security deposit of $_____ Dollars is due and payable at the time the rental agreement is signed. This money is to be held to satisfy any claim for the damage to the property or the removal of any litter left at the time of move-out or for any damage or loss sustained as a result of a breach or default by the Tenant.
III. **TERMINATION OF LEASE**
   This lease may be terminated as follows:
   A. The RESIDENT may terminate this Lease Agreement by giving OWNER/MANAGER _____ days written notice prior to the time of the RESIDENT'S departure.
   B. The OWNER/MANAGER may terminate this lease by giving RESIDENT 30 days written notice.
   C. If the RESIDENT shall not depart the premises after _____ days written notice, RESIDENT shall be deemed to be holding over against the OWNER/MANAGER and the RESIDENT shall be liable for all legal costs, expenses, including attorney fees, occasioned by RESIDENT's refusal to depart. Upon removal of the RESIDENT'S manufactured home from the above prescribed leased premises, any items left on the above described leased property shall after _____ days, become the property of the OWNER/MANAGER.
IV.   **TRANSFER OR SUBLETTING**
   A. Since your home site (lot) is rented to you as an individual, it is not transferable to another party. There shall be no assignment, transfer, lease or sublease of your home. Any individual desiring to reside in your home must fill out a new application which in turn must be approved by management.
   B. Manufactured homes that have been sold on a rented site must be moved off the site at time of sale unless the purchaser thereof applies for his own rental agreement and is granted same by the OWNER/MANAGER. No commercial activity will be allowed nor will any manufactured home be used for illegal or immoral purposes.
   C. The management specifically reserves the right to approve or reject all applications to this community, however, no considerations shall be based on race, color, creed or ethnic origin.
V.   **EVENTS OF DEFAULT**
   Any of the following shall be deemed an Event of Default:
   A. The failure to pay any installment of rent when the same becomes due and the failure continues for 5 days.
   B. Residents failure to perform or observe any other covenant, term or condition of this lease or the Rules and Regulations to be performed or observed by Resident and if curable, the failure continues for 15 days after notice thereof is given to Resident.
   C. Abandonment of the Leased Premises.
   D. The filing or execution or occurrence of:
      (1) An involuntary petition in bankruptcy against Resident and the failure of Resident, in good faith, to promptly commence and diligently pursue action to dismiss the petition.
      (2) A petition against Resident making a reorganization, arrangement, composition, readjustment, liquidation, dissolution or other relief of the same or different kind under any provision of the Bankruptcy Act, and the failure of Resident in good faith to promptly commence and diligently pursue action to dismiss the petition.
      (3) A general assignment for the benefit of creditors by Resident.
VI.   **OWNER/MANAGER'S REMEDIES**
   A. Upon the occurrence of any Event of Default, OWNER/MANAGER may, at its option, in addition to any other remedy or right it has hereunder or by law re-enter the Leased Premises, without demand or notice, and resume possession by an action in law or equity or by force or otherwise and without being liable in trespass or for any damages and without terminating this Lease. OWNER/MANAGER may remove all persons and property from the Leased Premises and such property may be removed and stored at the cost of the Resident.
VII. **ATTORNEYS FEES**
   In the event that the OWNER/MANAGER should be required to go to court to recover any delinquent rent or other charges or to enforce any term of this Agreement, or the Rules and Regulations as herein incorporated, RESIDENT shall be liable for all court costs, any reasonable attorney fees and any other charges incurred by OWNER/MANAGER in such action.
VIII. **RULES AND REGULATIONS**
   The RESIDENT, his family, guests, agents and the like shall comply with all rules and regulations established by the OWNER/MANAGER, a copy of which is attached hereto as Exhibit "A", and made a part hereof as if set forth herein. Failure to comply with any of the rules and regulations set forth in Exhibit A shall constitute a breach of this agreement and may result in the termination of this lease.
IX.   **CONSTRUCTION OF TERMS**
   Words of any gender used in this lease shall be held to include any other gender, and words in the singular shall be held to include the plural when the sense so requires.
X.   **BINDING OF OTHER PARTIES**
   This lease shall be binding upon the parties hereto, their heirs, administrators, executors, successors and assigns. This provision, however, shall not be construed to permit the assignment of this Lease except as may be permitted hereby.
XI.   **GOVERNING LAW**
   This agreement shall be construed under and in accordance with the laws of the State of Indiana.
XII. **WAIVER**
   Waiver of one breach of a term, condition or covenant of this Lease Agreement by either party shall be limited to the particular instance and shall not be limited to the particular instance and shall not be deemed to waive past or future breaches of the same or other terms, conditions or covenants.
XIII. **GENERAL AGREEMENT OF THE PARTIES**
   The RESIDENT is required to abide by all Federal, State, County and local laws and ordinances. All RESIDENTS are further obligated to comply with and abide by the State Board of Health Rules and Regulations.
   Notices to be given hereunder shall be deemed sufficiently given when in writing and (a) actually served on the party to be notified or (b) placed in an envelope directed to the party to be notified at the following addresses and deposited in the United States mail by certified or registered mail, postage prepaid:

   1. If to OWNER/MANAGER at _____

   2. If to RESIDENT at _____
   Such address may be changed by either party by written advise as to the new address given as above provided. If there is more than one Resident, their obligation shall be joint and several.
IN WITNESS WHEREOF, the parties hereto have set their hands in duplicate, each of which shall be deemed an original the day and the year first above written.

I hereby acknowledge that I have read, understand, agree to and will comply with all of the rules and regulations of _____ as stated herein and in the Rules, Regulations and Community Guidelines of said Community. Any breach of same by myself or member of my party shall be construed to be a failure to perform or express conditions of the terms of my tenancy. The owner or management may terminate this tenancy for any infraction of said rules by notification in accordance with State Law.

   IN WITNESS WHEREOF, the parties hereto have executed and received a copy of this Agreement on this _____ day of _____, 19_____.

RESIDENT: OWNER/MANAGER:

_____   By _____

_____   Title _____

FIG. 15.3 Used by permission of the Indiana Manufactured Housing Association, Inc.

MANUFACTURED HOME COMMUNITY GUIDELINES

The following Rules and Regulations are to be read in conjunction with and are considered a part of the formal rental agreement of all Residents of the _____ Manufactured Home Community:

I. **YOUR NEW MANUFACTURED HOME**
    A. All manufactured homes will be skirted with skirting approved by management within twenty (20) days of moving into the community. Samples of acceptable skirting are at the office.
    B. All manufactured homes will be anchored according to state and Federal regulations. Installation of earth anchors and attachment of mobile homes thereto is the responsibility of the home owners.
    C. The placement, maintenance and repair of all steps to the home are the sole responsibility of home owner.

II. **PROHIBITED ACTIVITIES**
    For the benefit of the other park residents, the following activities are specifically prohibited in the community:
    A. Loud parties or disturbances.
    B. Speeding vehicles.
    C. Automobile, boat, trailer or vehicle repairs, which can not be completed the same day as started.
    D. Air rifles, B-B guns, fireworks.
    E. Drunkenness and immoral conduct.
    F. Disabled and unlicensed vehicles parked at your home.
    G. Peddling, soliciting, canvasing distributing literature by a religious group or any other form of commercial enterprise without the permission of the Park Management.
    H. Removal of any plants or shrubs from a lot.
    I. Truck-tractors or semi-trailers permitted in the park beyond the storage lot or assigned parking area.
    J. Any violation of any Federal, State, County or City Ordinance, or Statute.

III. **HOOK-UPS**
    Each resident is responsible for water, sewer, oil, gas and electrical installation upon his lot and will be charged for expense of replacing or servicing same where damage is caused due to neglect or improper use on the part of the resident. The RESIDENT will make his own application for all utilities, such as telephone, gas, electric and pay all statements rendered by said companies.

IV. **MANUFACTURED HOME SITES**
    A. Manufactured homes will be placed or removed only by authorized personnel under direct supervision by management. All homes shall be placed on each lot as determined most appropriate by management.
    B. All awnings, appurtenances, porches, steps, storage buildings and skirting must be approved in writing prior to installation or may be subject to removal.
    C. Any trees or shrubs or any temporary or permanent concrete or masonry work must be approved beforehand, and when approved shall not thereafter be removed from premises.
    D. All garbage must be placed in proper fly tight, rigid receptacles. Garbage receptacles must be kept in storage buildings or at the rear of each house except on days when garbage is picked up.
    E. Each resident is cautioned against driving rods, stakes, pipes, etc. into the ground or against digging in an area without first checking with the office. Many types of underground installations might be endangered by indiscriminate action. Any damage of this type will be charged to the resident.
    F. Each Resident is responsible for the maintenance of yards. All yards must be neat and attractively maintained at all times. Management reserves the right to mow yards and impose a charge for mowing against residents and/or owner to be paid at next lot rent payment.
    G. Manufactured homes must be maintained in a neat and attractive condition.

FIG. 15.4 Guidelines also known as rules and regulations. Used by permission of the Indiana Manufactured Housing Association, Inc.

V. **PETS**

A manufactured home community is not the best place to raise a pet. If you wish to have a pet in the community, prior permissions must be obtained from the Management.

No pets shall be permitted to create a nuisance in the community. Pet owners are responsible for cleaning up waste deposits of pets.

VI. **TIRES AND AXLES**

Residents must retain ownership of their home's tires and axles. Tires and axles must be stored underneath each home or in an appropriate storage building.

VII. **GUESTS**

Residents shall be responsible and held liable for the conduct of their guests while in the manufactured home community.

VIII. **VACATING**

Your manufactured home community is planned for permanent residence, but if you must leave, it will require thirty (30) days notice or your security deposit is forfeited. The Manager must be notified by the resident and the mover at least forty-eight (48) hours prior to the manufactured home toter arriving in the park. It is also up to the Resident to get a moving permit from the County Treasurer's Office signifying that all property taxes have been paid on the home for the current year and to pay any back rent due before a home can be moved.

IX. **RULES VIOLATION**

Violation of any park rule or regulation can result in resident eviction. Indiana Code allows owners of manufactured home communities the right to eject persons. "The owner, operator or caretaker of any mobile home park may eject any person from the premises for non-payment of charges or fees for accommodations, for violations of any regulation of the State Board relating to mobile home parks or for any violation of any rule of the park which is publicly posted with the park." (Indiana Code 13-1-7-Sec. 34)

X. **PARK RESPONSIBILITIES**

While the Management and owners of your community will strive to assure the safety of residents and the property, they are not responsible for losses due to fire, theft or accident. You the resident are hereby notified that you assume the risk in such matters.

For any accident or injury on any lot, the resident of such lot shall indemnify and hold management harmless of any and all claims by any person.

XI. **CREDIT CHECK**

Home sites shall only be rented to manufactured home owners. Qualifications for site rental will be based on the credit, income, etc. of the manufactured home owners.

I _____ do hereby give permission and authorization for the Management of _____ Home Community to check my credit and all records concerning rental of a manufactured home site.

XII. **AMENDMENTS TO RULES AND REGULATIONS**

Park Management reserves the right to alter, add to or amend such rules and regulations from time to time, but such changes shall not take effect until written notice thereof is posted within the manufactured home community, or written notice to this effect is delivered to the RESIDENTS home, 30 days prior to implementation.

I have read, understand and agree to abide by these rules set forth by _____ for the benefit of its residence.

_____
       (Name)   (Lot)   (Rent)

FIG. 15.4 *(Continued)*

Date_____

REQUEST FOR SERVICE
WORK ORDER

Resident_____

Address_____

Service Requested: _____

_____

_____

_____

_____

_____

_____

_____

_____

Work Performed: _____

_____

Work Completed ☐   Repaired Temporarily ☐   Parts On Order ☐   Recommendations: _____

_____

_____

Work Performed By_____

(*a*)

FIG. 15.5(a)   Standard real estate management form.

PAST DUE RENT NOTICE

Name _____

Address _____

_____

Site #_____

Date of Notice	Rent Due	Late Charges	Previous Balance	TOTAL AMOUNT DUE

THANK YOU . . .For your immediate payment of the Total Amount Due   ▲
                                                                    PAY THIS AMOUNT

Property Management Form #112
Copyright Mar. 1993

DMN Publishing, Inc.
P.O. Box #47024 — Indianapolis, IN 46247

(*b*)

FIG. 15.5(b)   Standard real estate management form.

MANUFACTURED HOME COMMUNITY RESIDENT APPLICATION

DATE _____

When Space Wanted _____

Full Name _____ Lot No. _____

In Case of Emergency Call _____ Phone No. _____

Social Security Number _____

Single _____Married _____Widowed _____Divorced _____Kind of Pet _____Size at Maturity _____Lbs.

Number of persons who will reside or spend
more than 36 consecutive hours at residence _____

Present
Present Address _____ Phone # _____

Name and Address of Present Landlord _____ Phone (_____) _____

Name and Address of Prior Landlord _____ Phone (_____) _____

EMPLOYER
Company Name _____ Phone (_____) _____

Company Address _____

Your Manager's Name _____Length of Employment _____

REFERENCES
Your Bank_____

Credit Card(s) _____

Store Credit _____ Phone (_____) _____

Personal _____ Phone (_____) _____

MANUFACTURED HOME Serial No. _____Color _____

Make Of Home _____ Year _____ Size _____ Value _____

Purchased from (Name) _____

(Address) _____ (Phone) _____

Home Financed With (Name) _____

(Address) _____

(Phone) _____

Current Needed _____110 _____ 220   Kind of Heat _____ AMPS   60   100   200

Names of persons who will reside or spend   Place of employment and address
more than 36 consecutive hours at residence

_____
_____
_____
_____
_____
_____
_____
_____

FIG. 15.6 Used by permission of the Indiana Manufactured Housing Association, Inc.

Cars	Model	Year	License No.	State

In consideration of space being rented to us, the undersigned and all persons occupying the lot shown above agree to abide by the rules and regulations of your park now in effect, or which may later be posted. We agree to hold the park operators harmless from damages caused by fire, windstorm, or other act of God, and from any losses resulting from theft or breaking in of tenant's property. We agree to leave park on request, without cause, and with the return of any un-earned money; to register guests who remain overnight, notifying park office on their departure. We understand rent is payable in advance. In addition to agreeing to leave the park on request, without cause, but with the return of any unearned money, we also understand that we may be ejected from the park for nonpayment of charges or fees for accommodations, or for violations of law or disorderly conduct, or for violation of any regulation of the Indiana State Board of Health relating to manufactured home parks, or for violation of any rule or regulation of the park which is now or may later be publicly posted within the park. We acknowledge and agree that we are to be liable to the park for any unpaid rent, late charges, legal fees, and any other fees or charges incurred by the park operator as a result of non-payment of rent, abandonment of the rented premises, or any other breach of this agreement, together with interest thereon at the rate of ten percent (10%) per annum and we further acknowledge that the park shall have an innkeeper's lien or hotel keeper's lien upon our property in the same manner and for the same purposes and subject to the same restrictions as statutory innkeeper's or hotel keeper's liens. The park operator shall have a lien upon any manufactured home or other article of value left upon or around the space being rented to us and that the park operator shall have the right to detain such manufactured home or other article of value until the amount of the unpaid rent, late charges, legal fees and any other fees or charges incurred by the park operator have been fully paid, and unless such charges shall have been paid within sixty (60) days from the time when the same accrued, the park operator shall have the right to sell the manufactured home or other article of value at public auction in compliance with Indiana law. It is also agreed by the applicant that there will be no assignment of the use of the lot to any other person, nor occupancy of the lot by any other person without first obtaining prior written consent of the park operator. The undersigned, by his signature hereto, acknowledges that he has received a copy of the Registration for himself and all persons occupying the lot shown above.

The undersigned hereby (verifies/verify) that the foregoing information is true and acknowledge(s) that any subsequent discovery of the falsity of the foregoing information or any other misrepresentation in this application shall be grounds for denial of this application or eviction if said discovery is subsequent to the granting of this application. In making this application, the undersigned authorize(s) the park owner to make whatever inquiry it deems necessary of any individual, company, agency, bank, credit institution or other entity, in addition to any credit bureau or credit reporting agency with regard to the undersigned applicant(s).

I, _____, Lot No. _____, have read and fully understand all park rules and will abide by said rules while living in _____ manufactured home park.

DATE _____

LOT DEPOSIT: $_____ LOT RENT: $_____

OTHER DEPOSITS: $_____ OTHER CHARGES: $_____

$_____

TOTAL AMOUNT DUE: $_____

AMOUNT PAID: $_____ TOTAL MONTH RENT: $_____

BALANCE DUE: $_____ COMMENTS: _____

BALANCE PAID: $_____

Signature of Occupant Verifying Statements

ARRIVED _____ _____
Husband

DEPARTED _____ _____
Wife
GIVEN COMMUNITY
GUIDELINES _____ _____
Signature of Manufactured Home Community Manager

FIG. 15.6 *(Continued)*

SUMMARY OF DELINQUENT ACCOUNTS

For Month of _____ , 19 ___

Property _____   Preparer _____   Manager _____

Unit #, or Address	Resident's Name	Telephone Number(s)	Total Amt. Owed, Incl (NSF & LC)	Late & NSF Charges	Date and Action (1)	Date and Action (2)	Date and Action (3)

This form available for purchase in tablet format.
Property Managerment Form #104
Copyright Jan 1989.

G.F.A
MANAGEMENT
P.O. Box 47024
Indianapolis, IN 46247

FIG. 15.7 A standard real estate management form.

- Accounts payable (A/P) records (paid invoices, etc.). See Fig. 15.8 for Invoice Distribution format.
- Purchasing-related documents, filled in Purchasing Comparsion Charts, and so on. See Fig. 15.9.

Every year, the property file should be purged of outdated and extraneous material. Do not be too quick to throw material away; rather, store it in file boxes for an additional year. *Note:* Do not dispose of documents relative to governmental and real estate transfer matters.

Depending on how much of the actual property accounting is performed onsite, additional property file categories could include bank account records, payroll files, insurance claim information, and various personnel records. It is important that all files be secured after normal business hours.

INVOICE DISTRIBUTION SUMMARY

Payable to: _____   Date _____

From: _____   Ck. NO. _____

Memo: _____   Approvals _____ / _____

Invoice No.	P.O. No.	Property	Chart of Acct#	Sub #	Memo	Net $

TOTAL $ PAID _____

This form available for purchase in tablet format.
Property Management Form #105
Copyright Jan 1989

GFA
MANAGEMENT
P.O. Box 47024
Indianapolis, IN 46247

FIG. 15.8   A standard real estate management form.

PURCHASING COMPARISON CHART

- for Products & Services -

_____
Product/Service Being Researched

_____
Potential Purchaser/User of Data

_____
Date(s) of Data

_____
Chart Preparer

Use this form to summarize data and as reference from year to year. Print or type all entries.

	Name/Address of Potential Vendor, Supplier	Telephone # and Contact Person	Pricing Data	Terms	Lead Time Warranty	Additional: References, Point of Origin
1.						
2.						
3.						
4.						
5.						
6.						
7.						
8.						
9.						
10.						
	Averages, Summary					

Footnotes:
This form available in tablet format.
Property Management Form #108
Copyright Jan. 1993

PMN Publishing, Inc.
P.O. Box #47024
Indianapolis, IN 46247

FIG. 15.9 A standard real estate management form.

Pending Files. This is the last major category of office files. Pending files include such desktop items as packing slips awaiting invoice match-up, rental prospect applications awaiting further documentation or approval, in-process maintenance work orders, and correspondence not yet signed or mailed, or copies not yet filed.

Rent Records. Although not a file as such, rent records are vital records of tenant or resident rent payment history. If rent is collected on-site, the rent records can be kept manually (as with a Onewrite or pegboard system or ledger account) or computerized. If individual rent payments are mailed to a central location (property management office, bank, property's owner, etc.), once again, the rent booking or accounting system can be manual or automated. Rent receipting also varies. Most community managers require payment by personal check or money order, allowing the cancelled check or money order receipt to serve as the renter's proof of payment. Many offices, however, continue to issue rent receipts for all payments, whether cash, check, or money order. When individual rent payments are mailed, the USPS cancellation stamp on the envelope is evidence of timely payment of a person's rent.

It is common practice for on-site managers to generate and use, if not provided by a central office, a delinquent rent or accounts receivable "aging" report. One format is shown in Fig. 15.7. This work sheet is used weekly, sometimes daily, by the on-site manager, to see that all outstanding rent balances are paid well before the end of the month in which they are due.

Forms

Several important property management forms have already been introduced in this chapter, shown as Figs. 15.2 through 15.9. Additional helpful management office forms are shown in Figs. 15.10 through 15.13. Following are brief descriptions of these property management forms.

1. *Incident-Accident Report.* An underutilized but valuable form when fully completed in a timely fashion. (See Fig. 15.2.)
2. *Lease for Mobilehome Rental Site.* Format varies from state to state, and province to province. Check with a local attorney and manufactured housing trade association for legal advice and guidance concerning local practice. (See Fig. 15.3.)
3. *Guidelines for Living (Rules and Regulations).* May or may not be part of lease, depending on local practice. Some jurisdictions require these to be posted in a public place, for example, on clubhouse bulletin board. (See Fig. 15.4.)
4. *Work Order Format or Request for Service.* Use whatever format works best. Not used as widely in manufactured home landlease communities as in apartments. Recommend using 1- or 2-copy NCR paper. (See Fig. 15.5a.)
5. *Past Due Rent Notice.* Simple format on NCR paper; when used regularly and appropriately, produces results. (See Fig. 15.5b.)
6. *Application to Rent.* Tailored to manufactured home tenancy. Usually has two exterior photos of present home and copy of title attached, or information about mortgagor. (See Fig. 15.6.)

PROPERTY INFORMATION SHEET

PROPERTY_____ PREPARER _____ DATE _____

I. ACCIDENT & CRIME

CATEGORY	IDENTIFCATION	PHONE NUMBER (S)
State Police		
Local Police		
County Sheriff		
Fire Department		
Ambulance Service		
Hospital		

II. UTILITIES

CATEGORY	IDENTIFCATION	PHONE NUMBER (S)
Water Company		
Electric Company		
Fuel (gas, oil)		
Telephone Company		
Cable TV Company		

III. SERVICES

CATEGORY	IDENTIFCATION	PHONE NUMBER (S)
Underground Cable Locator		
Answering Service		
Electrician		
Furnace Repair		
Plumber		
Air Conditioning		
Sewer (clean-out)		
Washer & Dryer Repair		
Glass Repair		
Equipment Rental		
Trash Removal Service		
Insurance Co.		
Attorney		
Pager Call #s		

IV. STAFF

CATEGORY	IDENTIFCATION	PHONE NUMBER (S)
Owner		
Manager On-Site		
Rental Consultant		
Maintenance		
Maintenance		
Property Manager		
Security		

This form available in tablet format.
Property Management Form #111
Copyright Jan. 1993

DMN Publishing, Inc.
P.O. Box #47024
Indianapolis, IN 46247

FIG. 15.10   A standard real estate management form.

7. *Summary of Delinquent Accounts.* The on-site manager's tool for delinquent rent collection; one of the property manager or owner's performance indicators. (See Fig. 15.7.)

8. *Invoice Distribution Summary.* Use this form to match up and summarize packing slips and invoices. (See Fig. 15.8.)

9. *Purchasing Comparsion Chart.* Makes product and service bidding, shopping, and comparsions a lot easier. Save from year to year as a ready, useful reference. (See Fig. 15.9.)

10. *Property Information Sheet.* A basic property information reference sheet for desktop and SOP use. (See Fig. 15.10.)

11. *ATTENTION, Contact Office Immediately.* Door hanger card adaptable for wide variety of purposes: delinquent rent collection reminder, note to move disabled and unlicensed vehicles, rules violation warning, and so on. (See Fig. 15.11.)

12. *Property Management Report Card.* Use once each year on-site, and send to every move-out, along with his or her returned security deposit. Include a personal letter and SASE (self-addressed stamped envelope) to encourage response. (See Fig. 15.12.)

FIG. 15.11   Format for posterboard tag to attach to door handles.

PROPERTY MANAGEMENT REPORT CARD

- for Multi-Family Rental Communities -

_____
Community Being Graded

_____
Date Report Graded

_____
Return Report Card to

_____
Grader (optional)

Please take a few minutes to grade this rental community. Your input is important and will help management do a better job. Simply check appropriate blocks and answer questions. Thanks!

PROPERTY-FACILITY   Poor   Avg   Good
Overall Cleanliness
Overall Appearance
Condition of Streets
Condition of Buildings
Condition of Laundry
Remarks: _____

STAFF & MANAGEMENT   Poor   Avg   Good
Courteous
Helpful
Responsiveness
Dependable
Personal Appearance
Remarks: _____

AMENITIES   Poor   Avg   Good
Swimming Pool
Playground
Other:
Remarks: _____

RESIDENT RELATIONS   Poor   Avg.   Good
Activity for Residents
Services for Residents
Communication Efforts
Remarks: _____

- Do or Would You Recommend this Rental Community to Friends and/or Relatives?
  _____ YES _____ NO   Why /Why Not: _____
- Should there be more Planned Social Activities for Residents:
  _____ YES _____ NO   Why/Why Not: _____
- What Daily Newspaper(s) do You Read?_____
- What Weekly Newspaper(s) do You Read?_____
- Anything Else You'd Like to Bring to Our Attention?_____

Footnotes:
This form available in tablet format.
Property Management Form #109
Copyright Jan. 1993

PMN Publishing
P.O. Box #47024
Indianapolis, IN 46247

FIG. 15.12   A standard real estate management form.

13. *Weekly Marketing and Operations Report.* One of the most comprehensive weekly "up the chain of command" report formats available. (See Fig. 15.13.)
14. *Standard Shopping Report.* A self-grading device, especially useful when completed by a disinterested third-party evaluator. (See Fig. 14.5.)
15. *Petty Cash Envelope and Slips.* Not shown here, but readily available in office supply stores. A must for loose cash accounting.

WEEKLY MARKETING AND OPERATIONS REPORT

FOR _____ (property)

For Week of _____ to _____

Date Prepared _____. Preparer _____

UNIT DATA   **# UNITS**   ***DESCRIPTION OF CONCESSIONS (who?)***

Number of Units in Rental Community: _____

Number of Concessions*, models: (-) _____

Number of Units Available: (=) _____

1. _____
2. _____
3. _____

MARKETING & SALES ACTIVITY*[1]

	M	T	W	T	F	S	S	Totals
1. #Ads Run (Size: ____ x ____)								
2. #Phone Inquiries*[2]								
3. #Prospect Visits								
4. #Applications Taken								
5. #Applications Approved								

PRODUCT AVAILABILITY (at time of report)

6. #Units Ready but Not Leased: _____

7. #Units Not Ready (Why? #20): _____

LEASING PROGRESS

8. Present # Occupied Units: _____

9. Present # Vacant Units: _____

10. #Move Out, Futrue (Why?#20) _____

11. #Pre-leased, Future Occupancy _____

12. # Move-ins this week, _____,   Unit ID #'s _____

13. #Move-out this week, _____,   Unit ID #'s _____

BANK DEPOSITS		PAYROLL	
Date	Amount	Empl.	Hrs.
_____	_____	_____	_____
_____	_____	_____	_____
_____	_____	_____	_____
_____	_____	_____	_____
_____	_____	_____	_____
_____	_____	_____	_____

DEMOGRAPHIC SURVEY: List Move-ins first, then Move-outs . . .

	Last Name	Age	Sex	Family Comp.	Occup.	Month Income	Coming From?	Why Move?	Length Resid.	Other Infor.
14.										
15.										
16.										
17.										
18.										
19.										

20. **NOTABLE INCIDENTS**: SEE #7 and #10 ABOVE, PLUS OTHER OCCURRENCES:

1* Conversion Percentages: Line #3 = #3 ÷ #2; Line #5 = #5 ÷ #3
2* Phone Inquiries: Attach Weekly Prospect Inquiry Report showing calls & visits

This form available for purchase in tablet form.
Property Management Form #102
Copyright Jan 1989

GFA
MANAGEMENT
P.O. Box 47024
Indianapolis, IN 46247

FIG. 15.13 A standard real estate management form.

Management Techniques

From a "big picture" perspective there are several, even many, ways to oversee, supervise, and manage a manufactured home landlease community and the staff associated with it. Time and space do not permit even a cursory summary of the varieties of style one might exercise. For the purposes of this chapter, it is sufficient to point out the need for a manager to be able to

Plan,

Organize,

Lead, and

Control.

• Planning cannot be overemphasized. All performance, good and bad, is influenced by the timeliness, depth, and accuracy of the planning step.

• In organizing, the emphasis should be on simplicity and flexibility.

• The ability to lead is also key. The astute leader becomes one who coordinates and communicates up and down the chain of command (i.e., organization chart) and laterally with peers and associates.

• Control is the proverbial icing on the cake of management. Here job performance is appraised according to known standards and previously agreed-upon goals. Steps are taken to ensure continued success or to further improve upon results.

One way to achieve management goals is to use the problem-solving procedure. This is simply a management version of the scholastic scientific process:

Select a Problem, a Task

Consider It a Challenge, An Opportunity

Define It: Document It

Ensure the Situation Is What It Appears

Study It; Question Every Detail

Break Problem Down into Parts

Research and Organize Data

Get the Facts; Use the Basic M's of Management

Refine and Digest Data

Internalize and Reflect on Alternatives

Produce and Rework Ideas

Weigh and Decide by Combining, Eliminating, Rearranging, Simplifying, Testing, and Selecting the Best Alternative(s) . . .

Scheduling and Setting Objectives

Standards of Performance

Implement and Monitor

Take Action (by) Adjusting and Modifying as Necessary

Evaluating Performance and Results

Follow-up and Recap Results

Review All Actions

Plan for the Future

One property management technique, that easily improves the effectiveness of manufactured home community management, is based on the idea of setting goals, using periodic supervision, and evaluation of results.

The MAP, or Management Action Plan, was popularized by Craig Hall in the early 1980s. The MAP is simply a memorandum that results from a face-to-face meeting between an on-site manager and a property manager, or even the property owner. A mutually agreed-upon list of tasks relative to the property is written down. The property manager or owner prioritizes those tasks, with the most important ones listed first. After penning a succinct one-sentence description of each proposed task, the responsible individual's initials are placed in the right margin along with a desired completion date. The list is typed on property or company letterhead, and the original is sent to the on-site manager, a copy is kept by the property manager for follow-up, and a copy is forwarded each month to the property owner as a reference and progress report. Then at successive meetings between the on-site manager and the property manager or owner, the MAP is updated by crossing off completed items, and adding new tasks at the bottom of the page, changing target completion dates as necessary. It usually takes 2 or 3 months before a MAP needs to be retyped. By this time it is likely that most tasks are completed and the MAP is all but illegible.

Manual Bookkeeping at the Property Level

Earlier mention was made of Onewrite or pegboard systems for rent collection. Onewrite creates all needed records, provides good control of income received, is fairly easy to use, has a good audit trail, can be used for billing as well as receipting, and contains ample account distribution columns.

Onewrite or pegboard system[9] users like being able to stack all four forms of the A/R system upon one another, then make a single pen entry that is imprinted identically, by carbon or NCR, on each part.

[9] Commercial systems are readily available from Safeguard, McBee, & many other office & form supply firms.

- The top form is usually a rent receipt, though many do not use receipts when rents are mailed to a property management office
- Under the rent receipt is the tenant rent record card
- Next is the rent ledger, also called the accounting journal or spread sheet, because it opens out to 24 or 25 inches in length.
- A long, narrow blank bank deposit slip, when used, can be inserted where desired.

When a resident walks into the rental office to pay rent, a hardbacked post binder, with ledger sheet or accounting journal already in place, is topped with the appropriate tenant or rent record card, taken from the unpaid rent tub or posting tray. Then the rent receipt is placed on the very top. Incidentally, the rent receipt can be imprinted with the property name and address. The labeled blocks are then filled in with the requisite information: date; name; unit number; period covered; and income description, such as base rent, garage rental, utilities, pet fees; there are also blank boxes to fill in as appropriate. Once the tenant card or rent record is completed, it is placed in the paid rent tub. This two-tub system makes it easy to keep track of delinquent renters, because their cards end up alone in the unpaid rent tub.

When properly filled out, the tenant ledger card is a wealth of information. The top portion includes not only tenant name, address, and phone number, but also employer information, emergency contacts, and the security deposit record as well. The bottom three-fourths of the form is simply a ledger that matches up with columns on the rent receipt, as described in the preceeding paragraph. The rent ledger or spread sheet also has the same columnar format as the rent receipt and tenant ledger card. The last and final form, the bank deposit slip, can have provision not only for the amount paid, but for the check identification number too.

Accounts payable (A/P), or cash disbursement, is handled in much the same fashion, using the Onewrite Pegboard system of accounting. The A/P system usually has three component forms in addition to the hardbacked post binder.

The top or first form is a business check customized with the property or property management firm's name, address, and phone number. Under this is the owner's record card of payment made for a particular property. This form is really necessary only when two or more properties or companies are paid out of the same general checking account. Each property has its own record card. The third form is the cash disbursement journal, a vital part of any firm's bookkeeping system. Again, written information—date, to the order of, check number, description and amount—is entered exactly the same on the owner's record card and in the cash disbursement journal. The only inconvenience is that this is not the sort of checkbook conveniently carried around in a purse or suit coat. It does, however, fit easily into a briefcase. Payroll can also be handled by the same Onewrite Pegboard system.

A final note: the cash disbursement form is a spread sheet that, when opened up, with columns properly headed, provides a convenient chart of accounts, making it easy to pen in appropriate disbursements of funds.[10]

Computerization

A major decision is whether to contract for the services of a local computer services bureau, or to do computer processing wholly on-site or via modem with the central property management office.

If the decision is made to convert from manual bookkeeping to computer, including tenant record maintenance and word processing, there are four criteria to consider.

1. Standards of performance (details follow)
2. Main components of the system
3. The conversion process itself
4. Suppliers of services, hardware, and software

As far as standards of performance are concerned, the Institute of Real Estate Management Foundation, in a research study titled *Minimum Standards for Property Management Accounting Software,* proposed eight mandatory characteristics:

1. Ability to handle all of the firm's important record-keeping and accounting needs
2. Ability to contain adequate controls, security procedures, and audit trails
3. Increased efficiency and productivity for the firm
4. Flexibility in processing and outputs
5. Performance that equals or exceeds the manual system it replaces
6. Ability to provide the firm with useful and necessary analytical tools
7. Capacity to generate needed reports on a timely basis
8. Support for the firm to maintain the confidence and respect of its clients[11]

These criteria are but a starting point. If the manufactured home landlease community is large enough to support computerization, it is probably a good idea. However, the manual system works well for most small to mid-size properties, and it is very important that on-site staff be intellectually capable and motivated to learn new systems. If not, computerization could be a serious waste of time, money, and effort.

[10] G.F. Allen, "Bookkeeping System Proves Valuable for Rent Collection and Management," *Manufactured Home Merchandiser,* Chicago, Illinois, March, 1989, pp. 56 & 57.
[11] G.F. Allen, *Mobilehome Community Management,* 2nd. ed (Indianapolis, IN: 1991), PMN Publishing, p. 66.

Another useful management technique has to do with leasing and sales. A Weekly Prospect Inquiry Report was introduced in Chapter 14. When this is used with every phone inquiry and visit by a rental or sales prospect, it becomes a very helpful tool. Not only is the volume of calls and visits tracked, by date and name, but the source or motivation of the inquiry is also identified. Once each week the conversion ratios for phone-to-visit and visit-to-approved application results are calculated. The scores can then be compared with industry performance standard averages (approximately 25% in each case), and the on-site leasing or sales consultant's job performance quantified. The weekly prospect inquiry data is put onto a Weekly Marketing and Operation Report (see Fig. 15.13) for further evaluation on-site, and sent to the property owner or property management office for review.

PERSONNEL MATTERS

Organization Chart

The military has a chain of command, electricians use wiring diagrams on their jobs, and professional property managers rely on organization charts to illustrate graphically how one job title or function relates to others within a particular firm or property.

An organization chart simply depicts the top-to-bottom and lateral positional relationships between employees, and their job responsibilities within a firm. The organization chart may be a basic sketch of one property's staffing (as in Fig. 15.14) or show several properties' relationship to one another and to upper management.

These charts are helpful when interviewing job applicants, evaluating staff changes, and planning future placements.

Job or Position Description

Job descriptions are written summaries of specific jobs, grouped under various company functions. When prepared in tandem with organization charts, they present a complete description of the company, the manufactured home landlease community. A job description also provides helpful guidelines in a hiring interview. The interviewer and job applicant review the job description, often together, to gauge the applicant's skills, past experience, and attitude toward the job in question. This review also provides the applicant an opportunity to size up the job being considered.

Once an employee is hired, the job description is a good pattern for job familiarization and, if necessary, for training in new skills. The job description, when designed to do so, can also be a performance evaluation tool, containing bench marks, objectives, or goals that employees and managers need to achieve to be fully productive on a given job assignment.

Typical Small to Mid-size Manufactured Home Landlease Community

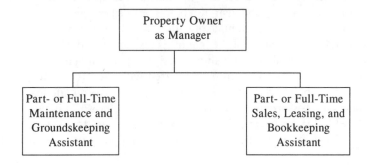

Typical Mid-size to Large Manufactured Home Landlease Community

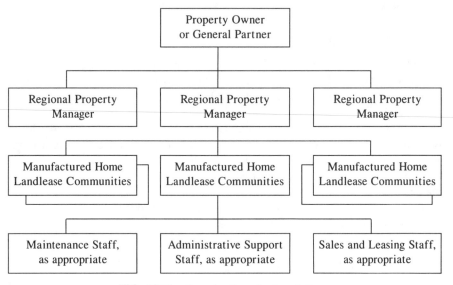

FIG. 15.14   Organization chart variations.

When are job descriptions prepared, and by whom? If a firm does not have job descriptions, now would be a good time to begin developing them. When a firm develops job descriptions, it is equally important to review them annually, so as to keep the written duties or responsibilities and standards of performance up to date.

Job descriptions are usually drafted jointly by the employee and his or her immediate supervisor. This can be easily done by having the employee keep a clipboard at hand for a few days, jotting down the various duties performed during that period of time. The supervisor should do the same, but these observations are generally oriented toward what should be taking place on the job being analyzed.

The two discuss and compare lists at least once a week for 2 weeks. After the second week, a typed "rough" should be prepared for an on-the-job review during the third week. A final draft is prepared during the fourth week.

When handled in a straightforward manner, with a positive attitude on the part of everyone involved, preparing a job description is an enlightening, helpful, and beneficial growth experience for both employee and supervisor.

A caution: Unless a particular job is very narrow in scope, there is a tendency for job descriptions to become long and detailed. When they do, the result is more of an operations procedure than a simple job description. Try to limit the job description to one single-spaced page or two double-spaced pages.

There can be as many as six parts to a job description, or fewer if sections are omitted or combined.

Description. This is the first part of the overall job description and usually includes the job title at the head of the page and one sentence, often beginning with the words "Responsible for . . ." In this sentence, the major job function is described and related to departments such as management, sales, manufacturing, operations, purchasing, and customer service. This section usually indicates whether the job is local (i.e., one property or community) or regional in nature.

Duties or Responsibilities. List regular duties first, then periodic ones. List job duties in order of declining importance and priority. Include just enough detail to ensure that duties are understood. Use "action verbs" to begin each duty description, for example: *approve, control, develop, inspect, lease, maintain, manage, operate, plan, promote, schedule, sell,* and *supervise.* It is vital to balance detail and brevity as each job duty or responsibility is identified and recorded. The ABC Rule of Good Communication, once again, is valid here. Strive to be Accurate, Brief, Clear—Concise—Complete.

Results or Standards of Performance. This section, addressing accountability, is optional in some job descriptions. Manufacturing firms use this section to establish engineered or comparative standards of production for individual workers. In other functions, such as maintenance and office work, it is sometimes difficult to set objective standards (i.e., specific number of pieces to be produced, maintained, recorded each working hour), so standards tend to be more subjective. Results or standards of performance are keyed directly to each listed duty or responsibility and, as stated earlier, should be achievable and mutually agreeable between employee and supervisor. During the annual employee job performance review, the Standards of Performance section is often used as an evaluation tool.

Reporting Relationships. In this section of a job description, work relationships are listed up, down, and laterally by individual name or job title. One of the easiest ways to demonstrate these work relationships, particularly to a prospective community manager or bookkeeper, is to reference the appropriate organization chart.

Employment Requirements. Here is where the specific ability and job experience needs of the position are defined. What specific skills, if any, are required? How much of what kind of experience is necessary to perform the job satisfactorily? A gauge of attitude or motivation is also important at this point. Does the prospect really have the appropriate aptitude? Is the individual operations or sales oriented, aggressive or reticent, and do these tendencies really matter for this particular job? These are key questions for the hiring interviewer and employee's future supervisor to consider.

Administrative. This final section merely contains the dates on which the job description was written and last reviewed, and the name or names of its preparers.[12]

The Hiring Process

The first step in the hiring process is to find candidates for jobs. Openings can be announced in classified ads in local newspapers, manufactured housing trade association newsletters, and industry periodicals. Recommendations from peers and other employees are common sources. It is usually a good idea to promote and transfer from within, when possible, but new hires often have to be brought in from outside, especially when management is dealing with a newly developed property and with turnaround challenges. Turnaround challenges, per se are usually poorly-performing income properties already in one's portfolio or may be REO (real estate-owned) properties purchased out of foreclosure from banks or other lending institutions.

A typical hiring interview checklist might use the following procedure when interviewing to fill any on-site position. The hiring interview itself is made up of three distinct parts, or *PI stages:* the *Pre-Interview, Private-Interview,* and *Post-Interview* stages.

The *Pre-Interview* stage of the hiring interview checklist begins with the interviewer's review of the candidate's application, or resume, and job references, in light of a prepared job description. During this phase also, the candidate should be given an opportunity to review the job description.

The *Private Interview* should be just that, private, between interviewer and candidate, with few or no interruptions. Interviewers should put the candidate at ease as much as possible. The very first thing to note is the candidate's personal appearance and handshake. Are they appropriate for the job being filled? Is the job applicant's personal appearance clean or dirty? Is the handshake forthright or shy? Briefly review the job description with the candidate, being careful to highlight key job responsibilities. Note the candidate's responses and questions about the various job duties. Ask leading questions and *listen* to the responses.

The Success Triangle concept of the Private Interview has been used for a number of years to gauge and guide personal and business success, and it is

[12] G.F. Allen, "Job Descriptions Can Benefit Community Managers," *Manufactured Home Merchandiser,* Chicago, Illinois, December, 1986, p. 36.

directly applicable to the hiring interview. Two sides of an equilateral triangle are labeled *Job Skills* (or Abilities) and *Job Experience* (Direct and/or Related), and the all-important base of the triangle is labeled *Job Motivation* or "attitude altitude" (see Fig. 15.15).

The hiring interviewer can use the Success Triangle to research and estimate an applicant's fitness for a particular job in the manufactured home landlease community and, possibly, his or her potential for success in that responsibility. Furthermore, managers can use interview data, in conjunction with the Success Triangle, to guide a new employee, through training and consultation, in the successful performance of his or her new job duties.

• *Job skills and abilities:* Are they commensurate with the job requirements? Can the abilities and skills be tested for verification and attainment level? Are job reference checks helpful and accurate at this point? Are the job skills technical and detailed in nature, or general and broad based, as needed in management positions? The interviewer should develop and record a definite opinion(s) at this point.

• *Experience:* Is it direct or related in some way? Is it also commensurate with the job requirements? How much depth is there to the individual's experience? These are all key questions for the interviewer to consider carefully. It is important to note that interviewers rarely encounter a candidate with a perfect balance of ability and experience in the job being filled. Often, it is a matter of comparing the two factors and deciding which candidate has the best balance for the job, then taking the third factor (motivation) into serious consideration.

• *Motivation and attitude:* Is the candidate overtly positive, or on the negative side? Is the candidate a leader or a follower, and which is needed for this job? Is he or she operations or sales oriented? Be very careful not to force a round peg into a square hole. Is this candidate a self-starter, or does he or she require close and regular supervision? Although this stage is the most subjective part of the hiring

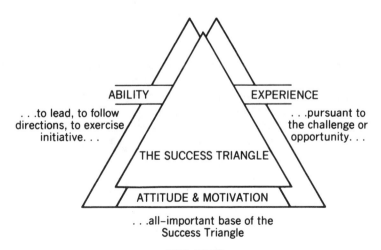

FIG. 15.15

interview, it is the most important. The well-motivated candidate, with appropriate attitude altitude, will be successful both personally and in job performance. Limited attention to these considerations can cause problems later. It is for good reason that motivation and attitude describe the base of the Success Triangle.

There are still more questions to consider. What does the candidate see as his or her personal job performance strength? Just about anyone will tell when asked. A candidate may mention punctuality, interpersonal relations, or high productivity, to name a few. The hard part is learning the self-perceived job performance weakness. Sometimes a candidate will offer a honest response, if convinced that the interviewer is going to perform a thorough reference check and find out anyway.

When hiring for a sales-related job, ask the candidate to identify his or her favorite hobby and talk about it for at least 1 minute. If the individual can do so without faltering, this person's eventual trainer stands a very good chance of developing him or her into an effective salesperson. On the other hand, if the candidate cannot talk 1 minute about something he or she claims to enjoy, then it is highly doubtful that this person is trainable or can be motivated to sell effectively. Interviewers have found that this strategy works, with rare exception.

Finally, if the job candidate has any military background at all, ask to see a DD214 form. This is a military job description and performance record that is issued to every service person upon separation from the active military forces. Beware of former military applicants who cannot produce the form.

Make sure to ask whether the person you are interviewing has any questions. One final review of the job description is an effective way of drawing out questions.

The *Post-Interview* is the wrap-up of the first two stages of the hiring interview. This is simply the interviewer's personal review of the hiring interview, which is best summarized in handwritten notes right on the job application or resume. This is also a good time to perform the job reference check, if it has not been done. Make the hiring decision when all the interviews are complete, and have the courtesy to let all candidates know how they fared.[13]

Staffing Requirements

Staffing a manufactured home landlease community is at the same time easier and trickier than planning the same for an apartment community. It is easier because a landlease community is less labor intense than income-producing properties with "brick and mortar" improvements (i.e., buildings), yards to maintain, and extra facilities to clean and repair. Conventional wisdom dictates, for conventional garden style apartments, that there be:

1 Maintenance person per 60 units
1 Rental consultant per 100 units[14]

[13] G.F. Allen, "Hiring Checklist," *Manufactured Home Merchandiser,* Chicago, Illinois, October, 1986, pp. 43 & 44.
[14] F. Basile and G. Caruso, *Multihousing Management* (Washington, D.C.: NANB, 1989), p. 20.

On the other hand, one maintenance person should be able to handle all the usual responsibilities associated with a landlease community of up to 200 homesites. This is because homesite renters (i.e., homeowners) are responsible for maintaining their residences and, usually, mowing their rental homesites. The maintenance person, or manager, supervises home move-ins and move-outs, polices the property continually for trash and debris, and effects minor street and utility repairs as needed. The job becomes more complicated, and staffing trickier, when there are swimming pools, wastewater treatment facilities, clubhouses, and water wells on-site.

Rental consultant staffing is related directly to property size, number of vacant rental homesites, and whether new and resale homes are sold on-site. If a mid-size property's physical occupancy falls below 90% to 95%, a full-time and effective leasing presence is justified. If a manufactured home landlease community is full (95% or more physical occupancy) and on-site home sales is not a factor, one individual can usually handle the leasing and related administrative responsibilities of a mid-size (approximately 200 homesites) property. In fact, given a manufactured home landlease community of 200, or even 300 or more, homesites, with public utilities and minimum amenities, a husband and wife team should be able to handle satisfactorily all management-related responsibilities. The only caveat is that office and working hours become critical. The ideal is for maintenance staff to start early in the day, by policing the property for trash and quitting in the midafternoon; the property office to open at 9:00 or 10:00 A.M., but closed to walk-in traffic until noon, and then open until 6:00 P.M. or later for rental and sales prospect traffic arriving after the workday.

Training and Certification

There are several good books available for on-site staff, property managers, and owners to use as operating guidelines and training references (see the Bibliography).

Property management training and certification is also available through the following organizations:

1. Certified Property Manager (CPM): A mid-to-upper-level professional real estate management designation available through the Institute of Real Estate Management (IREM), Box 109025, Chicago, IL 60610; (312) 661-1930.
2. Accredited Resident Manager (ARM): The on-site or resident manager designation, also available through IREM.
3. Certified Apartment Manager (CAM): The designation is the same level as the ARM and RAM (to follow), but available through state apartment associations affiliated with the National Apartment Association, 1111 14th Street, N.W., #900, Washington, DC 20005; (202) 842-4050.
4. Registered Apartment Manager (RAM): This designation is sponsored by the National Association of Homebuilders through affiliated companies and organizations. For more information, contact NAHB at 1201 15th Street N.W., Washington, DC 20005; (800) 368-4242.

The manufactured housing industry has three property manager certification courses available for on-site and mid-level managers and property owners.

5. Accredited Community Manager (ACM): Designation via the Manufactured Housing Educational Institute, 1745 Jefferson Davis Highway, #511, Arlington, VA 22202; (703) 979-6620.
6. Accredited Mobilehome Community Manager: Designation is available from the Western Mobilehome Association, 1760 Creekside Drive, #200, Sacramento, CA 95833; (916) 641-7002.
7. Manufactured Housing Manager (MHM): Designation is an inexpensive, correspondence program for home or office study. Available from PMN Publishing, Box 47024, Indianapolis, IN 46247.

Initial on-the-job training and continuing education are important to successful property management in the manufactured home landlease community environment. The preceeding management certification courses, and texts listed in the Bibliography, can provide a healthy start and in a tangible display of effort and dedication. The conscientious on-site community manager, however, must remain sensitive to learning opportunities relative to the manufactured housing industry as a whole, and specialized issues in particular; for example: Fair Housing regulations, ADA, collections and advertising regulations, computers, and the best in effective sales and leasing techniques.

There is much more that could be said about personnel matters in this arena. Subjects such as variations in management style, job performance evaluations and annual reviews, compensation package guidelines, and contract labor matters are covered in specialty texts dealing with these and related property management topics.

RESIDENT RELATIONS

Resident relations, as an ownership and management priority, must rank on a level with return-on-investment. Happy home owners and good resident relations make it much easier to market and operate successfully a profitable landlease community. Although there are many ways to promote resident relations in the manufactured home landlease community environment, there is a seven-step procedure that has proven particularly helpful:

Step 1: Residents have to be the number one priority.

Learn what attracts rental prospects to the manufactured home landlease community in the first place, and what keeps them happily living there.

To find out what attracts prospects, make sure that leasing consultants always ask callers and visitors how they heard of the landlease community. This should be a regular part of their leasing and sales presentations.

Leasing consultants will find it easy to remember to do this if they complete a Guest Card for each rental and sales prospect they talk to on the telephone or interview in person. Keep a Weekly Prospect Inquiry Record, or a traffic report of some sort, on a clipboard next to the telephone.

Be especially sensitive to any mention of referrals, whether they come from present residents, local manufactured home retailers, chamber of commerce, or even other rental communities.

It is also important to know what keeps residents satisfied. One way is to ask them to respond to a periodic questionaire. A better way is the technique suggested by popular business writer Tom Peters: Management by Wandering Around (MBWA). Regularly walk or drive through the landlease community and chat with residents.

Once it is understood what attracts prospects to the property, and what keeps the residents happy, zero in on those areas of management to further strengthen marketing and resident relations.

Step 2: Think of those who live in the manufactured home landlease community as residents, not simply tenants; and think of inquirers as prospective renters and buyers, not just consumers.

Get to know prospects by name as soon as possible, especially during the initial telephone inquiry. Using the prospect's name during that first conversation conveys the friendliness of the community, and taking note of prospects' names provides a practical means for follow-up later. Find out what the prospects' housing needs are. Here again, the Guest Cards are helpful aids.

Just as it is important to know and use a prospect's name, it is also helpful to know and use the names of current residents in conversation.

If the landlease community has an occupancy problem, check the information center hours. More often than not, information centers are open from 9:00 A.M. to 5:00 P.M. on weekdays and closed at lunchtime. Yet many prospective renters and buyers also have 9-to-5 weekday jobs and cannot come in when the information center is open.

Consider shifting information center hours to 10:00 A.M. through 6:00 P.M., or 11:00 A.M. to 7:00 P.M., to accommodate prospects who want to visit after work. In addition, have a trained leasing consultant on duty during the lunch hour, when some working prospects are likely to call or visit.

Just as it is important to think in terms of residents rather than tenants, it is also important to use up-to-date, positive terminology in conversations and correspondence.

It would be another step in the right direction to stop referring to resale homes by size (e.g., 70 × 14 or 14 × 70), the year of manufacture, or even the manufacturer's name in classified advertising. Rather, talk about them in conventional housing terms when and where possible.

Step 3: Make it a high priority to keep residents satisfied.

Community owners need to identify and, if necessary, change or eliminate any policies or procedures that cause continual dissatisfaction among residents.

Take a tip from the Satisfaction Guarantee promised by Hampton Inns, the well-known hotel chain: "We guarantee high quality accommodations, friendly and efficient service, and clean, comfortable surroundings. *If you're not completely satisfied, we don't expect you to pay."* How many landlease community owners or managers can or would offer such a guarantee? Martin Newby of Sarasota, Florida, owns and manages more than a dozen landlease communities. He promises to respond in a positive way, within 1 hour, to every resident complaint, question, or request for assistance.

Not every issue can be resolved within an hour, but Newby instructs his on-site managers to give residents a specific verbal commitment, any time, day or night, as to how and when the matter will be resolved—and they keep their commitments.

Interestingly, on rent collection day, Newby's managers treat their residents to free coffee and doughnuts at the information center, and the community manager takes a bag of doughnuts to elderly shut-in residents when going to their homes to collect rent.

Step 4: Ensure that all employees have the opportunity to experience the community from the resident's prospective.

Managers and other employees who live on-site experience firsthand both the good and the bad, right along with other residents. They too face any maintenance problems. In fact, some states require that the identified caretaker reside in the landlease community.

Employees' understanding is enhanced when they are required to pay rent like other residents, rather than have it waived or concessioned as part of their compensation. The experience of being rent-paying employees raises their awareness of the need to correct on-site problems quickly. Moreover, many property owners have stopped giving employees rent and utility concessions because these indirect forms of compensation are rarely appreciated for their full value beyond the first month of employment. Offering free water, electricity, and phone service to employees also encourages waste and discourages conservation and efficiency.

It is important that employees who deal directly with residents have good skills in dealing with people. According to Bobbie Gee, writing in an issue of *SAM's Buying Line,* likable people:

- Smile easily and often
- Have a good sense of humor
- Are themselves, without pretense
- Are fun
- Compliment easily and often
- Know how to use commonsense etiquette
- Show self-confidence
- Engage others in conversation about themselves
- Are able to laugh at themselves
- Are approachable and touchable
- Are good listeners

Employees who are deficient in these areas may need counseling, retraining, or even replacement.

Step 5: Organize the working environment so that on-site managers have the authority to perform their assigned jobs as efficiently as possible.

Assigning managers duties to perform without giving them sufficient accompanying authority is like asking them to drive a heavy 6-inch steel spike with a lightweight plastic hammer—it simply cannot be done. Job responsibilities must be matched with an appropriate measure of authority. When this balance is achieved, the results are less failure and frustration, and more personal success, job satisfaction, and properly completed tasks.

Step 6: Let residents know that management appreciates their tenancy.

There are many ways to demonstrate appreciation, which can be summed up in two short phrases: *tell 'em* and *show 'em*.

Tell 'em. Periodic letters from management should start with a "Welcome Aboard" message inserted in the initial packet of community information that residents receive upon moving in.

A Letter of Appreciation should be sent when residents renew their rental agreements—a milestone decision that should not be taken for granted.

When it is apparent that residents are going to extra expense and effort to beautify their home and the grounds around it, make it a point not only to send them a letter of appreciation, but also to speak to them personally. A Thank-You note is an appropriate enclosure with the returned security deposit check when tenancy ends.

Show 'em. As the budget allows, be open to sponsoring a variety of projects to improve resident morale. Among these are publishing a community newsletter, which can pay for itself through local advertising; holding seasonal parties, geared toward children in family-oriented communities and seniors in all-adult communities; supporting resident participation on local softball teams or bowling leagues; and offering free transportation to nearby shopping malls and medical centers.

Step 7: Recognize top-performing managers and staff, with enthusiasm and worthwhile recognition, on a regular basis.

Increasingly, multiple-property firms are realizing the importance of giving credit where credit is due. ROC Properties in Englewood, Colorado, has set the pace for several years with its Manager Recognition Program. Manager performance is gauged and evaluated monthly, against previously set goals, and interim awards are presented as earned. Then, at the firm's annual management conference, the top performers who have met personal and property performance goals for the year are singled out for membership in the exclusive President's Club.

Implementing the seven steps can build an effective resident relations program. Use these ideas as a springboard for planning a truly effective and comprehensive resident relations program.[15]

What happens when resident relations are ignored or abused? Management becomes more difficult, occupancy may well suffer, and, worst of all, rent control and landlord-tenant legislation may result. Granted, poor resident relations alone will not precipitate rent control; rent control legislation is usually the consequence of

[15] G.F. Allen, "Seven Steps to Effective Resident Relations," *Manufactured Home Merchandiser,* Chicago, Illinois, September, 1992, pp. 34–37.

abuses such as too large or too frequent rent increases, unnecessary and unjustified management heavy-handedness, and just plain breakdown in communication between ownership, management, and the resident.

What is meant by rent control and landlord-tenant legislation? The state and local governments have authority to limit the amount of rent and related charges billed to lessees (homeowners-renters), and to codify just how property owners and managers will relate to their rental property's residents.

What are the consequences? Rent control generally slows or halts new construction, lowers property values, reduces tax revenues, increases condominium conversions, increases the number of abandonments and demolitions of low-cost housing, causes higher property taxes, increases the transient population, and leads to more deferred maintenance, a higher crime rate, fewer property loans made, and higher property operating costs—to support said regulations.

The best two ways to prevent rent control and landlord-tenant legislation is to practice good resident relations and keep the lines of communication open at all times.

Obviously, a great deal has been covered in this chapter. Proper property management of a manufactured home landlease community need be no more difficult than operating and supervising any other type of income-producing property. Learn and use most of the tools and aids outlined in this chapter, and the new community will be headed in the direction of success.

CHAPTER 16

FINANCIAL MANAGEMENT

Start-up and ongoing property management operations are but half the challenge of successful manufactured home community operations. Setting up the books and closely monitoring financial performance are key responsibilities to ensure satisfactory and enhanced return on investment.

SETTING UP THE BOOKS

There are two main elements to a manufactured home landlease community's financial management system:

1. *A historical tracking and reporting system.* This system is characterized by monthly operating statements, showing the previous month's income and expense performance, and performance year to date, in the same categories. Some operating statements also relate the current and annual figures to earlier budget projections. See Appendix G for an example of how Clayton, Williams and Sherwood tracks the financial performance of its landlease communities.

2. *A forecasting system.* This system is characterized by an annual budget broken into monthly increments as well as financial projections (i.e., spread sheet) relative to sales, leasing, and other income-performance target areas.

There are also system design basics to be considered when setting up the financial management system.

Chart of Accounts

A chart of accounts is the sequential listing of all elements of the accounting system, with each element assigned a numerical code or line item number. The four main parts of an overall chart of accounts are:

- Assets
- Liabilities
- Income
- Expenses

A typical landlease community income and expense chart of accounts is as follows:

Income

- Rental income
- Service income
- Service labor income
- Additional source(s) of income

Operating Expenses

Management Fee. Any nonsalary and nonwage fee paid to a firm or individual functioning as a management subcontractor.

Administrative and Wages. All office-related, on-site salaries and wages paid for leasing, bookkeeping, and management. This category also includes outside accounting and legal expenses.

Administrative Costs. Includes travel and entertainment, dues and subscriptions, bad debt expense, office supplies and postage, contributions, and on-site computer supplies.

Telephone. Basic telephone charges and long-distance carrier service fees. Does not include Yellow Page ad fees.

Advertising. Newspaper classified and display ads, telephone directory Yellow Page ads, brochures, business cards, special signage, radio and TV ads.

Operating Supplies. Pool chemicals, lawn fertilizers and seed, ice-melting chemicals, and so forth.

Heating Expense. Natural or propane gas, fuel oil for office, clubhouse, and maintenance facility.

Electricity. Street lights, pumps and blowers, building lights—and heating, if appropriate.

Water/Sewer. Public or private system-related fees and/or costs.

Maintenance/Repair. Trash removal, snow removal, grass cutting, street repairs. Do not include cost depreciable items in this category.

Maintenance Wage. If not included in Administrative and Wages, as may be the case with a small landlease community, this category includes wages for maintenance supervisor and staff, groundspersons, and, possibly, swimming pool lifeguards.

Real Estate Tax. Manufactured home landlease community's real estate taxes.

Other Taxes, Licenses, and Fees. Business-related taxes (e.g., personal property), and fees and licenses required to operate the property.

Property Insurance. Liability and business coverage as desired; also group and workmen's compensation insurance, if not included in the Administrative and Wages category.

Subcontract. Specialty maintenance needs (electrician, plumber), sometimes even refuse removal. Can include wastewater treatment plant operator if not on staff.[1]

Accounting System. A decision will also have to be made as to the type of accounting system to use.

- Manual, using traditional double-entry system, or a one-write, single-entry system.
- Automated, using one or another of the hardware and software variants available.
- Cash-basis, the simplest system most commonly used by small to mid-sized properties.
- Accrual-basis, where income is booked when received and operating expenses are accrued at the time obligation is incurred.
- Modified-accrual, simple to administer.

In any event, an accountant's advice should be sought in these matters.

---

[1] G.F. Allen, "Manufactured Housing Communities Prove a Better Investment Than Apartments," *Mfd. Home Merchandiser,* Chicago, Ill., Aug. 1992, pp. 26–27.

MANAGING BY THE NUMBERS

There are more than a dozen helpful formulae for property managers, at all levels, to use to gauge job performance, measure market indicators, effect product and service price comparisons, value an income-producing property, and estimate financial security parameters. Although a few of these have been introduced in other parts of this text, *all* formulae are included here under the following categories:

- Marketing and leasing/sales related
- Operations and return on investment related
- Valuation related
- Acquisition finance or refinance related

Most of the formulae use data specific to the following subject property. Annual figures are indicated, unless otherwise noted.

300 homesite landlease community
280 physically occupied rental homesites
$250/month site rent
$900,000 annual income, assuming 100% physical occupancy; for example, $250/month × 300 sites × 12 months
$360,000 in operating expenses, assuming 40% OER (operating expense ratio)
$450,000 annual debt service or mortgage payment
12% local area "cap," or capitalization rate
$4,500,000 value of subject property, based on capitalization of income
$600,000 original equity, or down payment, to purchase subject property

Marketing and Leasing/Sales Related

1. *Physical Occupancy*
   Formula:

$$\frac{\text{\# occupied sites}}{\text{\# total sites}}$$

Example:

$$\frac{280}{300} = 93.3 \text{ or } 93.3\%* \text{ physical occupancy}$$

Note: The reciprocal of 93.3 is 6.7, or 6.7% physical *vacancy* rate. Occupancy or vacancy rate? Depends on whether one's perspective is to think of how full or how empty something is. Multifamily property owners tend to think in terms of "occupancy" and commercial property investors in terms of "vacancy."

2. *Economic Occupancy*
Formula:

$$\frac{\text{\# occupied sites} - \text{\# delinquent and concessioned sites}}{\text{\# total sites}}$$

Example:

$$\frac{280 - 20}{300} = \frac{260}{300} = 86.7 \text{ or } 86.7\%^* \text{ economic occupancy}$$

> **Note:* Again, the reciprocal of 86.7 is 13.3, or an economic *vacancy* rate of 13.3%. The economic occupancy rate, although more difficult to quantify at times, is a far better "acid test" of a property's true "occupancy level" than the conventional physical occupancy percentage.

3. *Break-Even Occupancy Ratio* (Use annual figures for this when possible.)
Formula:

$$\frac{\text{operating expense \$} + \text{mortgage payment for same period}}{\text{rental income \$ total for same period}}$$

Example:

$$\frac{\$360M + \$450M}{\$900M} = \frac{\$810M}{\$900M} = .90 \text{ or } 90\%^* \text{ break-even occupancy ratio}$$

> **Note:* 90% is the level of economic occupancy this property needs to achieve to effect "break-even," where there is enough real income to cover anticipated operating expenses and established mortgage payment.

4. *Conversion Percentages*
Formula:

$$\frac{\text{\# on-site visits by prospects}}{\text{\# phone calls by prospects}} = \text{conversion rate}$$

Example:

$$\frac{20 \text{ visits}}{80 \text{ calls}} = .25 \text{ or } 25\% \text{ conversion rate}^*$$

Formula:

$$\frac{\text{\# approved applications}}{\text{\# on-site visits by prospects}} = \text{conversion rate*}$$

Example:

$$\frac{5 \text{ approved applications}}{20 \text{ visits}} = .25 \text{ or } 25\% \text{ conversion rate}$$

Note: All factors introduced in these two formulae should be for the same period of time, usually weekly. Furthermore, 25% is considered an acceptable "industry average" minimum in apartment and manufactured home landlease community leasing.

5. *Turnover Ratio*
Formula:

$$\frac{\text{\# move-outs/year}}{\text{average \# of occupied sites}} = \text{turnover ratio}$$

Example:

$$\frac{20}{280} = .07 \text{ or } 7\% \text{ annual turnover ratio*}$$

Note: This formula is also adaptable to computing employee turnover; for example, 2 separated employees in a year's time ÷ average of 6 on payroll = 33.3, or 33 1/3% employee turnover.

Operations and Return on Investment Related

6. *Operations Expense Ratio or OER%*—computed annually overall, or per line item monthly.
Formula:

$$\frac{\text{\$ operating expense}}{\text{\$ total income}} = \text{OER}$$

Example:

$$\frac{\$360M}{\$900M} = .40 \text{ or } 40\% \text{ OER}$$

Note: OER is also known as "expense ratio," where an operating expense line item is divided by a net sales figure. When other businesses refer to "net profit margin" (NPM) they are simply stating the reciprocal of the OER; for example,

$$\frac{\$ \text{ operating profit (or NOI*)}}{\$ \text{ total sales}} = \frac{\$540}{\$900} = .60, \text{ or } 60\% \text{ NPM}$$

Note: Net Operating Income

7. *Per Unit Cost Comparison*—computed annually overall, or per line item monthly.

Formula (annually overall):

$$\frac{\text{annual \$ operating expense}}{12 \text{ months}} \div \# \text{ sites} = \$/\text{unit month}$$

Example:

$$\frac{\$360,000}{12} \div 300 \text{ sites} = \$100/\text{site month}$$

Formula (particular line item):

$$\frac{\text{month total \$}}{\# \text{ sites}} = \$/\text{site month}$$

Example:

$$\frac{\$800}{300} = \$2.67/\text{site month}$$

8. *Net Operating Income*
Formula:

Gross collected income − total operating expense
(not including mortgage) = net operating income or NOI

Example:

$$\$900,000 - \$360,000 = \$540,000 \text{ NOI}$$

Note: NOI is the first "bottom line" performance measurement indicator. NOI is also one of the three primary factors needed in the "income capitalization formula" to estimate property value. See formula 12 to follow.

9. *Cash Flow (CF) Before Taxes*
Formula:

$$\text{annual \$ NOI} - \text{annual mortgage \$} = \text{CF before taxes}$$

Example:

$$\$540,000 - \$450,000 = \$90,000 \text{ CF before taxes}$$

Note: This is the second "bottom line" performance measurement indicator. This is revenue available to ownership, after mortgage payment, for reinvestment or distribution.

10. *Cash-on-Cash Return* (first year)
Formula:

$$\frac{\text{cash flow \$ before taxes}}{\text{original equity or down payment}}$$

Example:

$$\frac{\$90,000}{\$600,000} = .15, \text{ or 15\% cash-on-cash return}$$

Note: This percentage, the third "bottom line" performance measurement indicator, is compared with rates of return available from other investment opportunities.

Valuation Related

11. *Gross Rent Multiplier (GRM)*
Formula:

$$\frac{\text{value \$}}{\text{annual receipts}}$$

Example:

$$\frac{\$4,500M}{\$540M} = 8.333 \text{ GRM factor}$$

Note: Value \$ can be sale price. Now relate the 8.333 GRM to another, similar nearby property, to estimate its GRM value; for example, \$600,000 annual receipts $\times$ 8.333 = \$4,999,800 estimated value of a similar neighboring property.

12. *Income Capitalization Method of Estimating Value* (also known as the IRV method)

Definitions: I   = annual NOI (see formula 8)

R = capitalization or "cap" rate

V = value estimation—either "asking" or sale price, depending on the perspective of the person using the formula

Formulae:

I   = R × V or .12 × \$4,500,000 sale price = \$540M NOI, or I

R = I ÷ V or \$540,000 ÷ \$4,500,000 = .12 cap rate, or R

V = I ÷ R or \$540,000 ÷ .12 = \$4,500,000 value, or V

Note: To estimate the local "cap," or capitalization rate, applicable to the subject property, for which the NOI is known, research I and V factors of nearby similar properties, recently sold. Compute the R in each instance (e.g., R = I ÷ V) and decide on an appropriate average or appropriately weighted R value (capitalization rate) to use with the subject property's NOI (e.g., V = I ÷ R) to estimate the value of subject property.

In light of the preceding formulae, how does a subject property or properties, or a planned project, possibly compare? One way to finetune such an analysis is to compare a given property's OER performance with national standards. Figure 16.1 shows four manufactured home landlease community studies and comparable apartment OER statistics. The expense categories or chart of accounts is the same as suggested earlier in this chapter.

Acquisition Finance or Refinance Related

13. *Debt Coverage (DC)*

Formula:

$$\frac{\text{annual NOI}}{\text{annual debt service (DS)}} = \text{DC}$$

Example:

$$\frac{\$540M}{\$450M} = 1.2 \text{ DC}$$

Note: In this case annual NOI exceeds annual DS (also known as mortgage payment) by 20%. Conservative lending institutions may require 1.3/1 (i.e., 30% cushion of NOI over DS), whereas a less conservative institution may be satisfied with 1.05/1 to 1.1/1, or only 5% to 10% coverage.

Comparing Operating Expense Ratios (OERs)

Expense Category	Manufactured Home Communities				Apartments	
	Texas A&M Guide	Horner Plan	National Survey III	Allen Model	IREMs Analysis	Apt. Model
ADMINISTRATIVE EXPENSES						
Management Fee	NA[1]	5.0%	5.0%	5.0%	4.5%	4.5%
Wages	9.0%	4.4%	4.3%	4.5%	8.4%[2]	8.0%
Admin. Costs	1.5%	2.6%	2.4%	2.5%	7.0%	6.5%
Telephone	NA	0.6%	0.5%	0.5%	NA	NA
Advertising	1.0%	0.2%	0.3%	0.5%	NA	NA
TOTAL	11.5%	12.8%	12.5%	13.0%	19.9%	19.0%
OPERATING EXPENSES						
Supplies	0.5%	1.3%	0.4%	0.5%	2.5%[3]	
Heating	9.0%	0.3%	0.3%	0.5%	0.9%[4]	0.9%
Electric	*[5]	0.8%	0.9%	1.0%	1.7%[6]	1.5%
Water/Sewer	*[5]	14.0%	9.2%	9.0%	3.1%[6]	3.0%
TOTAL	9.5%	16.4%	10.8%	11.0%	8.2%	7.9%
MAINTENANCE EXPENSES						
Repairs	7.0%	3.4%	5.8%	5.0%	8.5%[7]	8.5%
Wages	*[8]	3.4%	3.0%	3.0%	5.8%[2]	
TOTAL	7.0%	6.8%	8.8%	8.0%	14.3%	14.0%
TAXES AND INSURANCE						
Real Estate Taxes	9.0%	5.4%	6.8%	6.5%	7.4%	7.5%
Other Taxes, Licensing	NA	NA	0.3%	0.5%	0.1%	0.1%
Property Insurance	0.5%	2.6%	0.9%	1.0%	1.6%	1.5%
TOTAL	9.5%	8.0%	8.0%	8.0%	9.1%	9.1%
SERVICE EXPENSES						
Subcontracts	NA	1.3%	NA	NA	NA	NA
TOTAL OER	37.5%	45.3%	40.1%	40.0%	51.5%[9]	50.0%

Footnotes:
1. NA—Not available in this study—but possibly included in the wage category.
2. 9.4% (payroll) plus 4.8% (other payroll) totals 14.2%; To ascertain proportions for lines #3 and #17, use data from column #3.
3. 0.3% (supplies), 1.2% (building services), 0.6% (other operations) and 0.4% (recreation and amenities) equal 2.5%.
4. 0.5% (heat fuel) and 0.4% (gas) equal 0.9% for common area only.
5. Texas A&M included electric and water/sewer expenses with heating expenses.
6. 1.7% plus 3.1% equals common area only.
7. 0.4% (security), 2.2% (grounds maintenance), 3.2% (maintenance and repair), and 2.3% (painting and decorating) equal 8.5%.
8. Texas A&M lumped maintenance wages with repair costs.

FIG. 16.1   Manufactured home landlease community OER performance compared with apartments.

14. *Loan-to-Value*
Formula:

$$\frac{\text{loan amount}}{\text{property value}}$$

Example:

$$\frac{\$3{,}600M}{\$4{,}500M} = .80, \text{ or } 80\% \text{ loan to value}$$

Note: Also known as debt-to-worth. The mortgage limit a lending institution is willing to underwrite for a particular property.

Miscellaneous

15. *Absenteeism*
Formula:

$$\frac{\#\text{ employee days absence}}{\#\text{ paid employee days}} = \text{absenteeism }\%$$

Example:

$$\frac{5 \text{ days absence}}{100 \text{ paid employee days}} = .05, \text{ or } 5\% \text{ absenteeism}$$

Note: Usually computed monthly; for example, 5 employees × 20 workdays = 100 paid days

16. *Gross Margin* (applicable when new manufactured homes are sold on-site)
Formula:

$$\frac{\text{Net sales }\$ - \text{cost of goods sold }\$}{\text{net sales }\$} = \text{gross margin}$$

Example:

$$\frac{\$600M - \$300M}{\$600M} = .50, \text{ or } 50\% \text{ gross margin}$$

Note: Although *net sales* is referenced in this example, other applications substitute *gross sales* into the equation.

MAXIMIZING ROI

There are four major elements of financial management that go a long way to maximizing ROI (return on investment) in a manufactured home landlease community:

- Budgeting
- Operating statement review
- How to maximize income
- How to minimize expense

Much has been written about the latter two, particularly as they apply to the manufactured home landlease community environment.

Operations budgets, when prepared annually, and capital spending budgets on 3- to 5-year cycles facilitate strategic planning and decision making relative to:

- Capital spending (e.g., clubhouse remodeling)
- Investments (e.g., timely refinancing, planning for the future)
- Rental rate adjustment, as to amount and timing
- Operating expenses (e.g., trim further or reinvest in the property)
- Cash flow analysis (e.g., evaluate profitability or estimate value of property)

There are three methods of researching and formulating the annual operations budget:

1. Historical cost-based method; for example, take August's year-to-date (YTD) $ total for each line item, divide by 8 (months) to estimate a raw monthly expense figure, then multiply by 12 (months) to annualize.
2. Zero-based method, also known as the "built-up method," assumes no historical data and necessitates researching a wholly new expenditure estimate for every expense line item.
3. Combination of both methods. Usually the best approach. Use historical data where there is a solid record of stable month-to-month data; for example, fixed expenses such as real estate taxes. And use the zero-based method, when time allows, to solicit vendor bids for providing product and services in the year ahead, and "build" an expense estimate.

Most landlease communities' fiscal year coincides with the calendar year, and operational budget planning usually begins in August and September, is completed in October and November, and is approved in December for distribution and implementation in January.

Operating statements are monthly status reports of a property's fiscal performance, relative to sales, leasing, and operational expense. As pointed out earlier, a monthly operating statement typically depicts monthly and YTD performance, along with variances to the monthly and annual budget projections. The key task for every owner, property manager, or on-site manager is to look closely at every line item, income and expense, to determine whether and how it could be improved in the months ahead. This is the essence of maximizing income and minimizing expense. See the Clayton, Williams and Sherwood example in Appendix G.

Income Maximization Measures

Maximizing income is tied to the property owner's investment philosophy. For example, at one extreme is "max profit at all costs," and at the other, "provide rental space almost as a social service." Other considerations include one's marketing plan as it relates to lease expirations, site turnover and vacancy estimates, and rent levels for new and renewing leases.

What are the possible rental rate adjustment philosophies among landlease community owners and property managers?

- "Follow the pack"—wait until everyone else has a higher rate, then follow suit, but remain behind.
- Raise $5, $10, or $15 a month, once each year, no matter what.
- Conduct regular market surveys to ascertain local rent levels and competitor's amenities, then peg the subject property at the middle or at the leading edge of the market rate and adjust accordingly.
- Given strong physical and economic occupancy (e.g., 95%+), raise rent upon each turnover until homesites will not lease; then rent new vacancies and raise lease renewals to the highest renting rate.

Each of these procedural philosophies has its pros and cons. It is easy to see, however, how some can lead to underperformance and, hence, undervaluation, whereas others, given market strength, could lead to enhanced profitability, or even abuse.

Some procedural matters also enhance the ability to maximize income.

- Rent to well-qualified individuals who can afford the community; this will minimize rent collection problems. Just be careful not to discriminate.
- Have a tight collection policy and clearly spelled-out procedures to ensure effective collections.
- Use significant late fees and NSF charges (e.g., $25 + $2/day) to discourage late payments and "insufficient funds" check payments. Collecting late fees and NSF charges on a large scale can become a worthwhile, though usually tedious, secondary income stream for a rental property.
- Use rent discounting. When lessees pay their rent during the month *prior* to when it is due, reward them with a $10 discount. This enhances cash flow

management, as 80%+ will generally avail themselves of the discount. Invest this "early income" and pay operating expense out of the remaining 20% of monthly rent as it is collected. Then transfer monies from savings when needed for mortgage payment and the balance of the month's operating expenses.

- Insist on a *No Cash* policy. This reduces on-site theft risk and usually eliminates the need for employee bonding insurance.
- Mailed-in rent does not necessarily boost income, but surely saves labor. Less time is spent at the desk in the on-site office, and fewer trips are needed to the bank to make deposits. Residents supply their own stamps and envelopes, and their cancelled checks serve as rent receipts.

Here are some ways to maximize income at a landlease community:

Rent-Related Revenue

Charge for additional (beyond two) residents per home; also for pets and for washing machines.

Charge a premium for more desirable homesites; for example, corner, lakefront, larger yard, secluded.

Rent the clubhouse to groups from outside the property.

Storage area available? Charge rent for it; also for storage sheds and carports.

Charge a security deposit and keep it in a separate, interest-bearing account.

Consider rental homes on-site *only* if very closely managed and controlled. Implement a rent-to-own program, to instill a measure of equity interest in the home on the part of homebuying residents.

Older, too small homesite? Rent to RVs or park model homes, or combine two small homesites into one and rent at a higher rate to a large singlesection or multisection home.

Labor and Property-Related Revenue

Sale and installation of skirting, porches, insulation. Grass cutting, snow shoveling, and even maid service, are all real possibilities.

Community Service Revenue

Laundry service, vending machines, pay phone commissions, video rental, cable TV franchise fees or rebates, and swimming pool fees, especially to outsiders.

Notary services.

Other Revenue Possibilities

Where permitted, recoup administration fees for reading water meters, computing, printing, and distributing water bills.

Broker new and resale homes.

Sell homeowner's insurance.

Perform manufactured home appraisals for a fee.

Have a nonrefundable application or entrance fee to offset credit check charges.

These are only some of the ways to maximize income.

Expense Minimization Measures

The following expense minimization measures are keyed to the previously described chart of accounts.

Management Fee. When the property is fee-managed by a third party, tie the property management fee to bottom-line performance—the NOI, not just to rent dollars collected. Reevaluate the management contract each year and attempt to lower the percentage charged. The goal should be to have the fee management company work itself out of a job by training topnotch on-site personnel. Incidentally, on-site personnel should be on the landlease community's payroll, and not on that of the fee management company.

If the owner manages, however, avoid "milking" the property with high salary and generous personal expenses reimbursement, as this only devalues the property over the long haul. Rather, make the decision to distribute the profit at the end of the year—as a personal bonus—and put an appropriate portion back into the property as a set-aside for capital budget improvements.

Administrative Costs. Run lean! A full manufactured home landlease community requires far less labor than one with vacant homesites to mow, utility risers to protect, and grounds to police. Remember, true labor cost is 125% to 140% of annual gross compensation—even more with rental and utility service concessions. Therefore, it is important to demand top performance from employees. Set goals and expect them to be achieved. A good example of this is the use of the "conversion percentage" formulae described earlier. Require office staff to clean the office and clubhouse weekly. Trim expenses relative to travel, entertainment, association dues, subscriptions, books, seminars, and postage. Do not write off bad debts too quickly. Make the newsletter pay its own way by soliciting advertising.

Telephone. Log all long-distance calls. Discourage personal calls on company time. Aggressively compare long-distance service rates. Keep fax transmissions to a minimum. Avoid the use of beepers, car phones, and CB radios, unless vital to the efficient operation of the property.

Advertising. Design ads carefully—for full effect. Beware of Yellow Page directory imitations. Keep track of phone and visit traffic, and closely monitor the various media to see which brings most results. Use both sides of business cards. On the reverse side, put a map (if the property is remote), a coupon (advertising a move-in "special"), a loan amortization chart (if homes are sold on site), or even next year's calendar. Encourage resident and retail sales center referrals, the cheapest and best form of advertising, as it is based on local reputation and performance.

Operating Supplies. Ask for a commercial or business discount. Where possible, combine purchases for several properties (i.e., use the group-buying principle). Ask for discounts for buying ahead. The Annual Procurement Planning Calendar (see Figure 16.2) is especially helpful here. Also use the Purchasing Comparison Chart (Figure 15.9) described earlier. Avoid using open accounts with local stores, as they are too easy to abuse. If they are used, require detailed and legible invoices, and signatures on packing slips. Have a tightly monitored petty cash fund especially for gasoline and office supply purchases. Never purchase hand tools for maintenance personnel.

Heating Expenses. Hire a utility bill audit specialist from time to time. Ensure proper, periodic maintenance of all equipment to keep breakdown to a minimum.

Electricity. Make sure that outside lights are off during the day, and that all electric lights are cycled properly. Wastewater treatment plant aeration blowers are often designed to operate intermittently and not continuously. Keep utility lines underground where possible.

Water and Sewer Service. Use individual metering when possible, as this cuts expenses up to 33%. Repair waterline and riser leaks and breaks immediately. Always identify other underground service lines *before* digging. In frigid areas, strictly enforce heat tape installation to reduce water waste via trickling faucets.

Maintenance and Repair. Evaluate outside vendors on a regular basis for price, service, and quality. Use the Purchasing Comparison Chart (Figure 15.9) as an aid. Ensure maintenance or management supervision of every move-in and move-out. Avoid any build-up of deferred maintenance (e.g., potholes in streets). Have a comprehensive PM (preventive maintenance) program for all equipment and vehicles. Make sure maintenance staff is literate (able to read work orders and repair manuals), experienced (ask to see appropriate hand tools before hiring), and motivated (looks the part, by being clean and in work uniform).

Maintenance Wages. The only time two men or women should be working together outside is when safety is a consideration, or the job clearly calls for a team. Avoid using rent and utility concessions as compensation.

Real Estate Taxes. Check the accuracy of tax computation cards. Hire an audit firm to review the taxes.

Month:

Annual Procurement Planning Calendar for Year _____ [Sample]

Product or Service	Jan.	Feb.	Mar.	Apr.	May	June	July	Aug.	Sep.	Oct.	Nov.	Dec.
Lawn care—chemicals and service	P	O	D	—	—	—	—	—	—	Stop		
Pool—chemicals, tags, parts		P	O	D	—	—	—	—	—	Stop		
Air conditioner—parts and supplies			P	O	D							
Exterior painting			P	O	D							
Street and sidewalk repairs			P	O	D							
Rock salt	—	—	Stop				P	O	D	—	—	—
Cleaning s. pplies	P	O	D			P	O	D				
Purch. operations manual review	✓			✓			✓			✓		
Quarterly performance report			✓			✓			✓			✓
Annual vendor report	✓											

Key: P—Plan, research O—Order D—Deliver

FIG. 16.2 A real estate management purchasing planning tool.

295

Other Taxes, Licenses, and Fees. Be vigilant; pay only what is owed. Try to pay membership fees, insurance premiums, and so on, based on number of occupied homesites, and not on the number of planned or total sites.

Property Insurance. Practice adequate loss control at all times. Reduce liability and damage exposure by:

- Avoidance—eliminate hazards (e.g., no diving board).
- Prevention—reduce hazards (e.g., have a lifeguard).
- Transfer—maintain adequate insurance coverage.
- Retention—use deductible on insurance policy.

Involve an insurance representative in the loss-control program to point out ways to reduce exposure, risk, and expense. Use the Incident-Accident Report (Figure 15.2) on a regular as-needed basis.

Subcontractor. A subcontractor may be hired if services are cheaper and better than those provided by on-site staff. Ensure property insurance coverage (liability and workmen's compensation) before allowing work to begin. Ask for a copy of a valid current certificate of insurance, and call the carrier to verify the subcontractor's coverage.

SOME FINAL THOUGHTS

- Some advocate the "collect quickly and pay slowly" approach. Although this may have short-term cash flow benefit to management, it often proves costly to reputation and to the ability to negotiate in the long run.
- Nonrecurring major expenditures are best handled with the documentation characteristic of purchase orders; whereas recurring major expenditures (e.g., utilities) generally have specific budget allocations.
- Keep all noninterest-bearing checking accounts at near-zero balance; using a "sweep account" helps here. Sweep accounts are automatically maintained at a predetermined dollar level, with excess transferred to an interest-bearing savings account.

Managing by the numbers can be one of the most exciting and rewarding aspects of manufactured home community management. It's a handy way to "keep score." Just don't lose sight of the other key aspects of effective property management, especially those pertaining to personnel, resident relations and marketing.

CHAPTER 17

PUTTING IT ALL TOGETHER

Planning, designing, constructing and licensing—according to the brochure distributed by a state Department of Public Health, these are the four steps to expanding or constructing a manufactured home community. Not so. This is a simplistic approach to land development that causes many such projects to go awry. It is the intent of this text to describe the manufactured home community development process in enough detail, not only to point would-be developers in the right direction from the very beginning of their projects, but also to warn of pitfalls and to help them avoid making costly mistakes. This chapter is a working summary of key material presented in earlier chapters, along with a few new twists to facilitate creative thinking, practical planning, and logical application.

A SUCCESS FORMULA

Much has been said about the manufactured housing industry in general and manufactured home communities in particular. At this point it may be useful to consider a management success formula that helps summarize one's mindset, how to best utilize resources, and plan effectively pursuant to successful land development planning and implementation.

The Management Success Formula

a.k.a. Entrepreneur's Success Formula

a.k.a. Business Success Formula

is simply the admonition to

Listen and Learn
Plan and Prepare
Motivate and Manage
with the
Right Product and Service
Right Location and Timing
Right Skills and Experience
Right Attitude and Motivation
Right Management and Staff
Right Methods and Resources[1]

When one looks at these couplets in light of manufactured home community development, marketing, and operations, it is easy to see how they interrelate.

1. *Listen and learn.* This is the main reason for reading this text. Smart developers will not stop here. They will read additional material on the subject, talk with successful developers, and learn from others' experiences.

2. *Plan and prepare.* This is the bulk of what this text has been about: project conceptualization, identification and evaluation of development sites, project feasibility studies, building site plans, zoning matters, business plan formulation, marketing, and property management planning.

3. *Motivate and manage.* These are the port and starboard sides of the manufactured home community development craft. Personal initiative and the ability to motivate others are important personal and team requirements from day one. Once the project is under way, it will be critical to effect that sensitive balance between just enough personal supervision, and the delegation of appropriate responsibility and authority to qualified, experienced, and motivated individuals.

4. *Right product and service.* This is one of those indispensable keys to business success. Early feasibility studies must make such selections clear and reasonable and potentially profitable. And the business plan must describe the selected products and services in a believable, understandable, and convincing fashion.

5. *Right location and timing.* The operative word here is *and.* As vital as location is for real estate investment projects of all kinds, timing is just as important. They work together hand-in-glove, ensuring that a well-located new development has sufficient numbers of qualified and capable prospects available to visit to buy or lease. And "right timing" must have right location as well.

6. *Right skills and experience.* This is perhaps the easiest couplet to overlook or shortchange. Personnel selection risks, even errors, may be easier to correct or adjust than marginal location and timing, or even wrong product and service, but such errors and shortfalls do take a toll on in-fill momentum, team morale, and limited resources. Select right the first time. Put marketing-oriented staff into sales and leasing positions, and operations-oriented individuals into property management and maintenance positions.

---

[1] George Allen's "Management Success Formula," GFA Management, Indianapolis, IN, 1985.

7. *Right attitude and motivation.* A proven entrepreneurial spirit, character-ized by personal initiative, endurance, and hard work, along with a willingness to risk, are all but indispensable to ensure project success. Such attitude and motiva-tion must be contagious to one's staff, to carry everyone through trying times to good times. Keep the attitude altitude high!

8. *Right management and staff.* Every manufactured home community devel-opment needs its chief and its braves, its leader and its followers. The most capa-ble, experienced, and motivated individual must take the lead—who, it is hoped, will be the project developer. The supporting staff, as described earlier, must pos-sess the appropriate job skills to sell, manage, or otherwise operate effectively within their job descriptions. When successful direct experience underscores the claimed and apparent skills, the entire manufactured home community benefits.

9. *Right methods and resources.* These are policies and procedures relative to every characteristic function of the new manufactured home community. From the very beginning of project conceptualization to site identification and re-search, to project feasibility and business plan drafting, it is vital to apply the best known, proven methods and resources available. Anything less is inviting failure, or less than complete success.

The Success Formula is but one way to effectively tie together all that has been presented as stand-alone segments of knowledge and to experience how they ulti-mately iterate as a dynamic whole, a practical working tool for the would-be developer.

A GLANCE BACK AND A LOOK FORWARD

Project Conceptualization

Just as a properly tuned automobile runs smoothly on all four or six cylinders, the ideal manufactured home community concept aligns a similar number of key fac-tors to effect smooth development.

The Housing Market. There must be a bona fide and demonstrable local need for manufactured housing in general, and a manufactured home community in particular, to make this a worthwhile and profitable undertaking. Anything less could end up being a waste of time and money at worst, or a slow in-fill or mar-ginal project at best. Ensure success by identifying and documenting a strong need for affordable housing in the local housing market.

Development Site Availability and Characteristics. There must be suit-able raw land, rightly located, upon which to build, or again the project might flounder. Land use restrictions and zoning problems notwithstanding, if there is strong enough local demand for affordable housing, even retirement housing, it may be well worth the time, effort, and expense to overcome regulatory barriers. Assess all these factors very carefully.

Overall Economic Considerations. The local economy—and even the broader economy—has to be able to support the development concept. Is this a growing, stable, or declining local market area, relative to employment opportunities, demographic trends, and infrastructure? What is the nature of local politics, and the prevailing attitudes toward land use and zoning planning, as far as manufactured housing and manufactured home communities are concerned? Find out early, not later.

Product Selection and Market Planning. Although treated in depth in earlier chapters, these are key considerations at the earliest stages of project conceptualization and planning. Is, in fact, the desired product line or lines available in anticipated quantities at a marketable price? How, where, and when can the housing and community be best marketed to targeted home buyers and potential lessees?

Development Site

The search for and identification of building site possibilities are moot if a would-be developer already has suitable, well-located, and zoned property in hand. However, that is not always the case, and the fruit of such a search often leads to the research and evaluation of several potential building sites within a local area appearing to have a need for affordable housing. Once the best site has been selected, it is necessary to option or purchase it for development planning to proceed.

Initial Project Feasibility

Once again, in determining feasibility, the local housing market demand comes to the fore. Such demand drives the computation of absorption rates—the estimated measure of supply and demand factors as they relate to project fill-in, on the sales and leasing side of the marketing equation. Targeted home buyers and potential lessees are clearly identified and quantified. Initial project costs are estimated for the first time. Marketing alternatives too are identified and quantified, and, if not effected beforehand, product pricing is estimated, examined, and massaged to ensure that it is the most attractive package available to consumers. It is also at this stage, if not determined earlier, that the decision is made as to whether the development will be landlease or some other form of multifamily community. Then work sheet computations are drawn up to account for all project feasibility factors.

Preliminary Building Site Plan

It is in the preliminary building site plan, also known as the revised concept plan, that the five or so major categories of the initial project conceptualization are revisited. Each is reexamined in light of any new information that affects the original planning and concept, whether there are better ways to accomplish this affordable housing project, or whether simply fine-tuning is called for at this point. These are the key points to review again:

1. *Housing market:* Is it the same as originally described or different? If different, how so? Are targeted buyers or lessees clearly known and quantified?

2. *Development and building site characteristics:* Are they supportive of the concept? Are development costs reachable, or better or worse than originally conceived? Is this the best location for this project in this time frame?

3. *Overall economic conditions of the area:* Are they improving, worsening, or remaining stable? What are the driving influences? What are their effects on the project?

4. *Local political relationships and land use planning:* Are these, as well as zoning or rezoning efforts, proceeding on schedule and as hoped for? Is there trouble ahead, or smooth sailing?

5. *Product selection and market plan:* Are these on track as well? What changes, if any, have been or will need to be implemented? Are there any new ways to improve performance prospects?

And the list, obviously, goes on. The key is to use this stage as an opportunity to pause and reflect on project progress to date. It may not be too late to turn back and regroup; yet this may be an ideal time to remotivate and redouble one's efforts at proceeding forward with the completion and operation of the new manufactured home community.

Zoning Matters

Assuming the construction or building site is under the developer's control, zoning or rezoning strategies become critical progress bench marks. Maximum attention is therefore focused on effective procedural considerations, sterling exemplary personal conduct, and professional appearing and sounding presentations that ensure success where success might indeed be had. This is one of those areas, as in seeking project financing, in which one's fate is truly in the hands of others, whether they be local politicians, planning commission members, zoning board members, even the public at large, or worse, remonstrators. It therefore behooves the would-be developer to prepare, rehearse, and present well; and given the opportunity, to develop and manage very well. In fact, much of what goes into this sort of presentation to local officials and the general public is applicable to the business plan that is prepared for investors and potential sources of project financing.

Business Plan

The business plan is a fairly straightforward document, described in tailored detail in Chapter 7. However, a brief review of the package and its main parts is in order.

Business Plan Package.[2] This consists essentially of a well-written letter that is accurate, brief, clear, and concise, along with a semipermanently bound plan of 20 to 40 pages of text and appendixed material. Each copy of the plan should be numbered consecutively, and as is often the case, marked "Confidential." This adds to the perceived value of the document, as it does indeed contain sensitive information.

Business Plan Proper[3]

1. *Executive Summary.* The scope of the business opportunity is presented here, with some sort of interest "hook" at the beginning to pique the reader's desire to read further. This is a clear verbal snapshot of the risks and rewards of the new development project.

2. *General Company and Project Description.* This includes background information on the company and its principals, a physical description of the prepared manufactured home community and product selection, and even some stated goals for the project. It is especially helpful when honestly couched in society-serving terms.

3. *Market Plan.* Here the housing demand is identified and quantified. The competitive edge, if any, is stated, along with the advertising and sales strategy and a timetable for a minimum of 2 years.

4. *Management Plan.* This section describes the organizational structure, as to who is responsible for what and to what degree, and for what compensation. An organization chart and/or job descriptions may be included here or referenced in an appendix.

5. *Operational Plan.* Here are found the nuts and bolts of the operation; for example, the sources of the product (new and resale homes, after-market products). A chronology of the development's construction and eventual operations is presented. Strengths and weaknesses of the plan are also described here.

6. *Financial Plan.* This is one of the most critical parts of the business plan. It must make clear sense to the reader—whether a potential investor or an institutional lender. What are the dollar needs, and how will they be met—with debt or equity financing? Present Profit-and-Loss statements for a minimum of 24 months and a pro forma cash analysis for 24 months. Clearly identify break-even points as well. Keep in mind that this project has to be a profitable venture or practically no one will sign on financially.

7. *Appendices.* Here include resumes of principals and key employees; additional information and descriptions (photos) of the housing product, and market research data not included in the plan proper. Also include an organization chart

[2] George Allen, "Creating Business Plans for Investors, Developers," *Manufactured Home Merchandiser,* Chicago, IL, May, 1992, pp. 23 & 24.
[3] George Allen, "Creating Business Plans for Investors, Developers," *Manufactured Home Merchandiser,* Chicago, IL, May, 1992, pp. 23 & 24.

and job descriptions (if they are not included in the plan proper), and sample policies, procedures, and forms.

The business plan is certainly one of the developer's most important documents to demonstrate probable project success. It forces the developer to give form and substance to earlier concepts, and provides the means to convince investors and possible finance sources to become an integral part of the project development team.

Building Site Acquisition and Development Financing and Engineering

At this point the property should be firmly in the control of the developer. The equity or debt capital decision has been made or provided for. The loan packaging, for the most part, relates directly to the business plan just described. And now due diligence, if not preformed earlier, moves to front-burner importance. Everything about the building site must check out or be clearly accounted for, from topography to floodplain to soil nature and quality to environmental issues, if any. This is really the tightening of loose ends just prior to the finalized concept, preliminary engineering (an intermediate step), and final engineering, with its construction drawings and specifications, approvals and permits, and contract document preparations.

Homebuyer Financing

The unique and somewhat complicated subject of chattel and, under certain conditions, real property financing, makes this aspect of manufactured home community development a real and special challenge. It is also an area that, when well understood and planned for, enhances the affordability of new and resale manufactured housing, and the profitability of both retail home sales and landlease community operations.

Construction Phase

The construction phase is an iterative stage from start to finish. Several of the characteristic tasks were begun much earlier in the development process, some tasks begin now, and others continue after the project is complete. A brief summary of these steps includes the following:

- Permits and approvals in hand
- Bids solicited and received
- Contract documents prepared
- Contractor and team selected and retained
- Project scheduling effected

- Construction commences
- Management meetings and inspections occur throughout
- Sales, leasing, in-fill, and property management begins

A word on home installation is appropriate here. Well before this stage, a decision was made as to whether homesites will be nonpermanent or permanent installations; construction reflects that decision in the nature of the effected improvements. Siting is important as manufactured homes are moved into the first phase of the community and attached to appropriate utility service connections: water, sewer, electric, natural gas, telephone, and possibly cable TV. Accessories and desired attachments are placed as well.

Marketing the New Community

In marketing the new community, the marketing basics of the business plan are revisited. Product, price, place, and promotion considerations and plans are updated with a new market survey, and advertising is effected. Assuming home sales and homesite leasing take place simultaneously, staff responsibilities are assigned accordingly and training and performance measurements are implemented as appropriate. Maximum attention, for a new manufactured home community, is given to promotion within the local neighborhood and community. A good positive image from the very beginning is irreplaceable and mandatory.

Sales and Leasing On-site

Sales and leasing on-site can now begin. Sales and leasing skills in general are basic to this stage, but they are also necessarily tailored to communicate the unique and positive features of manufactured housing as an affordable housing alternative, and manufactured home communities as desirable and convenient environments for families and retirees.

As long as on-site sales and leasing professionals continually follow the ABC guideline, . . . "Always Be Closing," throughout these six levels of a sale or lease, they will do well:

- Announcement
- Telephone contact
- Personal contact
- Demonstration
- Agreement
- Renewal and referral

Besides learning to be an effective "closer," each member of the sales and leasing staff must keep track of prospects and follow up appropriately by telephone and letter.

Start-up and Ongoing Operations

There are several unique principles that relate to property management of manufactured home communities. They are the keys to ensuring rising profitability, when applied consistently and conscientiously. The basics of start-up, otherwise, are not very different from those used for other forms of multifamily residential properties, nor are management office operations. However, there are significant differences relative to personnel and manager skills and staffing, resident relations (i.e., relating to homeowner-renters, and not simply renters), and the financial (i.e., cash flow) management of manufactured home landlease communities. Beyond all this, the ownership and management of such income properties can be enjoyable, personally fulfilling, and profitable experiences.

Manufactured home communities are reflections of the homes and residents who live in them. Develop and manage a quality community with spacious homesites and new or upscale resale homes, and lease or sell to appropriately screened and qualified consumers, and wind up with a multifamily housing community of which one can be proud—and a profitable business venture as well.

APPENDIX A

Carlson's Column

Exploding 10 Myths About Factory-Built Homes

By Don O. Carlson
Editor & Publisher

1. *Factory-built home quality is poor:* **False.** Regardless of whether we're talking about factory-built panelized, modular, HUD-Code, dome, log or other styles, in-plant quality of construction is invariably superior to what can be done in the field. There is no way you can compare the precision of cut with a $10,000 radial arm saw or $100,000 component cutter in a factory with a hand saw or a hand-held power circular saw at a job site. Factory fastening methods are also demonstrably superior because they use pneumatic tools which drive fasteners to precise depths-- no under-driving and no shiners. What's more, factory inspections cover every detail from floor framing to final paint, and the average number of inspections per house run over a dozen. The best that can be hoped for at a job site is three or four, providing the on-site inspector has time to get there. In the factory, the inspectors work there full time or are trained third party inspectors who come in unannounced to check every phase of the work.

2. *Factory-built materials are second rate:* **False.** The average factory builder can't even consider green lumber because too many pieces are too warped or bent to fit into their precise jigs for wall panels or trusses. In many site building locations green lumber is still used; and the ultimate homeowner inherits its problems for decades after the building is finished. Factory building materials, are the same as used at the site, except they are constantly protected from the weather damage during construction in the factory so their final quality is bound to be superior.

3. *Factory-built units are not strong:* **False.** In the modular unit, we have the strongest of all construction methods based on the 2X4 platform framing system. This is partially because modulars by tradition are over built. But, even the panelized and HUD-Code units are of necessity stronger than site built because they must be handled by cranes without falling apart, or hauled on wheels over roads whose motion imparts forces in excess of healthy earthquakes. The fact the units remain intact is another indication that both HUD-Code and modulars are exceedingly well built.

4. *Factory-built homes are difficult to finance:* **False.** Factory-built homes, are very easy to finance because they have a long track record. When the homeowner wants the Acme Plan 3A from a factory with some variations, chances are the local banker has seen it before and knows the value. HUD-Code units today can be financed in parks with a chattel mortgage or on permanent foundations with real estate-type 30-year mortgages. Bankers also like the idea that factory-built homes are well insulated which means the ultimate buyer won't go broke paying utility bills. Some bankers allow a half point lower mortgage interest rate for factory-built homes because of their superior energy saving package.

5. *Factory-built homes take too long to build:* **False.** The average double-section HUD-Code home can be placed in a park and ready for occupancy in a couple of days; the average double-section modular or HUD-Code home can be placed on a foundation and ready for occupancy within a week; the average closed panel or open panel home can be ready for occupancy in about six to eight weeks; the average site built home takes three to six months to complete.

6. *Factory-built homes don't appreciate in value:* **False.** All phases of factory-built housing appreciate in value in lock step with site built homes providing neighborhood factors, principally location, are equal. Studies show HUD-Code homes built as long as 15-years ago have appreciated in value, thereby destroying the myth that HUD-Code units, like some cars, decline in value.

7. *Factory-built homes are not safe:* **False.** If you are in earthquake or tornado country, probably the safest type of home to be in is modular because of the construction technology of glue-nailed sheathing and decking plus additional framing members which makes them most likely to succeed under nature's onslaughts. Panelized homes are better resisters of natural forces because they have been more precisely cut and fit and fastened in the factory. The frame work of today's HUD-Code homes is the same as site built homes or panelized units, and they are engineered for safe use in the specific geographic region where they are sold. HUD-Code homes may be the safest on the market because of the federal laws requiring smoke detectors, escape windows and incombustible materials around furnaces and kitchen ranges. Many site built homes go up in areas where not even smoke detectors are required by local law.

8. *Factory-built homes don't last:* **False.** There are endless examples of factory-built homes that have been in continuous service for 50, 60 and 70 years. One example: The homes built by National Homes through the midwest 50 years ago, which originally sold for $7,000, $8,000 and $9,000 complete, today are still in use; the major change has been that they have increased ten-fold in value.

9. *Factory-built homes don't look good:* **False.** Over 90% of all panelized homes today are customized to meet the buyer's desires. They look as good, and in many cases, better than anything that can be built at job sites. Some panelizers are producing spectacular mansions of over 10,000 sq. ft. Modular home units are routinely stacked to resemble any type of architecture the buyer may want from a New England salt box to ante bellum mansion. HUD-Code units are being finished with stucco walls, tile roofs, and exterior design features which defy their detection from site designs. Designwise, what the buyer wants and can afford he can get from a factory home builder.

10. *Factory-built homes are not the wave of the future:* **False.** America is a nation which understands factory fabrication. When we buy a washing machine, a microwave oven, a VCR or a car, we don't expect it to be dumped in parts in our backyard for us to assemble. We expect these products to come factory-made and factory-inspected and ready for instant use. It's ridiculous to assume that in future years home buyers will cling to the idea of costly piece-by-piece fabrication of homes at job sites. Site building is the wave of the past; factory home building is inevitably the wave of tomorrow.

APPENDIX B

MANUFACTURED HOME COMMUNITY DEVELOPMENT SITE ACQUISITION CHECKLIST

1. GENERAL:

Proposed Community Name: _____

    Address: _____

    City or Township: _____

    County or Parish: _____

    Phone Number: _____

Name of Developer(s): _____

    Address: _____

    City, State, Zip: _____

    Phone: _____

Current Zoning of Site: _____

    Authority: _____

    Date Granted: _____

Conditional Use Permit? _____

Form of Ownership: _____

Rate of Absorption: _____

Average Comparative Rents: _____

% Family Residents: _____

% Empty Nesters: _____

% Retirees: _____

% School-Age Children: _____

Tax Map Reference: _____

Assessor's Parcel(s) #: _____

2. SIZE:

Total Number of Sites: _____

Total Acreage: _____

Number Sites This Phase: _____

   Acreage: _____

Sites Additional Zoned Land: _____

   Acreage: _____

Acres Commercial Land: _____

Other Vacant Land: _____

Description of Layout: _____

Type Community: _____

   Adult Section: _____

   Adult Only: _____

   Family Section: _____

   Mixed: _____

Developer Owned Homes: _____

3. SITES:

Typical Site Dimensions: _____

   Singlesection: _____

   Multisection: _____

Prior Use of Property: _____

Type of Water System: _____

Metered: _____

Regulating Agency: _____

    Address: _____

    City, State, Zip: _____

    Phone: _____

Water Tested: _____

Type of Sewer System: _____

Regulating Agency: _____

    Address: _____

    City, State, Zip: _____

    Phone: _____

Percolation test: _____

4. OTHER UTILITIES:

    Garbage: _____

    Payment: _____

    Pickup Date: _____

    Community T.V.: _____

    Cable T.V. Available: _____

        Address: _____

        City, State, Zip: _____

        Phone: _____

        Basic Rate: _____

        Premium Services: _____

5. HOME SALES:

    In Community Sales: _____

    Number of Community Retailers: _____

    Number of Sales Models: _____

    Number of Area Retailers: _____

    Proximity to Retailers: _____

6. SCHEDULE OF FEES AND CHARGES:

Monthly Rent or Lot Price: _____

   Single: _____

   Multi: _____

   Waterfront: _____

   Golf Course: _____

   Large Lot: _____

   Treed Lot: _____

   Premium Lot: _____

Monthly Maintenance Fee: _____

Entrance Fee: _____

Reservation Fee: _____

Security Deposit: _____

Setup Fees: _____

Lot Preparation: _____

   Driveway: _____

   Electrical Hookup: _____

   Plumbing Hookups: _____

   Lot Lighting: _____

Mailbox Location: _____

Name Plate: _____

Snow Plowing Fee: _____

Lawn Maintenance Fee: _____

Late Payment Fee: _____

Insufficient Funds Fee: _____

Violation of Rules Fee: _____

Extra Resident Fee: _____

Pet Fee: _____

Lot Maintenance Fee: _____

7. TENANTS ASSOCIATION:

    Representative: _____

      Address: _____

      City, State, Zip: _____

      Phone: _____

    Regular Meeting Date: _____

    Place of Regular Meeting: _____

8. GOVERNING AGENCIES:

    Agency Governing M/H Comm: _____

    Landlord-Tenant Regulations: _____

    Rental Rate Controls: _____

    Closed Community Sales: _____

    Removal of Older Homes: _____

    Entrance Fees: _____

    Right of Resales: _____

    Security Deposits: _____

    Leases: _____

    Tenants Right to Purchase: _____

    Eviction Notice: _____

    Mayor/Town Manager: _____

      Address: _____

      City, State, Zip: _____

      Phone: _____

    County Courthouse and Name: _____

      Address: _____

      City, State, Zip: _____

      Phone: _____

Tax Assessor's Name: _____

   Address: _____

   City, State, Zip: _____

   Phone: _____

Code Enforcement Officer: _____

   Address: _____

   City, State, Zip: _____

   Phone: _____

Mobile Home Commission: _____

   Address: _____

   City, State, Zip: _____

   Phone: _____

Zoning and Planning Agency: _____

   Address: _____

   City, State, Zip: _____

   Phone: _____

Chamber of Commerce: _____

   Address: _____

   City, State, Zip: _____

   Phone: _____

9. BROKERAGE:

How Was Property Referred: _____

Seller: _____

   Address: _____

   City, State, Zip: _____

   Phone: _____

Seller's Broker Representative: _____

   Address: _____

   City, State, Zip: _____

   Phone: _____

Seller's Attorney: _____

   Address: _____

   City, State, Zip: _____

   Phone: _____

Seller's Accountant: _____

   Address: _____

   City, State, Zip: _____

   Phone: _____

Buyer's Broker: _____

   Address: _____

   City, State, Zip: _____

   Phone: _____

10. TERMS:

   Asking Price: _____

   Purchase Terms: _____

   Assumable Mortgages: _____

   Purchase Money Mortgage: _____

   Inspection Contingency: _____

   Financing Contingency: _____

   Rent Roll Contingency: _____

   Verification of Income/Expense: _____

   Letter of Intent: _____

   Purchase and Sale Agreement: _____

   Closing Date: _____

   Extensions of Closing: _____

11. LAND USE REGULATIONS:

   Zoning of Site: _____

   Conditional Use Permit: _____

Floodplain Status: _____

Home Installation Inspections: _____

Water Agency: _____

Sewer Agency: _____

Setup Requirements: _____

Fuel Storage Requirements: _____

Inspections Required: _____

12. TAXATION:

Last Year's Real Property Tax: _____

Due Date: _____

Last Year's Personal Tax: _____

Due Date: _____

Taxed as: _____

Assessed Value/Market Value: _____

Current Tax Rate: _____

Date of Last Valuation: _____

M/H Tax: _____

   Personal: _____

   Commercial: _____

   Real Property: _____

   Motor Vehicle: _____

Yearly Mobile Home License Fee: _____

Other Taxes: _____

   Local: _____

   County: _____

   State: _____

   School: _____

13. DEMOGRAPHICS:

   Community Description: _____

   Form of Local Government: _____

   County Population: _____

   City Population: _____

   Growth Rate: _____

   Stability of Economy: _____

   Major Employers: _____

   _____

   _____

   _____

   _____

   Average Family Income: _____

   Unemployment Rate: _____

14. PHYSICAL:

   Grade School: _____
      Location: _____

   Jr. High (Intermediate) School: _____
      Location: _____

   High School: _____
      Location: _____

   Private Schools: _____
      Location: _____
      Location: _____
      Location: _____

   Nearest Shopping Center: _____

   Nearest Regional Mall: _____

   Nearest Regional Airport: _____

Proximity to Major Highways: _____

Distance to City Center: _____

Urban or Suburban: _____

Military Bases: _____

State Employment Centers: _____

Federal Employment Centers: _____

Major Employers: _____

Clinics: _____

Hospitals: _____

Police Precinct: _____

Fire Station: _____

Type of Fire Protection: _____

   Full-Time Staff: _____

   Volunteer: _____

15. LOCAL CONDITIONS:

Price for Entry Level Housing: _____

Rental Rate for 2 Bdr., 2 Bath: _____

Apartment Vacancy Rates: _____

Competitive Communities: _____

_____

_____

_____

_____

Ave. Rent Comp. Community: _____

Vacancy of Competition: _____

Community Attitudes: _____

General Soil Conditions: _____

General Topography: _____

Archeological Problems?   _____

Environmental Problems?   _____

16. CHECKLIST:

- ☐ Legal Survey of Site
- ☐ Deed to Property
- ☐ Photographs of Site
- ☐ Preliminary Title Report
- ☐ Existing Mortgages
- ☐ Other Liens
- ☐ Copy of Rules and Regulations
- ☐ Copy of Lease Agreement
- ☐ Copy of Prospectus
- ☐ Copy of Increase Letters
- ☐ Service and Maintenance Contracts
- ☐ Insurance Policies
- ☐ Lawsuits or Claims
- ☐ Accounts Payable
- ☐ Accounts Receivable
- ☐ Copies of All Licenses and Permits
- ☐ Map of Area
- ☐ Site Plan of Community
- ☐ Appraisal Available
- ☐ Feasibility Studies Completed
- ☐ Rent Roll Available
- ☐ Operating Statement (Current)
- ☐ Operating Statement (Previous Year's)
- ☐ Phase I Archeological Report Required?
- ☐ Phase I or II Environmental Survey Completed?
- ☐ Copy of Zoning Ordinances
- ☐ Copy of Landlord/Tenant Act
- ☐ Rent Roll

- ☐ Engineering Drawings
- ☐ Letters from Utility Companies
- ☐ Letter of Compliance from Zoning
- ☐ Copy of Latest Appraisal
- ☐ Copy of Latest Boundary Survey
- ☐ Legal Description (If Not on Deed)
- ☐ Other: _____
- ☐ _____
- ☐ _____
- ☐ _____
- ☐ _____

APPENDIX C

PLANNING AND ANALYSIS
AID IN MOBILEHOME
COMMUNITY DEVELOPMENT*

The following material and tables are based on research prepared by manufactured home community developer and owner Tom Horner, Jr., of Leawood, Kansas. This pro forma financial plan for landlease community development utilizes construction and operating cost data based on average Midwest economic conditions, Kansas City rental rates, Horner's personal in–fill experience, and strategic selection of suitable real estate for development in a relatively tight leasing market.

Here are the given or known factors used in the following paragraphs and calculations:

GENERAL

1. Real estate parcel: approximately 40 acres in size.
2. Planned unit density: 5½ manufactured homes per acre.
3. Total number planned units: 220 homesites, e.g., 40 acres × 5.5 manufactured homes per acre.
4. Site rental rate at beginning: $160 per month, until 95% occupancy achieved. This rate should lag slightly behind the prevailing market site rent rate to stimulate new move-ins.
5. Fill-up rate: approximately 39 months with 5+ net move-ins each month.
6. Subsequent site rental rates (after 95% occupancy achieved):
   - Year 4 = $175/month
   - Year 5 = $190/month

* Originally published in *Mobile/Manufactured Home Merchandiser*, Chicago, IL, September, 1988, pp. 24–34.

- Year 6 = $205/month
- Year 7 = $220/month

7. Number move-ins on community opening: 20—a combination of new and late model resale homes in excellent condition, all owner occupied.

INVESTMENT-RELATED

1. Developer must have or develop a good working relationship with a knowledgeable and willing lender.
2. Developer is contributing the land to the project, or at the very least the loan package, and the lender is willing and able to lend the development money or financing in two phases:
   a. Construction loan for approximately a 3-year term at 10.5% interest and 80% coverage (enough ready cash to finance 80% of the construction financing needed), with the possibility of 2 discount points having to be paid by the developer.
   b. Mortgage, end loan, or permanent financing (after development step is completed); again 60% to 80% loan-to-value coverage, possibly at 10.5% interest, with monthly payments calculated on a 30-year amortization schedule and balloon payment due in 5 years. Again, the developer should expect to pay 2 discount points to secure the loan at the desired terms.
3. Debt coverage ratio will have to see the net operating income (NOI) at least 25% greater than the principal and interest payment for the same period, either monthly or annually. Another way of expressing the debt coverage ratio is 1.25:1, or $1.25 of NOI to every $1 of principal and interest (P&I) paid.

LAND AND RELATED COSTS

Land available at $7,000 per acre, zoned for manufactured home community construction or purchased "subject to" appropriate zoning.

Calculation: 40 acres × $7,000/acre = $280,000 land cost ÷ 220 homesites (see General #3) = $1,272 per site land cost.

IMPROVEMENTS

Following hard costs, assume the developer will be intimately involved in community development as the general contractor or has someone thoroughly knowledgeable supervising the construction activity.

1. Estimated hard cost per site = $ 7,000
   See Table C.1 for detailed breakdown.
2. Estimated contractor markup of 20%
   ($7,000 × .20)   1,400
3. Estimated other costs
   (financing or contingencies)   1,000
4. Clubhouse and swimming pool
   ($24,000 + $40,000 ÷ 220 sites)   290
5. Total estimated cost of improvements per homesite $ 9,690
6. Plus land cost
   (see Land #1)   +1,272
7. Total estimated cost per site $10,962

TABLE C.1   Typical Construction Costs

Estimate of Individual Actual Site Construction Costs	Per Site
Supervision and management	$ 200
Initial planning, engineering, surveys, etc.	505
Site preparation, overall grading, etc.	450
Sidewalks	250
Curbing (24" lazy-back or equivalent)	225
Streets (either 40' wide to accommodate parallel on-street parking, or narrower street with off-street parking for two cars on each site)	850
Preparation for concrete flat work on individual sites	80
Patio, mobile/manufactured home runners, individual site access, sidewalks from curb to patio, etc. Single = $1,100 Double = $1,565	
Sewer system	481
Water distribution system (master metered)	381
Natural gas distribution system	250
Electrical distribution system (at least 100 amp)	650
Crushed rock between concrete runners	150
Miscellaneous: installation of cable TV underground work	100
Underground telephone installation	50
Individual yard lights	125
Seeding and/or sodding individual sites	250
Landscaping	125
General cleanup	150
Storm drain	250
Mailbox facilities or units	100
Total for single site = $6,722 double site = $7,187	+
Estimated average cost	$7,000 per site

At this point, the known factors and calculations of the previous paragraphs are applied to the phased development plan for the proposed manufactured home community.

FIRST YEAR

The developer usually spends more than the proportionate amount of construction funds per site, because much of the site work is heavy on the front end, required early in the development of the community.

All site grading must be done. This includes utility distribution and collection lines (water, sewer). Estimate that 50% of the construction funds will be spent during the first year of the 3-year development period.

$9,690/site improvement cost $\times$ 220 sites,	
or a total of $2,131,800 $\times$ 50% =	$1,065,900
Land cost	+ 280,000
Total first-year investment	$1,345,900

SECOND YEAR

Additional 25% of $2,131,800 improvements	$ 532,950
Plus amount used during first year	+1,345,900
	$1,878,850

THIRD YEAR

Final 25% of $2,141,800 improvement costs	$ 532,950
Plus amount used first 2 years	+1,878,850
	$2,411,800

Summary: $280,000 land costs, plus $2,131,800 total improvements costs equals total development costs of $2,411,800.

At this point, it is necessary to change gears, so to speak, and look at the three pro forma displays or charts that estimate rental income, operating expenses, NOI, and cash flow before taxes over the first 7 years of the community's development.

Table C.2 is a simple spread sheet that estimates Early Years Rental Income Until Achieving 95% Occupancy. It is fairly self-explanatory. The total annual income figures—such as Year #1 = $91,200 through Year #7 at $551,761—appear again in Table C.4.

Table C.3 is a simple summary that estimates Operating Expenses as a Percentage of Income under normal manufactured home community operating

TABLE C.2 Rental Income Pro Forma

		Jan.	Feb.	March	April	May	June	July	Aug.	Sept.	Oct.	Nov.	Dec.	Total
		Early Years Rental Income Until Achieving 95% Occupancy												
Year #1 @ $160/month*1		20*2 $3,200*3	25 $4,000	30 $4,800	35 $5,600	40 $6,400	45 $7,200	50 $8,000	55 $8,800	60 $9,600	65 $10,400	70 $11,200	75 $12,000	$91,200
Year #2 @ $160/month		80 12,800	85 13,600	90 14,400	95 15,200	100 16,000	105 16,800	110 17,600	115 18,400	120 19,200	125 20,000	130 20,800	135 21,600	$206,400
Year #3 @ $160/month		140 22,400	145 23,200	150 24,000	155 24,800	160 25,600	165 26,400	170 27,200	175 28,000	180 28,800	185 29,600	190 30,400	195 31,200	$321,600
Year #4 @ $175/month		200 35,000	205 35,875	209*4 36,575	same	same	same	same	same	same	same	same	same	$436,625
Year #5 @ $190/month		39,710	same	same	same	same	same	same	same	same	same	same	same	$476,520
Year #6 @ $205/month		42,845	same	same	same	same	same	same	same	same	same	same	same	$514,140
Year #7 @ $220/month		45,980	same	same	same	same	same	same	same	same	same	same	same	$551,760

Footnotes:
*1 monthly site rent
*2 number of occupied sites
*3 estimated monthly rental income
*4 209 is 95% or 220 home sites

✓TABLE C.3   Line Item and Bottom Line OERs

Operating Expenses as a Percentage of Income

Typical operating expenses for a mobile/manufactured home community of 200 to 500 sites, with 95% occupancy, with sewer and water (and gas and electric) being paid by tenant.

Account #	Description	Percentage
301	Rental Income	100%

Operating Expenses

400	Supervision and property management	5.000
401	Accounting and bookkeeping	.067
402	Resident manager and related expenses	4.420
403	Legal fees	.528
411	Rental expenses	.288
412	Insurance	2.579
413	Telephone and communications expenses	.600
414	Taxes, real estate and other	5.379
415	Office supplies and postage	.400
416	Advertising and promotion	.166
420	Maintenance, labor expenses	3.356
421	Maintenance, materials and repairs	2.463
423	Maintenance, outside services	1.298
424	Swimming pool and playground expenses	.922
425	Clubhouse or rental units expense	.030
430	Security	1.278
432	Trash service	1.327
433	Miscellaneous expenses	.043
440	Water	N/A
441	Sewer	N/A
442	Natural gas	.252
443	Electricity	+.787
Total operating expense percentage		31.18 rounded to 30%

Note: If sewer and water are furnished by the community, add approximately 14% to the 30%, for a revised expense ratio of 44%.

conditions, once the development stage is completed. Again, these are fairly self-explanatory, though costs will vary significantly, category by category, depending on local market and operating conditions and circumstances. The 30% total operating expense ratio (e.g., 30% of rental income collected) figures directly into the net income calculation shown in Table 4, beginning with the third year. The estimate for the first 2 years is simply too elusive to pin down.

Table C.4 literally pulls it all together, as far as the previous two pro forma spread sheet/summaries are concerned. The "net cash or cash flow before taxes" line shows clearly, albeit in estimated fashion, what the dollar loss (first 3 years

TABLE C.4 Protected Operating Statements

7-Year Pro Forma Operating Statement

Year # & Rent / Category	1 $160	2 $160	3 $160	4 $175	5 $190	6 $205	7 $220
Annual income collected @ 95%	$91,200	$206,400	$321,600	$436,625	$476,520	$514,140	$551,760
Vacancy factor[1]	N/A	N/A	N/A	N/A	N/A	N/A	N/A
Operating expenses @ 30% ratio	-$50,000 (rough est.)	-$75,000 (rough est.)	-$96,480	-$130,987	-$142,956	-$150,000	-$150,000
Net operating income (NOI)	$41,200	$131,400	$225,120	$305,638	$333,564	$364,140	$401.760
First loan during construction[2]	-$111,919[a]	-$167,879[b]	-$250,299[c]	N/A	N/A	N/A	N/A
Permanent loan payment	N/A	N/A	N/A	-$248,645[4]	-$248,645	-$248,645	-$248,645
Net cash or cash flow before taxes	($70,719)[3]	($36,479)	($25,179)	$56,993	$84,919	$115,495	$153,115

Footnotes:

1. Income figured at 95% occupancy so no vacancy adjustment necessary at this point.
2. a. 10½% on $1,345,900 improvement costs first year, less $280,000 land cost = $111,919 interest.
   b. 10½% on $1,878,850 improvement costs first 2 years, less $280,000 land cost = 167,879 interest.
   c. 10½% on $2,411,800 improvement costs first 3 years, less $280,000 land cost = $250,299 interest.
3. Deficits during construction period—e.g., interest during construction, some of which will be covered by or offset against income, and then absorbed by permanent loan or mortgage. See footnote 4.
4. Permanent loan amount and payment completion:

   Deficit during 3-year construction period: $ 132,377
   Improvements amount: $9,690 × 200 sites   2,131,800
   Total amount of permanent loan or mortgage $2,264,177

   This could be on a 30-year term at 10½ with a 5-year balloon. Payment will be $20,720.46/month or $248,645.57 annually.

TABLE C.5   Estimated ROI

Return on Investment
Related Assumptions

1. *Computation of "equity" investment*

Land by Owner/Developer	$280,000
2 loan points paid by owner	53,238
(2% of approx. $2 million in loans)	+_____
Owner equity	$333,238

2. *Computation of return on investment*

Year #1	No return, no additional cash loss as it was made part of mortgage	-0-
Year #2	Same as above	-0-
Year #3	Same as above	-0-
Year #4	$56,993 net cash ÷ $333,238 equity	= 17.10%
Year #5	$84,919 net cash ÷ $333,238 equity	= 25.48%
Year #6	$115,495 net cash ÷ $333,238 equity	= 34.66%
Year #7	$153,115 net cash ÷ $333,238 equity	= 45.95%

only) and profit (before taxes) picture is through the first 7 years of the manufactured home community development and operation.

Table C.5 summarizes the anticipated Return on Investment (ROI), as based on aforementioned and related assumptions. The table graphically points out how great a risk the real estate developer takes on a venture such as this, and how significant the ROI can be once the project is well under way and filling up on schedule.

Table C.6 simply takes the mathematical calculations a few steps further by demonstrating the Loan-to-Value Ratio and Debt Coverage Ratios of the subject community from Years #4 through #7.

This illustrates a manufactured home community development pro forma financial planning and analysis vehicle, from start to finish. But remember, all the data shown will vary widely from market to market, is subject to economic climate and conditions, and must be carefully tailored to the developer's philosophy and method of conducting business.

TABLE C.6   Key Performance Ratios

Ratios That Are Important to Lenders

Loan-to-Value Ratio

This is just what it says—the ratio between the value of the property and the amount of the loan against the property. Considering this is a new mobile/manufactured home community and competitive in the market area, for calculation purposes, use a 9.5% income capitalization rate (cap rate) to estimate the income value of this property.

Year #1 = Construction
Year #2 = Construction
Year #3 = Construction
Year #4 = During in-fill, NOI = $305,638 ÷ .095 cap = $3,217,240 estimated value
Year #5 = During in-fill, NOI = $333,564 ÷ .095 cap = $3,511,200 estimated value
Year #6 = During in-fill, NOI = $364,140 ÷ .095 cap = $3,833,050 estimated value
Year #7 = During in-fill, NOI = $401,760 ÷ .095 cap = $4,229,050 estimated value

Because the permanent loan amount is $2,265,177, the loan-to-value relationships are:

Year #1 = Construction, N/A
Year #2 = Construction, N/A
Year #3 = Construction, N/A
Year #4 = $2,265,177 loan ÷ $3,217,240 value = 70.40%
Year #5 = $2,265,177 loan ÷ $3,511,200 value = 64.51%
Year #6 = $2,265,177 loan ÷ $3,811,050 value = 59.44%
Year #7 = $2,265,177 loan ÷ $4,229,050 value = 53.56%

These percentages will be slightly more favorable as some small reduction in loan principal occurs during each of these years (#4 through #7) as monthly mortgage payments are made on the loan.

Debt Coverage Ratio

This is the ratio between NOI and amount of P&I loan payment.

Year #4 = $305,638 ÷ $248,645 = 1.23-to-1
Year #5 = $333,564 ÷ $248,645 = 1.34-to-1
Year #6 = $364,140 ÷ $248,645 = 1.46-to-1
Year #7 = $401,760 ÷ $248,645 = 1.62-to-1

The higher the ratio, the greater the ability of the income property to meet its long-term mortgage obligations.

APPENDIX D

LIST OF STATE FLOOD INSURANCE AGENCIES

Alabama Department of Economics and Community Affairs
State Planning Division
P.O. Box 2939
3465 Norman Bridge Road
Montgomery, AL 36105-0939
(205) 284-8735

Alaska Department of Community and Regional Affairs
Division of Municipal and Regional Affairs
949 East 36 Avenue, Suite 400
Anchorage, AK 99508
(907) 561-8586

Arizona Department of Water Resources
Flood Control Branch
99 East Virginia, Second Floor
Phoenix, AZ 85004
(907) 561-8586

Arkansas Soil and Water Conservation Commission
#1 Capitol Mall, Suite 2D
Little Rock, AR 72201
(501) 371-1611

California Department of Water Resources
P.O. Box 388
Sacramento, CA 95802
(916) 445-6249

Colorado Water Conservation Board
State Centennial Building
1313 Sherman Street, Room 823
Denver, CO 80203
(303) 866-3441

Connecticut Department of Environmental Protection
Water Resources Unit
165 Capitol Avenue
Hartford, CT 06106
(203) 566-7245

Delaware Department of Natural and Environmental Control
Division of Soil and Water Conservation
Richardson and Robbins Building
89 Kings Highway
P.O. Box 1401
Dover, DL 19903
(302) 736-4411

District of Columbia
Department of Consumer Regulatory Affairs
614 H Street N.W.
Washington, DC 20001
(202) 727-7577

Florida Department of Community Affairs
Division of Resources Planning and Management
2571 Executive Center Circle East
Tallahassee, FL 32301
(904) 488-9210

Georgia Department of Natural Resources
19 Martin Luther King Jr. Drive, SW Room 400
Atlanta, GA 30334
(404) 656-3214

Guam Office of Civil Defense
P.O. Box 2877
Agana, Guam 96910
(011-671) 477-9841

Hawaii Board of Land and Natural Resources
Department of Land and Natural Resources
P.O. Box 373
Honolulu, Hawaii 96809
(808) 548-7539

Idaho Department of Water Resources
State House
Boise, ID 83720
(208) 334-4470

Illinois Department of Transportation
Division of Water Resources
Local Floodplain Programs
300 North State Street, Room 1010
Chicago, IL 60610
(312) 232-4160

Indiana Department of Natural Resources
608 State Office Building
Indianapolis, IN 46204
(317) 232-4160

Iowa Department of Water, Air and Waste Management
Wallace State Office Building
Des Moines, IA 50319
(515) 281-5029

Kansas State Board of Agriculture
Division of Water Resources
109 Southwest Ninth Street
Topeka, KS 66612
(913) 296-3717

Kentucky Department of Natural Resources
Division of Water
18 Reilly Road
Fort Boone Plaza
Frankfort, KY 40601
(502) 564-3410

Louisiana Department of Urban and Community Affairs
P.O. Box 44455, Capitol Station
Baton Rouge, LA 70804
(504) 925-3730

Maine Bureau of Civil Emergency Preparedness
State House
187 State Street
Augusta, ME 04333
(207) 289-3154

Maryland Department of Natural Resources
Water Resources Administration
Tawes State Office Building D-2
Annapolis, MD 21401
(301) 269-3826

Massachusetts Water Resources Commission
Division of Water Resources
State Office Building
100 Cambridge Street
Boston, MA 02202
(617) 727-3267

Michigan Department of Natural Resources
Water Management Division
P.O. Box 30028
Lansing, MI 48909
(517) 373-3930

Minnesota Department of Natural Resources
Division of Waters
444 LaFayette Road
St. Paul, MN 55101
(612) 296-9226

Mississippi Research and Development Center
3825 Ridgewood Road
Jackson, MS 39211
(601) 982-6376

Missouri Department of Natural Resources
1101 R. Southwest Boulevard
P.O. Box 1368
Jefferson City, MO 65102
(314) 751-4932

Montana Department of Natural Resources and Conservation
32 South Ewing Street
Helena, MT 59601
(406) 444-6646

Nebraska Natural Resources Commission
P.O. Box 94876
Lincoln, NE 68509
(402) 471-2081

Nevada Division of Emergency Management
Capitol Complex
Carson City, NV 89710
(702) 885-4240

New Hampshire Office of State Planning
2½ Beacon Street
Concord, NH 03301
(603) 271-2231

New Jersey Department of Environmental Protection
Division of Water Resources
P.O. Box CN 029
Trenton, NJ 08625
(609) 292-2296

New Mexico State Engineer's Office
Bataan Memorial Building
Santa Fe, NM 97501
(505) 827-6140

New York Department of Environmental Conservation
Flood Protection Bureau
50 Wolf Road, Room 422
Albany, NY 12233
(518) 457-3157

North Carolina Department of Natural Resources and Community Development
Division of Community Assistance
P.O. Box 27687
Raleigh, NC 27611
(919) 733-2850

North Dakota State Water Commission
State Office Building
900 East Boulevard
Bismarck, ND 58505
(701) 224-2750

Ohio Department of Natural Resources
Floodplain Planning Unit
Fountain Square
Columbus, OH 43224
(614) 265-6755

Oklahoma Water Resources Board
10th and Stonewall, 12th Floor
Oklahoma City, OK 73105
(405) 271-2533

Oregon Department of Land Conservation and Development
1175 Court Street, N.E.
Salem, OR 97310
(503) 378-2332

Pennsylvania Department of Community Affairs
551 Forum Building, Room 317
Harrisburg, PA 17120
(717) 787-7400

Puerto Rico Planning Board
P.O. Box 41119, Minillas Station
Santurce, PR 09940
(809) 726-7110

Rhode Island Office of State Planning
Statewide Planning Program
265 Melrose Street
Providence, RI 02907
(401) 277-2656

South Carolina Water Resources Commission
3830 Forest Drive
P.O. Box 4440
Columbia, SC 29240
(803) 758-2514

South Dakota Department of Military and Veteran Affairs
Division of Emergency and Disaster
State Capitol
Pierre, SD 57501
(605) 773-3231

Tennessee Department of Economic and Community Development
Division of Local Planning
1800 James K. Polk Office Building
505 Deadrick Street
Nashville, TN 37219
(615) 741-2211

Texas Department of Water Resources
P.O. Box 13087, Capitol Station
1700 North Congress Avenue
Austin, TX 78711
(512) 475-2171

Utah Office of Comprehensive Emergency Management
1543 Sunnyside Avenue
Salt Lake City, UT 84108
(801) 533-5271

Vermont Environmental Conservation Agency
Division of Water Resources
State Office Building
Montpelier, VT 05602
(802) 828-2761

Virginia State Water Control Board
P.O. Box 11 143
Richmond, VA 23230
(804) 257-0075

APPENDIX E

PERT SCHEDULING

Project: WILLIAMS

Williams Estates

12–Jun–1985

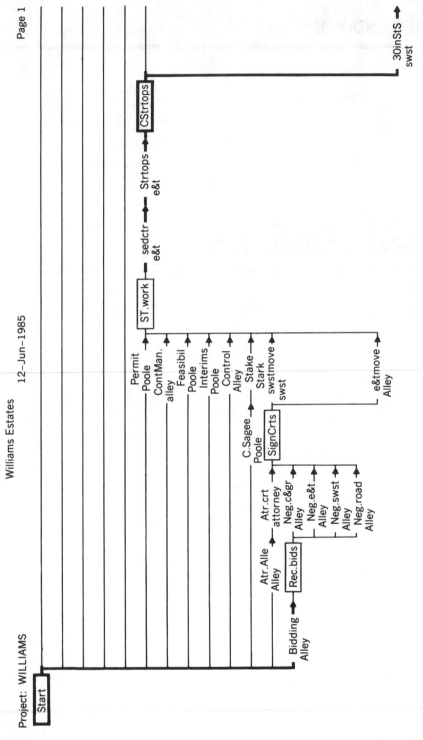

Project: WILLIAMS

Williams Estates   12-Jun-1985

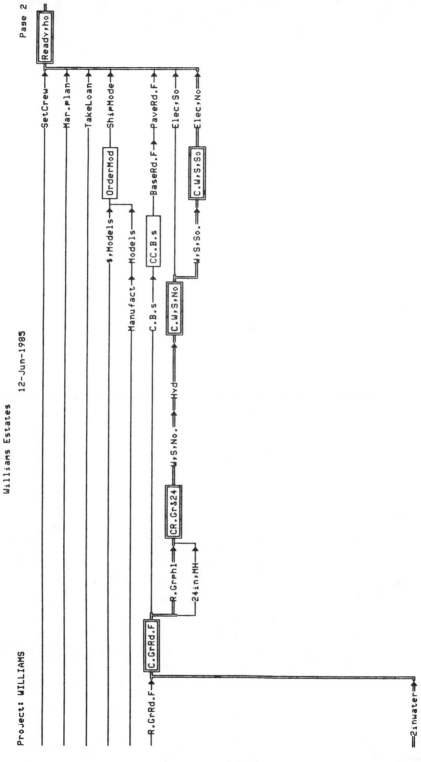

Project: WILLIAMS

=Setmodel⇒ Sales

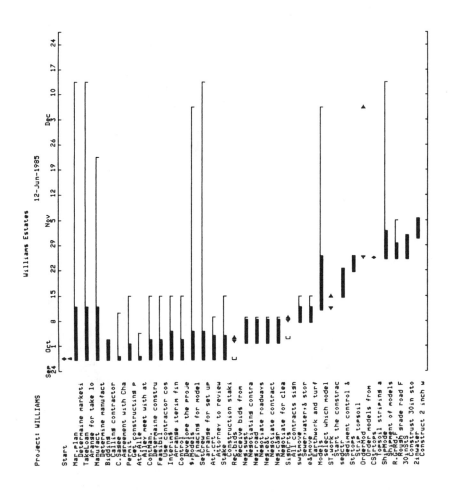

Project: WILLIAMS

Williams Estates   12-Jun-1985

340

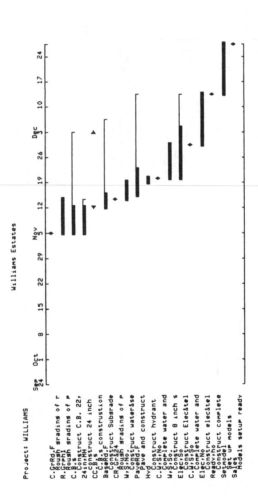

Project: WILLIAMS   Williams Estates   Page 2

C.,GRd,F
R.,Rough grading of r
C.,Rough grading of P
C.,B.,s
24inChstruct C.B. 22,
CC Construct 24 inch
Base,B.,s construction
BaseRd,F
CRCRS124 uct Subgrade
W.,No.,Rough grading of P
Pav,Rd.,Fruct waterase
Pave and construct
Hyd,Construct hydrant
C.,No.,Construct hydrant
W.,Complete water and
W.,So.,Construct 8 inch s
El Construct Electatel
C.,W.,SoComplete water and
El Construct water and
Ready,hoConstruct elecatel
Se Construct complete
Se model Construct complete
Sales set up models
Models setup ready

Project: WILLIAMS

Williams Estates
12-Jun-1985

Name	Responsible Code	Duration Description	Slack	Start Date	Finish Date	% Complete
Start			0.00 Dys W		27-Sep-1984 12:00 PM	
Mar. plan	Poole	10.00 Dys W Determine marketing plan	46.00 Dys W	27-Sep-1984 12:00 PM	11-Oct-1984 12:00 PM	0
Take Loan	Poole	10:00 Dys W Arrange for loan on homes	46.00 Dys W	27-Sep-1984 12:00 PM	11-Oct-1984 12:00 PM	0
Manufact.	Poole	10.00 Dys W Determine manufacturers whose homes will be sold	31.00 Dys W	27-Sep-1984 12:00 PM	11-Oct-1984 12:00 PM	0
Bidding	Alley	3.00 Dys W Calling contractors for bids	0.00 Dys W	27-Sep-1984 12:00 PM	2-Oct-1984 12:00 PM	0
C.Sagee	Poole	1.00 Dys W Agreement with Charle Stark inspection & surveying	8.00 Dys W	27-Sep-1984 12:00 PM	28-Sep-1984 12:00 PM	0
Permit	Poole	2.00 Dys W Get constructing permit from county	10.00 Dys W	27-Sep-1984 12:00 PM	1-Oct-1984 12:00 PM	0
Atr. Alley	Alley	1.00 Dys W Alley meet with attorney review plan, spec, contracts	4.00 Dys W	27-Sep-1984 12:00 PM	28-Sep-1984 12:00 PM	0
Cont. Man.	Alley	3.00 Dys W Determine construct management plan	9.00 Dys W	27-Sep-1984 12:00 PM	2-Oct-1984 12:00 PM	0
Feasibil.	Poole	3.00 Dys W Use contractor cost, market update for final economic feasibility	9.00 Dys W	27-Sep-1984 12:00 PM	2-Oct-1984 12:00 PM	0
Interim $	Poole	5.00 Dys W Arrange interim financing	7.00 Dys W	27-Sep-1984 12:00 PM	4-Oct-1984 12:00 PM	0

341

Williams Estates
12-Jun-1985

Project: WILLIAMS

Name	Responsible Code	Duration	Description	Slack	Start Date	Finish Date	% Complete
Control	Alley	3.00 Dys W	Develop the project control model	9.00 Dys W	27-Sep-1984 12:00 PM	2-Oct-1984 12:00 PM	0
$, Models	Poole	5.00 Dys W	Financing for models	46.00 Dys W	27-Sep-1984 12:00 PM	4-Oct-1984 12:00 PM	0
Set Crew	Poole	5.00 Dys W	Arrange for setup crew	51.00 Dys W	27-Sep-1984 12:00 PM	4-Oct-1984 12:00 PM	0
Atr. crt.	Attorney	3.00 Dys W	Attorney to review & draft contract documents	4.00 Dys W	28-Sep-1984 12:00 PM	3-Oct-1984 12:00 PM	0
Stake	Stark	3.00 Dys W	Construction staking of first phase	8.00 Dys W	28-Sep-1984 12:00 PM	3-Oct-1984 12:00 PM	0
Rec. bids			Receive bids from contractors	1.00 Dys W	2-Oct-1984 12:00 PM	2-Oct-1984 12:00 PM	0
Neg. swst	Alley	4.00 Dys W	Negotiating contracts, sewer, water, storm	1.00 Dys W	2-Oct-1984 12:00 PM	8-Oct-1984 12:00 PM	0
Neg. road	Alley	4.00 Dys W	Negotiate roadways	1.00 Dys W	2-Oct-1984 12:00 PM	8-Oct-1984 12:00 PM	0
Neg. e&t	Alley	4.00 Dys W	Negotiate contracts for earthwork and turf establishment	1.00 Dys W	2-Oct-1984 12:00 PM	8-Oct-1984 12:00 PM	0
Neg. c&gr	Alley	4.00 Dys W	Negotiate for clearing and grubbing, removals contracts	1.00 Dys W	2-Oct-1984 12:00 PM	8-Oct-1984 12:00 PM	0
Sign Crts			All contracts signed	1.00 Dys W	8-Oct-1984 12:00 PM	9-Oct-1984 12:00 PM	0

Williams Estates
12-Jun-1985

Project: WILLIAMS

Name	Responsible Code	Duration Description	Slack	Start Date	Finish Date	% Complete
swst move	swst	4.00 Dys W	1.00 Dys W	8-Oct-1984 12:00 PM	12-Oct-1984 12:00 PM	0
		Sewer, water, & storm sewer contractor move on site				
e&t move	Alley	4.00 Dys W	1.00 Dys W	8-Oct-1984 12:00 PM	12-Oct-1984 12:00 PM	0
		Earthwork and turf est. contractor move on site				
Models	Poole	10.00 Dys W	31.00 Dys W	11-Oct-1984 12:00 PM	25-Oct-1984 12:00 PM	0
		Select which models will be placed on sales center and sold				
St. work			1.00 Dys W	15-Oct-1984 12:00 PM	15-Oct-1984 12:00 Pm	
		Start the construction of grading, storm, sewer, water				
Sedctr.	e&t	5.00 Dys W	0.00 Dys W	15-Oct-1984 12:00 PM	22-Oct-1984 12:00 PM	0
		Sediment control & storm water management phase 1				
Strtops.	e&t	3.00 Dys W	0.00 Dys W	22-Oct-1984 12:00 PM	25-Oct-1984 12:00 PM	0
		Strip topsoil				
Order Mod.			31.00 Dys W	25-Oct-1984 12:00 PM	7-Dec-1984 12:00 PM	
		Order models from manufacturer				
CStrtops.			0.00 Dys W	25-Oct-1984 12:00 PM	25-Oct-1984 12:00 PM	
		Topsoil striping and stock piling complete				
Ship Mode	Poole	5.00 Dys W	31.00 Dys W	25-Oct-1984 12:00 PM	1-Nov-1984 12:00 PM	0
		Shipment of models to site				
R. GrRd. F	e&t	2.00 Dys W	5.00 Dys W	25-Oct-1984 12:00 PM	29-Oct-1984 12:00 PM	0
		Rough grade road F				
30 in. water	swst	3.00 Dys W	0.00 Dys W	31-Oct-1984 12:00 PM	5-Nov-1984 12:00 PM	0
		Construct 30 in. storm sewer and outlet				

Project: WILLIAMS

Williams Estates
12-Jun-1985

Name	Responsible Code	Duration	Description	Slack	Start Date	Finish Date	% Complete
2 in. water	swst	3.00 Dys W	Construct 2 inch water main	0.00 Dys W	31-Oct-1984 12:00 PM	5-Nov-1984 12:00 PM	0
C. GrRd. F			Rough grading of road F complete	0.00 Dys W	5-Nov-1984 12:00 PM	5-Nov-1984 12:00 PM	
R. Grph 1	swst	7.00 Dys W	Rough grading of phase 1	0.00 Dys W	5-Nov-1984 12:00 PM	14-Nov-1984 12:00 PM	0
C.B.s	swst	5.00 Dys W	Construct C.B. 22, 23, 24, 27, and leads	15.00 Dys W	5-Nov-1984 12:00 PM	12-Nov-1984 12:00 PM	0
24 in, MH	swst	5.00 Dys W	Construct 24 inch storm sewer and MH	2.00 Dys W	5-Nov-1984 12:00 PM	12-Nov-1984 12:00 PM	0
CC.B.s			C.B.s construction complete	15.00 Dys W	12-Nov-1984 12:00 PM	3-Dec-1984 12:00 PM	
Base Rd. F	swst	4.00 Dys W	Construct Subgrade and base for road F	15.00 Dys W	12-Nov-1984 12:00 PM	16-Nov-1984 12:00 PM	0
Cr. Gr & 24			Rough grading of phase 1 and 24 inch storm & MH #2 complete	0.00 Dys W	14-Nov-1984 12:00 PM	14-Nov-1984 12:00 PM	
W, S, No.	e&t	3.00 Dys W	Construct water & sewer serve north of road F	0.00 Dys W	14-Nov-1984 12:00 PM	19-Nov-1984 12:00 PM	0
Pave Rd. F	swst	5.00 Dys W	Pave and construct curb on road F	15.00 Dys W	16-Nov-1984 12:00 PM	23-Nov-1984 12:00 PM	0
Hyd	e&t	1.00 Dys W	Construct hydrant north of road F	0.00 Dys W	19-Nov-1984 12:00 PM	20-Nov-1984 12:00 PM	0

Project: WILLIAMS

Williams Estates
12-Jun-1985

Name	Responsible Code	Duration Description	Slack	Start Date	Finish Date	% Complete
C. W, S, No.			0.00 Dys W	20-Nov-1984 12:00 PM	20-Nov-1984 12:00 PM	
Complete water and sewer north of road F						
W, S, So.	e&t	8.00 Dys W	0.00 Dys W	20-Nov-1984 12:00 PM	30-Nov-1984 12:00 PM	0
Construct 8 inch sewer, water and sewer serves south of road F						
Elec, So	Poole	10.00 Dys W	8.00 Dys W	20-Nov-1984 12:00 PM	4-Dec-1984 12:00 PM	0
Construct Elec. & tel. north side						
C. W, S, So			0.00 Dys W	30-Nov-1984 12:00 PM	30-Nov-1984 12:00 PM	
Complete water and sewer south of road F						
Elec, No		10.00 Dys W	0.00 Dys W	30-Nov-1984 12:00 PM	14-Dec-1984 12:00 PM	0
Construct elec. & tel. south side						
Ready, ho			0.00 Dys W	14-Dec-1984 12:00 PM	14-Dec-1984 12:00 PM	
Construct complete site ready for home placement						
Set model	Poole	10.00 Dys W	0.00 Dys W	14-Dec-1984 12:00 PM	28-Dec-1984 12:00 PM	0
Set up models						
Sales			0.00 Dys W	28-Dec-1984 12:00 Pm	28-Dec-1984 12:00 PM	
Models setup ready to sale from						

APPENDIX F

A DESCRIPTION OF THE DEFUNCT WOODALL STAR MANUFACTURED HOME COMMUNITY RATING SYSTEM

In the early 1970s, when the 950-page *Woodall Mobile Home Park Directory* ceased publication, 13,000 of the 24,000 mobile home communities then in operation were listed and rated for consumer reference. Although the directory has not been published for almost 2 decades, a sufficient number of property owners, real estate brokers, appraisers, and lending institutions cite Woodall's one-star through five-star rating system, to make its reference worthwhile here.

Frankly, few if any allusions to "five-star quality" in a landlease community's advertising, prospectus, or value appraisal report have any direct relation to the original quality gradients. Read and see for yourself. The following guidelines are quoted from the 1970 edition of the *Woodall Mobile Home Park Directory*.

WOODALL ONE-STAR PARK

The most important consideration for a one-star park is overall appearance. If it is not a decent place to live, it will not be listed in Woodall's *Directory*. The following are general requirements:

1A. Fair overall appearance.

1B. Patios on most lots. May be concrete, asphalt, wood, or some suitable material.

1C. Grass, rock, or shell to cover ground.

1D. Streets fair to good. May be dirt, asphalt, or gravel in reasonable condition.

1E. Rest rooms clean, if any.

1F. Adequate laundry or laundromat nearby.

1G. If fences allowed, must be neat.

1H. Mail service.

1I. Homes may be old models but show evidence of care.

1J. Managers available some hours of each day.

WOODALL TWO-STAR PARK

In addition to the requirements for a one-star park, a two-star park will have the following:

2A. Landscaping—some lawns and shrubs.

2B. Streets in good condition. Must be dust free, of crushed rock, gravel, or shell minimum.

2C. Neat storage.

2D. Well-equipped laundry or laundromat nearby.

2E. 220-volt connections available.

2F. If children accepted, park should have play area.

2G. Park free of clutter, such as old cars and other abandoned equipment.

2H. Well maintained and managed.

WOODALL THREE-STAR PARK

What a three-star park does, it does well but not as uniformly as higher-rated parks. Many three-star parks were once rated higher, but original construction does not allow for today's 10-foot, 12-foot, and double-wides, or the 55-foot and 60-foot lengths. If children are allowed, there should be an adequate play area. However, the disarray caused by children may at times be the determining factor that keeps a three-star park at that level when it otherwise could be rated higher.

In addition to the requirements for one- and two-star parks, a three-star park must have the following:

3A. Attractive entrance.

3B. All mobile homes must be in good condition.

3C. Awnings and cabana rooms on some homes in Southern areas.

3D. Some spaces for large mobile homes.

3E. Paved or hard-surfaced streets.

WOODALL FOUR-STAR PARK

(There are two categories. See item 4K.)

Four-star parks are luxury parks. In addition to the requirements for one-, two-, and three-star parks, a four-star park must have the following:

4A. Good landscaping.

4B. Most homes skirted with metal skirts, concrete block, ornamental wood, or stone.

4C. Paved streets, edged or curbed.

4D. Uncrowded lots.

4E. Underground utilities if permitted by local conditions and authorities.

4F. Most tanks, if present, concealed.

4G. Any hedges or fences must be attractive and uniform.

4H. Awnings, cabanas, or porches on most homes in Southern areas (excepting double-wide units).

4I. Most lots to accommodate large mobile homes.

4J. Where row parking of homes exists, all must be lined up uniformly.

4K. Community hall and/or swimming pool and/or recreation program. If a park is four star in all but this requirement, the fourth star will be printed as an open star indicating a four-star park without park-centered recreation.

4L. Excellent management.

WOODALL FIVE-STAR PARK

Five-star parks are the finest. They should be nearly impossible to improve. In addition to the requirements for one-, two-, three-, and four-star parks, a five-star park must have the following:

5A. Well-planned and laid-out spacious appearance.

5B. Good location in regard to accessibility and desirable neighborhood. In some locations park should be enclosed by high hedges or ornamental fence.

5C. Wide paved streets in perfect condition. Curbs or lawns edged to street, sidewalks, street lights, street signs.

5D. Homes set back from street.

5E. Exceptionally attractive entrance and park sign.

5F. Patios at least 8 × 30 feet (excepting double-wide units).

5G. Paved off-street parking, such as carports or planned parking.

5H. All homes skirted.

5I.   All hitches concealed. Any existing tanks concealed.

5J.   Recreation, some or all of the following: swimming pool (excepting areas with long, cold winters), shuffleboards, horseshoe pitching, golf course, hobby shop, hobby classes, games, potlucks, dances, or natural recreational facilities.

5K.   Beautifully equipped recreation hall with kitchen. Room for community gatherings, tiled rest rooms, etc.

5L.   Uniform storage sheds or central storage facilities.

5M.   All late model homes in excellent condition.

5N.   At least 60% occupancy in order to judge quality of residents, which indicates park's ability to maintain a five-star rating between inspections.

5O.   All empty lots grassed, graveled, or otherwise well maintained.

5P.   If pets or children allowed, there must be a place for them to run and play without cluttering the streets and yards. Most five-star parks are for adults only.

5Q.   Superior management interested in comfort of residents and maintenance of park.

Here is a sample entry from the 1970 edition of the *Woodall Mobile Home Park Directory*.

> ** Sunny Lake Park, 123 Fourth St., 5 mi.n.b.c. WW HS 100L, Ch,
> FS.NP.ONS 10 R.

This would indicate that the Sunny Lake Park is 5 miles north of the business center, at 123 Fourth Street. It deserves a two-star rating, has accommodations for 100 homes, laundry, community hall, separate section for families, and does not permit pets. It has 10 spaces for travel trailers and maintains rest rooms. The "WW" notation was an additional rating of the overnight or vacation facilities, which ranges from one through four Ws.

How were these star ratings determined? In 1970, 21 teams of Woodall people visited every mobile home park in the country. The directory editor also used postcard pages in the directory proper, encouraging mail-in opinions from park owners and managers as well.

CLAYTON, WILLIAMS & SHERWOOD'S OPERATING AND RELATED FINANCIAL STATEMENT SAMPLES

TABLE G.1 A Clayton, Williams & Sherwood Property
Manufactured Home Landlease Community (237-Homesite Adult Community)

STATEMENT OF INCOME
FOR THE PERIOD ENDING November 30, 199___

	Current Month			Year to Date		
	Actual	Budget	Variance	Actual	Budget	Variance
Revenues:						
412000 Potential Rent	43,832.00	41,712.00	2,120.00	455,989.61	458,832.00	(2,842.39)
412500 Resident Concessions	(176.00)	.00	(176.00)	(1,936.00)	.00	(1,936.00)
Net Rental Income	43,656.00	41,712.00	1,944.00	454,053.61	458,832.00	(4,778.39)
420000 Laundry Income	35.95	40.00	(4.05)	626.54	440.00	186.54
480000 Interest Income	(103.13)	300.00	(403.13)	945.61	3,300.00	(2,354.39)
490000 Service Fees	.00	10.00	(10.00)	56.00	110.00	(54.00)
494000 Late Fees	.00	.00	.00	66.00	.00	66.00
Other Income	(67.18)	350.00	(417.18)	1,694.15	3,850.00	(2,155.85)
Total Revenues:	43,588.82	42,062.00	1,526.82	455,747.76	462,682.00	(6,934.24)
Operating Expenses:						
721032 Workers Compensation	.00	633.00	633.00	9,426.54	13,525.00	4,098.46
721051 Commissions	.00	167.00	167.00	1,700.00	1,837.00	137.00
721053 Managers Bonus	855.00	.00	(855.00)	4,416.88	5,420.00	1,003.12
721054 Managers Home	562.91	483.00	(79.91)	5,032.58	5,313.00	280.42
721055 Managers Insurance	105.90	350.00	244.10	3,324.77	3,850.00	525.23
721056 Payroll Taxes	357.37	292.00	(65.37)	3,238.69	3,901.00	662.31
721063 Salaries-Maintenance	1,344.88	504.00	(840.88)	8,228.64	6,699.00	(1,529.64)

351

STATEMENT OF INCOME
FOR THE PERIOD ENDING November 30, 199___

		Current Month			Year to Date	
	Actual	Budget	Variance	Actual	Budget	Variance
721065 Sal-Office Assistant	661.50	147.00	(514.50)	2,328.63	1,691.00	(637.63)
721067 Salaries-Property Mgr.	818.40	2,233.00	1,414.60	23,263.86	26,797.00	3,533.14
721069 Salaries-Training	325.00	250.00	(75.00)	650.00	2,750.00	2,100.00
Payroll and Benefits	5,030.96	5,059.00	28.04	61,610.59	71,783.00	10,172.41
728001 Accounting	52.18	98.00	45.82	1,096.80	1,078.00	(18.80)
728002 Advertising	25.97	75.00	49.03	589.90	825.00	235.10
728004 Auto and Truck	51.68	167.00	115.32	1,124.25	1,837.00	712.75
728024 Office Expense	512.56	260.00	(252.56)	3,011.48	2,860.00	(151.48)
728027 Repairs and Maintenance	151.44	450.00	298.56	5,822.24	4,950.00	(872.24)
728029 Telephone	163.58	300.00	136.42	1,550.42	3,300.00	1,749.58
728030 Tools and Supplies	602.09	420.00	(182.09)	4,391.12	4,620.00	228.88
728052 Home Set Up	.00	.00	.00	8.44	.00	(8.44)
728053 Marketing	39.83	200.00	160.17	1,577.33	2,200.00	622.67
Controllable Expenses	1,599.33	1,970.00	370.67	19,171.98	21,670.00	2,498.02
730005 Bank Charges	107.50	83.00	(24.50)	1,259.52	913.00	(346.42)
730011 Dues, Books, Subscriptions	.00	55.00	55.00	592.93	605.00	12.07
730017 Insurance	987.37	955.00	(32.37)	9,731.11	10,505.00	773.89
730019 Legal Fees	.00	200.00	200.00	450.00	2,200.00	1,750.00
730021 Licenses and Fees	.00	100.00	100.00	1,240.20	2,876.00	1,635.80
730022 Meals and Entertainment	.00	40.00	40.00	141.39	440.00	298.61
730026 Property Taxes	4,075.72	2,877.00	(1,198.72)	32,845.72	31,647.00	(1,198.72)

STATEMENT OF INCOME
FOR THE PERIOD ENDING November 30, 199__

		Current Month			Year to Date		
		Actual	Budget	Variance	Actual	Budget	Variance
730028	Security	.00	.00	.00	900.00	816.00	(84.00)
730031	Travel	226.53	175.00	(51.53)	2,106.50	1,925.00	(181.50)
Other Park Operating		5,397.12	4,485.00	(912.12)	49,267.37	51,927.00	2,659.63
731001	Accounting	434.00	434.00	.00	4,774.00	4,774.00	.00
731007	Business Development	220.00	210.00	(10.00)	2,420.00	2,310.00	(110.00)
731022	Meals and Entertainment	.00	10.00	10.00	48.81	110.00	61.19
731024	Office Expense	55.00	55.00	.00	605.00	605.00	.00
731029	Telephone	.00	55.00	55.00	626.86	605.00	(21.86)
731031	Travel	.00	95.00	95.00	1,142.35	1,045.00	(97.35)
731051	Management Fees	2,200.00	2,103.00	(97.00)	24,708.10	23,133.00	(1,575.10)
Corporate Allocations		2,909.00	2,962.00	53.00	34,325.12	32,582.00	(1,743.12)
732012	Electric	1,334.93	1,370.00	35.07	14,496.81	15,070.00	573.19
732053	Gas	18.49	9.00	(9.49)	154.12	99.00	(55.12)
732054	Rubbish	1,508.68	2,036.00	527.32	17,431.27	19,298.00	1,866.73
732055	Sewer	1,112.52	525.00	(587.52)	5,391.69	5,775.00	383.31
732056	Water	192.50	400.00	207.50	2,965.99	4,400.00	1,434.01
Utilities Expense		4,167.12	4,340.00	172.88	40,439.88	44,642.00	4,202.12
Total Operating Expenses:		19,103.53	18,816.00	(287.53)	204,814.94	222,604.00	17,789.06
Net Operating Income/(Loss):		24,485.29	23,246.00	1,239.29	250,932.82	240,078.00	10,854.82

STATEMENT OF INCOME
FOR THE PERIOD ENDING November 30, 199___

	Current Month			Year to Date		
	Actual	Budget	Variance	Actual	Budget	Variance
734008 Capitalizable	253.17	.00	(253.17)	31,900.12	32,050.00	149.88
734027 Repairs and Maintenance	.00	200.00	200.00	.00	2,200.00	2,200.00
734052 Debt Service	10,903.69	12,593.00	1,689.31	131,271.09	138,523.00	7,251.91
734437 Tax Returns/Franchise Tax	.00	.00	.00	1,478.02	2,450.00	971.98
738053 Payroll Taxes-Sales Mgr.	(39.83)	.00	39.83	.00	.00	.00
Other Operating Cash Items	11,117.03	12,793.00	1,675.97	164,649.23	175,223.00	10,573.77
Income/(Loss) From Operations	13,368.26	10,453.00	2,915.26	86,283.59	64,855.00	21,428.59
735007 Capitalizable Other	.00	.00	.00	600.00	.00	(600.00)
735066 PY Expenses	.00	.00	.00	510.60	.00	(510.60)
Adjustments for Net Income	.00	.00	.00	1,110.60	.00	(1,110.60)
Income/(Loss)	13,368.26	10,453.00	2,915.26	85,172.99	64,855.00	20,317.99

BALANCE SHEET
AS OF November 30, 199__

	Ending Bal. Current Month	Ending Bal. Prior Month	Net Change for Month	Beginning of Year Bal.	Net Change for Year
Assets:					
Operating Cash					
101001 Cash/Ckg.-Independence	.00	.00	.00	18,440.46	(18,440.46)
101003 Cash/Ckg.-B of A	70,677.24	87,904.17	(17,226.93)	.00	70,677.24
102008 Cash/MM-Liberty	103.13	.00	103.13	.00	103.13
102011 Cash/MM-California Federal	.00	.00	.00	46,952.51	(46,952.51)
104000 Cash-Petty Cash	1,301.90	800.00	501.90	800.00	501.90
104001 Petty Cash	.00	501.90	(501.90)	501.90	(501.90)
107000 Cash-Depository	1,010.00	1,422.76	(412.76)	3,549.89	(2,539.89)
Total Operating Cash	73,092.27	90,628.83	(17,536.56)	70,244.76	2,847.51
Restricted Cash					
109026 Cash Rst/Imperial	.00	.00	.00	3,152.77	(3,152.77)
Total Restricted Cash	.00	.00	.00	3,152.77	(3,152.77)
Total Cash	73,092.27	90,628.83	(17,536.56)	73,397.53	(305.26)
Fixed Assets					
150000 Land	404,000.00	404,000.00	.00	404,000.00	.00
150500 Space Improvements	1,616,000.00	1,616,000.00	.00	1,616,000.00	.00
153000 Personal Property	20,939.75	20,939.75	.00	20,939.75	.00
153087 Personal Property 1987	17,967.45	17,967.45	.00	17,967.45	.00
153088 Personal Property 1988	17,300.26	17,300.26	.00	17,300.26	.00
153089 Personal Property 1989	6,394.12	6,394.12	.00	6,394.12	.00
153090 Personal Property 1990	11,217.82	11,217.82	.00	11,217.82	.00
153091 Personal Property 1991	17,570.00	17,570.00	.00	17,570.00	.00
Total Cost	2,111,389.40	2,111,389.40	.00	2,111,389.40	.00

356

BALANCE SHEET
AS OF November 30, 199___

DATE/TIME PREPARED: 12/18/9___ 01:54 pm
REPORT #:006
PAGE #: 2

		Ending Bal. Current Month	Ending Bal. Prior Month	Net Change for Month	Beginning of Year Bal.	Net Change for Year
158005	A/D-Space Improvements	(736,896.04)	(736,896.04)	.00	(736,896.04)	.00
158030	A/D-Personal Property	(17,681.08)	(17,681.08)	.00	(17,681.08)	.00
158087	A/D-Personal Property 87	(13,109.92)	(13,109.92)	.00	(13,109.92)	.00
158088	A/D-Personal Property 88	(14,969.00)	(14,969.00)	.00	(14,969.00)	.00
158089	A/D-Personal Property 89	(3,487.00)	(3,487.00)	.00	(3,487.00)	.00
158090	A/D-Personal Property 90	(4,350.00)	(4,350.00)	.00	(4,350.00)	.00
158091	A/D-Personal Property 91	(2,511.00)	(2,511.00)	.00	(2,511.00)	.00
	Total Accum Depreciation	(793,004.04)	(793,004.04)	.00	(793,004.04)	.00
	Net Fixed Assets	1,318,385.36	1,318,385.36	.00	1,318,385.36	.00
	Other Assets					
110037	ICO-1406/7010	(2,011.43)	(1,973.69)	(37.74)	(268.66)	(1,742.77)
120000	Accounts Receivable	(990.00)	(3,278.00)	2,288.00	92.00	(1,082.00)
120004	Other Accounts Receivable	.00	.00	.00	9.00	(9.00)
120008	Insurance Proceeds Rec.	(103.13)	.00	(103.13)	.00	(103.13)
135013	Due Fr (to) CWS MHS	.00	26.61	(26.61)	1,508.60	(1,508.60)
160500	Closing Costs	25,650.46	.00	25,650.46	.00	25,650.46
161500	Loan Fees	.00	42,750.00	(42,750.00)	42,750.00	(42,750.00)
166010	A/A-Legal Closing	.00	(2,850.00)	2,850.00	(2,850.00)	2,850.00
166015	A/A-Loan Fees	.00	(14,249.54)	14,249.54	(14,249.54)	14,249.54
182000	Park Clearing	3,000.00	3,000.00	.00	3,000.00	.00
183500	Prepaid Expenses	.00	.00	.00	178.02	(178.02)
	Total Other Assets	25,545.90	23,425.38	2,120.52	30,169.42	(4,623.52)
	Total Assets:	1,417,023.53	1,432,439.57	(15,416.04)	1,421,952.31	(4,928.78)

BALANCE SHEET
AS OF November 30, 199___

	Ending Bal. Current Month	Ending Bal. Prior Month	Net Change for Month	Beginning of Year Bal.	Net Change for Year
	Liabilities:				Current Liabilities
200000 Accounts Payable	45.03	1,559.33	1,514.30	2,377.04	2,332.01
200500 Other Payables	1,500.00	.00	(1,500.00)	856.00	(644.00)
202500 Property Tax Payable	.00	28,770.00	28,770.00	.00	.00
209000 Year End Payable	.00	.00	.00	4,185.37	4,185.37
Total Current Liabilities	1,545.03	30,329.33	28,784.30	7,418.41	5,873.38
Long Term Debt					
234000 1st Trust Deed Payable	1,248,474.00	1,248,474.00	.00	1,248,474.00	.00
235000 2nd Trust Deed Payable	196,000.00	196,000.00	.00	200,000.00	4,000.00
235050 Accrued Interest-2nd TD	54,000.00	54,000.00	.00	54,000.00	.00
Total Long Term Debt	1,498,474.00	1,498,474.00	.00	1,502,474.00	4,000.00
Total Liabilities:	1,500,019.03	1,528,803.33	28,784.30	1,509,892.41	9,873.38
	Equity:				
Partners' Equity	(168,168.49)	(168,168.49)	.00	(87,940.10)	80,228.39
Current Year Earnings	85,172.99	71,804.73	(13,368.26)	.00	(85,172.99)
Total Equity:	(82,995.50)	(96,363.75)	(13,368.26)	(87,940.10)	(4,944.60)
Total Liabilities and Equity:	1,417,023.53	1,432,439.57	15,416.04	1,421,952.31	4,928.78

LET'S GO SHOPPING

George Allen, CPM, is president of GFA Management, Inc., in Indianapolis, Indiana. GFA Management is a professional management firm specializing in residential and commercial property management and consulting.

GFA
Management
Box # 47024
Indianapolis, IN
46247

"Wake me up when it's Friday!"

The poster slogan on the wall behind the leasing consultant's desk all but shouted its message. And the leasing effort which followed parodied the sleeping bear depicted on the poster. No qualifying of the prospect or identifying rental needs was done; no attempt at benefit selling was made; and worst of all, no effort to close with an application to complete or commitment to a tentative move-in date was presented. This was a complete leasing flop, especially as the prospect was a professional shopper.

Treat every rental prospect like a professional shopper! Such simple advice, yet it is a mindset, a motivator that continues to elude the best of property managers. Why? Because it is hard to be up on one's toes every time someone walks through the information center door. There is also the continual turnover of employees,

Reprinted with permission from the *Journal of Property Management*, published by the Institute of Real Estate Management.

the misleading comfort of an occasional tight market, and the changing priorities of property managers.

All these circumstances give rise to a need to regularly have one's properties shopped, either by in-house staff members or by outside professionals.

In his book *Tenant's Revenge* (Boulder, Colorado: Paladin Press, 1983), Andy Kane describes how to effectively shop a property.

"If you inspect an apartment with the leasing agent and are considering renting it, you should leave, drive around the block, and return. The manager will think you have gone. Go to an adjoining unit, and knock on the door. Ask the tenant what he or she thinks of the building. Are there roaches and crime? Is there heat in winter? Does the owner fix things? Ask anything else that may interest you."

How would your property or properties fare under such scrutiny?

WHO SHOULD SHOP?

Here are at least four ways to find out: Shop it yourself. The obvious drawback is that you will be recognized, and you are really too close to the forest to see the trees.

Have a friend or peer do the shopping. But do they know what to look for and will they compromise the whole evaluation program?

Use in-house personnel. (Remember, your secretary can do anything.) But they may have a similar problem of being recognized.

Finally, retain a qualified, experienced shopping service from outside the firm. Some private companies perform shopping services, as do state apartment associations. The only problem here is that a property management firm often winds up financing someone else's education at doing this sort of assignment, and one's competitors benefit from such largesse 6 months down the road.

In addition, these amateur shoppers are usually easily spotted as they ask too many of the right questions, tend to lead the leasing conversation (something authentic rental prospects rarely do), and linger too long as they stretch for details to include in their report.

The two most reliable sources for professional shopper service continue to be property management firms and real estate management consultants who specialize in this type of assignment. Both are usually well experienced and capable. Such firms can provide references and sample past reports to verify the quality of their performance. The drawback with the property management firm, however, is the potential conflict of interest when a property's management contract is up for renewal.

SUPPORTING DOCUMENTATION

Norvik Management Services of Elm Grove, Wisconsin, is a property management firm that offers professional shopping services. In Norvik's case, the client receives a detailed shopper's report of the rental property as compiled by one of the company's 1,000 qualified shoppers. The report contains objective and subjective information relative to a telephone inquiry of the property, a trip to the property (off-site factors and curb appeal), and an on-site tour of the property.

During the three information gathering phases of the company's report preparation, attention is paid to leasing technique; signage; condition of models, grounds, and leasing office; and follow-up effort by staff. By developing a standardized shopping report, participants help ensure that the most common problems among leasing agents are addressed.

Professional shoppers will generally wrap up their visit with two additional steps. After the personal on-site interview, they tour the property once again (assuming they drove through it), this time photographing instances of deferred maintenance (potholes in the street), marginal curb appeal (uncut grass), and possible rules violations (bedsheet curtains). These photos become an addendum to the report sent to the property owner or property management firm who hired the shopper.

A shopper will also attempt to casually interview at least two residents of the property during the final drive-through. The shopper simply asks, "What do you like about living here? Are there problems I should know about before I move in?" Some of the most salient insights and otherwise hidden defects are uncovered during these impromptu conversations.

POTENTIAL PROBLEM AREAS

Melinda Brody of Melinda Brody and Associates, Orlando, Florida, specializes in sales training and has shopped leasing and sales consultants for several years. In the September/October 1989 issue of *Units,* she summarized the problem areas she encounters most while "mystery shopping," as she calls it, income property leasing staffs:

• *Poor phone skills.* The phone conversation is not exciting! Leasing consultants respond mostly to questions asked and do not paint enough word pictures to whet the caller's appetite to visit. Rarely is an appointment set.

• *Lack of qualifying and rapport building prior to demonstration.* Leasing consultants are still too quick to grab the keys and run out to show the model. They should learn to use the Guest Card to build rapport and discover the prospect's hot buttons.

• *Difficulty in handling objections and assertively asking for the order.* Generally, leasing consultants are not prepared with answers to typical objections. The most common objections seem to be size and price. They need to relate more benefits and explain what the price includes. Closing always seems to be difficult. Not enough closing questions are asked during the presentation.

As these three basic problems seem to reappear often in shopping efforts, the shopping report should be structured to emphasize these concerns. Shopping reports may also be customized to address particular problems at a specific property.

TELEPHONE SALES TECHNIQUE EVALUATION

Once the rental prospect who is telephoning has been properly greeted, his or her specific needs ascertained, background qualified, and interest stimulated, the bottom line goal is to get an appointment! For without an appointment, the phone interview with an otherwise qualified prospect has been valueless. If they commit to an appointment to visit the property and talk further about a lease, the consultant has a second opportunity to close the sale.

Additional considerations during the telephone interview are to get the prospect's name, address, and phone number for follow-up purposes. Also, the consultant needs to give clear travel directions to the prospect, and ask how he or she heard of the rental community. The last question is very important, as it is management's best opportunity to gauge the advertising effectiveness of whatever media is being used to further the marketing plan at the time.

INTERVIEWING THE PROSPECT

How the leasing consultant conducts him- or herself from the moment the prospect walks in the door is another vital area a shopper should scrutinize. What could be more important?

The consultant should greet the prospect confidently and spend time asking about living needs and putting the prospect at ease. When properly used, the Guest Card can be a helpful aid to this end.

Finally, did the consultant make one or more attempts to close the lease transaction? Books are written on this aspect of selling and leasing—such as Zig Ziglar's *Secrets of Closing the Sale* (Revell, 1982). It's that important.

A FINAL NOTE

If a supervising manager gets every leasing consultant to believe and perform job responsibilities as if everyone who walks through the office door were a shopper, conversion percentages would improve, vacancy rates would decline, and advertising dollars would be well spent. Employing a professional shopping service is one way to ensure these goals are met.

And remember, what a property manager doesn't know is happening to rental prospects can and will hurt in occupancy, turnover, resident relations, and ultimately, return on investment.

APPENDIX I

THE ALLEN REPORT ON THE LARGEST COMMUNITY OWNERS

George Allen is president of GFA Management in Greenwood, Ind. GFA special-izes in residential and commercial real estate management. For more information, contact Allen at GFA management, Box 47024, Indianapolis, Ind. 46247.

More than 100 owners and managers of multiple manufactured housing rental community portfolios responded to the 1992–93 Allen Report survey questionnaire.

More than 1,800 communities and 450,000 sites are owned or managed by the 126 companies listed in the accompanying chart. Overall, the average survey size is 247 sites, a repeat of 1991–92 figures.

The top 101 firms boast impressive portfolios in excess of 1,000 sites apiece. The average rental community size among this large group is 254 sites.

The remaining 25 companies have a minimum of two communities apiece (500 sites) in their portfolios. The average number of home sites in this group is 139.

The portfolio size in this list ranges from one showcase property to a mega-portfolio of 80 manufactured housing rental communities.

Thirty-five states are represented this year, 6 more than in last year's survey. California leads the pack with 27 companies followed by Michigan (14), Illinois (9), Florida (8), New York (7), Ohio (6), Colorado (5), Arizona, Georgia and Wis-consin (3 each). Some 67% of the firms listed operate in at least one of these 10 states.

Alberta and British Cclumbia are the two Canadian provinces included in the report.

Five firms that appeared in the 1991–92 survey were not included in this year's list. At the same time, 32 new firms were added (identified by the NR symbol on the chart).

This list represents only a third of the community owners and mangers who have property portfolios containing a minimum of 500 sites or more than one community. Many of the firms listed in the survey are leaders in various manufactured housing associations.

The accuracy of the statistics is dependent on the reporting accuracy of the respondents. Every reasonable effort was made to check community and site counts. (If you find errors, please let us know.)

1993 Rank	Firm Name	State or Prov.	# Sites Owned or Managed	# Comm. Owned or Managed	States or Prov.	1992 Rank
1	Lautrec Ltd.[2]	Mich.	22,436	56	9	2
2	Clayton, Williams & Sherwood[2]	Calif.	20,457	51	9	1
3	ROC Properties[1,3]	Colo.	18,745	80	32	12
4	Ellenburg Capital[2]	Ore.	17,563	61	14	3
5	Uniprop[1]	Mich.	14,300	38	12	4
6	Mobile Home Communities Inc.[2]	Colo.	12,837	42	16	5
7	DeAnza Assets Inc.[2]	Calif.	12,551	31	6	6
8	Bloch Realty[1]	Mich.	12,012	32	9	7
9	Aspen Enterprises	Mich.	11,913	27	5	9
10	Angeles Corp.[2]	Calif.	11,676	15	6	8
11	Chateau Land Development	Mich.	10,032	20	2	10
12	Carlsburg Properties[2]	Calif.	9,313	33	21	15
13	Clayton Homes Inc.	Tenn.	8,551	?8	7	33
14	Kingsley Mgmt.[3]	Utah	8,500	27	7	11
15	Bessire & Casenhiser Inc.[1,2]	Calif.	8,000	47	3	14
16	R&S Property Mgmt.	Calif.	8,000	7	3	NR
17	Merrill Lyncy Hubbard Inc.[1,2]	N.Y.	7,807	17	3	17
18	Sundance Enterprises[1]	Mich.	7,600	28	6	NR
19	Light House Home Center	Ind.	6,655	12	3	21
20	Wilder Corp.	Fla.	5,881	20	3	23
21	Colo. Real Estate & Investment	Colo.	5,710	28	6	19
22	United Mobile Homes[1]	N.J.	5,200	22	5	20
23	Evans Mgmt.[1,2]	Calif.	5,117	29	2	22

NR = not ranked previously

1. Firms that fee-manage communities for other property owners or function as managing partners for properties possibly included in the portfolio of another firm listed in the chart.

2. Firms with one or more certified property managers on staff.

3. Name or address changed from last year.

1993 Rank	Firm Name	State or Prov.	# Sites Owned or Managed	# Comm. Owned or Managed	States or Prov.	1992 Rank
24	J&H Asset Property Mgmt.[1,2]	Calif.	5,107	39	1	NR
25	Kentland Corp.	Mich.	4,856	17	2	25
26	Choice Properties	Mich.	4,439	16	4	34
27	Storz Mgmt.[1,2]	Calif.	4,433	37	3	26
28	Garden Homes Mgmt. Corp.	Ct.	4,430	66	3	27
29	Buchanan Mgmt.	Mich.	4,121	13	3	51
30	Meadows Mgmt. Co.	Calif.	4,086	9	3	29
31	Intercoastal Comm.	Fla.	4,066	9	1	72
32	Brandenburg, Staedler, Moore & Butters	Calif.	4,000	15	1	31
33	LaCumbre/LCM Mgmt.[1]	Calif.	3,973	25	2	NR
34	Steiner & Assoc.[1]	Fla.	3,827	21	1	30
35	PM Realty Advisors[2]	Calif.	3,800	7	3	NR
36	Horner & Assoc.[1,3]	Kan.	3,730	13	4	44
37	Franklin Group	Mich.	3,717	24	2	35
38	McDay Corp.	Calif.	3,515	8	4	36
39	5005 Properties	Minn.	3,475	21	11	43
40	Chesapeake Homes	Md.	3,409	16	3	38
41	Martin Newby Mgmt.[1]	Fla.	3,400	13	1	39
42	Zeman MHC[1]	Ill.	3,350	19	2	42
43	Countryside Mgmt.[2]	Colo.	3,277	11	6	24
44	Homefree Village	Colo.	3,200	3	1	41
45	Katahdin Corp.	Maine	3,200	13	5	40
46	The Blair Group	Fla.	3,142	4	1	45
47	Capital Development	Ill.	3,110	9	4	32
48	Tunnell Cos.	Del.	3,052	6	1	47
49	Ashford Mgmt. Group[1]	N.Y.	3,000	17	7	48
50	E.T. Consultants	Calif.	2,904	8	5	50
51	Western MHP Mgmt.	Calif.	2,700	13	2	NR

1993 Rank	Firm Name	State or Prov.	# Sites Owned or Managed	# Comm. Owned or Managed	States or Prov.	1992 Rank
52	Harshaw Asset Mgmt. Corp.[2]	Texas	2,650	17	1	NR
53	Richards & Assoc. Ltd.	Calif.	2,605	14	4	53
54	Pegasus Group[1]	Calif.	2,400	10	6	46
55	Newport Pacific Capital Property Corp.[2]	Calif.	2,293	17	2	68
56	Heritage Financial Grp. Inc.	Ind.	2,188	17	4	60
57	Capital Investments Corp.[3]	Va.	2,181	11	6	28
58	Park Mgmt. Specialists Corp.	Ohio	2,060	11	3	58
59	Calif. MH Park Mgmt.	Calif.	2,000	13	1	55
60	Oakwood Land Development Corp.	N.C.	2,000	4	3	56
61	Silver King Cos.[1]	Ariz.	1,986	20	3	59
62	Jennings Real Estate	Ill.	1,940	6	4	81
63	Harvey J. Miller Inc.	Calif.	1,938	7	5	52
64	Balcor/Amer. Express[1]	Ill.	1,909	5	4	49
65	Dolphin Real Estate Grp.	Calif.	1,849	26	4	57
66	Essex Investments	N.Y.	1,794	9	7	61
67	Mason Properties	N.Y.	1,793	24	5	74
68	Ballerina Park Home Comm.	Okla.	1,785	11	3	62
69	Apollo Properties Inc.[1,2]	Ariz.	1,756	9	1	NR
70	QCA Mgmt.	Okla.	1,750	9	6	63
71	Patterson Mgmt. Grp.[1,2]	Ga.	1,593	3	1	NR
72	Goldstein Properties	Calif.	1,577	5	1	67
73	Holiday Homes[3]	Ohio	1,574	6	2	73
74	P.I.C.[1,2]	Wash.	1,562	19	2	70
75	D.R.S. Realty	Mich.	1,500	8	4	71
76	Keystone Mgmt.	Mich.	1,500	15	2	77
77	Ridgewood Properties Inc.	Ga.	1,500	6	1	65
78	Vortex Properties	Vt.	1,483	11	3	78
79	Cannon MH Group Inc.	Ga.	1,460	7	1	NR

1993 Rank	Firm Name	State or Prov.	# Sites Owned or Managed	# Comm. Owned or Managed	States or Prov.	1992 Rank
80	The Boston Grp.	Utah	1,450	9	1	75
81	A.L.S. Properties	Minn.	1,401	6	4	79
82	Bryn Mawr Properties	Wash.	1,400	11	3	76
83	American MH Comm.	Ill.	1,350	9	2	NR
84	Park/Cook Investments	Ohio	1,300	17	3	80
85	Real Estate Investment Partners	Ill.	1,275	9	3	NR
86	Hall Financial Grp.	Texas	1,228	3	2	54
87	Canadian Heritage Homes	Alberta	1,210	7	2	88
88	Goldman & Associates[1]	Ill.	1,200	5	2	82
89	Miland Inc.	Kan.	1,200	7	1	NR
90	Novinger & Co.	Kan.	1,200	8	5	83
91	Billings Properties	Calif.	1,124	8	4	93
92	Starview Sales Inc.	Pa.	1,124	10	1	86
93	Kaufco Inc.	Maine	1,095	6	3	85
94	Bertakis Dvpmt.	Mich.	1,093	4	1	NR
95	Asset Dvlp. Grp.	Wis.	1,088	5	2	87
96	Kahn Dvlp. Co.[2]	S.C.	1,072	7	1	NR
97	Nationwide Investment Co.	Ill.	1,048	3	2	NR
98	Northern Properties Ltd.[2]	Mich.	1,044	7	1	NR
99	Hanover Grp.	Ind.	1,036	6	1	NR
100	Trailer Mart Inc.	Ohio	1,012	2	1	NR
101	Ashwood Comm.[3]	Wis.	1,001	9	1	NR
102	Grossman Properties	Ariz.	991	3	2	91
103	Maumee Valley Homes	Ohio	990	12	1	89
104	Richard Kellam Assoc. Inc.	Va.	900	3	2	92
105	Mel Riff Enter.	Fla.	893	3	1	66
106	Homewood Manor Enter. Inc.	Miss.	892	6	1	NR
107	Orangewood Lakes MH Comm.	Fla.	852	4	1	NR

1993 Rank	Firm Name	State or Prov.	# Sites Owned or Managed	# Comm. Owned or Managed	States or Prov.	1992 Rank
108	Jay Gelb Co.	N.Y.	850	6	3	94
109	Jim Clayton	Tenn.	850	5	2	84
110	MH Parks of J.P. Ossen[3]	Ct.	850	10	2	95
111	Bush, Carr & McAdoo	Calif.	760	6	1	98
112	Investors Realty	Del.	700	6	1	99
113	Heron Cay	Fla.	600	1	1	NR
114	Landsman Grp.	Md.	600	3	2	NR
115	Steenburg Homes	Wis.	600	3	1	101
116	Willette Properties	N.C.	583	5	1	100
117	Sky Harbor	N.Y.	576	3	1	NR
118	Dennis Ohnstad[1]	Ill.	500	4	1	NR
119	Urban Assets	Calif.	400	2	1	96
120	Act III Investments[1]	Ind.	365	6	1	NR
121	Kenneth Everett Rentals	Ala.	347	4	2	NR
122	Triton Valley Estates	N.Y.	314	4	1	NR
123	White Properties	Nev.	255	3	2	NR
124	Jim Beck	Ohio	239	2	1	NR
125	Flummerfelt Properties	Iowa	225	4	1	NR
126	R&L MH Inc.	Okla.	162	2	1	NR

VENDOR RESOURCE DIRECTORY OF PRODUCTS AND SERVICES FOR MANUFACTURED HOME COMMUNITIES

APPRAISAL AND COST ESTIMATION SERVICES

Boeckh Building—Cost Manual
E.H. Boeckh
Box 510291
New Berlin, WI 53131
800-809-0016

Datacomp Appraisal Systems
5250 Northland Drive, N.E.
Grand Rapids, MI 49505
(616) 363-8454   Ted Boers

F. W. Dodge Division
McGraw-Hill Publishers
1221 Avenue of the Americas
New York, NY 10020
(212) 512-2000

Kelley Blue Book
5 Oldfield
Irvine, CA 92718
(800) 444-1743

Marshall and Swift's Valuation
   Services
911 Wilshire Blvd., 15th Floor
Los Angeles, CA 90017
(213) 683-9000

Mobile/Manufactured Home
   Blue Book
29 North Wacker
Chicago, IL 60606
(800) 621-9907

Moser Group
1805 Sardis Road N., #111
Charlotte, NC 28270
(704) 841-8400   Dennis Moser

N.A.D.A. Appraisal Guide
Box 7800
Costa Mesa, CA 92628
(714) 556-8511   Vince Pulsipher

Auctions: Manufactured Homes &
  Manufactured Home
  Communities
The Miles Company
Box 2228
Salisbury, NC 28145
(704) 637-2828   Jim Cox

APPRAISERS—REAL ESTATE

Act III
55 N., 200 W.
Lebanon, IN 46052
(317) 482-3984   Sharon Niccum

Allen & Associates
2000 N. Woodward Ave.,
  Suite 310
Bloomfield Hills, MI 48304
(810) 433-9630
Laurence Allen, MAI

Brown, Chudleigh & Schuler
744 Cardley Ave.
Medford, OR 97504
(541) 772-8566   Greg Schuler

Charles M. Ritley & Associates
23875 Commerce Park Road
Beachwood, OH 44122
(216) 464-8686   Roger Ritley, MAI

Cushman & Wakefield, Appraisal
  Division
150 S. Wacker Drive, Suite 3100
Chicago, IL 60606
(312) 551-1770   Mike Schaeffer

Field Adjusting, Inc.
112 Norcross St., Ste. H
Roswell, GA 30075
(800) 864-0523   D. Arnold

Laurencelle Appraisal Co.
725 S. Adams Rd. #244-A
Birmingham, MI 48009
(810) 540-4036
Tim Laurencelle, MAI

Palmer, Groth & Pietka
110 SW Yarnhill St.
Portland, OR 97204
(503) 226-0983   T. Wright

Pardue, Heid, Church, Smith,
  Waller
4915 W. Cypress Street
Tampa, FL 33607
(813) 287-1020

Sheets, Hendrickson & Associates
3333 Henderson Boulevard,
  Suite 230
Tampa, FL 33609
(813) 871-3216   Bob Behrle

**COIN-OPERATED LAUNDRY
SERVICES**

Automatic Laundry Co.
Box 39365
Denver, CO 80239
(303) 371-9274

Macke Laundry Service
122 Messner Drive
Wheeling, IL 60090
(800) 622-2141

WEB Service Co.
3690 Freemar Boulevard
Redondo Beach, CA 90278
(800) 421-6897

COMPUTER SOFTWARE AND COOPERATIVE PROCESSING SERVICES

American Computer Software
802 W. Broadway, #204
Madison, WI 53713
(608) 221-9449

Rent Manager
London Computer Systems
3246 Woodlake Court
Cincinnati, OH 45140
(800) 669-0871   Dave Hegemann

MRI Property Management
   Systems (cooperative processing)
23945 Mercantile Road
Cleveland, OH 44122
(216) 464-3225   Fred Goodman

PC Manager, The
170 East 17th Street, Suite 212
Costa Mesa, CA 92627
(714) 548-0303   Jim Washington

PRISM Computers
8515 Douglas, #17
Des Moines, IA 50322
(515) 270-0388

CONVERSION CONSULTANTS AND RESOURCES

Blair Group
5600 US 98 N., #7
Lakeland, FL 33809
(800) 274-5564   Bill Gorman

Brandywine Mobile Home
   Community Services
2637 McCormick Drive
Clearwater, FL 34619
(813) 726-8868   Tod Eckhouse

Community Association Institute
   (CAI)
1630 Duke Street, #300
Alexandria, VA 22314
(703) 548-8600

Van Alfus Financial Services
83 Montgomery Street
Jersey City, NJ 07302
(201) 434-6629   Art Goldberg

Florida Institute* ·
2530 State Road, #580
Clearwater, FL 34621
(813) 576-9480   Fred Yonteck
*a.k.a. National Society of
   Homeowner Associations, Inc.

Lee Jay Celling & Associates, PA
20 N. Orange, #700
Orlando, FL 32801
(800) 330-1234

National Association of Housing
   Cooperatives (NAHC)
1614 King Street
Alexandria, VA 22314
(703) 549-5201

National Cooperative Bank
1401 Eye Street, N.W., Suite 700
Washington, DC 20005
(202) 336-7700

PMC Financial Services
2365 Skyfarm Drive
Hillsborough, CA 94010
(415) 375-8043   Deane Sargent

CREATIVE MARKETING BROCHURES

Greco Writing
902B Ridgefield Circle
Clinton, MA 01510
(508) 368-1022   Patti Greco
(Marketing communications
  consultant)

CREDIT INFORMATION

Credit Information Corp.
5550 McKelvey Road, Suite 210
St. Louis, MO 63044
(800) 899-6396

Credit Interfaces
15050 Avenue of Science, #230
San Diego, CA 92128
(800) 456-4008

DEMOGRAPHICS

Claritas
53 Brown Road
Ithaca, NY 14850
(800) 234-5973

Equifax
5375 Mira Sorrento Place, #400
San Diego, CA 92121
(800) 866-6510

Market Statistics
355 Park Ave. South
New York, NY 10010
(800) 266-4714

DIRECTORIES

Fleets Guide to Financing
15020 Shady Grove Road,
  Suite 500
Rockville, MD 20850
(301) 279-6800 Ext. 105
Damiann Bilotta

Manufactured Home
  Merchandiser(supplier)
203 N. Wabash, #800
Chicago, IL 60601
(312) 236-3528   Herb Tieder

RV & MH Aftermarket Association
11 S. LaSalle St., #1400
Chicago, IL 60603
(312) 553-0300

DUE DILIGENCE

Credit Quality & Financial
  Consulting, Inc.
4334 Magnolia Street
Palm Beach, FL 33418
(407) 622-5893
George Gall, CPA

**ENERGY MANAGEMENT &
WATER CONSERVATION**

Enviro-Check, Inc.
7121 Grand National Drive, #101
Orlando, FL 32819
(407) 352-2266

**ENGINEERING AND LAND
PLANNING SPECIALISTS**

Alley and Associates
Box 897
Palm Harbor, FL 34682
(813) 787-3388   Dave Alley

Donald Westphal
512 Madison Avenue
Rochester, MI 48307
(810) 651-5518

Flint Survey & Engineering
5370 Miller Road, Suite 13
Swartz Creek, MI 48473
(810) 230-1333   Curt Karlson

Franklin Engineering
151 W. Jefferson Street
Franklin, IN 46131
(317) 736-7168   Steve Williams

Gerald Kessler and Associates
3760 Vance, #301
Wheat Ridge, CO 80033
(393) 756-1536   Gerald Kessler

IRIC
11 June Terrace
Lake Forest, IL 60045
(708) 234-8020   Herbert Behrend

McDermott Engineering
303 N. Placentia Avenue, Suite E
Fullerton, CA 92631
(714) 572-0376

QCI Development Consultants*
6541 N. Glade Way
Parker, CO 80134
(303) 840-9192   Bruce Melms
*a.k.a. Custom Comark Homes

Urban Research and Development
28 Bethlehem Plaza
Bethlehem, PA 18018
(215) 865-0701   Martin Gilchrist

Vaughn Shahinian & Associates
11185 Mora Drive
Los Altos, CA 94024
(415) 941-8592
Vaughn Shahinian

**ENVIRONMENTAL
CONSULTANTS**

ATEC
8665 Bush Road
Indianapolis, IN 46256
(317) 577-1761

ENVIROTEL
1000 Nutt Road
Phoenixville, PA 19460
(610) 935-9177   Robert McIntyre

Federated Environmental
  Associates, Inc.
1314 Bedford Avenue
Baltimore, MD 21208
(410) 653-8434
Jim Gossweiler, Sr. V.P.

Paragon Environmental
153 Washington Street
E. Walpole, MA 02032
(508) 660-8888

EXPERT WITNESS REGISTRY

TASA
1166 DeKalb Pike
Blue Bell, PA 19422
(800) 523-2319

FEASIBILITY CONSULTANTS

Consultants Resource Group
7520 W. Waters Avenue
Tampa, FL 33615
(813) 888-6341   Ed Hicks

Danter Co., The
30 Spruce Street
Columbus, OH 43215
(614) 221-9096   Kenneth Danter

Palmer, Groth & Pietka
2143 Hurley Way, #150
Sacramento, CA 95825
(916) 641-2206   Tim Wright, MAI

Rhodes Associates
9708 Carriage Road
Kensington, MD 20895
(301) 870-3505   George Rhodes

FEE MANAGEMENT FIRMS

Apollo Properties
307 W. 2nd Street
Mesa, AZ 85201
(602) 898-1939
Steve Pappas, CPM

Ashford Management Group
501 Main Street
Utica, NY 13501
(315) 724-4900   Russ Petralia

Bessier & Casenhiser
725 Brea Canyon Road, #6
Walnut, CA 91789
(714) 594-0501
R. Bessier, CPM, and
  K. Casenhiser, CPM

Evans Management Services
871 38th Avenue
Santa Cruz, CA 95602
(408) 475-0335   Greg Evans

Love Realty
2951 Flowers Road S., #220
Atlanta, GA 30341
(404) 457-4395   Bob Love, CPM

Martin Newby Co.
3801 Bee Ridge Road
Sarasota, FL 34233
(941) 923-1456   Martin Newby

MDL Group
516 S. 6th Street, Suite 100
Las Vegas, NV 89101
(702) 388-1800   Tim Behrendt

Star Mobilehome Park
  Management
22992 Millcreek Road, Suite A
Laguna Hills, CA 92653
(714) 951-9565   Mike Cirillo

Steiner and Associates
5012 W. Lemon Street
Tampa, FL 33609
(813) 289-0500   Nelson Steiner

Storz Management Co.
9152 Greenback Lane, #3
Orangevale, CA 95662
(916) 989-5333   Jerry Storz

FINANCING FOR REAL ESTATE

Acquisitions Mortgage Co.
3146 Bristol Road
Warrington, PA 18976
(215) 343-9180

Belgravia Capital Corp.
19900 MacArthur Boulevard,
  #1100
Irvine, CA 92715
(714) 724-8700   Erik Paulson

Bloomfield Acceptance Co.
260 E. Brown Street, #350
Birmingham, MI 48009
(810) 644-8838   Dan Bober

Collateral Mortgage, Ltd.
524 Lorna Square
Birmingham, AL 35216
(205) 978-1843   Chris Dyson

Crown Capital Group
620 Crown Oak Centre Drive
Longwood, FL 32750
(407) 767-9553   Dean Hauck

Gorham Financial Corp.
1415 Nohilae Drive, #290
Minneapolis, MN 55422
(612) 546-9121   Frank Commers

Heller RE Financial Services
500 West Monroe Street, 15th
Chicago, IL 60661
(312) 441-6761

Local Federal Bank, FSB
Commercial Loan Department
P.O. Box 26480
Oklahoma City, OK 73126-0480
800-375-1243, Ext. 2329
Alan Goss

Love Funding Corp.
1220 19th Street NW, #801
Washington, DC 20036
(202) 887-8475

Manufactured Housing
  Community Bankers
1401 Dove Street, Suite 670
Newport Beach, CA 92660
(714) 261-1772   David Young

Manufactured Housing Resources
  Group
525 Canyon Boulevard, Suite A
Boulder, CO 80302
(303) 592-4363   Roderick Knoll

Monte Klein Co.
Box 7481
Menlo Park, CA 94026
(415) 854-6355

SJS Realty Services
51 Sherwood Terrace
Lake Bluff, IL 60044
(708) 615-2250   Mark Siegel

Suburban Mortgage
7316 Wisconsin Avenue, #208
Bethesda, MD 20814
(301) 654-8616   Kyle Poole

FORMS AND BOOKKEEPING SYSTEMS

Business Forms of America
9321 Kirby Drive
Houston, TX 77054
(800) 231-0329

Deluxe Business Forms and
  Supplies
980 Elkton Drive
Colorado Springs, CO 80907
(800) 843-4294

Jenkins Business Forms
Box "B"
Mascoutah, IL 62258
(800) 851-4424

McBee Systems
299 Cherry Hill Road
Parsippany, NJ 07054

NEBS Business Forms and Supplies
500 Main Street
Groton, MA 01471
(800) 843-4294

Peachtree Business Forms
Box 13290
Atlanta, GA 30324
(800) 241-4623

PMN Publishing
Box 47024
Indianapolis, IN 46247
(317) 888-7156

Professional Publishing
122 Paul Drive
San Rafael, CA 94903
(800) 288-2006

Reynolds & Reynolds
3555 S. Kettering Boulevard
Dayton, OH 45439
(800) 531-9055

Safeguard Business Systems
Box 7501
Ft. Washington, PA 19034
(800) 523-6660

Thompson Business Forms
2200 Warner Street
San Antonio, TX 78201
(800) 842-0191

HERITAGE GROUP

RV/MH Heritage Foundation and
  Museum
801 Benham Avenue
Elkhart, IN 46516
(219) 293-2344   Carl Ehry

HUMAN RESOURCES ASSESSMENT

Stoneham Associates
235 Pine, Suite 1300
San Francisco, CA 94104
(415) 383-4820   Donna Stoneham

INDUSTRY STATISTICS

Berlin Research
731 Pacific Street, #1
San Luis Obispo, CA 93401
(805) 541-0171   Bronson Berlin

Business Trend Analysis
2171 Jericho Turnpike
Commack, NY 11725
(516) 462-5454

Dr. Thomas Nutt-Powell
100 Crescent Boulevard
Needham, MA 02194
(617) 449-7752

Dr. Waldo Born
Eastern Illinois University
Charleston, IL 61920
(217) 581-6201

Foremost Insurance Co.
5800 Foremost Drive, Box 2450
Grand Rapids, MI 49501
(800) 527-3905
(616) 956-8188   Ann Calomeni

George Carter and Affiliates
767 Park Avenue
Oradell, NJ 07649
(201) 265-7766

John DeWolf
11424 Waterview Cluster
Reston, VA 22090
(703) 437-0711

Joint Center for Housing Studies
79 John F. Kennedy
Cambridge, MA 02138
(617) 495-7908   William Apgar

Kammrath & Associates
1202 E. Missouri Avenue, #15
Phoenix, AZ 85014
(602) 263-5340   Bob Kammrath

Manufactured Housing Institute
2101 Wilson Boulevard, Suite 610
Arlington, VA 22201
(703) 558-0400   Jerry Connors

National Conference of States on
  Building Codes and Standards
  (NCSBCS)
505 Huntmar Park Drive, #210
Herndon, VA 22070
(703) 437-0100

Packaged Facts(reports)
625 Avenue of the Americas
New York, NY 10011
(212) 627-3228   David Weiss

PMN Publishing, "The Allen
  Report"
Box 47024
Indianapolis, IN 46247
(317) 888-7156   Nora Freese

Robert Siegel and Associates
26 Trianon Drive
Kenner, LA 70065
(504) 586-2000

Statistical Surveys, Inc.
1693 Sutherland Drive, S.E.
Grand Rapids, MI 49805
(616) 281-9898   Tom Walworth

Timberline Associates
11027 Timberline Drive
Shelby Township, MI 48316
(810) 731-2964   Paul Thacher

Welford Sanders
2658 N. Sherman Boulevard
Milwaukee, WI 53210

**INSTALLATION SPECIALISTS
AND EQUIPMENT**

Manufactured Housing Resources
Box 9
Nassau, DE 19969
(302) 645-5552   George Porter

Soiltest, Inc. (pocket penetrometer)
Box 8004
Lake Bluff, IL 60044
(800) 323-1242

Stabilizer Systems, Inc.
2205 Artesia Street
San Bernardino, CA 92408
800-451-8647
Jeff Lorenz, General Manager

INSURANCE INFORMATION

Barrett & Associates
7 W. Square Lake Road
Bloomfield Hills, MI 48302
(810) 452-9881   Mark Barrett

Hogg Robinson of Michigan
Box 5007
Southfield, MI 48086
(313) 948-5650   Mark Barrett

John Carriero & Son
Box 312
Mechanicville, NY 12118
(518) 664-9882

LaRue Insurance
3089 Fairview Road
Greenwood, IN 46142
(317) 889-1000   Gary Cleveland

INVESTMENT INFORMATION RESOURCES

John T. Reed
342 Bryan Drive
Danville, CA 94526
(800) 635-5425
RE-related publications

LAKE MANAGEMENT SUPPLIES

Aquatic Control
Box 100
Seymour, IN 47274
(812) 497-2410

LANDSCAPING INFORMATION

American Nurseryman
77 W. Washington, #2100
Chicago, IL 60602
(800) 621-5727

LOAN AMORTIZATION TABLES

Financial Publishing Co.
82 Brookline Avenue
Boston, MA 02251
(800) 247-3214

MAILBOXES

Salsbury Mailboxes
1010 E. 62nd Street
Los Angeles, CA 90001
(800) 323-3003

MANAGEMENT CONSULTANTS

GFA Management, Inc.
Box 47024
Indianapolis, IN 46247
(317) 791-8114
George Allen, CPM

JLT & Associates
9 Elmwood
Irvine, CA 92714
(714) 297-2921   John Turzer

Manufactured Housing Solutions
3325 Bonnie Hill Drive
Los Angeles, CA 90068
(415) 968-7626

Mike Campbell RE Services
7777 N. Wickham Rd. #12-311
Melbourne, FL 32940
(407) 752-6398   Mike Campbell

John Lehman
820 Sylvan Ave.
Mountainview, CA 94041
(415) 968-7626

Robert Sage
Box 7783
Winter Haven, FL 33883
(813) 299-9941

MANAGEMENT RESOURCES

Construction Bookstore
  (mail order)
Box 2959
Gainesville, FL 32602
(800) 253-0541

"Find People Fast"
INFOMAX, Inc.
4600 Chippewa, #244
St. Louis, MO 63116
(314) 481-3000

Institute of Real Estate
  Management
430 N. Michigan Avenue
Chicago, IL 60610
(312) 329-6000
CPM & ARM Programs

J. Wiley & Sons, Inc.
605 Third Avenue
New York, NY 10158
(212) 850-6000

Lincoln Graduate Center
Box 12528
San Antonio, TX 78212
(800) 531-5333   Dr. Gary Dean

Manufactured Housing
  Educational Institute
2101 Wilson Boulevard, Suite 610
Arlington, VA 22201
(703) 558-0400   Ann Parnham
ACM Program

National Apartment Association
1111 14th Street N.W., Suite 900
Washington, DC 20005
(202) 842-4050
CAM Program

National Association of
  Homebuilders
1201 15th Street N.W.
Washington, DC 20005
(800) 368-5242
RAM Program

National Association of Real
  Estate Investment Trusts
1129 Twentieth Street, N.W.,
  Suite 705
Washington, DC 20036
(202) 785-8717

PMN Publishing,
  "The Allen Letter"
Box 47024
Indianapolis, IN 46247
(317) 888-1703   Nora Freese

Texas Real Estate Research Center
Texas A & M University
College Station, TX 77843

Urban Land Institute
625 Indiana Avenue N.W., #400
Washington, DC 20004
(202) 624-7000

NEWSLETTERS

Newsletter Express
3500 DePauw, LL 1900
Indianapolis, IN 46268
(317) 876-8916

OUTDOOR FURNITURE

Texacraft Outdoor Furnishings
Box 741558
Houston, TX 77274
(800) 231-9790

PARKING CONTROL SUPPLIES

Peachtree Business Products
1284 Logan Circle
Atlanta, GA 30318
(800) 241-4623

PERSONNEL RECRUITING

Techention-Spangler and
   Associates
Box 718
Camdenton, MO 65020
(314) 346-4165

Vernon, Sage and Associates
Box 24582
Fort Worth, TX 76124
(817) 451-8785   Tony Vernon

PIERS—STEEL

C & R Pier Manufacturing
275 S. Rancho Avenue
Colton, CA 92324
(909) 872-6444

PROPERTY TAX RESEARCH AND APPEAL

Cocon, Inc.
Box 159
Belleville, MI 48112
(313) 699-3430

Easley McCaleb and Stallings
3980 DeKalb Technical Parkway,
   #775
Atlanta, GA 30340
(800) 843-0139
(404) 454-9998

Ennes & Associates
3275 N. Arlington Heights Road,
   #410
Arlington Heights, IL 60004
(708) 577-6500   Carl P. Pharr

RENTAL UNIT SALES

Homes Direct, Inc.
216 Third Avenue South
Jacksonville Beach, FL 32250
(904) 246-6688   James Stock

RESIDENT RETENTION

Let's Party! c/o Williams Design
P.O. Box 277
Yuma, AZ 85366
(520) 329-1262   Mindy Williams
(Activities Guide)

RESIDENT SCREENING

Americhek, Inc.
7825 North Dixie Drive
Dayton, OH 45414
(513) 454-1700

RETAIL SALES AND MARKETING CONSULTING SERVICES

The Housing Marketplace
145 W. Christina Boulevard
Lakeland, FL 33813
(813) 648-1487   Joe Adams

JCA
Box 704
Bettendorf, IA 52722
(800) 336-0339
Bill and Judy Carr

Developing Attitudes
9648 Kingston Pike #2
Knoxville, TN 37922
(423) 539-1504   Les Grebe

Nancy J. Friedman
"Telephone Doctor"
30 Hollenberg Court
Bridgeton, MO 63044
(800) 882-9911

Roger Huddleston
Box 739
Mahomet, IL 61853
(217) 586-4444

R.S. Associates
2507 Eastland Avenue
Nashville, TN 37206
(800) 356-7065   Robert Skillen

Salesmaker Associates
Americus Center, #705
6th and Hamilton Streets
Allentown, PA 18101
(215) 434-2643
Grayson E. Schwepfinger

Sales & Marketing Magic
36473 US 19 North
Palm Harbor, FL 34684
(813) 784-9469   (learning aids)

SCALE MODEL HOMES

Scale Model Homes Co.
Box 47024
Indianapolis, IN 46247
(317) 888-7156   Ron Freese

SIGNS

Como Signs & Supplies
Box 5337, 806 Jefferson Street
Lafayette, LA 70502
(800) 232-0448

Grimco, Inc.
3928 Delor Street
St. Louis, MO 63116
(314) 481-4404

Mobile Advertising Sign & Display
Box 8952
Mattoon, IL 61938
(217) 967-5436   Don Dominix

Tri-Safety Symbol Signs
Box 45134
Baton Rouge, LA 70895
(504) 927-1478   Anne Stentiford

Vulcan Signs
Box 850
Foley, AL 36536
(800) 633-6845

SURVEYOR

AES Group, Inc.
605 State St.
Newburgh, IN 47630
(800) 867-8783   Tina Williams

SWIMMING POOL
CONSULTANTS AND SUPPLIES

Bel-Aqua
750 Main Street
New Rochelle, NY 10805
(914) 235-2200

Form Management Services (tags)
150 Airport Drive, #9
Westminster, MD 21157
(800) 541-2361

Recreation Supply Co.
Box 2757
Bismarck, ND 58502
(800) 437-8072

Recreonics
Box 34575
Louisville, KY 40232

Spear Corporation
Box 3
Roachdale, IN 46172
(317) 522-1126

Water Environment Federation
601 Wythe Street
Alexandria, VA 22314
(800) 666-0206

WATER LEAK DETECTION

Hydro-Tech, Inc.
805 S.E. 15th Street
Deerfield Beach, FL 33441
(954) 425-0954   Earl King

WATER METER INSTALLATION
AND BILLING

Aquameter, Inc.
1630 Grandview Avenue
Columbus, OH 43212
(800) 860-0008   Kathleen Lyden

B & B Water/Wastewater
4402 S. Division Street
Moline, MI 49335
(616) 877-4196

Digital Metering, Inc.
8551 154th Avenue, NE
Redmond, WA 98052
(206) 885-0900

Edison Micro-Utilities
2400 East AZ Biltmore Circle
   Drive
Suite 2230
Phoenix, AZ 85016
(602) 381-8221   Bill Robertson

Park Utilities, Inc.
Box 998
Carmichael, CA 95609
(916) 944-1824   Tom Grant

SLC Water Meter Co.
3059 Dixie Highway
Pontiac, MI 48055
(313) 673-8539

Universal Utilities
1610 Crescent Drive
Flint, MI 48503
(810) 238-3964   John Ball

U.S. Energy
500 Sun Valley Dr., #H-2
Roswell, GA 30076
(404) 998-3996

WaterMaster of Columbus
1255 North High Street
Columbus, OH 43201
(800) 444-9283   Tracy Harvey

DIRECTORY OF NATIONAL, REGIONAL, STATE, AND PROVINCIAL MANUFACTURED HOUSING RELATED ASSOCIATIONS AND INSTITUTES

DIRECTORY OF NATIONAL, REGIONAL, STATE, AND PROVINCIAL MANUFACTURED HOUSING RELATED ASSOCIATIONS AND INSTITUTES*

—NATIONAL ASSOCIATIONS—

American Association of Housing Educators   —no phone—
College of Architecture
Texas A&M University
College Station, TX 77843

American Builders Consortium   (717) 533-5935
227 Townhouse
Hershey, PA 17033

---

* Researched and prepared by George Allen of GFA Management, Inc. and the staff of IMHA/RVIC, Indianapolis, Indiana.

American Consulting Engineers Council   (202) 347-7474
1015 15th Street, NW, Suite 802
Washington, DC 20005

American Mobile Home Association   (303) 232-6336
12929 West 26th Ave.
Golden, CO 80401

American Planning Association   (312) 955-9100
1313 60th Street
Chicago, IL 60637

Appraisal Institute   (312) 335-4100
875 North Michigan Avenue
Chicago, IL 60611

Association for Investment Management & Research   (804) 980-3647
Box 7947
Charlottesville, VA 22906

Association for Regulatory Reform   (202) 783-4087
1331 Pennsylvania Avenue, NW, Suite 524
Washington, DC 20004

Institute of Real Estate Management   (312) 329-6000
430 North Michigan Avenue
Chicago, IL 60610

Manufactured Housing Educational Trust   (714) 935-1900
500 North State College Blvd., Suite 1020
Orange, CA 92668

Manufactured Housing Institute   (703) 558-0400
2101 Wilson Blvd., Suite 610
Arlington, VA 22201

Mortgage Bankers Association of America   (202) 861-6554
1125 15th Street, NW
Washington, DC 20005

Multi-Family Housing Institute   (202) 857-1142
1200 19th Street
Washington, DC 20036

National Association of Home Builders   (202) 822-0200
15th & M Streets
Washington, DC 20005

National Association of Real Estate Investment Managers   (310) 479-2219
11755 Wilshire Blvd.
Los Angeles, CA 90025

National Association of Real Estate Investment Trusts   (202) 857-1142
1129 Twentieth St., NW, Suite 705
Washington, DC 20036

National Foundation of Manufactured Home Owners   (206) 885-4650
Box # 33
Redmond, WA 98073

Pension Real Estate Association   (203) 657-2612
95 Glastonbury Blvd.
Glastonbury, CT 06033

Property Management Network   (317) 888-7156
Box # 47024
Indianapolis, IN 46247

Urban Land Institute   (202) 624-7044
625 Indiana Avenue, NW
Washington, DC 20004

—CANADIAN ASSOCIATIONS—

Canadian Manufactured Housing Association   (613) 563-3520
150 Laurier Avenue West, Suite 200
Ottawa, Ont., CN K1P5J4

Manufactured Home Registry (government)
940 Blanchard Street
Victoria, BC, CN V8W3E6

Manufactured Housing Association of Alberta/   (403) 347-8925
Saskatchewan
Suite 201, 4921-49 Street
Red Deer, AB, CN T4N1V2

Manufactured Housing Association of British Columbia   (604) 850-1353
Suite 302, 32463 Simon Ave.
Abbotsford, BC, CN V2T5E3

Manufactured Housing Association of Nova Scotia   (902) 835-9125
67 Eaglewood Drive
Bedford, NS, CN V4A3B3

Manufactured Housing Association of Ontario   (519) 245-2000
Box 54
Sirathray, Ont., CN N7G3B1

Mobilehome Park Association of New Brunswick   (506) 458-8119
c/o Kelly's Cove
Fredrickton, NB, CN E3B6A5

Manufactured Home Park Owners Association of British Columbia
c/o Aldine Larsen
Crispen Bays
7790 King George Highway
Surrey, BC, CN V3W5Y4

—STATE and REGIONAL ASSOCIATIONS—

Alabama Manufactured Housing Institute   (334) 264-8755
60 Commerce Street, Suite 1212
Montgomery, AL 36104

Manufactured Housing Industry of Arizona   (602) 966-9221
1801 South Jen Tilly Lane, Suite B-2
Tempe, AZ 85281

Arizona Manufactured Housing Association   (602) 952-1102
4700 East Thomas Road Suite 103
Phoenix, AZ 85018

Greater Arizona Manufactured Housing Association   (520) 887-0591
3833 North Fairview Ave., Suite 129
Tucson, AZ 85705

Arkansas Manufactured Housing Association   (501) 771-0444
2500 McCain Place, Suite 203
North Little Rock, AR 72116

California Manufactured Housing Institute   (909) 987-2599
10630 Town Center Drive, Suite 120
Rancho Cucamonga, CA 91730

California Manufactured Home Park Owners Alliance   (916) 441-1882
7311 Greenhaven Drive, Suite 100
Sacramento, CA 95831

Western Mobilehome Association   (916) 448-7002
1007 7th Street, 3rd floor
Sacramento, CA 95814

Colorado Manufactured Housing Association   (303) 832-2022
1410 Grant St.
Denver, CO 80203

Colorado MH Parkowners Association   (303) 757-2614
3592 South Hillcrest Dr.
Denver, CO 80237

Delaware Manufactured Housing Association   (302) 678-2588
Treadway Towers, Suite 309
Dover, DE 19901

First State Manufactured Housing Institute   (302) 674-5868
Box 1829
Dover, DE 19903

Florida Manufactured Housing Association   (904) 222-4011
115 North Calhoun, Suite 5
Tallahassee, FL 32301

Georgia Manufactured Housing Association   (770) 955-4522
1000 Circle, 75 Parkway, Suite 060
Atlanta, GA 30339

Manufactured Housing Association of Hawaii
1051 7th Avenue
Honolulu, HI 96816

Idaho Manufactured Housing Association   (208) 343-1722
PO Box 8605
Boise, ID 83707

Illinois Manufactured Housing Association   (217) 528-3423
3888 Peoria Road
Springfield, IL 62702

Illinois Housing Institute   (708) 824-2224
140 North River Road
Des Plaines, IL 60016

Iowa Manufactured Housing Association   (515) 265-1497
1400 Dean Avenue
Des Moines, IA 50316-3938

Indiana Manufactured Housing Association   (317) 247-6258
3210 Rand Road
Indianapolis, IN 46241-5499

Kansas Manufactured Housing Association   (913) 357-5256
214 SW 6th Street, Suite 206
Topeka, KS 66603

Kentucky Manufactured Housing Institute   (502) 223-0490
2170 US 127 South
Frankfort, KY 40601

Louisiana Manufactured Housing Association   (504) 925-9041
4847 Revere Avenue
Baton Rouge, LA 70808

Manufactured Housing Association of Maine   (207) 622-4406
3 Wade Street, Lescomb Building
PO Box 1990
Augusta, ME 04330-6318

Manufactured Housing Institute of Maryland   (301) 797-5341
PO Box 1158
Hagerstown, MD 21740-1158

Michigan Manufactured Homes, Recreational Vehicles, &
Campground Association   (517) 349-8881
2123 University Park Drive, Suite 110
Okemos, MI 48864

Minnesota Manufactured Housing Association   (612) 222-6769
555 Park Street, Suite 400
Saint Paul, MN 55103

Mississippi Manufactured Housing Association   (601) 355-1879
PO Box 12227
Jackson, MS 39236-2227

Missouri Manufactured Housing Institute   (314) 636-8660
PO Box 1365
Jefferson City, MO 65102

Montana Manufactured Housing &
Recreational Vehicles Association   (406) 442-2164
PO Box 4396
Helena, MT 59604

Nebraska Manufactured Housing Association   (402) 475-3675
5300 West O Street
Lincoln, NE 68528

Nevada Manufactured Housing Association   (702) 737-7778
3160 East Desert Inn Road, Suite 3-165
Las Vegas, NV 89121

Nevada Mobilehome Park Owners Association   (702) 731-1900
4055 South Spencer Street, Suite 107
Las Vegas, NV 89119

New Jersey Manufactured Housing Association   (609) 588-9040
2382 Whitehorse-Mercerville Road
Trenton, NJ 08619

New Mexico Manufactured Housing Association (505) 299-4070
Box 11607
Albuquerque, NM 87192-0607

New York Manufactured Housing Association, Inc. (518) 464-5087
421 New Karner Road
Albany, NY 12205-3809

North Carolina Manufactured Housing Institute (919) 872-2740
PO Box 58648
Raleigh, NC 27658-8648

North Dakota Manufactured Housing Association (701) 667-2187
PO Box 2681
Bismarck, ND 58502

Ohio Manufactured Housing Association (614) 258-6642
906 East Broad Street
Columbus, OH 43205

Manufactured Housing Association of Oklahoma (405) 521-8470
PO Box 32309
Oklahoma City, OK 73123

Oregon Manufactured Housing Association (503) 364-2470
2255 State Street
Salem, OR 97301

Manufactured Housing Communities of Oregon (503) 391-4496
3857 Wolverine St., NE, Suite 22
Salem, OR 97305

Pennsylvania Manufactured Housing Association (717) 774-3440
PO Box 248
New Cumberland, PA 17070

Manufactured Homes Institute of South Carolina (803) 794-5570
PO Box 5885
West Columbia, SC 29171-5885

South Dakota Manufactured Housing Association   (605) 224-2540
PO Box 7077   (605) 224-4022 (fax)
412 W. Missouri, Suite 8   (800) 657-4352
Pierre, SD 57501

Tennessee Manufactured Housing Association   (615) 242-7395
240 Great Circle Road, Suite 322
Nashville, TN 37228

Texas Manufactured Housing Association   (512) 459-1222
PO Box 14428
Austin, TX 78761

Utah Manufactured Housing Association   (702) 737-7778
3160 East Desert Inn Road, Suite 3-165
Las Vegas, NV 89121

Virginia Manufactured Housing Association   (804) 750-2500
8413 Patterson Avenue
Richmond, VA 23229

Manufactured Housing Communities of Washington   (360) 753-8730
509 12th Avenue, SE, Suite 7
Olympia, WA 98501

Washington Manufactured Housing Association   (360) 357-5650
PO Box 621
Olympia, WA 98507

Washington MH Dealer Association
PO Box 68397
Seattle, WA 98168

West Virginia Manufactured Housing Association   (304) 727-7431
205 First Avenue
Nitro, WV 25143

Wisconsin Manufactured Housing Association   (608) 255-3131
202 State Street, Suite 200
Madison, WI 53703

Central Wyoming Mobilehome Association
PO Box 40
Casper, WY 82602

APPENDIX L

ALLEN MANUFACTURED HOUSING RETAIL SALES LOAN AMORTIZATION CHARTS

ALLEN LOAN AMORTIZATION CHARTS
for
New and Resale Manufactured Home Sales into
Manufactured Home Communities
and
Loan-and-Home Sales Finance Packages[1]

New and resale manufactured homes sited on nonpermanent foundations, such as piers, concrete slabs, or runners, usually in manufactured home landlease communities, are most often financed with personal property loans or chattel mortgages. These loans are characterized by shorter terms (e.g., 5 to 20 years) and slightly higher interest rates (e.g., 8% to 16%) than are typical of conventional real estate mortgages. Figure L.1 shows the Loan Amortization Chart that has been specifically configured for new and resale manufactured home loan monthly repayment of principal and interest only.

How to use? Given a manufactured home priced out at $30,000, deduct a cash down payment of $3,000. This leaves $27,000 to be financed at prevailing market terms; in this case, 10% over 12 years. Refer to the Loan Amortization Chart (Fig. L.1) and locate the appropriate factor where the 10% horizontal line and 12-year vertical column intersect; in this case, a factor of 11.96. That's $11.96, to be paid monthly over the term (12 years) of the loan, for each $1,000 borrowed. Since 27 thousand dollars is being borrowed (i.e., the mortgage amount), multiply 27 times $11.96 to calculate a monthly mortgage or debt service payment of $322.92. Simple

[1] A heretofore unpublished article by George Allen, scheduled for publication in the *Journal of Manufactured Housing* during 1993.

YRS =	5	6	7	8	9	10	11	12	13	14	15	16	17	18	19	20
8	20.28	17.54	15.59	14.14	13.02	12.14	11.42	10.83	10.34	9.92	9.56	9.25	8.99	8.75	8.55	8.37
8 1/4	20.40	17.66	15.72	14.27	13.15	12.27	11.56	10.97	10.48	10.06	9.71	9.40	9.14	8.91	8.70	8.53
8 1/2	20.52	17.78	15.84	14.40	13.28	12.40	11.69	11.11	10.62	10.20	9.85	9.55	9.29	9.06	8.86	8.68
8 3/4	20.64	17.91	15.97	14.53	13.42	12.54	11.83	11.24	10.76	10.35	10.00	9.70	9.44	9.21	9.02	8.84
9	20.76	18.03	16.09	14.66	13.55	12.67	11.97	11.39	10.90	10.49	10.15	9.85	9.59	9.37	9.17	9.00
9 1/4	20.88	18.15	16.22	14.79	13.68	12.81	12.10	11.53	11.05	10.64	10.30	10.00	9.75	9.53	9.33	9.16
9 1/2	21.01	18.28	16.35	14.92	13.81	12.94	12.24	11.67	11.19	10.79	10.45	10.15	9.90	9.68	9.49	9.33
9 3/4	21.13	18.41	16.48	15.05	13.95	13.08	12.38	11.81	11.34	10.94	10.60	10.31	10.06	9.84	9.65	9.49
10	21.25	18.53	16.61	15.18	14.08	13.22	12.52	11.96	11.48	11.09	10.75	10.46	10.22	10.00	9.82	9.66
10 1/4	21.38	18.66	16.74	15.31	14.22	13.36	12.67	12.10	11.63	11.24	10.90	10.62	10.38	10.16	9.98	9.82
10 1/2	21.50	18.78	16.87	15.45	14.36	13.50	12.81	12.25	11.78	11.39	11.06	10.78	10.54	10.33	10.15	9.99
10 3/4	21.62	18.91	17.00	15.58	14.49	13.64	12.95	12.39	11.93	11.54	11.21	10.94	10.70	10.49	10.31	10.16
11	21.75	19.04	17.13	15.71	14.63	13.78	13.10	12.54	12.08	11.70	11.37	11.10	10.86	10.66	10.48	10.33
11 1/4	21.87	19.16	17.26	15.85	14.77	13.92	13.24	12.69	12.23	11.85	11.53	11.26	11.02	10.82	10.65	10.50
11 1/2	22.00	19.30	17.39	15.98	14.91	14.06	13.39	12.84	12.38	12.01	11.69	11.42	11.19	10.99	10.82	10.67
11 3/4	22.12	19.43	17.52	16.12	15.05	14.21	13.54	12.99	12.54	12.16	11.85	11.58	11.35	11.16	10.99	10.84
12	22.25	19.56	17.66	16.26	15.19	14.35	13.68	13.14	12.69	12.32	12.01	11.74	11.52	11.32	11.16	11.02
12 1/4	22.38	19.69	17.79	16.40	15.33	14.50	13.83	13.29	12.85	12.48	12.17	11.91	11.68	11.49	11.33	11.19
12 1/2	22.50	19.82	17.93	16.53	15.47	14.64	13.98	13.44	13.00	12.64	12.33	12.07	11.85	11.67	11.50	11.37
12 3/4	22.63	19.95	18.06	16.67	15.62	14.79	14.13	13.60	13.16	12.80	12.49	12.24	12.02	11.84	11.68	11.54
13	22.76	20.08	18.20	16.81	15.76	14.94	14.28	13.75	13.32	12.96	12.66	12.40	12.19	12.01	11.85	11.72
13 1/4	22.89	20.21	18.33	16.95	15.90	15.08	14.43	13.91	13.48	13.12	12.82	12.57	12.36	12.18	12.03	11.90
13 1/2	23.01	20.34	18.47	17.09	16.05	15.23	14.58	14.06	13.63	13.28	12.99	12.74	12.53	12.36	12.21	12.08
13 3/4	23.14	20.48	18.61	17.23	16.19	15.38	14.74	14.22	13.80	13.45	13.15	12.91	12.71	12.53	12.39	12.26
14	23.27	20.61	18.75	17.38	16.34	15.53	14.89	14.38	13.96	13.61	13.32	13.08	12.88	12.71	12.56	12.44
14 1/4	23.40	20.74	18.88	17.52	16.49	15.68	15.05	14.53	14.12	13.78	13.49	13.25	13.05	12.89	12.74	12.62
14 1/2	23.53	20.88	19.02	17.66	16.63	15.83	15.20	14.69	14.28	13.94	13.66	13.43	13.23	13.06	12.92	12.80
14 3/4	23.66	21.01	19.16	17.81	16.78	15.99	15.36	14.85	14.44	14.11	13.83	13.60	13.41	13.24	13.10	12.99
15	23.79	21.15	19.30	17.95	16.93	16.14	15.51	15.01	14.61	14.28	14.00	13.77	13.58	13.42	13.29	13.17
15 1/4	23.93	21.29	19.44	18.10	17.08	16.29	15.67	15.18	14.77	14.44	14.17	13.95	13.76	13.60	13.47	13.36
15 1/2	24.06	21.42	19.58	18.24	17.23	16.45	15.83	15.34	14.94	14.61	14.34	14.12	13.94	13.78	13.65	13.54
15 3/4	24.19	21.56	19.72	18.39	17.38	16.60	15.99	15.50	15.10	14.78	14.52	14.30	14.12	13.96	13.84	13.73
16	24.32	21.70	19.87	18.53	17.53	16.76	16.15	15.66	15.27	14.95	14.69	14.48	14.30	14.15	14.02	13.97

COMPUTED BY FINANCIAL PUBLISHING COMPANY, BOSTON, MASS. 02215

Property Management Form #113

DMN Publishing, Inc.
P.O. Box 47024
Indianapolis, IN 46247

FIG. L.1 Allen loan amortization chart for new and resale manufactured home sales.

isn't it? And home buyer mortgagors should realize that over the term of the loan, assuming they don't pay it off early, they'll pay $46,506.24 for the $27,000 loan. How is this computed? Simply 144 months (12 years × 12 months) × $322.92. As sobering as that is, it's really just the price (i.e., $46,506.24 − $27,000) of $19,506.24 to borrow $27,000 over 12 years at 10% interest. And don't forget to add back the down payment (e.g., $3,000) to estimate the overall true cost of the home, or $46,506.24 plus $3,000 equals $49,506.24, for the original home negotiated to the $30,000 sale price.

Now let's take a look at the increasingly popular land and home sales package. In this case the cost of the homesite proper is packaged, for conventional mortgage loan computation purposes, with the sale price of the manufactured home that is to be permanently installed (i.e., on a permanent foundation) upon the home buyer's real estate parcel or homesite.

These mortgages are characterized by longer terms, (e.g., 10 to 33 years) and generally lower interest rates (e.g., 5% to 20%). Figure L.2 displays the Loan Amortization Chart that has been specifically configured for land and home monthly mortgage payment of principal and interest only.

How to use? Given a land and home sales package of $60,000, deduct $6,000 cash down payment. This leaves $54,000 to be financed at prevailing market terms, in this case, 8% over 20 years. Refer to the Loan Amortization Chart (Fig. L.2) and locate the appropriate factor where the 8% horizontal line and the 20-year vertical columns intersect; in this case a factor of 8.37. That's $8.37 to be paid monthly over the term (e.g., 20 years) of the loan for each $1,000 borrowed. Since 54 thousand dollars is being borrowed (i.e., the mortgage amount), multiply 54 times $8.37 to calculate a monthly mortgage or debt service payment of $451.98. Simplicity once again. And as before, the home buyer mortgagor should comprehend that he or she will be paying $108,475.20 (that's 240 months × $451.98) for the $54,000 loan; and when the $6,000 cash down payment is added back, the overall true cost of the land and home package is approximately $114,475.20.

Another point bears mention here. The foregoing calculations have been for the first two letters of the well-known PITI home buying acronym. P and I represent "principal" and "interest," principal being repayment of actual dollars borrowed and interest the price or cost to borrow said principal. The T and I represent "taxes" (i.e., usually real estate taxes) and home owners "insurance" premiums, calculated monthly amounts and often paid along with the P and I payments each month, hence the overall acronym PITI.

YRS =	10	11	12	13	14	15	16	17	18	19	20	21
5	10.61	9.87	9.25	8.74	8.29	7.91	7.58	7.29	7.04	6.81	6.60	6.42
5 1/4	10.73	9.99	9.38	8.86	8.42	8.04	7.71	7.43	7.17	6.95	6.74	6.56
5 1/2	10.86	10.12	9.51	8.99	8.55	8.18	7.85	7.56	7.31	7.08	6.88	6.70
5 3/4	10.98	10.25	9.63	9.12	8.68	8.31	7.98	7.70	7.45	7.22	7.03	6.85
6	11.11	10.37	9.76	9.25	8.82	8.44	8.12	7.84	7.59	7.37	7.17	6.99
6 1/4	11.23	10.50	9.89	9.38	8.95	8.58	8.26	7.98	7.73	7.51	7.31	7.14
6 1/2	11.36	10.63	10.02	9.52	9.09	8.72	8.40	8.12	7.87	7.65	7.46	7.29
6 3/4	11.49	10.76	10.16	9.65	9.22	8.85	8.54	8.26	8.01	7.80	7.61	7.44
7	11.62	10.89	10.29	9.79	9.36	8.99	8.68	8.40	8.16	7.95	7.76	7.59
7 1/4	11.75	11.02	10.42	9.92	9.50	9.13	8.82	8.55	8.31	8.10	7.91	7.74
7 1/2	11.88	11.15	10.56	10.06	9.64	9.28	8.96	8.69	8.45	8.25	8.06	7.90
7 3/4	12.01	11.29	10.69	10.20	9.78	9.42	9.11	8.84	8.60	8.40	8.21	8.05
8	12.14	11.42	10.83	10.34	9.92	9.56	9.25	8.99	8.75	8.55	8.37	8.21
8 1/4	12.27	11.56	10.97	10.48	10.06	9.71	9.40	9.14	8.91	8.70	8.53	8.37
8 1/2	12.40	11.69	11.10	10.62	10.20	9.85	9.55	9.29	9.06	8.86	8.68	8.53
8 3/4	12.54	11.83	11.24	10.76	10.35	10.00	9.70	9.44	9.21	9.02	8.84	8.69
9	12.67	11.97	11.39	10.90	10.49	10.15	9.85	9.59	9.37	9.17	9.00	8.85
9 1/4	12.81	12.10	11.53	11.05	10.64	10.30	10.00	9.75	9.53	9.33	9.16	9.01
9 1/2	12.94	12.24	11.67	11.19	10.79	10.45	10.15	9.90	9.68	9.49	9.33	9.18
9 3/4	13.08	12.38	11.81	11.34	10.94	10.60	10.31	10.06	9.84	9.65	9.49	9.35
10	13.22	12.52	11.96	11.48	11.09	10.75	10.46	10.22	10.00	9.82	9.66	9.51
10 1/4	13.36	12.67	12.10	11.63	11.24	10.90	10.62	10.38	10.16	9.98	9.82	9.68
10 1/2	13.50	12.81	12.25	11.78	11.39	11.06	10.78	10.54	10.33	10.15	9.99	9.85
10 3/4	13.64	12.95	12.39	11.93	11.54	11.21	10.94	10.70	10.49	10.31	10.16	10.02
11	13.78	13.10	12.54	12.08	11.70	11.37	11.10	10.86	10.66	10.48	10.33	10.19
11 1/4	13.92	13.24	12.69	12.23	11.85	11.53	11.26	11.02	10.82	10.65	10.50	10.37
11 1/2	14.06	13.39	12.84	12.38	12.01	11.69	11.42	11.19	10.99	10.82	10.67	10.54
11 3/4	14.21	13.54	12.99	12.54	12.16	11.85	11.58	11.35	11.16	10.99	10.84	10.72
12	14.35	13.68	13.14	12.69	12.32	12.01	11.74	11.52	11.32	11.16	11.02	10.89
12 1/4	14.50	13.83	13.29	12.85	12.48	12.17	11.91	11.68	11.49	11.33	11.19	11.07
12 1/2	14.64	13.98	13.44	13.00	12.64	12.33	12.07	11.85	11.67	11.50	11.37	11.25
12 3/4	14.79	14.13	13.60	13.16	12.80	12.49	12.24	12.02	11.84	11.68	11.54	11.43
13	14.94	14.28	13.75	13.32	12.96	12.66	12.40	12.19	12.01	11.85	11.72	11.61
13 1/4	15.08	14.43	13.91	13.48	13.12	12.82	12.57	12.36	12.18	12.03	11.90	11.79
13 1/2	15.23	14.58	14.06	13.63	13.28	12.99	12.74	12.53	12.36	12.21	12.08	11.97
13 3/4	15.38	14.74	14.22	13.80	13.45	13.15	12.91	12.71	12.53	12.39	12.26	12.15
14	15.53	14.89	14.38	13.96	13.61	13.32	13.08	12.88	12.71	12.56	12.44	12.33

COMPUTED BY FINANCIAL PUBLISHING COMPANY, BOSTON, MASS. 02215

Property Management Form #114

FMA Publishing, Inc.
P.O. Box 47024
Indianapolis, IN 46247

FIG. L.2 Allen loan amortization chart for land and manufactured home sales.

YRS =	22	23	24	25	26	27	28	29	30	31	32	33
5 **	6.26	6.11	5.97	5.85	5.74	5.64	5.54	5.45	5.37	5.30	5.23	5.17
5 1/4	6.40	6.25	6.12	6.00	5.89	5.78	5.69	5.61	5.53	5.45	5.39	5.32
5 1/2	6.54	6.40	6.27	6.15	6.04	5.94	5.84	5.76	5.68	5.61	5.55	5.48
5 3/4	6.69	6.54	6.41	6.30	6.19	6.09	6.00	5.92	5.84	5.77	5.71	5.65
6	6.84	6.69	6.56	6.45	6.34	6.24	6.16	6.08	6.00	5.93	5.87	5.81
6 1/4	6.98	6.84	6.72	6.60	6.50	6.40	6.31	6.24	6.16	6.10	6.03	5.98
6 1/2	7.13	7.00	6.87	6.76	6.65	6.56	6.48	6.40	6.33	6.26	6.20	6.14
6 3/4	7.29	7.15	7.03	6.91	6.81	6.72	6.64	6.56	6.49	6.43	6.37	6.31
7	7.44	7.30	7.18	7.07	6.97	6.88	6.80	6.73	6.66	6.60	6.54	6.49
7 1/4	7.59	7.46	7.34	7.23	7.14	7.05	6.97	6.89	6.83	6.77	6.71	6.66
7 1/2	7.75	7.62	7.50	7.39	7.30	7.21	7.13	7.06	7.00	6.94	6.88	6.83
7 3/4	7.91	7.78	7.66	7.56	7.46	7.38	7.30	7.23	7.17	7.11	7.06	7.01
8	8.07	7.94	7.83	7.72	7.63	7.55	7.47	7.40	7.34	7.29	7.24	7.19
8 1/4	8.23	8.10	7.99	7.89	7.80	7.72	7.64	7.58	7.52	7.46	7.41	7.37
8 1/2	8.39	8.27	8.16	8.06	7.97	7.89	7.82	7.75	7.69	7.64	7.59	7.55
8 3/4	8.55	8.43	8.32	8.23	8.14	8.06	7.99	7.93	7.87	7.82	7.77	7.73
9	8.72	8.60	8.49	8.40	8.31	8.24	8.17	8.11	8.05	8.00	7.96	7.92
9 1/4	8.88	8.77	8.66	8.57	8.49	8.41	8.35	8.29	8.23	8.18	8.14	8.10
9 1/2	9.05	8.93	8.83	8.74	8.66	8.59	8.52	8.47	8.41	8.37	8.32	8.29
9 3/4	9.22	9.11	9.01	8.92	8.84	8.77	8.70	8.65	8.60	8.55	8.51	8.47
10	9.39	9.28	9.18	9.09	9.01	8.95	8.88	8.83	8.78	8.74	8.70	8.66
10 1/4	9.56	9.45	9.35	9.27	9.19	9.13	9.07	9.01	8.97	8.92	8.89	8.85
10 1/2	9.73	9.62	9.53	9.45	9.37	9.31	9.25	9.20	9.15	9.11	9.07	9.04
10 3/4	9.90	9.80	9.71	9.63	9.55	9.49	9.43	9.38	9.34	9.30	9.26	9.23
11	10.08	9.98	9.89	9.81	9.74	9.67	9.62	9.57	9.53	9.49	9.46	9.43
11 1/4	10.25	10.15	10.06	9.99	9.92	9.86	9.81	9.76	9.72	9.68	9.65	9.62
11 1/2	10.43	10.33	10.25	10.17	10.10	10.05	9.99	9.95	9.91	9.87	9.84	9.81
11 3/4	10.61	10.51	10.43	10.35	10.29	10.23	10.18	10.14	10.10	10.06	10.03	10.01
12	10.78	10.69	10.61	10.54	10.47	10.42	10.37	10.33	10.29	10.26	10.23	10.20
12 1/4	10.96	10.87	10.79	10.72	10.66	10.61	10.56	10.52	10.48	10.45	10.42	10.40
12 1/2	11.14	11.05	10.98	10.91	10.85	10.80	10.75	10.71	10.68	10.65	10.62	10.60
12 3/4	11.33	11.24	11.16	11.10	11.04	10.99	10.94	10.91	10.87	10.84	10.82	10.79
13	11.51	11.42	11.35	11.28	11.23	11.18	11.14	11.10	11.07	11.04	11.01	10.99
13 1/4	11.69	11.61	11.53	11.47	11.42	11.37	11.33	11.29	11.26	11.24	11.21	11.19
13 1/2	11.87	11.79	11.72	11.66	11.61	11.56	11.52	11.49	11.46	11.43	11.41	11.39
13 3/4	12.06	11.98	11.91	11.85	11.80	11.76	11.72	11.68	11.66	11.63	11.61	11.59
14	12.24	12.17	12.10	12.04	11.99	11.95	11.91	11.88	11.85	11.83	11.81	11.79

COMPUTED BY FINANCIAL PUBLISHING COMPANY, BOSTON, MASS. 02215

Property Management Form #115

D∕∖∕ Publishing, Inc.
P.O. Box 47024
Indianapolis, IN 46247

FIG. L.2 (*Continued*)

Allen Loan Amortization Chart for Land and Manufactured Home Sales

Factors per $1,000.00

YRS =	10	11	12	13	14	15	16	17	18	19	20	21
14	15.53	14.89	14.38	13.96	13.61	13.32	13.08	12.88	12.71	12.56	12.44	12.33
14 1/4	15.68	15.05	14.53	14.12	13.78	13.49	13.25	13.05	12.89	12.74	12.62	12.52
14 1/2	15.83	15.20	14.69	14.28	13.94	13.66	13.43	13.23	13.06	12.92	12.80	12.70
14 3/4	15.99	15.36	14.85	14.44	14.11	13.83	13.60	13.41	13.24	13.10	12.99	12.89
15	16.14	15.51	15.01	14.61	14.28	14.00	13.77	13.58	13.42	13.29	13.17	13.08
15 1/4	16.29	15.67	15.18	14.77	14.44	14.17	13.95	13.76	13.60	13.47	13.36	13.26
15 1/2	16.45	15.83	15.34	14.94	14.61	14.34	14.12	13.94	13.78	13.65	13.54	13.45
15 3/4	16.60	15.99	15.50	15.10	14.78	14.52	14.30	14.12	13.96	13.84	13.73	13.64
16	16.76	16.15	15.66	15.27	14.95	14.69	14.48	14.30	14.15	14.02	13.92	13.83
16 1/4	16.91	16.31	15.83	15.44	15.12	14.87	14.65	14.48	14.33	14.21	14.11	14.02
16 1/2	17.07	16.47	15.99	15.61	15.30	15.04	14.83	14.66	14.51	14.39	14.29	14.21
16 3/4	17.23	16.63	16.16	15.78	15.47	15.22	15.01	14.84	14.70	14.58	14.48	14.40
17	17.38	16.79	16.32	15.95	15.64	15.40	15.19	15.02	14.88	14.77	14.67	14.59
17 1/4	17.54	16.96	16.49	16.12	15.82	15.57	15.37	15.21	15.07	14.96	14.86	14.79
17 1/2	17.70	17.12	16.66	16.29	15.99	15.75	15.55	15.39	15.26	15.15	15.05	14.98
17 3/4	17.86	17.28	16.83	16.46	16.17	15.93	15.74	15.58	15.44	15.34	15.25	15.17
18	18.02	17.45	17.00	16.64	16.34	16.11	15.92	15.76	15.63	15.53	15.44	15.37
18 1/4	18.18	17.61	17.17	16.81	16.52	16.29	16.10	15.95	15.82	15.72	15.63	15.56
18 1/2	18.35	17.78	17.34	16.98	16.70	16.47	16.28	16.13	16.01	15.91	15.82	15.76
18 3/4	18.51	17.95	17.51	17.16	16.88	16.65	16.47	16.32	16.20	16.10	16.02	15.95
19	18.67	18.12	17.68	17.33	17.06	16.83	16.65	16.51	16.39	16.29	16.21	16.15
19 1/4	18.84	18.28	17.85	17.51	17.24	17.02	16.84	16.70	16.58	16.48	16.41	16.34
19 1/2	19.00	18.45	18.02	17.69	17.42	17.20	17.03	16.88	16.77	16.68	16.60	16.54
19 3/4	19.17	18.62	18.20	17.86	17.60	17.38	17.21	17.07	16.96	16.87	16.80	16.74
20	19.33	18.79	18.37	18.04	17.78	17.57	17.40	17.26	17.15	17.07	16.99	16.93

COMPUTED BY FINANCIAL PUBLISHING COMPANY, BOSTON, MASS. 02215

Property Management Form #116

DMN Publishing, Inc.
P.O. Box 47024
Indianapolis, IN 46247

FIG. L.2 (*Continued*)

Allen Loan Amortization Chart for Land and Manufactured Home Sales

Factors per $1,000.00

YRS =	22	23	24	25	26	27	28	29	30	31	32	33
14	12.24	12.17	12.10	12.04	11.99	11.95	11.91	11.88	11.85	11.83	11.81	11.79
14 1/4	12.43	12.35	12.29	12.23	12.19	12.14	12.11	12.08	12.05	12.03	12.01	11.99
14 1/2	12.62	12.54	12.48	12.43	12.38	12.34	12.31	12.28	12.25	12.23	12.21	12.19
14 3/4	12.81	12.73	12.67	12.62	12.57	12.54	12.50	12.47	12.45	12.43	12.41	12.39
15	12.99	12.92	12.86	12.81	12.77	12.73	12.70	12.67	12.65	12.63	12.61	12.60
15 1/4	13.18	13.12	13.06	13.01	12.97	12.93	12.90	12.87	12.85	12.83	12.81	12.80
15 1/2	13.37	13.31	13.25	13.20	13.16	13.13	13.10	13.07	13.05	13.03	13.02	13.00
15 3/4	13.56	13.50	13.44	13.40	13.36	13.32	13.30	13.27	13.25	13.23	13.22	13.21
16	13.75	13.69	13.64	13.59	13.56	13.52	13.50	13.47	13.45	13.44	13.42	13.41
16 1/4	13.95	13.89	13.83	13.79	13.75	13.72	13.70	13.67	13.65	13.64	13.62	13.61
16 1/2	14.14	14.08	14.03	13.99	13.95	13.92	13.90	13.87	13.86	13.84	13.83	13.82
16 3/4	14.33	14.27	14.23	14.18	14.15	14.12	14.10	14.08	14.06	14.04	14.03	14.02
17	14.53	14.47	14.42	14.38	14.35	14.32	14.30	14.28	14.26	14.25	14.24	14.23
17 1/4	14.72	14.67	14.62	14.58	14.55	14.52	14.50	14.48	14.46	14.45	14.44	14.43
17 1/2	14.91	14.86	14.82	14.78	14.75	14.72	14.70	14.68	14.67	14.66	14.64	14.64
17 3/4	15.11	15.06	15.02	14.98	14.95	14.92	14.90	14.89	14.87	14.86	14.85	14.84
18	15.31	15.26	15.21	15.18	15.15	15.13	15.11	15.09	15.08	15.06	15.05	15.05
18 1/4	15.50	15.45	15.41	15.38	15.35	15.33	15.31	15.29	15.28	15.27	15.26	15.25
18 1/2	15.70	15.65	15.61	15.58	15.55	15.53	15.51	15.50	15.48	15.47	15.47	15.46
18 3/4	15.90	15.85	15.81	15.78	15.75	15.73	15.72	15.70	15.69	15.68	15.67	15.66
19	16.09	16.05	16.01	15.98	15.96	15.94	15.92	15.91	15.89	15.88	15.88	15.87
19 1/4	16.29	16.25	16.21	16.18	16.16	16.14	16.12	16.11	16.10	16.09	16.08	16.08
19 1/2	16.49	16.45	16.41	16.39	16.36	16.34	16.33	16.31	16.30	16.30	16.29	16.28
19 3/4	16.69	16.65	16.61	16.59	16.56	16.55	16.53	16.52	16.51	16.50	16.49	16.49
20	16.89	16.85	16.82	16.79	16.77	16.75	16.74	16.72	16.72	16.71	16.70	16.70

COMPUTED BY FINANCIAL PUBLISHING COMPANY, BOSTON, MASS. 02215

Property Management Form #117

DMN Publishing, Inc.
P.O. Box 47024
Indianapolis, IN 46247

FIG. L.2 *(Continued)*

GLOSSARY

Absorption[2]   The filling of space, such as the rental of units or sale of a tract. The time or rate must be estimated and considered as part of the owner's (usually the builder) costs.

Acquisition costs[2]   Costs of acquiring property other than purchase price.

Ad valorem   "according to value." Using the value of item taxed to ascertain amount of tax.

Agent   One authorized to represent or act in behalf of another (the principal), usually in business matters.

Amenity   A feature or benefit in addition to the basic homesite; e.g., swimming pool, clubhouse.

Amortization   Gradual repayment of a debt (i.e., principal of a loan) through a series of payments made over a period of time.

Ancillary income   Income received from on-site sources other than homesite rent.

APR[1]   Annual payment rate. The true percentage of interest charged on an annualized basis.

ANSI[1]   American National Standards Institute. The national coordinating institution for voluntary standardization in the United States.

Appraisal   An opinion of value based on a factual analysis of the personal or real property being valued.

* Indicates terms generally associated with manufactured housing.
[1] *The Mobilehome Salesmakers Guide II*
[2] *The Real Estate Dictionary.* (Boston, MA: Financial Publishing Co.)

Appreciation   Increase in value over a period of time, usually caused by inflation, economic factors, and improvements to property.

Back money[1]*   Refers to profit that retailer receives other than the sale of a manufactured home or accessories, on which he or she pays no sales commission. The two major items in back money are retailer reserve (participation) and insurance commissions.

Balloon mortgage   Long-term loan paid off in a lump sum at a specified term.

Berm   Earthen mound used to control drainage or as a screening buffer between properties.

BOCA   Building Officials and Code Administrators.

Break-even   Percentage of income necessary for an income property to pay all operating expenses and mortgages.

Broker   One licensed by a state to conduct business as a broker of real estate, insurance, securities, etc.

CABO   Council of American Building Officials

Cap or Capitalization rate   A current rate of return calculated by dividing the net operating income of a property by its estimated value.

Capital[2]   Money used to create income, either as an investment in a business or income property.

Cash flow   Flow of cash through a company; also the money a property owner can pocket after paying all expenses and mortgage.

Catch Basin   A receptacle located where a street gutter opens into a storm sewer, designed to convey stormwater.

CC&Rs   Conditions, covenants, and restrictions relating to a piece of real property.

Chattel   Personal property, as contrasted with real property.

Collage   Graphic grouping of photos in a display for marketing or information purposes.

Collateral security   Valuable consideration in addition to personal obligation of a borrower.

Comprehensive plan   Social, physical, and economic development of a community described in a compilation of goals, policies, and maps.

Condominium   Individual property ownership of a specific homesite or apartment with an individual interest in the land and other parts of the structure or common area with other owners.

Construction loan[1]   A loan to finance the improvement of real estate.

Contingencies   Plans subject to the occurrence of specified but uncertainly timed events.

Contour map[2]   A map which uses lines (most always curved) to outline the configuration and elevation of surface areas.

Cooperative or **Co-op**   Right to occupy a unit or site is based on purchase of stock in the corporation owning the property or building.

Cul de sac   A street open at only one end, usually with a large, rounded end.

Curb appeal   How a rental property looks to the casual passerby; its overall appearance, good or bad.

Curb cut   Apron of a driveway. Where curb has been cut away.

Curtailment*, or **Reduction**   in principal owed on floor planned manufactured homes in a retailer's inventory. This is in accord with bank and manufacturer's repurchase agreement, stipulating that principal be reduced per wear and tear and aging of homes.

Curvilinear   Having boundaries of curved lines; architectural design.

Debt service   Mortgage payment, interest and principal paid each month to mortgagor.

Decedents   Ones who have died.

Demographics   Statistical information relative to planning new business or expansion of same.

Density   Number of dwelling units in a given area of land.

Depreciation   Decrease in value owing to deterioration and or obsolescence.

DER   Department of Environmental Regulation.

Due diligence   The process of property inspection and evaluation of financial records between time a bona fide offer to purchase is made and accepted, and actual consummation of the transaction.

Earthwork   The moving and reshaping of surface contours.

Easement   A right one has in the land of another, created by grant, agreement, prescription, reservation, or necessary implication.

Effluent   Flow of treated sewage from a wastewater treatment facility.

Elevation   Exterior design of a structure as viewed from the front or side.

Encumbrance   Lien, charge, or claim against real property, but does not present transfer of title.

EPA   Environmental Protection Agency.

Equity   Market value of real property less any debts and liens.

Escrow[1]   An instrument in the hands of a third party that is held for delivery until certain acts are performed or conditions fulfilled.

FDIC   Federal Deposit Insurance Corporation; insures deposits at commercial and savings banks.

FED   Federal Reserve Board; nation's central bank.

Fee simple   The most complete form of real property ownership.

FEMA   Federal Energy Management Administration.

FHA   Federal Housing Administration; provides a variety of home and loan insurance programs to lending institutions through the U.S. Department of Housing and Urban Development.

FHBM Flood Hazard Boundary Map.

FHLMC Federal Home Loan Mortgage Corporation, a.k.a. "Freddie Mac." Increases the availability of mortgage credit and provides greater liquidity for savings institutions.[1]

FIA Federal Insurance Administration (part of FEMA).

FIRM Flood Insurance Rate Map.

Fixed expenses Expenses that do not vary with occupancy; e.g., taxes and insurance.

Floodplain[2] The extent of the land adjoining a river, which, because of its level topography, would flood if the river overflowed its banks.

Floor plan Layout of a structure, indicating size of rooms and purposes for each.

Floor planning Inventory financing of a retailer's manufactured housing stock. Usually simple interest rates, 1 or 2 points over prime rate.

FMHA Farmers Home Administration. Makes loans for rural housing, community facilities, etc.

FNMA[1] Federal National Mortgage Association, a.k.a. "Fannie Mae." Establishes a market for the purchase and sale of first mortgages for housing.

Foundation fascia a.k.a. skirting. Visual screening and weather barrier, of permanent or semipermanent material, covering the air space between bottom of a manufactured home and the ground.

Frost line Depth to which soil freezes.

FTC[1] Federal Trade Commission. A federal enforcement agency which promulgates trade regulations and rules.

GNMA Government National Mortgage Association, a.k.a. "Ginnie Mae." A source of mortgage money backed by and insured by the federal government.

Groundwater[2] Water in the subsoil or of a spring or shallow well.

Hardpan[2] A compacted layer of soil, usually containing clay, through which it is difficult to drain or dig.

Highest and best use Property condition or development bringing greatest profit to its owner.

Holdback Part of a loan commitment held back until additional requirement(s) are met.

Home owners association Usually associated with PUD, condominium, and co-op properties, but can include any group of home owners working together.

Homesite Parcel of improved land upon which a manufactured home is permanently or temporarily sited. Usually complete with infrastructure utilities, piers, driveway.

HUD[1] Department of Housing and Urban Development. Oversees most federally sponsored housing programs.

Hydrology The science dealing with the occurrence, circulation, distribution, and properties of the waters of the earth and its atmosphere.

ICBO International Conference of Building Officials.

Infiltration The movement of water through the soil surface into the soil; also used to describe movement of water through the soil into sanitary sewer lines through pipe cracks or separated connections.

Infrastructure All common improvements and community features, such as water and sewer lines, streets, schools, and government facilities.

Iterative Involving repetition, as with verbal and/or written actions and plans.

Land and home package Occurs when a manufactured home is purchased for placement upon homeowner's parcel of real estate.

Landlease The transfer of possessory and right to use real property rights to a tenant for a specific period, in return for rent compensation.

Landscaping Modification of the landscape through grading, trees, etc.

Laterals The sewer lines branching off the main sewer line.

Lease Agreement between lessor and lessee whereby the former gives up right of possession and use for a period of time in exchange for specified consideration or rent.

Leasehold[2] An estate in realty held under a lease. In some states considered to be personal property.

Lessee A person to whom a lease is given in exchange for rent.

Lessor Property owner or agent granting the lease for a consideration (rent).

Leverage Effecting an investment with as little cash (i.e., down payment) as possible and maximum debt.

Lien A charge placed upon a property for payment of a debt.

Loess Deposits of windblown organic silt.

Lotline[2] The boundary line of a lot in a subdivision.

Lotting plan A plan showing the lot (or homesite) layout and street arrangement in a subdivision or landlease community.

MHCSS Manufactured Home Construction and Safety Standards.

MHI Manufactured Housing Institute.

Mortgagee Party borrowing the money and granting the mortgage.

Mortgage The legal instrument used to obligate property to secure a loan.

Mortgagor Party lending the money and receiving the mortgage.

MSO Manufacturer's Statement of Origin. Manufacturers initiated document which originates title to a manufactured home.

Net operating income Amount left after adjustments and deductions for vacancy, credit loss, and operating expenses, but before mortgage is paid.

NFIP National Flood Insurance Program.

NFPA National Fire Protection Association.

Non-recourse financing[1]* The party arranging the loan assumes sole liability should the retail consumer default. In order to provide non-recourse financing, the lending institution may secure its position by obtaining mortgage guarantee insurance.

Option Right to purchase property at a negotiated price within a specified time period, in exchange for a consideration.

Ordinance Simply a law or statute.

Percolation[2] The absorption of liquid into soil by seepage.

Pier Integral part of the foundation system for many manufactured home installations. Usually concrete block material.

Piezometer tube A tube placed in the ground to measure groundwater levels.

PITI Principal, Interest, Taxes, Insurance.

Plat a.k.a. plot plan. General street map of a community.

PMI Private mortgage insurance.

Points An additional loan charge put on a loan to increase the yield to the lender. One (1) point equals 1% of face value of a loan amount.

PRD Planned Residential Development.

Principal Money still owed on a loan at any given time, not including interest.

Pro rata or pro rate[2] To divide into appropriate shares, such as taxes, insurance, rent and other items.

PUD Planned Urban Development. Characterized by intensive unified use of land and site design with combination of private and common area improvements.

Purchase money mortgage[2] A mortgage given by the buyer to the seller as part of the purchase consideration, as opposed to a hard money mortgage.

Real property Land and anything permanently attached to it.

Realtor[2] A designation given to a real estate broker who is a member of a board associated with the National Association of Realtors.

Rectilinear A community layout wherein straight streets run parallel and at right angles to each other.

Remonstrators Citizens in attendance at planning commission and board meetings who generally are against approving a particular land use approval or change.

Repurchase Agreement[1]* The Manufacturer's Repurchase Agreement is a written agreement between the manufacturer and bank whereby the manufacturer agrees to repurchase units in the retailer's inventory should the retailer default on his obligations or go out of business. A Retailer Repurchase Agreement is a written agreement between the dealer and lender whereby the dealer agrees to buy back manufactured homes from the bank in which the retail consumer has defaulted on loan payments.

Retailer Individual or firm in the business of marketing and selling new and resale manufactured homes.

Retailer buy rate[*1]   The difference between the cost of the financing to the retailer and the cost of financing to the consumer by the lending institution is known as the "buy rate." A good quality retail operation will normally have a more preferential buy rate, which allows the retailer to make more on participation, while charging the same interest rate to the consumer as a competitor might charge. Typically, if a retailer's buy rate is $6\frac{3}{4}\%$, cost to the consumer would be $7\frac{1}{2}\%$ to $8\frac{1}{2}\%$, depending upon how much the retailer can charge and still make the sale.

Retailer reserve[*1]   (Participation) A fixed amount of the interest rate set aside by the lending institution on behalf of the retailer to protect the lender on future repossessions should the dealer go out of business. If the retailer remains in business, the reserve generally belongs to him or her once the loans are paid off.

Return-on-investment   Annual earnings on original cash down payment.

Right-of-way[2]   A strip of land used as a roadbed, either for a street or railway.

ROC   Resident-owned community, usually characterized by cooperative or condominium ownership.

SBCCI   Southern Building Code Congress International.

SCS   Soil Conservation Service.

Security agreement[*1]   A security agreement, as specified by the Uniform Commercial Code (UCC), replaces the trust receipt. A security agreement between the lender and retailer eliminates the need of having an individual document (trust receipt) initiated for each home floor planned. While most states accept the Uniform Commercial Code, finance companies, banks and savings and loan institutions have been slower to change from the traditional trust agreement, which gives them more legal protection.

Seed money   Money needed for preliminary plans, reorganizing, controlling the site, and completion of feasibility studies.

Setback   The distance a structure must be set back (i.e., distanced from) a street, lotline, or property, to conform to a zoning or building code.

Simple interest[1]   Interest charged on an annual basis, payable monthly, on the unpaid balance remaining.

Skirting   Same as *foundation fascia.*

Soft market   Market condition when supply exceeds demand.

Streetscape   A pictorial view of or from a street.

Subdivision[2]   A division of a single parcel of land into smaller parcels by filing a map describing the division.

Subordination   Willingness of a lien holder (e.g., mortgagee) to accept payment after another creditor.

Swale   A valleylike intersection of two slopes in a piece of land.

Tag-along/tag section[1]   A third section to a manufactured home.

Tiedown   An anchoring device used to secure a manufactured home to the homesite anchoring system, whether it be earth anchors or hardware secured in concrete.

Tight or **hard market**   Market condition when demand exceeds supply.

Topography   Land surface contour.

Transporter   Single-axle over-the-road tractor designed to transport manufactured homes.

Trust deed[1]   An instrument that is evidence of the pledge of real property as security for a debt where the title to the real property is held by a third party in trust, while the debtor repays the debt to the lender.

Turnover ratio   Number of move-outs in a 12-month period as compared with total number of homesites.

UCC   Uniform Commercial Code.

USCG   United States Coast Guard.

USDA   United States Department of Agriculture.

USGS   United States Geological Survey.

VA   Department of Veterans Affairs; guarantees loans made to veterans.

Variable expenses   Expenses that fluctuate in proportion to physical occupancy, seasons, etc.

Water table[2]   The depth measured from the surface, at which natural underground waters are found.

Wetlands   Lands that have a wet and spongy soil, as with a marsh, swamp, or bog.

Wraparound mortgage[2]   A second or junior mortgage with a face value of both the amount it secures and the balance due under the first mortgage.

Zero lotline   The construction of a building on any of the boundary lines of a lot.

Zoning   Planned division of a community into areas designed for designated uses, e.g., residential, commercial, industrial.

BIBLIOGRAPHY

Allen, George, *Mobilehome Community Management,* 2nd ed. Indianapolis, Ind.: PMN Publishing, 1991.

Allen, George, *Real Estate and Property Management.* Monograph #1. Indianapolis, Ind.: PMN Publishing, 1993.

Allen, George, *Development, Sale and Purchasing of Manufactured Home Communities.* Monograph #2. Indianapolis, Ind.: PMN Publishing, 1993.

Allen, George, *Daily Management of Manufactured Home Communities.* Monograph #3. Indianapolis, Ind.: PMN Publishing, 1993.

Allen, George, *Upper Management Related Reports and Directories for Manufactured Home Communities.* Monograph #4. Indianapolis, Ind.: PMN Publishing, 1993.

Allen, George, and David Blakley. 1990. *Appraisal Guide for Mobilehomes.* Scottsdale, Ariz.: NAREA.

Branson, Gary, *The Complete Guide to Manufactured Housing.* Cincinnati, Ohio: Betterway Books, 1992.

Compliance Systems Publications Inc., *Complete Guide to H.U.D. Mobile Home Standards Program,* 2nd ed. Atlanta, Ga., 1977.

Cooke, P.W., R.D. Dikkers, H.R. Trechsel, H.K. Tejuja, and L.P. Zelenka, *Model Documents for the Evaluation, Approval, and Inspection of Manufactured Buildings.* NBS Building Science Series 87. Washington, D.C.: National Bureau of Standards, 1976.

Cushman and Robin, *Property Management Handbook.* New York: John Wiley & Sons, Inc., 1985.

Cymrot, Allen, *Street Smart Real Estate Investing.* Mountain View, Calif.: CR Publishing Co., 1993.

de Heer, Robert, *Realty Bluebook,* 29th ed. San Rafael, Calif.: Professional Publishing Corporation, 1993.

U.S. Department of Housing and Urban Development, *Design and Construction Manual for Residential Buildings in Coastal High Hazard Areas.* Washington, D.C.: HUD, January 1981.

Downs, J., *Principles of Real Estate Management.* Chicago, Ill.: IREM, 1990.

Federal Emergency Management Agency, *Design Guidelines for Flood Damage Reduction.* FEMA 15. Washington, D.C.: Government Printing Office, December 1981.

Federal Insurance Administration, National Flood Insurance Programs, *Elevated Residential Structures.* Reducing Flood Damage Through Building Design: A Guide Manual, 1976.

Federal Emergency Management Agency, *Flood Insurance Study: Guidelines and Specifications for Contractors.* Washington, D.C.: Government Printing Office, September 1982.

U.S. Department of Defense, *Flood-Proofing Regulations.* Washington, D.C.: Government Printing Office, 1984.

U.S. Department of Housing and Urban Development, *Guidelines for Improving the Mobile Home Living Environment.* Washington, D.C.: Government Printing Office, 1977.

Guidelines for Mobilehome Park Development and Operations. College Station, Tex.: Real Estate Center, Texas A & M University Press, 1988.

Hall, Craig, *The Real Estate Turnaround.* Englewood Cliffs, N.J.: Prentice-Hall, 1978.

Hicks, Edward, *How to Get an FHA 207(m) Mobile Home Lot Rental Community Loan Guarantee From HUD.* Portland, Maine: _____ 1991.

Hoffman, Richard M., *Mobilehome Earthquake Bracing Systems in California.* Mountain View, Calif.: Hoffman Books, 1993.

Jordan, Sloan, *Property Management Tactics in Manufactured Housing Communities.* Carlsbad, Calif.: SJ Publishing, 1990.

King, Langerden & Hummell, *The Successful On-Site Manager.* Chicago: IREM, 1984.

Kovacs, William D., and Felix Y. Yokel, *Soil and Rock Anchors for Mobile Homes: A State-of-the-Art Report.* NBS Building Science Series 107. Washington, D.C.: National Bureau of Standards, 1979.

Krigger, John, *Your Mobilehome Energy and Repair Guide.* Mont.: Saturn Resource Management, 1992.

Dodge Construction Cost Information System, *Manual for Building Construction Pricing and Scheduling,* annual ed. Princeton, N.J.: McGraw-Hill Information Systems Company, 1992.

U.S. Department of Housing and Urban Development, *Manual for the Construction of Residential Basements in Non-Coastal Flood Environs* (CR-997). Washington, D.C.: NAHB Research Foundation, March 1977.

National Concrete Masonry Association, *Manual of Facts on Concrete Masonry* (A), 1983.

NCSBCS/ANSI A225.1, NFPA 501A, *Manufactured Home Installations.* Washington, D.C.: NCSBCS,

McKie, Clint, *Do's and Don'ts of Mobilehome Repairing,* vols. 1 and 2. (   ), Mo.: CM Publishing, 1990.

Federal Trade Commission, Bureau of Consumer Protection, *Mobile Home Sales and Service.* Washington, D.C.: Government Printing Office, August 1980.

Colorado Manufactured Housing Association, and IREM, *Mobilehome Community Maintenance.* Denver, Colo.: Colorado Manufactured Housing Association, and IREM, 1986.

American Appraisal Association, *Mobile-Manufactured Housing Cost Guide.* Milwaukee, Wis.: Boeckh, 1993.

National Forest Products Association, "National Design Specification for Wood Construction," National Forest Products Association, 1982 edition.

Pappas, Stephen, *Managing Mobile Home Parks.* Chicago, Ill.: Institute of Real Estate Management, 1991.

U.S. Department of Defense, *Protecting Mobile Homes from High Winds* (TR-75). Washington, D.C.: Government Printing Office, February 1984.

American Society of Planning Officials, *Regulation of Modular Housing, with Special Emphasis on Mobile Homes.* (   ): AMSPO, 1971.

Marshall and Swift Company, *Residential Cost Handbook.* Los Angeles, Calif.: M&S Publishing, 1992.

Robinson, Leigh, *Landlording.* El Cerrito, Calif.: Express, 1988.

Sanders, Welford, *Manufactured Housing Site Development Guide*. Planning Advisory Service Report #445. Chicago, Ill.: American Planning Association, 1993.

Commerce Clearing House, *State Tax Handbook*. Chicago, Ill.: 1992. (Updated annually.)

Vellozzi, Joseph W., Manufactured Housing Institute, "Review of Proposed 1980 ANSI A58.1 Standard on Wind Forces Relative to Federal Mobile Home Construction and Safety Standards." Washington, D.C.: May 1980.

Waldrip, Travis G., *Mobile Home Anchoring Systems and Related Construction*. June 1976.

Wallis, Allan, *Wheel Estates: History of the Manufactured Housing Industry*. New York: Oxford University Press, 1991.

Yokel, Felix Y., Riley M. Chung, Frank A. Rankin, and Charles W.C. Yancey, *Load Displacement Characteristics of Shallow Soil Anchors*. NBS Building Science Series 142. Washington, DC: National Bureau of Standards, 1981.

Yokel, Felix Y., Charles W.C. Yancey, and Christopher L. Mulen, *A Study of Reaction Forces on Mobile Home Foundations Caused by Wind and Flood Loads*. NBS Building Science Series 132. Washington, DC: National Bureau of Standards, 1981.

Yokel, Felix Y., Riley M. Chung, and Charles W.C. Yancey, *NBS Studies of Mobile Home Foundations*. NBSIR 2238. Washington, D.C.: National Bureau of Standards, 1981.

PERIODICALS

Allen Letter (The), PMN Publishing, P.O. Box 47024, Indianapolis, IN 46247. Monthly paid subscription newsletter for owners and managers of manufactured home communities in the United States and Canada.

ARR Newsletter, Association for Regulatory Reform, 1331 Pennsylvania Avenue N.W., 508, Washington, DC 20004. Membership newsletter.

Automated Builder, Box 210, Carpinteria, CA 93013. Free manufacturer-oriented monthly magazine targeting factory-built housing of all types.

FMO News, Florida Mobilehome Owners Association, Box 5350, Largo, FL 34649. Monthly manufactured homeowner magazine.

Journal of Manufactured Housing, Box 288, Manchester, GA 31816. Southeast regional tabloid publication for manufactured housing interest groups. Publishes several columns written by manufactured housing industry specialists.

Journal of Property Management, Institute of Real Estate Management, 430 Michigan Avenue, Chicago, IL 60601. Monthly paid subscription magazine for Certified Property Managers.

MANUFACTS, California Manufactured Housing Institute, 10390 Commerce Center Drive, 130, Rancho Cucamonga, CA 91730. Manufactured housing industry's cutting-edge publicist of product and community design.

Manufactured Home Merchandiser, 203 N. Wabash, 800, Chicago, IL 60601. Manufacturer, supplier, and retailer-oriented monthly trade publication. Features Community Corner column for landlease community owners and managers.

Manufactured Housing Newsletter, 17236 N.E. 4th Street, Bellevue, WA 98008. Regional modular-oriented publication.

Manufactured Housing Today, Box 836, Forest Grave, OR 97116. Regional consumer-sales oriented tabloid.

MHI Newsletter and *Manufacturing Report,* Manufactured Housing Institute, 1745 Jefferson Davis Highway, Arlington, VA 22202. Member newsletter and manufactured home shipment report.

Mobile Home Digest, Ste 1600, 150 Second Avenue N, St. Petersburg, FL 33701. A quarterly newsletter.

Mobilehome Parks Report, 3807 Pasadena Avenue, 100, Sacramento, CA 95821. Paid subscription newsletter for western manufactured home community owners and managers.

Professional Builder, Box 5080, Des Plaines, IL 60017. Monthly magazine targeting homebuilders.

Shelter, 88 Old Street, London, Great Britain EC1V9AX (magazine).

Western Mobile News, 4043 Irving Place, Culver City, CA 90230. Consumer-oriented publication.

WMA Reporter, Western Mobilehome Association, 1760 Creekside Oaks Drive, Sacramento, CA 95833. Monthly magazine for West Coast owners and managers of manufactured home communities.

INDEX

schedule an appointment, 223
second ring, 223
signage, 231
six-levels, 219, 304
smile!, 223, 233
staff compensation, 95
standard shopping report, 231–232
Sales commission, 94–95
Sanders, Welford, 12
Sanitary Sewer Collection Plan, 111
Satisfaction Guarantee, 275
SBCCI, 198
Scattered lots, 133, 212. *See also* Homesites
Secondary market, 133, 155
  FNMA and FHLMC secondary market
    programs, 155–156
  Government National Mortgage Association
    (GNMA), 155
Septic tank, 119–120
Sewer plant, *see* Wastewater treatment
Shopper service, 233, 358–361. *See also*
  Sales and leasing
Signage, 111
  off-site, 215, 217
  on-site, 215, 217
Singlesection manufactured home, 2, 8. *See*
  Manufactured housing
Site-built homes, 4, 11, 35, 93
  compared with manufactured housing,
    6, 92
  condominiums, 92
Site-delivered housing, 2
Skirting, 9, 194–195, 224, 239–240
  curtain wall, 9
  foundation fascia, 9, 194–195
  foundation siding, 9
  installation charges, 292
  perimeter fascia, 9
Small Business Administration (SBA),
  216
Snow shoveling, 292
Snow storage, 73
Snowplowing, 73
Soil:
  bearing capacity, 198
    model codes, 198
  erosion control plan, 124
    check dams, 124
    hay bales, 124
    matting, 124
    sedimentation traps, 124
    silt fences, 124
    swales, 124
  permeable surfaces, 123

problem soils, 198–199
maps, *see* Maps
soil borings, 115
soil testing, 115, 125
Soil Conservation Service, 115, 123
  TR-55 and TR-20, 123
Southwest, 122
Speculation homes, 211
Stationery, 215–216
Storm Sewer Plan, 111
Storm water, 68, 111, 122–123
  25-year event, 64
  detention, 47, 64, 123
  down stream flooding, 123
  drainage, 78, 114, 122–123
  drainage basin, 123
  dry ponds, 124
  erosion, 123
  filter media, 124
  impermeable surfaces, 123
  littoral zone, 124
  management regime, 64
  percolation, 124
  permeable surfaces, 123
  pollutants, 64, 124
  post development runoff, 124
  rainfall events, 122, 124
  retention, 47
  storm sewer system, 122
  surface grades, 122
  swales, 124
  wet ponds, 124
State Capitals, 37
Street dealer, 9
Street Smart Real Estate Investing, 15
Streets, 63, 69. *See also* Manufactured home
  community
  acceleration, 64
  aggregate base, 125
  curvilinear, 70–71
  deceleration, 65
  design, 63, 66, 84, 116, 125–126, 248
  deterioration, 240–241
  entrance, 65, 74, 78, 92, 111
  parking, 126
  paved streets, 125
    asphalt, 125
    concrete, 125
  rights-of-way, 110, 116
  roadway system, 65, 82, 111, 122
  stacking facilities, 65
  subgrade, 125
  traffic patterns, 63, 76
  turn lanes, 65